D1071837

Critical Sociology:
European Perspectives

IRVINGTON CRITICAL SOCIOLOGY SERIES

Series Editor: J. W. Freiberg, Boston University

Critical Sociology:

European Perspectives

edited by

J. W. FREIBERG

Boston University and Centre d'Etude
des Mouvements Sociaux, Paris

IRVINGTON PUBLISHERS, INC., NEW YORK

HALSTED PRESS Division of
JOHN WILEY & SONS, Inc.
NEW YORK   LONDON   SYDNEY   TORONTO

Distributed by Halsted Press
A division of John Wiley & Sons, Inc., New York

Library of Congress Cataloging in Publication Data

Main entry under title:

Critical sociology.

    1.   Sociology—Addresses,   essays,   lectures.   2.
Sociology—Methodology—Addresses, essays, lectures. I. Freiberg,
J. W. [DNLM: 1. Sociology. HM51 C934]
HM24.C73 1978   301   78-8481
ISBN 0-470-26425-X

Printed in the United States of America

This book is dedicated to the
Centre d'Etude des Mouvements
Sociaux, whose Director, Researchers
and Staff have graciously included me
for nearly a decade.

CONTENTS

PART II
The Critique of Social Process: Applying the Critical Paradigm

ACKNOWLEDGMENTS

Gratitude is due to the following journals and publishers for permission to translate and/or reprint some of the essays appearing in this book:

Anouar Abdel-Malek's "The Concept of Specificity: Positions" appeared in *Cultures,* Vol. 3, No. 4, 1976.

John O'Neill's "For Marx Against Althusser" appeared in *Human Context,* Vol. 6, No. 2. Summer 1974.

Göran Therborn's "Social Practice, Social Action, Social Magic" appeared in *Acta Sociologica,* Vol. 16, No. 3. 1973.

Alain Touraine's "Eight Ways to Eliminate the Sociology of Action" appeared in *Neue Hefte für Philosophie,* 1975.

Manuel Castells and Emilio de Ipola's "Epistemological Practice and the Social Sciences" appeared in *Economy and Society,* Vol. 5, No. 2, 1976.

Claus Offe and Volker Ronge's "Theses on the Theory of the State" appeared in the *New German Critique,* No. 6, Fall 1975.

Nicos Poulantzas' "The Political Crisis and the Crisis of the State" appeared as the introduction to his edited book *La Crise de l'Etat,* published by Presses Universitaires de France, 1976.

PREFACE:

On the Origins and Development of This Book

This book grows directly out of "The Special Summer Sessions In Social Theory," a series that I organized at Boston University. Alain Touraine and Franco Ferrarotti visited during the first summer (1974), Anthony Giddens and Claus Offe during the second, Manuel Castells and Nicos Poulantzas the third, Ralph Miliband and Hans Peter Dreitzel the fourth, and now in the fifth summer, Göran Therborn and Robin Blackburn. During the regular academic year colloquia, I have had the pleasure of inviting and listening to Hans Peter Dreitzel, Michael Mann, John O'Neill, Vicente Navarro, and especially Henri Lefebvre, who, in the autumn of his years, kept us spellbound with a week of splendid lectures.

So this book recreates in print what were for us live and vital experiences; I hope that the spirit with which these ideas were presented is found in the reading. Following this preface is a brief biographical and bibliographical note on each author. I want to offer my deepest gratitude to those dedicated graduate students who attended these sessions; they consistently gave their very highest intellectual commitment and helped make the seminars experiences none of us will forget. My particular thanks to S. M. Miller, then chairperson of the Department of Sociology, and to the Boston University Summer Session; they gave me not only

the administrative green light but also their personal encourage-
ment. So many other individuals helped in so many ways: the sessions would have bogged down a dozen times without the skill of
the departmental and summer term staffs. The contributions of
the teaching assistants were equally important. Finally, I am in-
debted to Deborah L. Kee for her help: I translated from French to
English, and she then translated my English into something
hopefully considerably closer to general usage.

J.W.F.

BIBLIOGRAPHICAL NOTES ON CONTRIBUTORS

ANOUAR ABDEL-MALEK is maitre de recherche at the Centre National de la Recherche Scientifique in Paris and vice-president of the International Sociological Association. He studied at the University of Cairo, at the University of London, and at the University of Paris. He has worked as a bank clerk, journalist, high school teacher, and script writer. His major works in English include *The Comparative Sociology of Civilizations* (with Benjamin Nelson) and *Nasser and Nasserism*; most of his work is not yet available in English, such as his *Sociologie de l'Imperialisme* and *La Dialectique Sociale.*

DANIEL BERTAUX had a technical education at the Ecole Polytechnique and the University of California at Berkeley. He studied sociology at the Sorbonne. He does research at the Centre d'Etude des Mouvements Sociaux in Paris. His article "Two and One-Half Models of Social Structure," is available in English in *Social Stratification and Career Mobility* (R. Müller and Mayer, eds.); his book *Destins Personnels et Rapports de classe* is not yet translated.

MANUEL CASTELLS was born in Spain but works in Paris: he is maître-assistant at the Ecole des Hautes Etudes en Sciences Soci-

ales, Paris, and a member of the Centre d'Etude des Mouvements
Sociaux. He holds a degree in law as well as in sociology from the
University of Paris. He has taught in the United States, Mexico,
Chile, and Canada. Among his many books, those in English in-
clude *The Urban Question, Urban Struggles, Monopoville,* and *The
Economic Crisis and American Society.*

HANS PETER DREITZEL is a professor of sociology at the Free
University of Berlin. He was educated at the University of Göttin-
gen, the Free University of Berlin, and the Institut des Sciences
Politiques in Paris. He is an editor of the International Yearbook
of Sociology of Religion and Sociology of Knowledge. His books
include the following edited works in English: *On the Social Basis
of Politics; Patterns of Communicative Behavior; The Social Organization of Health; Family, Marriage, and the Struggle of the Sexes; and
Childhood and Socialization.* He, along with Alain Touraine and associates, has recently written *Beyond Crisis.*

FRANCO FERRAROTTI is a professor of sociology at the University of Rome, president of the Italian Sociological Association,
and editor of *La Critica Sociologica.* He studied in Turin, London,
and Chicago. His most important publication in English to date is
Social Research and Industry in Europe. His major statement, *An
Alternative Sociology,* will soon be published in English by Irvington Publishers.

J. W. FREIBERG is assistant professor of sociology and Director
of Graduate Studies at Boston University. He was educated at the
University of California at Berkeley and Los Angeles, and at the
Ecole Pratique des Hautes Etudes in Paris. He is a member of
Alain Touraine's Centre d'Etude des Mouvements Sociaux in
Paris. His principal study, *Class Relations in the French Press,* will
soon be published. His articles and essays have appeared in vari-
ous journals of critical social thought, such as *L'Homme et la
Societe, The Bulletin of Concerned Asian Scholars, Dialectical An-
thropology, The Insurgent Sociologist, Consciousness and Culture,
City Magazine* (Hong Kong), etc.

ANTHONY GIDDENS is at King's College, Cambridge. He was
educated at the University of Hull and at the London School of
Economics. His books include *Capitalism and Modern Social
Theory, Politics and Sociology in the Thought of Max Weber, The
Class Structure of the Advanced Societies, Elites and Power in British*

Society (with P. Stanworth), *New Rules of Sociological Method,* and *Studies in Social and Political Theory.*

URS JAEGGI is professor at the Free University of Berlin. His "Development and Interaction between American and German Sociology" was recently published in *Social Research.* His many books, the most recent being *Theoretische Praxis: Probleme eines Strukturalen Marxismus,* have not yet been translated into English.

HENRI LEFEBVRE has been one of the grand intellectuals of France for the last forty years; his split with the Communist party was of major importance in the anti-Stalinist movement. Over the years, he has written more than forty books on an amazing range of topics. He was educated at the University of Paris, and is now a professor of sociology there. His works that appear in English include *Dialectical Materialism, The Sociology of Marx, The Explosion,* and *Everyday Life in the Modern World.* As productive as ever, he has recently written three volumes on the capitalist state.

MICHAEL MANN was educated at Oxford and has a chair in sociology at the London School of Economics. He is editor of the British Sociological Association's "Studies in Sociology." He has led a life of quiet desperation within the British Labour party. His principal work is *Consciousness and Action in the Western Working Class.*

VICENTE NAVARRO is professor of health and social policy at the Johns Hopkins University in Baltimore. He is a member of the Executive Committee of the International Association of Advanced Studies on the Political Economy of Health Care. He was educated at Barcelona University, Karolinska Center (Sweden), the University of Edinburgh, and the Johns Hopkins University, He is editor-in-chief of the *International Journal of Health Services.* He has been a consultant to many progressive governments, including Cuba and Allende's Chile. His books include *Medicine Under Capitalism; The Political Economy of Social Security and Medical Care in the U.S.S.R.; Social Class, Policy Formation and Medicine: A Historical and Contemporary Analysis of the Medical Sector in Great Britain*; and *Health and Medical Care in the U.S.: A Critical Analysis.*

CLAUS OFFE is a professor at the University of Bielefeld, West

Germany. He was educated at the Free University in Berlin, and is an editor of *Leviathan* and *Kapitalistate*. His works in English include "The Theory of the Capitalist State and the Problem of Policy Formation" (in Lindberg and associates, *Stress and Contradiction in Modern Capitalism)* and *The Achievement Principle and Industrial Work.*

JOHN O'NEILL is a professor at York University in Toronto. He was educated at the London School of Economics and at Stanford University. He is an editor of *Philosophy of the Social Sciences.* His principal works are *Sociology as a Skin Trade, Making Sense Together: An Introduction to Wild Sociology, On Critical Theory,* and *Modes of Individualism and Collectivism.*

NICOS POULANTZAS was educated in Greece as well as at the University of Paris. He is currently maître de conferences de sociologie at the University of Paris (VIII), and at the Ecole des Hautes Etudes en Sciences Sociales. His *Political Power and Social Classes, Classes in Contemporary Capitalism, Fascism and Dictatorship,* and *The Crisis of the Dictatorships* are available in English.

GÖRAN THERBORN is a professor at the sociologiska institutionen of Umeå University in Sweden. He is probably best known to the English-speaking world for his articles in *New Left Review,* especially "Structure and Conflict in *das Kapital.* " New Left Books has recently published his *Science, Class and Society* as well as his *What Does the Ruling Class Do When It Rules?*

ALAIN TOURAINE was educated at the Ecole Normale Superieure, and is a professor of sociology at the Ecole des Hautes Etudes en Sciences Sociales and director of Le Centre d'Etude des Mouvements Sociaux in Paris. He founded the Journal *Sociologie du Travail.* Of his many books, several have been translated into English: *The May Movement* (Irvington Publishers), *Post-Industrial Society, University and Society in the U.S.,* and, most recently, *The Self-Production of Society.*

EDITOR'S INTRODUCTION:
CRITICAL SOCIAL THEORY
IN THE AMERICAN CONJUNCTURE

J. W. FREIBERG

I. IDEOLOGICAL HEGEMONY IN THE UNITED STATES

The reason for inviting a series of Europeans to participate in the summer seminars and in this edited book is that they have something special to tell us, something that we are not likely to hear from an American. This is because the social and political conjuncture in Europe is so radically different from that of the United States that the social researchers who are raised and educated in Europe take a strikingly different approach to social research than do most American researchers. There is no possible way in which this collection of articles could have been written by Americans, although there are an increasing number of critically minded individuals working hard to comprehend the social world in terms of social relations and class struggle.

One primary question for a critical sociology of knowledge in the United States is to investigate the conditions that limit our critical imaginations and silence our critical tongues. Why are social researchers here as likely to uncritically accept the reified categories of the bourgeois worldview as is the average individual?

What is it in the American experience that has produced such overwhelmingly conformist and conservative social thought? No *one* answer will be found, for our uncritical perspective is highly overdetermined—that is, it is simultaneously a product of numerous social processes and historical events. If one wanted to trace the social and historical roots of the American ideological conjuncture, it would seem worthwhile to investigate the contributions of such factors as:

1. The absence of a feudal tradition, which means that one set of social relations (aristocracy/peasantry) present in European history never occurred in the United States. Although feudal social relations certainly play a progressively smaller role in most European countries, they do act to prestructure a way of perceiving social relations in terms of *social classes*. Where Americans tend to perceive society as a conglomeration of individuals, some of whom are successful (Horatio Alger), Europeans tend to perceive society as the interplay of social classes, some of which rule over others.

2. One would certainly emphasize the peculiar and singular history of the American labor movement, particularly the extraordinarily violent repression of the movement that is associated with such incidents as the Great Railroad Strike (1877), Homestead and Coeur d'Alene (1892), Pullman (1894), Ludlow (1913), the Southern Tenant Farmers Union (1935), the Memorial Day Massacre (1937), and so on. When describing the apolitical, antisocialist unionism of the workingmen's parties (1830s), Terence Powderly and the Knights of Labor (1880s), Samuel Gompers and the American Federation of Labor (1930s), John L. Lewis and the Congress of Industrial Organizations (1930s), or their descendants, one should stress that the social and political timidity of American unionism resulted from the fact that it was subjected to the most violent repression by both private (Pinkerton) and state (National Guard) armed forces of any Western labor movement. At times, workers stood their ground and fought back, particularly, of course, the Industrial Workers of the World (IWW); but after World War I, with many states passing criminal syndicalism laws (1917–1918) and the federal government soon following with its Sedition and Espionage acts, these struggles were doomed to fail.

3. The presidential system provides a unique ability, compared with parliamentary systems, to reduce formal political participation to a one-day event every four years and to structure stability during crises (in contrast to the fall of governments in a parliamentary system). One also should look carefully at the two-party system, which, in conjunction with the presidential system, makes the formation of temporary alliances between smaller parties impossible. Only three national governments are older than the United States; this long-term stability not only indicates the success of this largely apolitical political process but has itself become a stabilizing factor. Americans cannot conceive of profound structural change in their political process; the French, in contrast, are currently in their fifth Republic.

4. Throughout U.S. history, administrative, legislative, and judicial repression have been directed at leftist parties, particularly the Communist Party. Blatant administrative intervention is exemplified in the Palmer Raids (1921), with the deportations of hundreds of radicals that ensued, and, of course, in the efforts of the Federal Bureau of Investigation under J. Edgar Hoover and President Richard M. Nixon to spy upon and directly interfere with the legal political practices of the small left parties. The federal government intervened not only with the Sedition and Espionage acts (160 convictions were obtained against the IWW for obstructing war efforts during World War I) but also with the McCarren Act. For much of American history, the Communist party has been outlawed as an agent of a foreign government, and Senator Joseph McCarthy's witch hunts are among many examples of the direct attacks on the Party and its sympathizers by the state. The courts also played their role, not only in enforcing these laws, but in establishing case law against union efforts. It is important to remind people that only due to the continuing class struggle, has judicial intervention developed from a Supreme Court ruling that union organizational efforts were an illegal "restraint of trade," to today's position that protects the organizational and negotiating rights of unions. The legislatures also played a role in this change, as for example, with the passage of the National Labor Relations Act. Legislative and judicial repression slackened (if not administrative—Watergate and the "Plumbers" were neither accidents nor exceptions) only because of labor's constant struggles and demands, within a framework of a bargain struck between labor unions and the state: the unions were granted legitimization at the cost of forsaking radical rhetoric and political action on class (as opposed to work) issues.

5. One also would want to recall the almost absurdly inappropriate pressures on the American Communist Party coming from the Soviet Union, and the Internationale (I am thinking of the experience of Harry Brauder in 1944), and from Stalin, in particular. If the American Communist party were to have meant anything and were to have built upon the progress of the 1930s and early 1940s, it would have had to be an open, democratic party that addressed itself to concrete American issues in a manner appropriate to the existing political and ideological conjuncture.

One also would investigate the dissolution of the once-powerful socialist parties which brought Eugene Debs 4 million votes. To what extent were his policies coopted, and to what extent were they dissipated by a merely superficial commitment to these ideas/ideals by the the Democratic party? At the turn of the century, there were more than two hundred socialist newspapers published in the United States; why and how was this press so utterly eliminated?

6. Another important factor in dissipating American political awareness and activism was, of course, the constant immigration of new laborers who were only too pleased to work for the wages that unions were condemning as absolutely insufficient. This flow of humanity provided a natural pool of strikebreakers and apolitical workers. And, of course, the "frontier experience" must be considered; if there has not been as much "upward mobility" in American society as some claim, there has been a great deal of geographical mobility. The constant western movement of industry depleted the ranks of labor activists; when conditions were bad or strikes were too long, it was easier to move to areas of lesser competition and concentration than to stay and fight.

7. In many ways, the American world view is directly linked with the eighteenth-century values and self-images of the rising European bourgeoisie: among them, the rights of "equality," "property," and "liberty." The ideological force of these values in the United States comes principally from two sources. First, under our common law legal system bolstered by the Bill of Rights, certain ideals are indeed realized for part of the population. Among these strata are the individuals who would presumably protest if this were not so. Those who write newspapers, books, and television news shows falsely assume that the advantages they enjoy are available to everyone, and so they erroneously, if in good faith, assure the general population that there is an almost complete adherence to these "American Values." This media whitewash reinforces a remarkably powerful national abil-

ity to ignore the palpable absence of these rights among various "marginal" sectors of the populace (African slaves as "two thirds" of a person in the United States Constitution, the confiscation of property from Japanese Americans during the World War II, the 50% unemployment rate among young, inner-city black males today.)

Two major ideological pillars play an equally important role in holding up this aging but still dominant world view: individualism, and a more recent addition, psychologism. Nowhere in the Western world—probably nowhere in the world—is there another society as epistemologically committed to an individualist perspective of social life. Americans tend to experience society as a collectivity of conscious individuals who enter into contact with one another in full awareness of the systems of laws and norms that structure their interaction.

A myriad of concepts reinforce this hyper-individualism; for example, the (anti-) philosophy of pragmatism (where Americans learned to distrust philosophical abstraction and to fear social theory), the mythology of Horatio Algerism, and the ideology of the self-sufficient frontiersman. It is in the light of this that we must see how open the United States has been to psychological discoveries from Wundt to Freud to Skinner. Psychology in Europe is a restricted discipline, a microstudy of human motivation; in the United States, psychology mixes with the individualistic world view to become a macroexplanation that subverts both popular social insight and professional sociological inquiry.

If pragmatism in part explains the positivistic deviation in social research (the reduction of sociology to methodology—history becomes "path analysis"), psychologism-individualism in part explains the social-psychological deviation in social research (the reduction of sociology to social psychology—social relations become "prestige scales"). This is important because the American world view I am sketching is entrapping for both the common person and most of the intelligentsia. Nothing else goes as far in explaining the American academic setting and the intellectual output of the United States as the insight that they are structured by the general American world view sketched above. American social science's fascination with "hard methods," experimental, small group research, behaviorist psychology, econometrics, and psychohistory, for example, can only be understood in relation to the world view within which it operates: individualistic, psychologistic, positivistic, pragmatic, etc.

Although the above is nothing more than a sketch, these points are the kinds of social, political, and ideological factors that have led to the ideologically closed society we experience today in the United States. Even this brief overview implies an enormous complexity to the historical development of America's "uni-dimensionality," or, better put, its highly dominant bourgeois world view (better because it reminds us that what is at issue is a relatively stable but still contradictory relation between social classes). It follows that the way out of this situation will be no less complex: it is a process that must happen concurrently on these many levels, or it will not happen at all. But in this essay, I want only to look at the smallest single aspect of this possible change: the way out of this stifling and restricting world view for American social theory and social research.

II. CRITICAL SOCIAL THEORY AND SOCIAL RESEARCH: CONSTRUCTING A MACROSOCIOLOGY

1. In Europe, critical notions are as much a part of the general world view as is Darwin's theory of evolution. People are as likely to think with critical social and political categories, that is, to experience the social world *through* these categories—almost irrespective of their personal politics—as they are likely to think with evolutionary categories about the biological world. Social classes are profoundly and visibly a part of everyday life; it is only in the United States thay they have become socially (and in turn sociologically) invisible. In Europe, class struggle is perennially present because labor unions, the left intelligentsia, the left press, and so forth, use, and therefore make available to the general public, critical categories for interpreting social and political events. The United States has no shortage of labor activism, but it is neither experienced nor interpreted as part of class struggle. Objectively, it *is* a manifestation of class struggle, but it is important to realize that the phenomena of institutional integration and ideological masking of most working-class activism prevent the politicization and polarization that these same occurrences would have in a different subjective setting.

One example of the degree to which critical categories of social thought are absent in the United States is that most Americans cannot distinguish between the three concepts: Marxism, Socialism, and Communism. In Europe, children learn these (and much finer) distinctions when using everyday political language.

In America, however, especially in the mass media, these three terms are synonyms applied to such varied objects as marginal political radicals, long-haired college students, and tanks. (In Vietnam, "Communist tanks" fought against "allied tanks.")

One source of the poverty of concepts that shackles the American political mind is clearly the mass media's refusal to speak in terms other than the accepted political banalities. The absence of critical categories in the American media should be contrasted with the European situation, particularly in southern Europe where, in the daily press (the least controlled of the mass media), even center and right papers presume a working knowledge of critical social categories on the part of the readers. In today's world, one is greatly limited in one's political thought if one is devoid of critical categories, for if politics means only Democrats and Republicans and the three or four pseudo issues of presidential campaigns, how can one possibly understand recent events in Italy, France, and Spain? For the great majority of Americans, it is epistemologically impossible to comprehend "Eurocommunism," for example, because they simply do not have an adequate command of the social and political categories needed to explain the complex issues of class relations that are involved.

2. There are two conceptual deprivations that contribute to the paucity of political understanding on the part of many Americans. The first, mentioned above, is the absence of the basic critical concepts of "social class" and "class struggle." The second is a lack of historical knowledge; if Americans know little about their own history, they know next to nothing about world history.

One contributing factor to the absence of the concepts of social class and class struggle, is that they have been replaced by other concepts. The concept of social class is replaced (or better, displaced) with concepts based on the human individual and the sanctity of his/her social interactions. Society is seen to be a direct product of the total set of the social interactions of its individual members. To the American mind, the individual is the absolute building block of all social relations; to challenge this belief with collectivist concepts is condemned as anti-American and anti-freedom. This hyper-individualism has its effects on social science as well: most American sociological work deviates towards social psychology from the true object of all social research: *social relations*.

Sociology has itself, therefore, played a role in subverting reference to the critical category of social class by inventing and popularizing a plethora of opposed concepts. We are all "middle class" living in a "consumer society" (and therefore, ipso facto, relations of production are no longer important); society is not divided into opposed social classes, but into "prestige" ranked occupational levels (which are complementary, in the Durkheimian sense of the division of labor); and we live in a society "with no barriers to upward mobility." Insofar as a good deal of American sociology has reinforced the displacement of the critical categories of "social class" and "class relations," it has become an ideological tool of the dominant class.

The United States operates with political categories of an earlier day. In one variant or another, the eighteenth-century liberal notion of pluralism remains pervasive. Our "individual liberties," we are told, are ensured by a contradictory counterbalancing of plural elites, by the checks and balances of the three branches of government, or by the supremacy of the market and the automatic balancing effect it has on the pressures of supply and demand. In short, contradiction is displaced from its actual functioning in the logic of class struggle to various spheres where it (quite to the contrary) is said to assure a "dynamic balance" of the status quo. Again, the sociologists and political scientists (whose own mental categories have been structured by this American sociopolitical epistemology), have produced discussion and rubric that play an integral role in the reproduction, legitimization, and "scientific confirmation" of the "classless" American society.

As I mentioned, Americans are deprived of history. European history is almost entirely unknown, and because the origins of American social and political institutions are almost entirely European, our ignorance of European affairs produces a break not only with the European past but also with its present. This has important ideological implications, since it renders Americans unable to compare their own experience with that of European countries. The French Revolution, the Restoration, the Reformation, the Russian Revolution, the rise of fascism—when these events are viewed from the shores of America (from the high school classroom, to be more precise), they seem as removed and as irrelevant as the Neolithic age.

3. I would like, then, to propose some first steps toward creating a viable, critical social science in the United States. The importance of doing so has been referred to above: when there are no critical categories of social experience to compete with hegemonic bourgeois categories, neither crisis nor conflict will by themselves lead to politicization of a polarization along class lines.

Toward an Indigenous Critical Social Science in the U.S.

—broaden the perspective

The deformed and anachronistic categories of American political experience are viable only as long as our view is restricted to
the United States. As soon as we speak of Western Europe, for example, the concepts of social class and class struggle, as well as
the clear necessity to chart all social thought historically, become self-evident. Furthermore, "social theory" as it is presented
in American universities is typically European works in translation. How can we possibly understand their content, let alone
their political implications, when they are read outside of the
geopolitical context in which they were written? The importance
of a world-level perspective has become all the more clear with
the changes in the internationalization of capital, as Immanuel
Wallerstein, Samir Amin and Christien Palloix, among others,
have demonstrated. To understand anything about the United
States, we must place it in the context of international relations
of domination and exploitation in which it plays a major role.

If we have lost our speaking competency in critical social analysis in the United States, perhaps we still have a listening competency. At any rate, it is clearly with the latter that we must begin.
That, of course, is the idea of this book, which presents many different types of European critical thought ; it is up to us to take
what is most relevant for the American experience and to create
an indigenous alternate "paradigm" in which to carry on social
science. It is important to realize, however, that critical social
theory cannot be imported as a finished and settled model. On
the contrary, European critical social analysis is in crisis, and this
discensus is positive and healthy. Critical social thought must be
always an open system of social insight, constantly renewing itself through a process of self-criticism. Nothing is more uncritical than dogmatism—both theoretical and political dogmatism.
Social thought, including critical social thought, must change as
social relations change; frozen critical thought becomes as anachronistic and counterproductive as any other blocked understanding.

—recreate history

In a critical paradigm, social sciences must become deeply historical. We must ignore the artificial academic boundary that ali-

enates us from history; as soon as the object of the social sciences is seen to be social relations (as opposed to reified objects of study in the various fields, such as "society" or, "government" or even "personality"), our mandate to reconstruct the historical development of these relations becomes self-evident. When social sciences cease to study *things*, but instead turn to investigate *processes* and *relations,* the need for an historical framework will turn us all into historians (as were our founding thinkers).

—intervene epistemologically

The inadequacy of the bourgeois categories of social experience must be demonstrated and explained. The most convincing way to accomplish this, however, is not an abstract presentation of critical categories; what is needed is a concrete demonstration of their greater explanatory power. Even granted a partial success of this effort, however, the social sciences will never exhibit the successive displacement of paradigms that both Thomas Kuhn and Karl Popper see happening in the natural sciences (although they disagree as to why and how fast this happens). Because social science "paradigms" are inseparable from their political implications, researchers are not going to be   convinced merely by the "greater explanatory power" of a given critical model over its conservative equivalent. Nevertheless, it is important to have the critical research paradigm at least *available* for interpreting concrete social events by researchers, students, and especially for popular consumers of the findings of social science.

—analyze concrete events

In the United States, given the antiphilosophical and antitheoretical aftereffects of pragmatism, it is particularly important to present critical analysis in the social sciences as insightful and synthetic analyses of concrete events. Critical categories will never be accepted here as a "philosophy" or as an "epistemology" as such, nor is critical social thought by its own nature meant to be presented or discussed in general and philosophical terms. On the contrary, the principle of historical specificity clearly indicates that critical social science investigates the meaning and sense of social events in the particular conjunctures in which they occur. Thus, for both strategic and logical reasons, critical social science in the United States must be based on concrete research that zeros in on specific social topics (always, of course, with the concern of relating the singular to the plural, the particular to the general); these studies can then be contrasted with those carried out from the paradigms of bourgeois social science. If critical epistemological categories and the general world view from which they are drawn become more widespread, readers will experience the critical analysis as fuller, more profound, and more convincing. Critical social research in the United States is therefore directly dependent on the growth of the social movements that question the relations of power, exploitation, and domination that only critical social analysis can satisfactorily explain.

III. CRITICAL SOCIAL SCIENCE AND SOCIAL MOVEMENTS

1. Critical social thought does not originate in the minds of petit bourgeois writers who have the training and time to produce articles and books on the subject. Critical thought, that is, the social categories, historical content, and dialectical logic of historical materialism, is a product of class relations, obviously mediated by individual writers with greater or lesser skill, broader or narrower perspective, deeper or shallower commitment. Critical social theory is fundamentally and ontologically different from other "sociological theories," which are philosophical constructions, whose descriptive power is wholly dependent on the imaginations of their creators.

Marx, for example, did not himself "create" the categories, content, and logic that make up his works; he experienced them in France and England. If he had not seen the revolutionary political movements of the French proletariat and the economic exploitation of the British working class, he would never have removed himself from the philosophical paradigm of his early utopian critiques. I am not claiming, however, that progress in critical theory comes only from the pens of men and women who are also political militants; such claims are either based on a bourgeois premise of the ultimate sanctity of the individual or are based on an anarchist premise of the primacy of activism. My point is that the basic categories of critical epistemology and critical social research, although noted and discussed by the "intelligentsia," are products of an historical epoch, and not the idiosyncratic products of individual writers.

The same can be—and must be—said for the great and noble notions of the rising bourgeoisie. "Freedom," "equality," "fraternity" were not notions "created" by Locke; Hume, Rousseau, and Montesquieu, among others. Ideas of an age, they were employed, not created, by these writers; they were expressions of the class relations between the rising bourgeoisie and the fading aristocracy. In other words, the definition of historical world views such as the bourgeois and dialectical world views, must never be confused with the wanderings of sociological imaginations that we know as "theory building." Profound sociological lessons are to be learned in contrasting the bourgeois and dialectical world views and, particularly, in studying the concrete social forces that produced these world views through the class relations, political struggles, and ideological debates of the past three centuries. This must not be confused with the smaller (but not unimportant) insights gained from observing microsocial phenomena with the help of such sociological theories as Erving Goffman's dramaturgical notions, Howard Becker's insights on labeling, and so on.

Critical social theory and the critical social research paradigm are directly dependent on social movements (social forces that represent popular causes in class struggle) because these movements call into question, by their real actions in the sociopolitical world, the power relations and the ideological discourse of the ruling class. Social power hides itself behind political legitimacy (the "divine right of kings," the "elected representative of the people") because, strategically, the more invisible it is, the more effective it is. For the same reasons, it also throws up a screen of ideological camouflage ("tradition," "patriotism") behind which the cultural choices made by those in power are presented as "neutral" and "natural." It is, historically, social movements—of slaves, peasants, industrial laborers, national minorities, racial minorities, etc.—that, by opposing the social and political domination and economic exploitation of their epoch, have brought into the light of day the (temporarily invisible) class origins of their dependency. The confrontation of these social movements with the ruling classes and class fractions forges the critical understandings of the period. These critical understandings are then expropriated and used in social description and analysis by the radical intelligentsia of the epoch, whether we think of organic intellectuals of the rising bourgeoisie, those of the rising proletariat, or even those of the new working class of our own epoch. World views are not created by the intelligentsia; on the contrary, the intelligentsia is in part structured by the civilizational definitions, epistemological categories, and socio-political assumptions of a given, class-bound, world view.

The resurgence of interest in critical theory and critical social research in the United States is directly due to the social movements that animate our times and question the power relations and ideological hegemony on both a local and a world level. Probably nothing, on the latter level, was more important than the protracted and finally successful struggles of the Vietnamese and Cambodian peoples. At the same time, within the capitalist countries, a remarkable phenomenon occurred in 1968. From New York to California, the student revolt that had begun at Berkeley in 1964 continued, but now almost identically motivated uprisings occurred in Mexico City, Paris, Rome, Tokyo, London, Berlin, Prague and so on. The internationalism of this movement was astounding; it provided an image of new class relations and therefore new class conflicts that had developed since World War II. Furthermore, in many capitalist countries, powerful movements of racial minorities, women, and regional separatists have also questioned other levels of manipulation and domination.

Critical social theory and social research in the United States re-emerged because of these social movements, but it must, if it is to have influence beyond the (still very limited number of) theorists and researchers themselves, be constantly related to the real struggles of concrete social groups. People can only be reached through their own experience; when critical analysis (i.e., critical sociopolitical categories and dialectical logic *applied* to guide the analyses and strategies of social movements) is not related to concrete life experiences of the very people involved, then indeed it seems like only another "theory." In the current ideological conjuncture, it is simply not possible to reach the American populace in the abstract: it is difficult to ask a housewife involved in the women's liberation movement to concern herself with the exploitation of men at work, or to ask the unemployed to see that their interests lie in aligning with those who are exploited in and through their employment, or to ask a black who in every sphere of his life is confronted, blocked, and managed by an institutional racism to align with working-class whites and liberated middle-strata housewives.

Therefore, critical social analysis in the United States must be organic and concrete: *organic* in that it is applied and used by the participants themselves of widely differing social movements, and *concrete* in that it best explains to such individuals the origins of their oppression and the directions of their rebellion. It is inherent in the dialectical epistemology of critical analysis that it be first employed as a method to unscramble the complexities and locate the primary contradiction in given specific instances of domination (historical specificity), and only later employed to construct a cogent world view that ties together such seemingly disparate oppression as that of the unemployed, the exploited employed, women, racial minorities, and so on. In other words, critical thought in the United States must be, and by its nature can be, two things at once. First, it must explain to participants in social movements the political economy of their particular situation of oppression—that is, of the concrete issues that to them are relevant, salient, and personal; second, it must relate their struggle to that of other groups through an analysis of the class relations, political practices and ideological discourse of the society as a whole.

This is not to say that critical social theory and research are synonymous with political activism. On the contrary, there is a relative autonomy of each sphere which must always be recognized. And yet it is in practice where ideologies are broken through and thus new understandings become possible. Critical social theory and research must turn these new insights into explicit understandings. Critical social theory has its own level of problems to solve; it must be organically related to the actual political practices of its historical conjuncture, but it must never be reduced to these practices as if it had no specificity of its own.

Critical social theory is not, therefore, just another sociological theory: it is integrally and organically related to the movement of society itself; it is as much a part of history, a product of history, as it is a study of history. That is why there must be a pluralism of paradigms for social research within critical social analysis. The operational processes and social relations of the modern capitalist and socialist states are complex; no given individual or school of thought can grasp and adequately conceptualize the full range of social phenomena which must be accounted for. Each school of thought, by virtue of its own concrete position in a given social-national-political conjuncture, is particularly well suited to perceive, describe, and analyze certain issues and to misperceive others. We therefore need many critical voices from many conjunctures so that working together, critical insights serve as critiques to each other, and hence extend the common project. That is the logic on which the present collection is based. Presenting authors from different European countries, this book demonstrates what considerable variation there is within the critical approach to social theory and social research. The authors, coming from varied national backgrounds and different political practices, each have their insights and areas of lucidity; the challenge is to critically synthesize their respective partial truths.

2. This application of the critical paradigm of social research to concrete topics does not mean that the empirical findings of different studies will not relate to one another. On the contrary, the critical paradigm is structured by the internal assumptions of the dialectical world view from which it is derived, and as such, all critical studies will be looking for certain patterns and regularities. Any research paradigm is similarly "biased" in the sense that it can only perceive and analyze the object of its study (i.e., produce its "facts") through the filters of its own assumptions and internal logic. There is, thus, no "disinterested" social research, nor any neutral techniques; it is impossible to even ask a sociological question that it is not structured by social and political assumptions. Critical social research has the possibility, all too often neglected, of at least being aware and open about its assumptions and premises. Let me mention three presuppositions of any critical social research that are in fact derived from the dialectical world view itself, rather than deduced from the concrete research to which the paradigm is applied:

a. Critical social theory and research explains social events, not in terms of the categories of everyday life, but in terms of the usually hidden but ultimately important effects of *social relations.* It is not that everyday life is an unimportant level of human social existence; on the contrary, the details of the concrete functioning of this level are crucial. But it simply does not follow that everything social can be explained on this level, as many sociological theories have assumed, particularly those emanating from the individualistically oriented United States. The effort to explain the totality of social events and practices on the level of everyday life is always a *reductionism,* and it can have no more success than other reductionisms, such as the biologism of Konrad Lorenz or the psychologism of B.F. Skinner. Durkheim long ago argued for the emergent properties of social phenomena, and even if his discussion was flawed by his positivist tendency to reify these phenomena instead of letting them be conceived of as relations, the veracity of his general point has been established throughout the history of science. Reductionism simply does not work; a residual content always remains that cannot be explained at a lower level of analysis, despite the interrelations of the various levels.

Similarly, although there is a relative autonomy in the interactions and conscious behaviors of everyday life, it does not follow that "social action" explains everything about social relations.

On the contrary, it is easily shown that cultural and social determinants pattern the general way in which "social actors" construct their interactions in everyday life.

Various sociological theories of everyday life have become
very popular in the United States, and this can only be understood in respect to the situation of hegemony discussed above.
To concentrate on everyday life without referring to the political
and economic structuring of its general patterns is, de facto, to
accept society as it is given. The critical paradigm lifts the sociological imagination from the blinding myriad of everyday events
to the basic processes of class relations, political struggles, and
ideological debates which structure not only the realities, but
even the possibilities, of everyday life. We can clearly, and I think
plausibly, assume that there is a certain autonomy of the individual within a given framework of social relations; the individual
bourgeois and the individual proletariat both manifest this autonomy, but they are not free to choose between identical sets of alternative social actions.

b. Critical social theory and research explains social events in
terms of contradictions. These are not logical contradictions, but
rather (as Lucio Coletti has pointed out) contrarities, conflicts between empirically existing positive social forces. Because the
critical worldview presumes that conflicts and struggle are endemic in any class society, it seeks to discover precisely *where*
and *how* this conflict is operative. It sees stability as a state of tension, and consensus as a managed hegemony.

"History," of course, is no more a "thing" than is "society"; it is
constructed from the assumptions and perceptions of a given
world view and research paradigm. From a critical perspective,
one of the principle aspects of history is a series of conflicts between the ruling classes, and their respective dominated classes.
Besides an analysis of this perennial inter-class struggle, critical
historical research also concentrates on intra-class struggle, as
Nicos Poulantzas, Maurice Zeitlin and others have argued. Marx's
concrete studies of 1848 and 1871 France make evident the extensive explanatory power of successfully accounting for the
interplay of inter- and intra-class conflict.

Critical social research must not sacrifice all concern with "system" in order to center on relations, since it must see society precisely as a *system of social relations*. As such, critical studies are
simultaneously synchronic and diachronic; that is, they pay equal
attention to the *systematic* nature of social relations and to the *historical development* of these relations.

Class conflicts occur at many levels, from the rare armed clashes between revolutionary forces and repressive armies of the ruling class, to conflicts between particular political movements and local police, to conflicts between individuals who are frustrated in their personal life situations and the society that confines and exploits them. The contradictions of society are not only present in overt conflict, however; they also are present in situations of negotiation and compromise, where classes and fractions of classes struggle bloodlessly in different institutional settings (labor contract negotiations, legislative battles, etc.).

The notion of class conflict is often misconceived and distorted. In no sense and in no historical period should this concept be seen as synonymous with armed struggle, although it may at rare times take this form. Class conflict is omnipresent in all institutional and organizational settings of a class society. Class struggle occurs not only in formulating the limits of the political processes of society, but also within the institutional processes. Similarly, the ideological confrontation between ruling class discourse and popular class rejection and ridicule of these concepts and self-serving explanations is a manifestation of class struggle.

Class struggle occurs in ideological phenomena: the films of François Goddard and Luis Buñuel, for example, have important critical content. Class struggle is evident in our schools in the subjects and topics that are taught, in the choice of teachers and professors who are hired, and in the books that are chosen. As social domination becomes more widespread with the incursion of class relations into the patterns and processes of consumption, the field of class conflict is extended. As the critical world view becomes progressively more available as an alternate social perspective to the bourgeois worldview, perhaps we could even speak of class conflict inside the minds of individuals who struggle to determine which perspective to employ.

The critical assumption of the omnipresence of conflict and contradiction reminds us that a particular social phenomenon we set out to study is not a social "thing"; rather it is a dynamic complex of social relations that is in constant tension as opposed social forces attempt to change its temporary composition in the direction of their interest. "Capital," said Marx, is not a thing, but a social relation. The "state," says Nicos Poulantzas in his article in this volume, is not a thing, but a social relation. One can go further: *there are no social "things,"* and therefore *no* political institutions, and *no* social organizations. There are only political institutional settings in which one level of social relations occurs (con-

flicting social classes and fractions of classes negotiating and compromising, thereby forming the "rules of the game"). These rules determine limits and goals for organizational settings in which another level of social relations occurs (management and subordinates carry out instrumental production). Organizational relations are a web of decisions, commands, and repression on the part of the authorities; of demands, subversion, and occasional rebellion by subordinates. At most times, a temporary state of compromise and tension allows for the functioning of the production process, while at times of crisis, which is endemic in capitalism, compromise gives way to conflict, and struggles over production conditions give way to struggles over authority relations.

c. Finally, critical social theory and research explain social events in terms of the system of social relations taken as a whole. "The truth is the whole," wrote Hegel. Society is such an intricately interlinked system of social relations that any effort to study a given social event in total isolation from other relations and processes is defeated before it begins. In bourgeois society, the analytic reigns supreme over the synthetic; the critical ideal is to harmonize these two variants of human thought.

One of the most tragic (and mammoth) examples of the intellectually self-destructive effects of the hegemony of analytic over synthetic (holistic) thought in our society, is the bourgeois university itself, with its innumerable "disciplines." Not only have the social sciences been completely divorced from the natural and health sciences, the humanities and arts, the schools of business and law, but they also have been irreparably divided from each other. The intellectual implications of this organization is that sociologists, historians, political scientists, anthropologists, and psychologists do not need to know anything about one another's work. Books are neatly labeled "sociology" or "political science" by publishers, placed on appropriate shelves by bookstore managers, and respectively perused by appropriately credentialed academics. It is very clear that one can get censored in bourgeois academia for "wandering" into neighboring domains; intellectual trespassing has its institutional punishments.

Critical social research, on the other hand, demands that these debilitating divisions be eradicated. It claims that it is impossible to understand "the market" or "government" or "society" without stepping back to focus on the complex system of class relations that takes economic, political, social, cultural, legal, and psychological manifestations. Critical social research rejects the bourgeois ideology that claims that the "knowledge explosion"

has necessitated the identity of insightfulness and expertise, and the definition of broader research as "interdisciplinary."

Thus, nothing is mysterious about the reference to "totality" on which the dialectical worldview insists. The assumption is simply that because the system of social relations can only be analyzed by studying the complex interrelations between the relatively autonomous processes of capital-labor conflicts, political struggles, and ideological debates, the meaning of each of these can only be grasped as a function of the system of social relations taken as a whole.

3. It is as easy to underestimate the importance of critical social theory as it is to overestimate it. It is overestimated when it is confused with the actions of the social movements that (informed by critical insights) are the agents of social change. Critical social theory, as such, is not a social force; it becomes viable and important only insofar as it is embodied in the practices and goals of various social movements.

Critical social thought, however, is underestimated when it is viewed as just another branch of sociology, just another sociological theory. The state-by-state fascistization of Latin America has documented that social research, particularly critical social research, is important to the juntas; critical social scientists by the hundreds have been murdered, tortured, imprisoned, and exiled. (At the time of this writing, one of the contributors to this volume, Emilio de Ipola, is lost somewhere in a Brazilian prison for the "crime" of his sociological ideas.) If social research, and critical social research in particular, were totally unimportant, why would the fascists fear it so?

It is feared because it speaks out at a particularly profound level of analysis. The psychological level, in contrast, is no threat; no one is pushing the cause for schizophrenia; therefore even if fascism were increasing the rates of schizophrenia, psychology qua psychology could not locate this relation. Similarly, sociology as such is not a threat; the Chilean junta is not repressing studies of social mobility along Blau and Duncan lines. The threat of critical social science is precisely that it destroys the academic barbed wire that marks off the various "disciplines." Critical social science is not interdisciplinary; it is antidisciplinary. It synthetically assembles a world view that explains in a coherent, unified fashion the relations between (to continue with the example of Chile) the internationalization of capital, the relations of national and internal bourgeoisie, the international "agreement" on Latin America between the United States and the

Soviet Union, the role of the international Latin American army trained and coordinated by the United States in Kansas and Panama City, the external economic presssures created by the American-directed manipulation of the international copper market and the World Bank, the internal political contradictions of the Allende government, the inability of his regime to mobilize around social issues and increase its legitimacy, the attacks on Allende of the bourgeois-owned press, and so on. These factors, taken together, explode the definitions and boundaries of the various bourgeois social sciences; yet only this type of macroexplanation could possibly give meaning to the role of any one single factor in which one was particularly interested.

Is there any proof that critical social research is similarly repressed in the United States? I submit that the fact that there are only a thousand (or am I wrong; is it five thousand?) critical scholars in the United States is itself proof of repression. We also can follow throughout American history the various purges of critical professors and writers during the incessant and recurrent periods of "red scare." We have recently learned about the Hoover/Nixon effort to sabotage the careers of critically oriented professors by such means as sending false "letters from interested parties" to deans and trustees.

4. Two tasks of critical social science are represented in this volume: that of the critique of social thought (the development of critical social theory), and that of critical concrete analysis (the application of critical social research). The critique of social thought has two principal branches, the first involving the critique of bourgeois thought, the second involving the critique of critical thought. The critique of bourgeois social thought demonstrates its social and political bias, its ideological origins and purpose, its superficial fixation with everyday life, and its usual ahistorical nature. However, the critique of bourgeois thought must never be seen as an automatic process of rejection, a simple battle of words.

On the contrary, critical social thought derives directly from bourgeois concepts; it searches for the rational kernel in the mystical shell. There was no better consumer of bourgeois thought than Karl Marx—but he was a picky eater. Perhaps only the concept of "labor power" is new to his work; all the rest was developed by bourgeois philosophers, political theorists, and political economists. What he did, of course, was to recombine these concepts in the logical framework of the dialectical world view, where they became critical, even explosive. (The *Theories of Surplus Value* represents, in effect, Marx's study notes—critiques as it were—of his critical reading of bourgeois political economy.) Thus, bourgeois thought in general and its social science in particular, are *not* to be rejected outright. They say much, both on and between the lines; it is up to the critical method to realize and to advance what is of value in the extensive literature, and to place it in a critical framework, where it will take on new and expanded meanings.

The second major target of critique involves the critique of critical thought itself: its anachronisms, omissions, and errors must be exposed, discussed, and resolved. Critical social thought, by its own logic, is meant to be anything but a collection of holy texts that require exegetical clarifications. The concepts of critical social research must be as dynamic and as changing as the social relations they denote. We must develop new concepts to deal with new conjunctures in class relations, and we must discard old concepts that no longer grasp the social world and that, therefore, impede both theoretical and practical advances. Errors must be openly discussed and critiqued on all levels: the theoretical errors of critical thought, the strategic errors of progressive social movements, and the political errors of socialist regimes.

The second task of critical social science is that of analyzing concrete social events and phenomena. Critical social research must not allow itself to be what it has so often been—a social philosophy, an abstract philosophy of society. Far more important and far more consistent with the internal logic of dialectical epistemology is that it be applied to concrete social research. Every area studied by bourgeois social science is fertile ground for the richest type of critique—the critique that does not, *a priori*, merely claim to be more adequate but that, *a posteriori*, proves itself to be more adequate to anybody willing to compare it with the bourgeois analysis of the same concrete problem. Of course, the politics of selecting the more adequate explanation is obvious, and the number of people who can be won over to the dialectical world view by its sheer explanatory power will be small indeed. As Kuhn explained, people do not substitute new research paradigms for old simply because the new is superior to the old. The change is social, not logical (as Popper would have it); but it also is not merely social (as Kuhn would have it). It is historical, and the historical movement of the social world as a whole is clearly in the direction of socialism. I suppose even the United States is slowly creating in its great womb its own appropriate form of socialism; in the meantime, American social scientists must sharpen their theoretical tools and must use them to assist in the most difficult job of midwifery that history has ever known.

PART I
THE CRITIQUE OF SOCIAL THEORY: REBUILDING THE CRITICAL PARADIGM

1.
THE CONCEPT OF SPECIFICITY

ANOUAR ABDEL-MALEK
Translated by J. W. Freiberg

ORIENTATIONS

There is hardly need to argue the need—both for the sciences of man and society, on the one hand, and societal practice, on the other hand—for a concept that can relate the particular to the universal, the sectorial to the general, in order to unify our vision and comprehension of the world. Never before have we been witness and partner to such an intensely variegated range of societal units and processes, and this, at the very time when gigantic strides in scientific discoveries and their technological applications are coupled with global systems, in the guise of ideologies, blueprints for world systems, prospective utopias, and the like.

This need is particularly felt in the hitherto nonparticipant areas of the world, that is, Asia, Africa, Latin America, or, in what we call the East (the Asian circle, around China; the Islamic circle, around the Arab World and its aura in Africa; and parts of Central and South America). It is in the non-participant areas of the world that the quest for authenticity and national identity is most forceful, as it is directly linked to the rise of national movements against the hegemony that the West imposed on them in the fifteenth century. Yet a parallel concern with the major types of social systems in the advanced countries is pushing to the fore the normative quest in that sector of the world too. This second aspect, that is, the resurgence of the normative quest in the West, has been accelerated by the rise of the East during our century. Thus, the need to investigate the interrelations between the particular and the universal, the sectorial and the general, can be said to be universally felt in present human societies.

Indeed, a very wide range of problems and questions exists.

How could we relate—if at all, and then, to what degree—the structure of power in new states (Papua New Guinea, Guyana, Jamaica); federal or confederal states; instances of the modern national states; ancient nation-states? Is there a bridge linking, in a comprehensive manner, the definition of cultural policy in France, Brazil, Egypt, Australia, Japan, and Mexico? Could we reach a consensus on a comparatist approach of, say, political pluralism and identity, the capacity for societal changes and transformations in societies as different as Canada, Paraguay, Indonesia, Madagascar? What is the potential capacity for intellectual creativity, scientific and technological innovations, resistance to change, the interplay of archaism-cum-modernity in nations like Mongolia and Italy, Hungary and Chile, Peru and India?

Key problems now relegated under the labor of "exceptionalism" are deeply perplexing to the traditional mind: for example, the role of the army in politics; the resurgence of the national dimension, specifically under the guise of the nationalitarian phenomenon; the subtle evolution of religions toward the cultural-ideological dimension; the growing awareness of the convergence of formally very different patterns of societal maintenance, such as the autocratic state, political pluralism, populist tribal consensus. There is hardly a major field of the sciences of man and society that remains immune from such ambiguities and from the quest for a relevant solution.

The following points, presented in outline form, bring together a number of positions, in order to clarify the major issues around what we submit is the key conceptual tool: the concept of specificity

A. THE FRAME OF COMPARATISM

The first and preliminary step onto the new path that we are ad-
vocating is to introduce some form of coherent typology of the
macrosocietal units to be compared. In other words, before comparing, we ought to know what, really, we are comparing. Three
major interwoven types of circles constitute the frame of comparatism.

1. *Civilizations.* This is the outer, more general circle defined
from Joseph Needham's approach as
    a. the circle of Indo-Aryan civilization
    b. the circle of Chinese civilization
This level of analysis leaves Latin America to be accounted for
later.

2. *Cultural areas.* This is the mediating circle, which is often
confused with the civilizational circle, as in Arnold Toynbee's
work. Broadly, the following cultural areas can be circumscribed.
    a. in the Indo-Aryan civilization circle
    —the Egyptian, Persian, Mesopotamian antiquities
    —the Greco-Roman antiquity
    —the European cultural area
    —the North American cultural area
    —major parts of the Indo-European cultural area in Latin
      America
    —the Sub-Saharan African cultural area
    —the Islamic cultural area, partially, that is, the Arab-Islamic
      and Persian-Islamic cultural areas (to the exclusion of the
      Asian-Islamic cultural area, which is linked with the Chi-
      nese civilization circle)
    b. in the Chinese civilization circle
    —China proper
    —Japan
    —Mongolia-Central Asia
    —the Indian subcontinent
    —Oceania (with the exception of Australia–New Zealand)
    —the Asian-Islamic cultural area (from Persia to the
      Philippines)
These two, outer major circles exemplify the historical and fundamental worlds of mankind: East and West.

In fact, "East" is composed of the following parts:
    a. the circle of Chinese civilization and its cultural areas
    b. the circle of Islamic civilization, which clearly is the one
      major link between the circle of Indo-Aryan civilization and

the circle of Chinese civilization, both as a mediation and as an area of maximal tensions

c. parts of the Indo-European cultural area of Latin America, that are directly linked with Africa, that is, specifically Brazil and the Caribbean

d. the Sub-Saharan African cultural area

The "West," therefore, is composed of the major sections of Indo-Aryan civilization.

3. *Nations* (or "national formations"). These are the basic units for the very existence, continuity, unfolding, and evolution of macrosocietal processes. Our typology suggests five categories

a. the fundamental nations, also described as renascent nations (Egypt, China, Persia, and Turkey; Vietnam, Mexico, Morocco)

b. the European, then Occidental, type of nation-state

c. the new nation-states heading toward unification. Both the new nation-states strictly speaking (Ethiopia, Ghana, Mali, Burma, Thailand, etc.), and the national formations within the framework of multinational ensembles (Armenia, Georgia, Ouzbekistan, etc.)

d. the dualistic Indian, then European, nation-state mainly in Latin America

e. the new states with a national vocation (mainly in several parts of Sub-Sahara Africa and a minor portion of Central and South America)

4. The key distinctions among the three circles cannot be dealt with here except in very broad outline.

a. Civilizational areas are defined by the general conception of the interrelation between cultures, nations, societal formations, on the one hand, and the time-dimension, on the other. It is this philosophic relation to "time, the field of human development," and its consequences, that distinguishes East from West.

b. Cultural areas can then be seen as societal ensembles sharing a common *weltanschauung,* more in terms of historical-geographical determinism through history (both ecological and geopolitical) than in terms of philosophy proper. These areas often conceptualize the world in terms of a limited set of dominant languages (Arabic, Chinese, English, Persian, Japanese).

c. Nations—or national formations—are easier to delimit, once agreement is reached on the indispensable structuring typology.

Yet once we posit these interwoven circles—the frame of comparatism—we have only posited a topographical description (anatomy) of the field for comparatism. We now must relate dialectically the different units within each of the three circles to the other two circles. This, precisely, is the purpose of our concept of specificity.

B. THE CONCEPT OF SPECIFICITY: STRUCTURE AND DYNAMICS

We propose to view the concept of specificity from its first global formulation in 1970:

The concept of specificity can be analyzed at three levels/moments:

1. The level/moment of general definition, as from the origin. In order to grasp the specificity of a given society, one should seek the pattern of societal maintenance of its socio-economic national formation, as, for example, from a critical study of its historical development. This particular pattern of societal maintenance is nothing else but the pattern of structuration and interaction among the four key factors that constitute every societal maintenance: the production of material life in the geographic and ecologic framework (the mode of production stricto sensu); the reproduction of life (sexuality); the social order (power and the state); the relation with the time-dimension (the limitedness of human life, religions, and philosophies). In that ensemble, the production of material life is decisive in the structuration of the whole pattern of maintenance, but only so in the last instance. By applying this model to different societies, we are better able to clarify the general picture, to qualify and to give color—through the introduction of dominant touches—the first analysis undertaken as from socio-economic criteria.

2. The level/moment of the emergence of spatio-temporal factors to conscious awareness. The study of specificity is not undertaken in the outer world of pure epistemology, but within the framework of the concrete evolution of given societies. This evolution puts the time factor in the forefront, therefore deriving the central importance of the notion of "depth of the historical field." It is easy to seek specificity in the case of an occasional society—a jamboree; student movements; an artificial state (Biafra), and so on. To talk of societal maintenance, however, we must address ourselves to the long duration of history, not to

contingency. By that we mean that one could validly speak of specificity in the old social-national formations—the ideal terrain for specificity—in those formations that have not yet or that have just reached the national level of evolution. One can thus see the vastness of the field: the immense majority of nations and peoples in our time. The social sciences will feel less at ease with the "space" factor because of the disfavor of geopolitics. However, the historical evolution of societies does not take place in the abstract space of the dialectics of the mind, neither does it unfold itself in the secluded field of epistemology. Societies, but only within the framework of their geographical conditions, can be considered under two aspects: localization, which leads to the appreciation of the place assigned to each society and to its state as compared to others, that is, geopolitics; and internal conditioning, that is, ecology, which indicates and quantifies resources and potentials that then have to be tempered by demographic factors.

3. The concept of specificity will be used both in the hegemonic area and in the dependent area.

Several problems should be located and studied because they constitute the structuring frame of specificity and are at the nodal point of meaningful social theory. These problems can be organized in two groups:

   a. the uses of the concept of specificity; that is, the relevance
   of the concept in different types of societies
   b. the definition of the priority areas for comparatism, using
   specificity as the main conceptual tool

C. SPECIFICITY AND AUTHENTICITY

The path from "universalism" to specificity remains in the field of exceptionalism because the prevailing assumptions of Western-centered theoretical self-assurance and reductionism cannot be expected to wither away, even in our fluctuating world.

Specificity, however, is here to stay.

We will pose the question in the following terms: Where, exactly, does specificity belong?

Specificity seems to be relevant to all existing societies. A glance at the growing body of literature gives a rather different image, for the accepted, or acceptable, concept of specificity is tamed to deal with non-Western, nonindustrialized national societies: China, the Indian sub-continent; Asia (with the excep-

tion of Japan); the Arab and Islamic worlds; Africa; hinterland
Latin America. Some form of theoretical *aggiornamento* seems to
have been attempted, from the now defunct *sociologie coloniale* to
the still affluent sociology of development (or "underdevelopment," or "Third World," etc.). Ethnicity in sociological garb.
This is how the concept of specificity is being conceived and applied. Several terms have been adopted or coined to show how
ideally relevant specificity is to marginal societies. Thus, the
Arabic sustantive *al-açalâh* (authenticity) has been introduced as
a synonym for specificity.

Let us look more closely. What, in a sociological perspective,
could be considered authentic? Manners and customs, social and
ethical values, traditional patterns; in other words, the whole
gamut of phenomena pertaining to the past, yet maintained more
or less intact, homogeneous and relevant, until our times. Thus,
in *açalâh* (vision); the values of Bedouinism, as the Arab form of
nomadism, stand side by side with the Arab concepts of honor;
sensuous love; political rhetoric; architecture; the mystic-cum-
erotic musical and vocal genre of the *muwasshahât;* the simul-
taneous capacity for cultural dialogue and cultural irredentism,
among other things, creating Arabian-Islamic authenticity.
Similar attempts have been at work to delineate the authenticity
of other national-cultural areas and national societies.

Now, we have really arrived at the sum total of major different
characteristics of one given societal ensemble (civilizations;
national-cultural areas, national societies) as compared to other
such ensembles. And yet when such catalogues are established,
they are mainly about non—Western societies. Attempts to compare the catalogues of two or more non-Western societies evalu-
ate each *quantitatively*—not interpret (*historicist-critical* or
historical-dialectical) their continued existence. Moreover, no attempt is made to understand the variations in the existence, impact, or style of evolution as they develop within one given frame
of societal maintenance, thus eluding the pattern of societal
maintenance of the unit under scrutiny. What we have amassed is
some sort of sophisticated list of "manners and customs" under
non-Western national flags, a compendium for the educated
traveler, businessman, or diplomat.

In the area of general, normalized comparatism, catalogues are
taking extreme statistical shapes, that is, numerical computa-
tions devoid of historical, or analytical-objective, background, as
exemplified in current "data programs."

Thus, we reach the stage where "new" conceptual tools serve

mainly to negate the vigorous process of opening up the hitherto sectorial, Western-centered field of vision to the whole world.

And yet the whole world is here for us to ponder, challenging us to readjust our theoretical tools to a global scale. The intellectual climate has provided the vital inspiration to delimit, define, and gradually elaborate the concept of specificity. But in our view, there is no time for restrictive, reductionist approaches. We need, in our visions and our ideas, and in the realm of politics, an instrument that can simultaneously:

I. account for the persistence and evolution of all societies—what we call the *pattern of societal maintenance,* and

2. do so from common, ascertainable factors that pertain to all national societies and work in each of them to varying degrees and shapes, as from the historical-geographical frame of existence within which each society has functioned and is functioning to this day.

Let us return to the type of instance that is illustrated by the above mentioned *al-açalâh.* '' As we know, literally dozens of such instances and denominations can easily be traced.

At times, they would refer to the prevailing ethnicist assumptions, which were, more or less, racialist and nearly always ethnocentrist, that is, Western-centered. In a more sophisticated manner and more recently, such shades of interpretation derive their credentials form the Weberian "idealtypus" conception: particularism was deemed to have its roots in the objectively different types of societies and social formations; and these differences were ascribed to the unfolding of history, as it were, of different ideal types of social formations, different historical personalities, from their structural, intellectual, and spiritual characteristics.

To many social thinkers, the Weberian approach is a more progressive rational one than the usual potpourri of preassumptions and prejudices. Yet it also means:

1. a recognition of the differences in all societies as against the reductionist assumption of universality and the subsequent policy of compulsory universality.

2. the unbridgeable gap between such different social formations, mainly under the guise of nations or national-cultural ensembles. Each unit being now nonreducible to other units, having been fully credited with its particularity, and this particularity itself defined as structurally different from other such particularities—structurally and not as a *result of the objective course of its historical development.*

Examples here abound following the so-called *açalâh*. We could cite in a tentative list: the accusation of militarism leveled against several nations and national-cultural ensembles of both East and West; the dreamy and sentimental character of, say, the Mediterranean ensemble; the elusive relation to the time-dimension in Latin America; the nonintegrative tendency said to obtain in Sub-Saharan Africa; rationalism in France; the historical and philosophical mind in Germany; pragmatism and experimentalism in the Anglo-Saxon world; the drive for new frontiers in the United States and the Soviet Union; the symbiotic, integrative vision of the world in the oldest nations (Egypt, China, Persia, etc.).

A tentative list—and one can easily think of additional items —yet even at this modest level, one can see how nonreducible are the variations. We are all deemed to be different, and condemned to remain so; separate and incapable of joining hands. The recognition of differences, this right to be different, leads to segregation, isolation, noncommunication. Our world appears to be a constellation of monads, unrelated and alien to each other because of their very differences.

Is there a way out from this mechanistic nightmare?

D. UNDERSTANDING THE GLOBAL DEPTH-REALITY

The concept of specificity can, and should, chart the path by which meaningful and relevant comparatism leads toward the restructuration of social theory. And it can do so by locating the priority areas for comparatism.

Which criteria should be selected?

I. Let us accept, and allow for, the widest possible range of pluralism: priorities and criteria in the social sciences are clearly defined, or delineated, under the direct influences of political power and the indirect influences of socio-economic factors. Obviously, legitimate institutional and personal scientific preferences and choices also are at work. The question of priorities and their criteria remains to be scrutinized.

Let us begin from the above statements.

A first range of priorities for comparatism, and therefore of criteria leading to the positing of such given priorities, will obviously lie in the near and medium range fields, that is, in the project—socio-economic, political, cultural—defined by any national society at one given stage of its historical evolution. The common characteristic of such an approach—which is, for practical purposes, inevitable and useful—is that it addresses itself to the field of the feasible, to social praxis and practical politics, using mainly quantitative tools, inasmuch as the long historical perspective seems of little immediate relevance here. Such appears to be what we would propose to term *operational comparatism*—or functional, tactical comparatism.

The depths remain unexplored, wherein lie the raw materials of social theory. And this is precisely where the concept of specificity can best be deployed, inasmuch as the *"depth of the historical field"* constitutes the very stuff of which this concept is composed, the source from which it stems, and without which the very thought of developing such a concept could not have arisen. If we accept this approach, we would then have a whole set of factors that leads to definitions of priorities and criteria. This level-form of comparatism we would propose to term *fundamental/ meaningful comparatism*—or civilizational, strategic comparatism.

2. The four key areas would constitute the mode of societal maintenance itself: production of material means of life; reproduction of human life; social power; relations with the time-dimension. Although a large number of phenomena and factors could indeed be grouped under those four headings, still there would remain an immense amount of factors and phenomena that are of an historically transient nature.

Several questions emerge:

a. Are all four areas equally important to the development of fundamental comparatism?

Here, we would have to look into the direct patterns of inter-relations between each one of these areas, on the one hand, and the necessities of social praxis, on the other. The area of production of material means of life cannot be separated from the very nature of practical politics, of immediate and continuing social praxis, and this is why, perhaps, Marx selected this as the ultimate decisive area in social dialectics. Moreover, this is so in spite of the fact that there is a specific mold to, say, socio-economic capitalistic formations and development in different national societies and national-cultural ensembles (Japan and Canada; Sweden and Egypt), which is, in turn, an expression, or actualization, of the particular specificity of each of these societies.

b. The other areas, or groups of factors, seem to be more permeated with specificity. They seem to constitute the level of the superstructure proper, although the reproduction of human life, that is, the whole field of sexuality, stands at the crossroads of economic production, on the one hand, and the power-cum-culture ensemble, on the other. One could note that an evolution has taken place in that complex balance: for whereas sexuality could be said to have been more directly linked with economic production in the precapitalist societies, where self-awareness was not magnified by the mass media and by the ethos of productivism and consumerism; and conversely, whereas sexuality can now be said to be immensely more attuned to, and permeated by, the changing images of the human condition, particularly to and by its relations with the time-dimension, philosophy, ideology, metaphysics, religion, mysticism, as well as to its transformation, literally, through the mounting struggle for the transformation of woman's condition in advanced societies.

c. Power in societies has vividly manifested its structural links with the hidden part of the iceberg, that is, the depth roots of national-cultural specificity, notably in, for example, the diverging paths of socialism as exemplified by the Soviet Union and China: the role of the army at the center of political power in the whole range of Nasserism (Egypt, Algeria, Peru, Argentina, Portugal, among others) as against the hitherto traditional reactionary obscurantist putschism prevalent in regions with weak national traditions; the fortunes of liberalism in Western capitalist countries; the postcolonial phase, as engaged in by the former colonial powers (notably, Great Britain, France, Portugal, Belgium); and American hegemonic imperialism (in Vietnam, as the most extreme case).

d. Nowhere, however, more than in the fourth area of the pattern of societal maintenance, as defined above—that is, the relations with the time-dimension—do we meet the same density of manifest specificity. For this is the very heart of the realm of culture and thought; it is the level where culture and thought reach their apex in a delicate network of sophisticated and systematic construction of religion and philosophy. Here, we experience but a limited need to explain different styles, shapes, molds, characters, for we obviously are treading on the familiar ground of ethnicity, coming to grips with the recognizable part of the iceberg.

Yet the significance of this massive evidence is not always

perceived. If culture and thought—revolving around the relation of man with time-dimension, as expressed in religions and philosophies—can show such a load of differences, such explicit types of specificity, then it must be that they express the sum total of societal maintenance, the global depth-reality, achievements, balance sheet, and potentials of a given society. The relevance of the evidence of such an exceptional load of specificity is a revealing phenomenon of paramount importance.

It follows, therefore, that the field of the combined aesthetic-intellectual superstructure proper—which expresses itself in religions, philosophies, metaphysics, ideologies, metapsychological and mystical forms—is where fundamental/meaningful comparatism—strategic civilizational comparatism—can best deploy its resources and reap the widest harvest. For here, more than in other fields, we can see the all-pervading central constitutive influence of the time dimension, of the depth of the historical field.

3. Thus, a preliminary attempt to define the priority areas for comparatism shows:

a. that the area/field/level of the greatest and most explicit differences—that of cultural and aesthetic intellectual superstructure, as exemplified in philosophies, religions, ideologies—can serve as the major starting point for fundamental/meaningful comparative research and inquiry;

b. that we therefore should be able to benefit from the work done at that level to clarify aspects of specificity in the two other superstructural areas—reproduction of physical life; power in societies—and to shed some light on the economic infrastructural domain;

c. that the broader and richer area could be defined as encompassing both the factor of man's relation to the time-dimension and the factor of power in society, for power seldom hesitates to relate itself to given religions, philosophies, ideologies—although it often conceals its organic links with the economic infrastructure, which is itself heavily permeated with technological advances that are easy to relate to different national-cultural areas.

4. One major example sheds some light on this highly complex field. Let us consider the range of societies that have come to be known as "hydraulic societies," which depend on artificial irrigation for the production of their food supplies. These societies are found mainly in the tropical, subtropical, and equatorial areas of the world from where the oldest societies and,

therefore, civilizations have sprung (Egypt, Mesopotamia, China, central and north India, Central America, central Africa). According to this theory, artificial irrigation—that is, the erection of dams, canals and drains—was the only way to control the major rivers, such as the Nile, the Yang-Tse Kiang, the Ganges, the Tigris, the Euphrates, the Congo. This need for persistent, continous, and systematic control of an immensely complex network of irrigation inevitably compelled sedentary societies to create an instrument for central unified control. It can be easily understood that after centuries, in fact after several thousand years, an inevitable autocratic character developed in these states. All and well. Yet, immediately, two major questions can be posed:

a. If the autocratic nature of state power in these regions can be seen in such a range of societies, does it not follows that the autocratic nature of state power all over the world and throughout the range of human history, except for brief interludes in restricted areas, is anything but a temporary condition? Is it not more appropriate to consider that the functions of the state are, per se, those of societal control, of the rationalized use of violence toward the maintenance of a given social order? To be sure, there are different degrees of autocracy. Yet to this day, the role of violence seems to have been persistent throughout history.

b. If we take the range of societies, as indicated above, could we really say that social and cultural institutions, phenomena, and processes are identical in, say, Vietnam and the Sudan, Pakistan and Morocco, Iraq and Cambodia? And if they are not how do we account for the differences, unless we accept superficial generalities and refuse the depths of the concpet of specificity that explore the dimension of both maintenance and transformation of each one of these societies and national-cultural groups?

Thus could end parochialism. Any advanced industrialized society does not need to negate or hide its load of authenticity, its *aṣalâh,* so to speak, or to consider its own "manners and customs" as constituting its specificity. The same is true of less industrialized, mainly non-Western societies. The concept of specificity appears to be the integrative conceptual tool par excellence—while better discovering what makes societies different through the whole course of their historical evolution. This is integrative and dialectically unifying—but not reductionist. Instead of data banks, which are valuable when informing basic historicist-critical analyses, the concept of specificity integrates the quantitative-statistical approach in our present synthetic view of our world and reaches in two major directions, vertically (historical evolution) and horizontally (civilizations, cultural areas, national societies).

2.

HABERMAS' CRITIQUE OF HERMENEUTICS

ANTHONY GIDDENS

Jurgen Habermas' writings are still only poorly understood in the English speaking world. This is in part because they often are treated as merely a latter-day offshoot of the so-called Frankfurt School, whereas in fact there are major differences between the works of Habermas and those of the "older generation" of Frankfurt philosophers. Another reason is that certain Marxist authors have dogmatically rejected the strongly marked revisionism integral to all of Habermas' endeavors without giving them the detailed consideration they deserve. There is, however, a third factor involved. Habermas writings draw extensively, albeit critically, on streams of thought that Anglo-Saxon philosophy has for the most part held at arm's length: in particular, Hegelianism and the tradition of the *Geisteswissenschaften.*[1] Here I shall use Habermas' critical connection with the latter as a mode of entry into his work.

GADAMER AND HERMENEUTICS

The tradition of the *Geisteswissenschaften,* or "hermeneutic tradition," has always been more or less closely tied to idealism in philosophy, although not specifically to Hegel's "objective idealism," which it antedates. If there is a central unifying notion involved, it is of course that of *Verstehen. Geisteswissenschaften* was coined by the German translator of J. S. Mill to render the latter's "moral sciences." Frederick Dilthey, whose earlier work culminates the first phase of development of the hermeneutic tradition, and whose later writings presage the more recent formulations of hermeneutics by Hans-Georg Gadamer, was by no means wholly opposed to Mill's views. While insisting on the differentiation of *Verstehen* (understanding) and *Erklären* (explanation) as established by Droysen, Dilthey was as certain as Droysen was that a precise science of history was needed. An emphasis on the necessary subjectivity of human action was to be complemented by an acknowledgment of the demand that the study of human conduct meet similar standards of "objective" assessment as those paramount in the natural sciences. For the early Dilthey, *Verstehen* was conceptualized as involving *Erlebnis,* the "reliving" or "reenactment" of the event by the historical analyst. The difficulties of reconciling *Verstehen* and *Erlebnis,* as it is dependent on an imaginative grasp of other subjective experiences and an objective foundation of the human sciences that would be comparable to that achieved in natural science, are obvious enough. Dilthey's struggle led him away from his early position. Max Weber, who from the beginning rejected the idea of the causal exclusiveness of natural science as favored by Dilthey, also tried to distance his version of the logic of *Verstehen* from the notion of reliving. That he was unsuccessful, however, is indidated by definite paradoxes to which his views give rise.[2]

The more recent revival of the hermeneutic tradition, as led by Gadamer, has been heavily influenced by the rise of phenomenology, although not in the form advocated by Husserl. It seems useful to distinguish three broad stages in the development of phenomenology.[3] The first was that established by Edmund Husserl's own program of transcendental phenomenology, the search for the basis of "knowledge free from presuppositions." In the second phase, several of Husserl's most prominent followers, including Johan Scheler, Jean-Paul Sartre, and Alfred Schutz, implicitly or explicitly abandoned such a quest in favor of an existential phenomenology, prefigured in Husserl's *Crisis of the*

European Sciences, in which the emphasis is on the primacy of the self in the lived-in world. The third phase is that of hermeneutic phenomenology, developed particularly in Martin Heidegger's later writings and by Paul Ricoeur, whose leading theme is the linguistic character of human "being in the world." In Gadamer's hands, hermeneutic phenomenology is used to formulate a radical rethinking of the idea of *Verstehen* and of the character of the *Geisteswissenschaften.*

While earlier authors treated *Verstehen* primarily as a method whereby historians or social scientists gain a systematic access to "subject matter," Gadamer regards it as the very condition and mode of human intersubjectivity. Language, not "reliving," is the medium of understanding, which is specifically not a "psychological" matter. For Gadamer, as for Heidegger, "language speaks its own being." The proper locus for an historically oriented hermeneutics is not in the behavior of individuals but in the reading of texts. Texts manifest the autonomy of language; they can be understood as meaningful products without any particular knowledge of their authors, for language is not the intentional creation of language-speakers; it is the public medium of social being. *Verstehen* can be represented as the mediation of traditions through dialogue, where "tradition" is the frame of meaning constituted by a language community—a "form of life." There is no escaping the historicity of traditions: hence, it is futile to seek a foundation in knowledge that is free from presuppositions. "Knowledge" is generated by, and is only possible within, traditions. The reading of a text that originates in a past tradition involves a creative mediation of traditions, a process that can never be "completed" because of the very historicity of human understanding. Hence, there cannot be an "objective" foundation for hermeneutics in the manner in which that term is conceived of in positivistic philosophies. However, according to Gadamer, the abandoning of "method" in hermeneutics does not entail the abandoning of "truth": the latter is guaranteed by the authenticity of the tradition from within which understanding is accomplished. It is exactly here that hermeneutics finds its task; hermeneutics is the universal principle of philosophy.[4]

HABERMAS ON THE "CLAIM TO UNIVERSALITY" OF HERMENEUTICS

Gadamer's claim about the universality of hermeneutics and its critique by K. O. Apel and by Habermas bear interesting similarities to the critical reception of the writings of Peter Winch by Ernest Gellner and others in Anglo-Saxon philosophy. Although Winch's views have not been worked out so elaborately as Gadamer's, they can be constructed as making a parallel case for the "universality of hermeneutics" in the explication of human action. Understanding human conduct is not a casual endeavor; it uncovers its intelligibility by relating it to the rules that constitute a form of life. The mediation of forms of life or language-games then emerges as a focal point of interest, although Winch's discussions of this are confined to problems of understanding alien cultures rather than oriented toward history.[5]

Gellner's polemical discussions of Winch's writings delineate some of the difficulties, especially the limitations, of a formulation of method in the social sciences that sees Winch as concerned with nothing more than the self-understanding of human beings in society. Such a perspective apparently precludes any possibility of examining the causal origins of social institutions, the divergent modes in which symbolic meanings are "interpreted" in the light of conflicting group interests, and the existence of forms of false consciousness or ideology.[6] But Gellner's attitude toward Winch's work is very largely negative: an outcome, it seems, of his earlier condemnation of Wittgensteinian philosophy.[7] Although his approach to Gadamer's hermeneutics follows similar lines, Habermas' critique of Winch is informed by the view that Gadamer's work, and hermeneutic issues more broadly, are of fundamental relevance to the social sciences. In this earlier work, particularly in *Zur Logik der Sozialwissenschaften* (1967), Habermas stresses the point that the generalizing sciences and hermeneutics have for a long while gone their separate ways; the problem is to show what logical relations connect them on the level of epistemology.[8]

In order to grasp the force of Habermas' discussion of hermeneutic phenomenology, it is first necessary to consider his theory that human knowledge is grounded in interests. In *Knowledge and Human Interests,* Habermas amplifies and makes more concrete the critique of positivism that has always been a leading theme of Frankfurt philosophy. Where positivism has triumphed, as it has for the most part in the philosophy of both the social and the natural sciences, knowledge is portrayed as independent both of interests and consequently, of the reflexive historical awareness of the knower. "Since Kant," writes Habermas, "science has no longer been seriously comprehended by philosophy. Science can only be comprehended epistemologically, which means as *one* category of possible knowledge. . . For the philosophy of science that has emerged since the mid-nineteenth century as the heir of the theory of knowledge is methodology pursued with a scientistic self-understanding of the sciences. 'Scientism' means science's belief in itself: that is, the conviction that we can no longer understand science as *one* form of possible knowledge, but must rather identify knowledge with science."[9] Thus portrayed, scientific knowledge actually conforms to only one type of knowledge-constitutive interest, that in the prediction and control of occurrences, or "technically exploitable" knowledge. It is only one logical form that the disclosure of reality can take and is directly connected with what Habermas calls "instrumental action," "purposive-rational action," or simply "labor."[10] Labor is one of three basic elements of the human self-formative process that Habermas distinguishes, the others being interaction and authority (or power).

Interest in technically exploitable knowledge, according to Habermas, is not specific to the natural sciences, although it is perhaps exemplified most clearly by them. An orientation to prediction and control implies generalizing explanation, that is, explanation that is expressed in causal laws. Such an orientation characterizes both the natural and the social sciences. In instrumental action, reality is perceived as being within a specific realm of experience that is organized conceptually in monological technical metalanguages that can in principle be expressed formally. To call such conceptual systems "monological" is to claim that their form is governed by identifiable rules of inference, which are in turn corrigible in the light of the results of measurement operations. Objectivity of knowledge is guaranteed, or at least sought after, through the interpretation of observations, procedures of measurement, and inferential rules.

Interaction, on the other hand, is founded in ordinary language communication, which is the organizing mode of intersubjectivity. The norms governing everyday communication are rooted in the practical demands of sustaining community existence. Language, and here Habermas agrees with Gadamer (and with Wittgenstein), is not merely a system of descriptions; it is the medium whereby an intersubjectively formed social life is carried on: language is a medium of "doing" things through communication with others. As such, to speak a language "correctly" means being able to use it in the contexts of day-to-day life in accordance with the norms of the language community. Whereas meanings in instrumental action are created artificially and connected only to the purposive-rational employment of "means," observers who confront interaction must recognize that they confront a world that is preinterpreted by the very people they wish to study. Interaction is dialogical rather than monological, and one cannot be concerned with it, without, in principle, being able to enter the dialogue. This is the locus of hermeneutics, which conforms to the knowledge-constitutive interest in understanding. Hermeneutic problems relate to the intertwining of language and experience in different forms of life, which ordinary language both expresses and mediates.

These two types of knowledge-constitutive interests generate two sorts of disciplines. First are the "empirical-analytic sciences," which are founded in concerns with prediction and control, and are derivable from knowledge that is nomological in form. In them, "Theories comprise hypothetico-deductive connections of propositions, which permit the deduction of lawlike hypotheses with empirical content."[11] The second are "historical-hermeneutic sciences," which are concerned with understanding traditions and their artistic and literary products. To these, however, must be added a third discipline: critical theory. Critical theory finds its task in the furtherance of an interest in emancipation, in the achievement of rational autonomy of action freed from domination. For Habermas, this is crucially bound up with the historicity of self-understanding as limited by unacknowledged causal conditions of interaction. Such unacknowledged conditions of interaction include the ideological framing of asymmetrical relations of dependence within systems of power. Critical theory renders the nomological bounds of interaction reflexively accessible to its participants in order to offer them the possibility of their transformation. It is concerned to ensure " that information about lawlike connections sets off a process of reflection in the consciousness of those whom the laws are about. Thus the level of unreflected consciousness, which is one of the initial conditions of such laws, can be transformed. Of course, to this end a critically mediated knowledge of laws cannot through reflection alone render a law itself operative, but it can render it inapplicable."[12]

We can represent this schematically as follows:

Ontological Elements of Self-Formative Process	Knowledge-Constitutive Interest	Type of Study
Labor (instrumental action)	Prediction and control	Empirical-analytical sciences
Interaction	Understanding	Historical-hermeneutic sciences
Authority (power)	Emancipation	Critical theory

Habermas considers reflexivity as fundamental to the interest in emancipation because it is in the course of self-reflection that the subject is able to grasp, and transform, the conditions under which he acts through embodying his knowledge of these conditions within the rationalization of his action. He has tried to explicate this further as expressing circumstances of *distorted communication:* initially, in the context of a psychoanalytic model of critical theory, and subsequently, through his notion of communicative competence (which is distinct from that employed by others, such as Hymes).

HABERMAS ON DISTORTED COMMUNICATION

Habermas' formulation of critical theory is based on an abstract analysis of shortcomings in Marx as well as on an elaboration of ideas derived from Freud. Habermas distinguishes two strands in Marx's account of the human self-formative process. One is the thesis that "man makes himself" through productive activity: that human beings separate themselves from animals insofar as they produce in creative interplay with their environment. The other is that human social development can be regarded as a reflexive project in which classes actively promote the self-transformation of society. Marx failed to work out a satisfactory metatheory that would relate these two elements, however, because he conceived of science only on the level of instrumental action. Hence, he was not able to develop the special significance of the critique of ideology, reducing the Hegelian emphasis on the primacy of self-reflection to the "materialist" theme of labor as the medium of social transformation.[13]

This collapse of labor and interaction in Marx can be opened again by treating psychoanalysis as the exemplar of "self-reflection as science." Freud's understanding of his own creation, itself limited, manifested as strongly a positivistic strain as Marx's writing did a generation earlier. But if appropriately refor- mulated philosophically, psychoanalysis nonetheless offers a comprehensive framework for the theoretical and practical tasks of the critique of ideology. Psychoanalysis is organized through dialogue between analyst and analysand; on one level, it operates as a hermeneutic investigation. Habermas points out that Freud, in fashioning his theory of dream interpretation, was in part in- fluenced by an analogy with philology, comparing such inter- pretation to the translation of foreign texts. Habermas relates Freud's account of unconscious imagery, and its recovery by the analyst, to Dilthey's treatment of hermeneutics as a method to explore the horizons of meaning that lie behind subjective con- sciousness. Freud's is a "depth hermeneutics."[14] According to psychoanalytic theory, the "text" of interaction as ordinary linguistic communication is distorted by repressions. In analyz- ing the nature of repressions, the clinician tends to move to a nomological level, using a mechanical terminology rather than an interpretative one phrased in terms of meanings. On this level, psychoanalytic procedure is concerned to identify as causal mechanisms the underlying deformations that restrict the analy- sand's consciously accessible self-understanding. Because Freud wished to present psychoanalysis as a natural science in the or- thodox sense which that term conveyed in his time, he treated psychoanalytic theory as something to universalize: when fully developed, psychoanalysis should become just another branch of medical science. From the point of view of Habermas' metatheoretical account of psychoanalytic procedure, however, it is only one moment in the emancipatory project of therapy. The aim of therapy is to extend the rational autonomy of the analysand by recovering those unconscious sources that impel the individual's behavior without the mediation of his reflexive consciousness. Self-understanding, autonomy of action (*Mun- digkeit*), and linguistic expression are all tied to one another, for it is the "translating" of unacknowledged causal conditions of ac- tion deriving from repressions into accessible self-understanding that makes it possible for the individual to achieve rational con- trol over influences that previously dominated his conduct. But this possibility can only be realized through language, which is the medium both of reflexivity and of communication with others. Thus, dialogue between analyst and analysand furthers the progress of emancipation and simultaneously expresses it because it permits an expansion of mutal understanding between the two parties. Anyone who practices psychoanalysis must first undergo analysis himself because the analyst most be freed from influences that might distort the analytic dialogue from his side rather than from that of the patient.

The grounding of the critique of ideology and power in the conditions of distorted communication is further pursued in the abstract theory of "communicative competence." The concept is parallel to Chomsky's ideal of "linguistic competence," which is not to be confused with linguistic performance; linguistic performance refers to what a speaker actually says, linguistic competence to an ideal-typical representation of his capabilities (or what Habermas calls "language reconstruction"). Noam Chomsky is concerned with the monological skills of language-speakers, Habermas with the conditions underlying the sustaining of dialogue. The communication of meaning in interaction demands far more than linguistic competence in Chomsky's sense; it involves mastery of features of the context in which interactions occur. Any situation of dialogue, Habermas claims, implicitly acknowledges three elements of interaction, which, if analytically combined to form a model of complete mutual understanding in an ideal speech situation, offer a baseline against which distortions in communication can be specified. Such an ideal speech situation involves the following: first, consensus arrived at solely through rational discussion; second, complete mutual understanding on the part of the participants in the interaction; and third, mutual recognition of the authentic right of the other to take part in the dialogue as an autonomous and equal partner. If in empirical circumstances of communication these features are contravened, through, for example, the power of one participant to impose his views on another in order to secure "consensus," then communication rests on distortions that the critique of ideology will bring to light. These ideas have recently been expanded and clarified in relation to a conception of what Habermas calls "universal pragmatics," in which he draws extensively from John Austin and John Searle on speech acts.[15] "Truth" here is no longer connected diffusely to the conditions of dialogue between traditions, as in Gadamer, but becomes one among several "validity claims" that can be redeemed in discourse. Truth relates to validity claims made in respect of constative speech acts and thus to the propositional content of statements. This is a "consensus theory of truth," but the phrase, as Habermas admits, is a bit misleading: truth does not consist in consensus but concerns the process of argumentation in discourse whereby validity claims of a constative form are redeemed. "The condition of the truth of assertions is the potential agreement of all others. . . . Truth involves the promise of reaching a rational consensus."[16] However, in principle rationality is not confined to statements but concerns other classes of. speech acts. There are four such classes, in which the redemption of validity claims concerns respectively *Verständlichkeit* (intelligibility), *Wahrheit* (truth), *Richtigkeit* (adequacy or correctness), and *Wahrhaftigkeit* (veracity or truthfulness). We have to be concerned not just with assertions, as properties of abstract discourse, but also with the rationality of norms as elements of practical action; and each in turn has to be connected to the intelligibility and veracity of the interchanges involved in the process of communication. When the intelligibility of an utterance is problematic, we ask such questions as: "What does that mean?" "How is that to be understood?" The answers to such questions supply interpretations of meaning (*Deutungen*). Where the truth of the propositional content of an utterance is problematic, we ask such questions as: "Are the facts of the matter as they are claimed to be?" We respond to such inquiries by assertations and explanations (*Erklärungen*). When it is the fairness of the normative grounding of a speech act that is problematic, we ask such questions as: "Why did you do that?" or "Were you right to do that?" The answers to such questions are justifications (*Rechtfertigungen*). Finally, where the veracity of an utterance, relating to the intentions of the speaker, is problematic, we ask such questions as: "Is he deceiving me?" "Is he trying to cheat me?" However, we characteristically address this latter type of question to a third person, although this type of interrogative also is used to "bring the untrustworthy person to account."[17]

This classification supplies the basis of a universal pragmatics. The latter, Habermas says, "has the task of identifying and reconstructing universal conditions of possible understanding."[18] Universal pragmatics differs from what Habermas calls the "empirical pragmatics" of Austin and Searle; whereas the latter is concerned mainly with the descriptive classification of speech acts in particular types of contexts, Austin attempts to reconstruct the rule systems that allow actors to communicate in any type of context.

The four classes of speech acts relate to four object domains: speech itself, external nature, society, and "internal nature." Consensual interaction can be carried on only to the extent that a speaker credibly sustains validity claims in each domain: truth in respect of the propositional content of what is said; legitimacy in respect of the norms justifying the speakers's right to say what he does; veracity in respect of his intentions; and intelligibility in respect of his meaning. Since understanding or intelligibility is in a sense "factually redeemed" whenever a process of communication occurs, Habermas treats this as an overarching category: the other three are elements *within* communication. (This threefold division again seems to reflect those represented schematically earlier.[19]) Among these three, validity claims relating to veracity have to be separated from the other two because validity is resolved in actual conduct: genuineness of intention is demonstrated by how one actually behaves. Validity claims concerning truth and fairness are open to redemption through discourse: these constitute what Habermas calls respectively "theoretical-empirical" and "practical" discourse. We can distinguish the following levels of argumentation in these two arenas of discourse:

	Theoretical-Empirical Discourse	*Practical Discourse*
Conclusions (C) Controversial	Statements	Precepts/evaluations
Validity Claim Demanded from Opponent	Truth	Correctness/propriety
	Explanations	Justifications
Data (D)	Causes (in respect of events) Motives (in respect of behavior)	Grounds
Warrant (W)	Empirical uniformities, hypothetical laws, etc.	Behavioral/evaluative norms or principles
Backing (B)	Observations, results of surveys, factual accounts, etc.	Interpretations of needs (values), inferences, secondary implications, etc.

Thus, adopting an example given by Stephan Toulmin, Habermas illustrates the form of theoretical-empirical discourse as follows. The statement "Harry is a British subject" (C) can be explained by the identification of a cause: "Harry was born in Bermuda" (D). This explanation is reached through the deductive application of a generalization: "A man born in Bermuda will generally be a British subject" (W). The plausibility of such a generalization can be indicated in terms of legal provisions of national status (B). Argumentation in practical discourses can be analyzed according to a parallel scheme, as indicated in the column on the far right. These systems of discourse allow us to order explanation and justification respectively in relation to specific ranges of phenomena. Assertions and normative evaluations can only be grounded as elements of such conceptual hierarchies. The grounding of arguments thus "has nothing to do with the relation between individual sentences and reality, but above all with the coherence between sentences within systems of speech."[20] In this connection, Habermas makes much of what he calls the "double structure" of speech acts. The illocutionary force and the proportional content of speech acts may vary independently of each other. The same propositonal content, as Austin originally pointed out, can be expressed in different forms of speech acts (assertions, commands, etc.). This "uncoupling" of illocutionary force and proportional content is now mutual understanding (intersubjectivity), and is differentiated from sensory experience or from the apprehension of an object world. The double structure of speech ties in with a basic feature of language: its inherent reflexivity. Insofar as speakers master the double structure of language, they have to conjoin the substance of what is communicated, to metacommunication about its illocutionary or practical application.[21]

If argumentation is to result in conclusions rationally arrived at, the form of the discourse must allow for continual revision or review. Here Habermas returns to the themes of *Knowledge and Human Interests,* claiming that each type of discourse must make possible a "step-by-step radicalization" of the self-reflection of the knowing subject.[22] This can be represented as follows:

Steps in Radicalization	Theoretical Discourse	Practical Discourse
Acts	Statements	Commands/prohibitions
Grounding	Theoretical explanations	Theoretical justifications
Substantive Language-Criticism	Metatheoretical transformation of language and conceptual systems	Metaethical/metapolitical
Self-Reflection	Critique of knowledge	Formation of rational political will

The first step in the "radicalization" of theoretical discourse is the incorporation of a statement or assertion, as an act, into a process of argumentation; the second is its theoretical clarification; the third is a transition form or modification of the language system initially adopted; the final, and "deepest," level of argumentation is reached when the nature of theoretical knowledge as such is reflected on (as an example, Habermas presents the controversy between Kuhn, Popper, and others in the philosophy of science).[23] The form of practical discourse is similar in respect to the self-reflection of the subject. Commands or prohibitions enter discourse when they become, or are made, problematic; the second level consists in their theoretical justification; a deeper level still is consideration of alternative normative conceptions or evaluations; the most profound level of argumentation concerns reflection on the nature of political will.

A consensus reached through argumentation, Habermas concludes, can only redeem a validity claim if it is possible to move freely between the different levels of discourse, which is the criterion of the ideal speech situation previously described. Habermas holds that psychoanalytic dialogue is directly relevant to the clarification of the circumstances preventing the realization of an ideal speech situation. Psychoanalytic dialogue accomplishes both less and more than usual discourse. Less in the sense that the patient is initially very far from being a full participant in the dialogue, which is guided by the analyst. A successful therapeutic "discourse" has as its first consequence that which is claimed by more conventional discourse: symmetry of changes of participation. Therapeutic dialogue is more than ordinary discourse, however, because it culminates in the redemption not just of claims to truth or correctness, but also claims to veracity—which, as Habermas has said before, cannot normally be discursively redeemed. "In accepting the proposals and the 'worked-through' interpretations of the analyst as valid and confirmed, the patient at the same time sees through his own self-deception."[24]

HERMENEUTIC UNDERSTANDING AND NOMOLOGICAL EXPLANATION

In remarking on Habermas' attempt to create a metatheory for a critical social science, I shall confine my attention primarily to the ideas sketched previously. That is to say, I shall not consider any of his discussions on the development of the legitimate order of bourgeois society or the crises to which that order is now exposed.[25] This does not mean, however, that such analyses bear no relation to Habermas' metatheory; on the contrary, they are obviously closely tied to one another as integral to his version of critical theory. Further, I shall not refer in any detail to the considerable critical literature, mostly in German, that Habermas' writings have stimulated. Habermas' works are not so clear as one would wish, and I shall concentrate on making a series of comments on what, if my formulation of Habermas' main concerns is accurate, appear to be difficulties that they raise, regardless of whether or not these are the same as those identified by other critics.

When *Knowledge and Human Interests* first appeared in English in 1972, some critics accused Habermas of adopting a misleading differentiation between the natural and social sciences, one that was based on the idea that whereas the former are "nomological" in their explanatory form the latter are "interpretative." But this rests on a misapprehension of Habermas' views. An interest in prediction and control is not specific to natural science and is not offered as a criterion for approaching traditional debates about divergences between the natural and social sciences. The point is to identify the two logically discrepant forms that claims to knowledge can assume and to substantiate the notion that the relation between the two is of an historical character, such that unacknowledged causal conditions of action can be transformed when these are made accessible to reflexive self-consciousness. Gadamer's "claim to universality" for hermeneutics has been matched, Habermas argues, with a comparable claim to universality emanating from positivism: that all happenings, whether in the social or in the natural world, are determined by the operation of causal laws. Neither of these competing claims recognizes the different type of knowledge-constitutive interest on which it itself rests: such recognition undermines each claim, without entirely repudiating either.

This is a persuasive viewpoint and, I believe, basically a correct one. Nonetheless, I do not think that Habermas' characterization of it is wholly acceptable. This can be shown by his treatment of each of the key concepts involved: the nomological and hermeneutic. If Habermas does not claim that the nomological form of explanation he identifies is peculiar to the natural sciences, he still tends to argue (as Horkheimer was prone to do) as if it is adequate to express the logic of method that they embody—albeit one that supplies only a partial and slanted self-understanding of the place of science within human culture as a whole. But this gives too much to positivism or, more accurately, to the "orthodox" hypothetico-deductive view of science.[26] The writings of such authors as Toulmin, Hesse, Kuhn, and others subjected this view to a major frontal assault and have left it largely in ruins—without having replaced it with an equally comprehensive alternative. Now in one important sense, this literature accords well with Habermas' emphases. Science, he says, presupposes the intersubjectivity of ordinary language communication, which can never be completely transposed into nomological formal languages. This was shown by Charles Peirce and again by the later Husserl. Such intersubjectivity constitutes what Apel calls the "*a priori* of communication." But writings such as those of Kuhn, which claim that scientific development involves a discontinuous series of paradigms, clearly imply that hermeneutic problems are as basic to science as they are to more sedimented "traditions." Science is certainly as much about "interpretation" as it is "nomological explanation": the former certainly cannot be disposed of as a transcendental a priori—as Gadamer has noted in commenting on Kuhn. "Explanation" in science is most appropriately characterized as the clarification of queries, not deduction from causal laws, which is only one subtype of explanatory procedure. In scientific analysis, "why questions" are normally answered by rendering a phenomenon intelligible or meaningful within the context of a paradigm or theory.[27] When the hermeneutic character of scientific theories and their mediations is recognized, it is seen that science is oriented in a fundamental way to "understanding"—which is precisely why it rivals other types of religious or magical cosmologies against the backdrop of which interaction, prior to the development of Western industrial culture, has been carried on. In sum, Habermas' view still retains too much of the old *Verstehen-Erklären* opposition, although in reworked form and supplemented by an "interest in emancipation."

Kuhn's discussion is confined to the internal history of science, while Gadamer's hermeneutic philosophy ranges much more broadly; however, clear similarities exist between "paradigms" and "traditions" and between each author's concern with his mediation. In a basic sense, Gadamer is legitimately able to claim the universality of hermeneutics and is puzzled by Habermas' rejection of the claim. This is precisely the sense in which all "knowledge," whether in science, literature, or art, is achieved within and by means of frames of meaning rooted in natural-langauge communities. If the "circular" character of knowledge as located in history is accepted, as Habermas does accept it, an epistemology of the form set out by Gadamer can be defended as necessary to *each* of the three forms of knowledge-constitutive interest identified by Habermas.[28] Habermas' position at this point seems to contain an unresolved, major difficulty, which is immediately related to his residual acceptance of a deductive-nomological version of scientific explanation. This concerns his view of the role of nomological analysis, rather than that of critical theory as such, which is what his attention is most concentrated upon. The "empirical-analytical sciences" study reality according to the knowledge-constitutive interest of prediction and control, organizing their "findings" in terms of hypothetico-deductive systems of causal laws. But what are the criteria by which such claims to knowledge are substantiated? For the "orthodox view" has an answer that Habermas has apparently (although, as it later turns out, not finally) rejected: correspondence to sensorily apprehended reality, grounded in the descriptions of a theory-neutral observation language. Can we say that, for Habermas, science can aspire to objectivity insofar as scientific theories increase prediction and control? Surely not, for a knowledge-constitutive interest in prediction and control is actually not logically tied to a nomological form of explanatory scheme in the way that Habermas apparently assumes it to be. I have already said that an interest in meaningful "understanding" is more integral to science than Habermas allows. This is the reverse side of the coin: the point that "prediction and control," as expressing constitutive interest or logical form of knowledge, are by no means limited to the sphere of the nomological. On the contrary, they are of primary significance in interaction itself and are manifestly crucial to the constitution of that form of knowledge (which I have elsewhere called generically "mutual knowledge"), whereby the understanding of others is achieved.[29] In this sense, the "predictability" of interaction, as well as the control of its course, is a contingent accomplishment of parties to interaction. I shall return to this later because it bears directly on Habermas' formulation of the notion of labor. What I have said leaves various loose ends that will be tied up later. One implication, however, is that Habermas' classification of disciplines into the "empirical-analytical" and the "historical-hermeneutic" is unsatisfactory. Hermeneutic problems cannot be confined to one class of disciplines; rather, they must span them all. If (as Habermas agrees) those fields of study that concern human action involve what I call a "double hermeneutic," the hermeneutic mediation of meaning-frames (paradigms) also must be regarded as posing central problems for any epistemology of natural science that seeks to go beyond the discredited formulas offered by logical empiricism.

LABOR AND INTERACTION

Habermas derives his distinction of "labor" and "interaction" in part from his critical assessment of Marx's transposition of self-reflection into the thesis of the self-constitution of humanity through production. Marx thereby reduces to one concept, that of "productive labor," two features of human social development that have to be analytically separated from each other. But while this permits Habermas to develop an incisive polemic against Marx's relapse into positivism, the mode in which he develops the distinction in his own theoretical scheme is less than satisfactory.

To differentiate labor and interaction, at least in the way that Habermas does, by treating the former as equivalent to strategic or instrumental action, seems to allow no conceptual mode of treating interaction as itself a "productive enterprise." This applies whether or not labor is regarded as generic to all activity or as a type of activity (social labor): for in neither sense can the "labor" that is put into the sustaining of meaningful interaction be treated simply as "purposive-rational action." Here it is necessary to stress, as against Habermas, the conceptual significance of Marx's observations on social life as praxis, although first these have to be clarified because they oscillate between an encompassing and a more limited conception of terms such as "production" and "productive labor." In his early writings in particular, Marx uses such terms very broadly, as elements of an ontology (one, of course, that owes much to Hegel). The distinctive characteristic of human beings, the special quality that differentiates humans from animals, is that human behavior is not tied to the merely "adaptive" character of instincts. At this point, Habermas' critique of Marx concentrates on showing that the idea of the "self-constitution" of human history through labor has no place for the reflexive awareness of conditions of action as the "human" mode of self-transformation. But he then goes on to connect labor with instrumental action and interaction with communication or dialogue. I consider that, in his writings, this has two consequences. First, it becomes difficult to make conceptually central those divergent interests—in the usual sense of the term—that are rooted in interaction since dialogue is conceived of basically as the symbolic communication of meaning. Second, it becomes difficult to treat interaction as *itself* always the product of 'labor,' in a broad sense of that term, since labor is conceptually tied in an abstract way to an ideal-typical formulation of purposive-rational action. The ramifications of these, I shall argue subsequently, run deep through the whole of Habermas' elaboration of the project of critical theory. What is supposedly at the very heart of Habermas' analysis—domination—tends to disappear from view. Or, expressed more precisely, the domination of some groups of men over others as founded in asymmetry of material interest slips away; it is replaced by the ideal of romination as equivalent to distorted communication. Power enters into interaction only as filtered through the ideological slanting of the conditions of communication, not as fundamental to the relations between actors, whereby interaction is constituted as an ongoing activity.

In some part, this can be traced back to the premises of Habermas' critique of Gadamer in *Zur Logik der Sozialwissenschaften*. In the conclusion of that book, Habermas acknowledges the force of the hermeneutic claim that language is the essential medium of intersubjectivity, but nonetheless he emphasizes it will not suffice to concern ourselves only with the connecting of disparate "traditions." Language is not just the medium of intersubjectivity; it "is *also* a medium of domination and social power"; insofar as it expresses power relations, "speech is *also* ideological."[30] But this cedes too much and too little to hermeneutics. Too much because, accepting the universality of language as the medium of being, it complements the mediation of traditions with an emphasis on power only at the cost of transmuting power into ideologically deformed communication; too little because it thereby fails to acknowledge the sense in which hermeneutics, insofar as it is concerned with all "meaningful comprehension," must be as basic to a critique of ideology as to any other human enterprise. Habermas appears to recognize this in his more recent writings (without drawing out its full consequences) since he separates *Verständlichkeit,* or intelligibility, from the three types of validity claims as the necessary basis of all dialogue.

Instead of equating labor with instrumental reason, and separating these analytically from interaction (both linked to "quasi-transcendental" cognitive interests), I think it important to place in the forefront the concepts of the productions and reproduction of interaction as contingent accomplishments of human actors. If, as I have outlined elsewhere, processes of production and reproduction are treated as involving the reflexive application of rules and resources in the realization of interests (wants), power emerges, together with symbolic meanings and normative sanctions, as integral to interaction rather than analytically separate from it.[31] The phrase "production and reproduction of society" has to be understood as equivalent to the encompassing sense of "labor" distinguished above and as integral to any and every case of interaction that is regarded as a skilled accomplishment. This frees the terms "labor" or "work" for the narrower and more orthodox sense of a distinctive social type of activity that may be contrasted to "play" and so forth. Reflexivity or self-reflection remains as central in this conceptual scheme as it does in that of Habermas, and it is treated as fundamental to the production and reproduction of interaction as rationalized human conduct. However, it is stripped of the Hegelian overtones that remain strongly defined in the ambiguous formulation of the subject as the "self" in "self-reflection," the latter term being used by Habermas to characterize the reflexive awareness both of "society" as a whole and of definite subjects.

REFLEXIVITY, AUTONOMY, AND CRITICAL THEORY

The concepts that Habermas develops in his theory of an ideal speech situation share a certain difficulty of application with

those comprising the trilogy of work, interaction, and communication. That is to say, they are offered as idealized notions
that clarify certain logical relations; but Habermas also seems to
want to use them in the service of concrete social analysis. It is
not clear, for example, how the theory of communicative competence can be applied to the study of actual circumstances of
communication, since it is an idealized form that, oriented to the
demands of grounding critical theory, abstracts from the contextual character of interaction.[32] But the contextual location of
ordinary-language communication, as Habermas himself emphasizes, is not just incidental to interaction. The reflexive use of
context, including within that latter term (temporarily extended)
"glossing" and conversational "formulation" as specified by
Harold Garfinkel, is quite basic to sustaining intersubjectivity in
interaction. However, I am not concerned with developing this
type of objection any more fully; in discussing the theory of communicative competence, I shall concentrate, as in the foregoing
section, on more substantive problems—ones that derive from
what I have already isolated as difficulties in Habermas'
metatheoretical scheme. These, as I have tried to make clear,
stem from the conceptualization of labor as instrumental rationality and that of interaction as communicative action or
dialogue. In this section, I shall trace some of their implications
for the third element in Habermas' tripartite division, the one that
absorbs him preeminently: critical theory, as involving the isolation of conditions of distorted communication.

Let us briefly recapitulate Habermas' exposition of knowledge-
constitutive interests. There are three categories of knowledge in
which reality can be apprehended, founded in three existential
conditions of social life: labor, interactions, and authority or
power. "Accordingly, the interests constitutive of knowledge are
linked to the functions of an ego that adapts itself to its external
conditions through learning processes, is initiated into the communication system of a social life-world by means of self-
formative processes, and constructs an identity in the conflict
between instinctual aims and social constraints."[33] There is no
way that interest can be canceled out, as presumed by positivistic
and some versions of hermeneutic philosophies. Knowledge is
always ultimately practical—or, in Habermas' expression, carries
within it a germinal ideal of the "good life." The practical impact
of positivistic philosophy facilitates the substitution of tmchnical
control, or technology *tout court,* for morally enlightened action,
that is guided by the thesis that all problems of social transforma-

tion can be reduced to technical decisions. A hermeneutics that
severs knowledge from interest (unlike that of Gadamer) merely
reinforces this succumbing to technicism, for it separates our
knowledge of the past from the demands of the present and
"locks up history in a museum." This dislocation of past from
present provides exactly the sort of rationale required by the
belief that contemporary social life can be guided by purely
technical, nonhistorical imperatives.

In each case, the ideal of "pure theory" has displaced recognition of the grounding of knowledge in interest: such recognition
can only be achieved precisely through the medium of the third:
emancipation. Here we reach the crux of Habermas' thesis: the
necessary connection between reflexivity and critical theory. "In
self-reflection," Habermas writes, "knowledge for the sake of
knowledge attains congruence with the interest in autonomy and
responsibility."[34] This is connected with the theory of communicative competence in two principal ways. One is via the
thesis that every actual situation of communication expresses
implicitly the intention of achieving perfect and unconstrained
consensus—that the 'validity' of statements expressed in
dialogue thus anticipates the "good life" of an emancipated
society. The other is through the thesis that the conditions of
distorted communication, as ideology, can be explicated through
nomological analysis as the unacknowledged ground of interaction and thus, being grasped reflexively by the subject, returned
to his control. I shall discuss the latter in this section, leaving the
former to the following section in relation to a critique of the
"psychoanalytic model."

The proximate source of Habermas' expostition of "self-
reflection" as an historical principle is Hegel, who considers
reflection as both an ontology and an epistemology: perhaps it is
even accurate to say that Hegel abandons the traditional differentiation between Kant's philosophy and Hume's empiricism. Self-
reflection in Hegel is the coming-to-itself of the Spirit. Now of
course Habermas breaks with this on the level of ontology, while
insisting that reflexivity must be accorded an independent
significance besides the self-transformation of human society
through labor. Reflexivity becomes, in fact, as I have just indicated, the very medium of the actualization of the knowledge-
constitutive interest in emancipation, for in self-reflection the impetus to the acquisition of knowledge becomes one with those of
autonomy of action and mutual understanding. The argument,
initially compelling, is shown to be weak when subjected to close

scrutiny. Habermas' indebtedness to Hegel conceals problems every bit as basic as those which he identifies in Marx's "transposition" of Hegel. In Habermas' scheme, ontology and epistemology are separated in the attempt to break free from Hegel's idealism. Self-reflection and the recovery of the alienated self are no longer regarded as elements of the constitution of reality itself but are instead treated as at the origin of the transformative capacity of critical theory. However, this leaves as only weakly elaborated, and apparently contingent, the relation between reflexive awareness of the conditions of action and the capability of really transforming those conditions.[35] This is a crucial matter, I think, and I shall try to show below that the psychoanalytic model adopted by Habermas helps to hide it from view, with rather profound consequences for the potential political relevance of Habermas' views.

Another way of expressing the above argument is to say that, although Habermas, in the context of his critique of Marx, makes clear a distinction between "self-reflection," on the one hand, and human "self-transformation" in praxis, on the other, he provides no conceptual means of reuniting them. In coming to reflexive awareness of previously unacknowledged conditions of his action, it seems as though the subject is thereby able to transform them in accordance with the interest in emancipation. This emphasis is quite distinct in Habermas, and he states it bluntly: self-reflection "releases the subject from dependence on hypostatized powers."[36] But of course, it does not. It may indeed free him from the hypostatization of those powers but not, in and of itself, from his dependence on them—or, alternatively, from their domination over him. I am not suggesting that Habermas is himself unaware of such an elementary distinction, which he mentions explicitly. Thus, with reference to the statement quoted above, he remarks: "Of course . . . a critically mediated knowledge of laws cannot through reflection alone render a law inoperative, but it can render it inapplicable." I am suggesting that the scheme he develops provides no conceptual vehicle for fully acknowledging its importance so that it is frequently glossed over.

The mode in which this glossing occurs in Habermas' writings can be illustrated in relation to the ambiguous character of the "self" in terms such as "self-reflection," "self-constitution," and so forth, which I have earlier alluded to. The question of who becomes reflexively aware of the conditions of his action—and the conditions under which he becomes so aware—is obviously crucial to the possible transformative effects of that awareness.

While it is acceptable to argue that such reflexivity offers a (potential) medium for expanding actors' autonomy of action, that
very autonomy can be used as a means of restricting others.
Habermas avoids such problems by moving unconcernedly between using self-reflection to refer to a total human project, in a
quasi-Hegelian way, and using it to refer to the reflexivity of
particular subjects.[37] It might be countered that the objection I
have made here is an unfair one since the whole object of critical
theory, as it is formulated by Habermas, is to make manifest the
underlying asymmetries in circumstances where the autonomy of
some is purchased at the expense of the autonomy of others. In
fact, Habermas' theory of ideological domination as distorted
communication shows with particular clarity the significance of
the differentiation I have made in the previous paragraph.

This can be illuminated by connecting it to another point made
earlier: "power" appears in Habermas' theory as the ideological
deformation of circumstances of communication. A reflexive
grasp of the conditions of action, it is held, is the mode in which
distorted communication is corrected on the level of interaction.
This tends to assimilate both the ways in which the conduct of
man is held in thrall through being dominated by acknowledged
causal conditions and the ways in which their autonomy is subject to domination by other men. The means of achieving
freedom from domination are not the same in two cases. The
first conforms more closely to Habermas' analysis of reflexivity
as the means of the transformation of action in the direction of
expanded autonomy. This is the sense of what I have called the
transformative capacity of human action. From this regard,
reflexive awareness of previously unacknowledged causal
grounds of action normally yields an increased autonomy of action on the part of human subjects. This is true insofar as much
awareness is incorporated into a reconstruction of the rationalization of action. Such a theorem does not hold where
power equals the domination of some over others, where that
domination is normally used not only to obfuscate the asymmetry of their interaction but also resist actively any attempts to
upset that asymmetry by those in a position of subordination.[38]

In a new preface to the fourth German edition of *Theory and
Practice,* Habermas admitted certain shortcomings in his original
formulations of reflexivity in the context of critical theory. "Self-
reflection," he now says, is not the same as "reasoned justification," which is a necessary adjunct to "self-reflection" if the
reflexive moment is to achieve practical impetus. The theoretical

knowledge that is necessary to grasp conditions of action must occur independently of, and in addition to, self-reflection as such. Such "theoretical discourse" is not supplied in psychoanalytic dialogue, where the reflexive autonomy attained by the patient in the course of successful analysis does not provide him with much of an abstract theoretical reconstruction of his newly expanded self-understanding.[39] But this is only a limited acknowledgment of the contingencies in the relation between reflexivity and action, and does not meet the objections I have registered previously. Habermas is evidently not inclined to introduce major modifications in the psychoanalytic model of critical theory, and it is appropriate at this juncture to turn to that model.

THE PSYCHOANALYTIC MODEL

Habermas' reworking of a traditional theme in Frankfurt philosophy—the complementarity of Marx and Freud—has already attracted a great deal of criticism. In order to assess how far any or all of it is justified, we first have to try to clarify Habermas' position. Habermas' use of Freud differs substantially from that of the earlier generation of Frankfurt philosophers, although the continuities also can be distinguished without difficulty. Habermas seems less interested in the content of psychoanalytic theory than in its form as critical dialogue (in the substance of his most recent writings, he borrows more from Piaget than from Freud). One could not justifiably say that his adoption of psychoanalysis is purely formal, regarding the latter as nothing more than an exemplar of the relations among the nomological, the hermeneutic, and the critical. It is not easy, however, to tell from Habermas' discussions of Freud how far he accepts the total corpus of Freudian theory, appropriately reconstructed as a reflexively founded therapeutic endeavor. Habermas' own model of psychoanalysis as critical theory is definitely, and quite deliberately, offered on an idealized level. He does not examine concrete clinical materials because the psychoanalytic model is offered as a metatheoretical framework for the rectifying of distorted communication. For this reason, he is able to avoid some rejoinders to his arguments that look to the actual practice of psychoanalysis. One might point out, for example, that there is a profound disagreement between analytic schools about proper modes of therapy, how far the patient should participate directly in the dialogue, and what form his participation should take. Or, from another aspect, we might say that psychoanalytic therapy is an authoritarian situation, monopolized and covertly manipulated by the therapist. We do not have to regard psychoanalysis as brainwashing[40] in order to recognize that the pretensions of analytic theory to uncover what is *in* the patient, rather than what is forcefully implanted by the analyst himself, can scarcely be accepted without more evidence than that given by clinical material as such. Habermas does not consider such issues of substance, but it is difficult to see how he could dismiss them as irrelevant to his case, insofar as his appeal to psychoanalysis does depend on acceptance of at least some of the concrete details of Freud's theory and his version of therapy.

Because Habermas' view seems elusive, it is probably more relevant to concentrate on the formal level of the metatheory of psychoanalysis as a model for ideology-criticism. Two major objections have been registered against this in the course of the interchanges among Habermas, Gadamer, and others.[41] Connected assertions are made that psychoanalysis is a dialogue between individuals, whereas a critical theory of society has to concern itself with relations between groups; the therapeutic dialogue is sustained voluntarily by both analyst and analysand, while group dependencies in society exist in a framework of coercion. Habermas' response to these assertions is to admit the force of the points, without conceding that they significantly undermine his position. Where others refuse to enter into dialogue, the confirmation of critical theory that is possible in the psychoanalytic encounter cannot be obtained: enlightenment is confined to those who share a common situation in conflict with others. Habermas adds that we can distinguish three components in the relation of theory and practice as they are mediated by the critique of ideology: the specification of modes of critical analysis of a given set of social circumstances; the appropriation of these reflexively by those to whom they refer; and the articulation of definite practical strategies of action. The differences among these three have been obscured in Marxism because European labor movements have been enmeshed as one overall historical project. There is no way to validate strategies on the level of theory because they have to be worked out in relation to particular conjunctures of circumstances.[42]

This attempted defense clarifies some of the problems that seem inherent in Habermas' theoretical scheme. In fact, it barely addresses itself to the objections made by critics of the psychoanalytic model and simply adds a third element to the differentiation between theoretical discourse and enlightened self-reflection: the element of strategy or tactics. Habermas severs strategy from enlightened self-reflection. But it is not clear what this implies. Quite clearly, the severance cannot be complete, or strategy would become an irrational matter. There must be some way in which "appropriate" strategy is suggested by theory, even if we acknowledge (as Habermas stresses in criticizing Georg Lukacs) that its validation does not rest on its successful application in any specific time and place. Habermas tries to turn into a virtue the distance that his analysis maintains from political involvement. But it really makes manifest the fact that the metatheoretical system he has constructed does not generate a political practice. There are reasons for this that concern Habermas' appraisal of modern capitalism more than his broader theory: having, like Herbert Marcuse, emphasized the all-encompassing grip of technical organization in which the modern social order is encased, Habermas has difficulty in pointing to any substantial avenues of potential transformation. I shall not consider this issue here but shall remain at the level of metatheory, where, as I argued earlier, Habermas' formulation of self-reflection has not been sufficiently freed from Hegel. As a consequence, the practical consequences of self-reflection remain as implicitly contingent—because of the manner in which Habermas develops the theme of the relation between social transformation and the reflexive grasp of the conditions of action. Habermas' differentiation among theoretical analysis, enlightened self-reflection, and strategies of action brings this more into the open but leaves unresolved the generic connections that have to be presumed to exist among the three.

Let us consider the criticisms of the psychoanalytic model made by Gadamer and others, developing them in the context of previous arguments. The first point concerns psychoanalysis as a dialogue between individual persons, not a relation between groups. This can be developed in various ways, but I shall only take up the one that seems to me to be most important: psychoanalysis basically as a conversation between two persons in which the only "practical grounding" of the interchange is in the reconstruction of the self-understanding of the patient. The psychoanalytic encounter, as it were, places an *epoche* on the interests (in the usual sense) and involvements of everyday life and reconstitutes them on a symbolic level as components, or deformations, of dialogue. Such a framework is thus peculiarly opposite to Habermas' conceptualization of interaction as "communicative action," or symbolic interchange, which also abstracts from the "material" context of practical day-to-day conduct. I have already stated my objections to this and have tried to trace through its implications regarding the complementary notion of labor. It is evident that, expressed in this way, the first critical rejoinder to Habermas' psychoanalytic model ties in closely to the second. For if group relations inevitably occur in a practical context of material interests, such interests also underlie the mode of ideological domination whereby asymmetries of power are legitimized; these are not, in any simple sense at least, entered into "voluntarily" by the subordinate groups. Now Habermas' response to this, as described above, is to declare that enlightened self-reflection and strategy operate at different levels (in his more recent writings, and in the debate with Luhmann, he has given more and more preference to an abstract category of "strategic action," distinguished from "instrumental action" as such). I have suggested that the contingent character of practical strategies of action is implied in Habermas' metatheoretical position itself. We can now see more clearly why such a view is inherently unsatisfactory: it provides no general mode of connection between social transformation and power. In other words, *power itself becomes merely another contingency in the relation between enlightened reflexivity and practice.*

In conclusion, we might return to the start of this discussion, Gadamer's hermeneutics. For Gadamer, "truth" resides in the mutuality of traditions and hence cannot claim any transcendental foundation. Habermas rejects the limitations that Gadamer's "claim to universality" of hermeneutics seems to place on the possibilities of critical theory. But there is more than a trace of Gadamer's version of truth in Habermas' attempt to construct a consensus theory of truth in conjunction with the theory of communicative competence. "Truth" refers to the conditions of argumentation whereby consensus is achieved: in theoretical discourse, every concrete communication between actors promises that agreement can be realized through autonomous and freely conducted dialogue. Gadamer's formulation of truth in reciprocity of dialogue is thus inadequate because it leaves unexamined distortions in the framework within which communication is conducted.

Habermas follows F. Ramsey and Peter Strawson (although without accepting the redundancy thesis of truth) in distinguishing between objects of experience and facts: the event of Caesar's death is thus separated from the fact "that Caesar died." Events or happenings are the objects of experience or action; facts are asserted in propositions. Facts presuppose the existence of objects, but when we say "so-and-so is a fact," we do not mean the existence of the relevant objects or events but the truth of the contents of the proposition. To state something as a fact is thus to make the claim that its propositional content could be discursively justified. Discourse brackets action, permitting only the argumentative examination of truth claims, in contrast to communicative action as such, in which truth claims are always implicit. "Truth *qua* justification of the truth claim inherent in a proposition does not reveal itself, like the objectivity of experience, in feed-back controlled action but only in a process of successful reasoning by which the truth claim is first rendered problematic and then redeemed. Facts are not happenings. That is why the truth of propositions is not corroborated by processes happening in the world but by a consensus achieved through argumentative reasoning." The nature of objectivity of experience must be explicated through a theory of object-constitution, while the theory truth has to be developed as a logical articulation of the conditions of discourse.

But the thesis that truth concerns the process of argumentation, while consensus is established in theoretical discourse, leaves unexplicated a basic element in Habermas' analysis of the differentiation of critical theory from hermeneutics. For while it is perhaps consistent with Gadamer's position to restrict "truth" to the achievement of dialogue between traditions, such a view does not conform to the requirements of a theory of distorted communication of the sort that Habermas tries to establish because he is required to penetrate below the dialogic process itself as understood by those participating in it. Presumably, Habermas wishes to claim that a disclosing of the distortions in the framework of dialogue is justified by showing that such dialogue diverges from the components of the idealized speech situation. But what then is the status of the nomological components of inquiry, or those elements that compose the "scientific discourse" that one is supposedly able to validate prior to and independent of the process of self-reflection? These cannot be validated simply by the successful achievement of enlightened self-reflection, if we also are to be able to acknowledge that the connection between them is not a logical but an historically contingent one. The question at issue is precisely that of the relation among the "objectivity of experience," the constitution of an object-world, and the redemption of truth claims, a matter that Habermas, having stressed the distinction between the two, passes over. The first demand here, although not the only one, is for an elaborated theory of reference.

Although Habermas' theory of truth seems only partially developed, so far he has not succeeded in generating a satisfactory defense against the charge—familiar enough in the context of any approach like his own—that he provides no means for distinguishing modes of substantiating truth claims from the nature of truth as such. In response to this sort of objection, he emphasizes that the consensus theory of truth universalizes the redemption of validity claims, rather than relating truth to specific modes in which statements may be supported. But this seems unlikely to meet the needs of what the analysis is designed to accomplish. Even if we accept that "truth" is a discursive justification of a particular type of validity claim, this would not in and of itself resolve the question of how theoretical-empirical discourse is validated independent of its potential incorporation within enlightened self-reflection. However, as it stands, the view is difficult to sustain. It is one thing to hold that the motion of truth necessarily implies discursive justification or its possibility; it is quite another to hold that this can provide an adequate mode of expressing its meaning.

In the concluding sections of this discussion, I have concentrated on critical commentary. Needless to say, this is not to dispute the importance of Habermas' writings. On the contrary, Habermas must rank as among the most preeminent contemporary social philosophers, one who has done more than any other to bridge the chasm between Continental and Anglo-Saxon philosophies. But Habermas' works must be judged on a level commensurate with their ambitiousness. Habermas' critique of hermeneutics, as well as the approach to critical theory that has in part emerged from it, embodies rather basic shortcomings. I have identified these as: a failure to break radically enough with the residue of the old *Erklären/Verstehen* opposition, with consequent difficulties for treating the interconnections of the nomologial and hermeneutic; the unsatisfactory character of Habermas' fundamental distinction between labor and interaction, which has the effect that the latter becomes treated as equivalent to symbolic or communicative action; the persistence of such a strongly marked Hegelian strain in the posited relations between "self-reflection" and autonomy, especially in Habermas' earlier works, that the transformative capacity of human action is not adequately connected to rational understanding of conditions of action; the associated reliance on a psychoanalytic model of ideology-critique that does not effectively illuminate the conjunction of differentials of power and asymmetries of material interests between groups in society; and the dearth of a theory of reference that would tie in Habermas' more recent discussions of truth as the redemption of validity claims in theoretical discourse to the themes of his preceding treatment of self-reflection.

It seems that Habermas' current preoccupations with universal pragmatics, the development of cognition and ego-identity in the child, and a scheme of evolutionary change are something of a departure from the emphases of his first works. In lieu of a direct statement from Habermas himself, it is difficult to assess how far he may have abandoned or substantially modified his earlier views. Certainly, a strong line of continuity in his works runs from his initial analysis of changes in the nature of public discourse (*Strukturwandel der Öffentlichkeit,* 1962) up to the present time, and it is difficult to resist the conclusion that several of the problems I have indicated remain deeply embedded in Habermas' most recent writings.

NOTES

1. In saying this, I do not ignore Bradley, Green, or T. F. Collingwood. But "British Hegelianism" was quite short-lived, and through the influence of Moore and Russell, British philosophy recovered its continuity with Hume and his successors. The "second revolution" in British philosophy, largely due to the later Wittgenstein, has undoubtedly created a more favorable climate to a renewed sympathy with these traditions.
2. See "My Hermeneutics, Ethnomethodology, and Problems of Interpretative Analysis," to appear.
3. Cf. Paul Ricoeur, *Husserl: An Analysis of His Phenomenology* (Evanston, Ill.: 1967).
4. Hans-Georg Gadamer, *Truth and Method* (London: 1975).
5. Peter Winch, *The Idea of a Social Science* (London: 1958); "Understanding a Primitive Society," *American Philosophical Quarterly,* Vol. I, 1964. Jurgen Habermas' views on Winch appear in *Zur Logik der Sozialwissenschaften* (Tubingen: 1967), pp. 134 ff; on Wittgenstein, see also the brief comments in *Habermas, Philosophisch-Politische Profile* (Frankfurt: 1971) pp. 141–146.
6. See various papers collected together in Ernest Gellner, *Cause and Meaning in the Social Sciences* (London: 1973); also *Legitimation of Belief* (Cambridge: 1974).
7. Ernest Gellner, *Words and Things* (London: 1968).
8. Jurgen Habermas, *Zur Logik der Sozialwissenschaften,* pp. 3 ff.
9. Jurgen Habermas, *Knowledge and Human Interests* (London: 1972), p. 4.
10. Jurgen Habermas, *Toward a Rational Society* (London: 1971), pp. 91 ff., and *Knowledge and Human Interest,* pp. 196 ff. See also *Zur Rekonstruktion des Historischen Materialismus* (Frankfurt: 1976), pp. 34 ff.
11. Habermas, *Knowledge and Human Interests,* p. 308.
12. Ibid., p. 310.

13. Jurgen Habermas, Cf. "Between Philosophy and Science: Marxism as Critique," in *Theory and Practice* (London: 1974).

14. It is worth remarking on the massive revival of concern with psychoanalysis that has attended the thesis that Freud's theories can be treated as expressing a "depth hermeneutics" in which language and its deformations are at the center. Psychoanalysis until quite recently has been more influential in the United States than elsewhere and has characteristically been moved in the direction of an "ego psychology." Authors such as Habermas, Arnold Lorenzer, Jacques Lacan, and Jacques Derrida, however, are much more interested in the reformulation of classical psychoanalytic concerns with the id, repressions, and the unconscious.

15. "Wahrheitstheorien," in Helmut Fahrenbach; *Wirklichkeit und Reflexion, zum Sechzigsten Geburtstag fur Walter Schulz* (Pfullingin: 1973); "Was Heisst Universalpragmatik?" in Karl-Otto Apel; *Sprachpragmatik und Philosophie* (Frankfurt; 1976). For an English version of some of the latter, see "Some Distinctions in Universal Pragmatics," *Theory and Society*, Volume 2, No. 2, 1976.

16. "Wahrheitstheorien," op. cit., p. 219. However, Habermas also holds that all speech has a "double structure," such that nonconstative speech acts have an implicit propositional content that can be made explicit. Cf. "Some Distinctions in Universal Pragmatics," op. cit., pp. 156–158.

17. Ibid., p. 221.

18. "Was Heisst Universalpragmatik?" op. cit., p. 174.

19. The continuity can be discerned in a paragraph in *Zur Logik der Sozialwissenschaften*, where Habermas connects labor with "external nature," "language" with intersubjectivity (subsequently differentiated into "intelligibility" as an overarching notion, and "practical discourse"), and domination with the repression of "inner nature."

20. "Wahrheitstheorien," op. cit., p. 245. According to Habermas, the forms of discourse connect to "cognitive schemata" of the sort described by Piaget. Such schemata also provide the basis of a speculative theory of evolution, which Habermas regards as essential to "rethinking historical materialism." This is at the center of his current preoccupations but falls outside the scope of my discussion here.

21. "Was Heisst Universalpragmatik?" op. cit., p. 213.

22. "Wahrheitstheorien," op. cit., pp. 252 ff.

23. Ibid., p. 264, n. 43.

24. Ibid., p. 260.

25. Jurgen Habermas, *Legitimation Crisis* (Boston: Beacon Press, 1975). (Note the excellent introductory essay by Tom McCarthy.) There is by now a very large critical literature, mostly in German, dealing with Habermas' writings. Moreover, Habermas' interchanges with Gehlen, Gadamer, and Luhmann also have generated secondary controversies. I shall not cite much of this literature directly. Among the more important items are; Habermas et al., *Hermeneutik und Ideologiekritik* (Frankfurt: 1971); Habermas and N. Luhmann, *Theorie der Gesellschaft oder Sozialtechnologie?* (Frankfurt: 1971). Rudiger Bubner et al., *Hermeneutik und Dialektik* (Tubingen: 1970). For a useful survey in English, see Fred R. Dallmayr, "Critical Theory Criticized: Habermas' *Knowledge and Human Interests* and Its Aftermath," *Philosophy of the Social Sciences*, Vol. 2, 1972; a fairly full bibliography appears in *Cultural Hermeneutics*, Vol. 2, 1975 (special issue on hermeneutics and critical theory).

26. Cf. the various contributions in M. Radner and S. Winokur, *Minnesota Studies in the Philosophy of Science*, Vol. 4, 1970.

27. Habermas now seems to acknowledge this more clearly but does not make much of it. Cf. "Was Heisst Universalpragmatik?" op. cit., p. 186.

28. Cf. Hans-Georg Gadamer, "From the hermeneutical standpoint, rightly understood, it is absolutely absurd to regard the concrete factors of work and politics as outside the scope of hermeneutics. The principle of hermeneutics simply means that we should try to understand everything that can be under-

stood." "On the Scope and Function of Hermeneutical Reflection," *Continuum*, Vol. 8, No. 3, 1972.

29. Anthony Giddens, *New Rules of Sociological Method*, New York, Basic Books, 1977, pp. 88 ff.

30. Habermas, *Zur Logik der Sozialwissenschaften*, p. 178.

31. *New Rules of Sociological Method*, pp. 118 ff.

32. In his discussion of universal pragmatics, Habermas says he accepts Searle's "principle of expressibility," according to which every speech act can be specified as a statement; but this principle seems compromised in a basic way by the ideal of "indefinite elaboration" as formulated in the writings of Harold Garfinkel and in a similar way in those of Fred Ziff.

33. Habermas, *Knowledge and Human Interests*, p. 313.

34. Ibid. p. 314.

35. Cf. Gadamer, "I cannot share the claims of critical theory that one can master the impasse of our civilization by emancipatory reflection." "Hermeneutics and Social Science," *Cultural Hermeneutics*, Vol. 2, 1975, p. 315.

36. Habermas, *Knowledge and Human Interest*, p. 310. One should perhaps point out that Habermas' relation to Hegel has occupied many of his critics, some of whom (like me) think he remains too much of an Hegelian, others of whom accuse him of not being Hegelian enough. The highly eclectic character of Habermas' writings is no doubt partly responsible for such debates.

37. However, Habermas has recently acknowledged, in a new edition of *Theory and Practice*, that he has, "in the works collected together here and also in later works, often used the idea of a human species, which constitutes itself as the subject of world-history, in an uncritical way." *Theorie und Praxis* (Frankfurt: 1971), p. 289.

38. *New Rules of Sociological Method*, pp. 110 ff.

39. "Introduction: Some Difficulties in the Attempt to Link Theory and Practice," in Habermas, *Theory and Practice*.

40. William Sargant, *Battle for the Mind* (London: 1956).

41. Hans-Georg Gadamer, "Replik," in Karl-Otto Apel, *Hermeneutik und Ideologiekritik* (Frankfurt: 1971).

3.
CRITICAL THEORY AND REVOLUTIONARY CONSCIOUSNESS

URS JAEGGI
Translated by Hans Fantel

After 1945, German sociology developed in a theoretical vacuum. At first, and for a long time thereafter, its cracks and holes were stuffed with American imports; there was thus a basic sociological understanding rooted in European thought, plus healthy common sense, minus a sound theoretical grounding. As a consequence, German sociology was trapped within a circle that, for lack of research facilities and qualified personnel, left the Europeans far behind. This situation changed when the neopositivists arrayed themselves against the Frankfurt School in their so-called methodological dispute. The debate turned into monologues that have already faded, leaving no afterglow. Yet the question still remains: "What about a Marxian sociology capable of developing a capable and adequate methodology?"

Under the aegis of the cold war, this question never even arose.

Even C. Wright Mills, the most prominent among the *engagé* sociologists in America, maintained that mainstream sociology had so incorporated the intellectual content of Marxism that the separation of the two had become a moot point. Moreover, the vulgar Marxism promulgated under Stalin in the socialist countries lacked all attraction as far as the West was concerned, not merely on the political but also on the theoretical level. It appeared as a straitjacket and a shackle. Despite all this, whoever did not wish to abandon the dialogue, usually confined himself to the classics: Marx and Engels. Nobody gave serious thought to the future of revolutionary movements. Ernst Bloch was alone in the early 1950s, when he said: "Revolution, after all, is not only the transformation of what falsely exists; revolution also signifies and effects by this transformation that man in history finally moves in his own orbit."[1] This was utopian thinking, sharply contrasting with dogmatism. The counterpart in the West—in Germany—was supplied by the so-called Frankfurt School, which at first operated in isolation. Later, Albrecht Wellmer summarized their position:

> Critical theory is guided by the idea of the "good life", which it always finds already present as a component of the historic-societal situations to be analyzed in terms of critical theory; a concept which as the idea of human recognition of each by each, as the idea of non-coercive, dialogic coexistence of men, had always been a design for the meaning of history, fragmentarily embodied in social traditions and institutions. It is this design for historical meaning which critical theory turns against existing society and the dominant forms of its unquestioned assumptions.[2]

This corresponds with both the "old" and the "new" traditions of the Frankfurt School. The point of departure is the thesis that critical theory conceives of itself as a relatively powerless protest against an apocalyptically self-sealing system of alienation and reification. This view is clearly exemplified in Horkheimer, Marcuse, and Adorno. The following remnant may form the link to Habermas: "The design of future praxis implied in critical theory can ultimately prove itself only in free recognition of those who have experienced societal changes guided by this theory as concrete liberation."[3] This implies the radical-democratic demand for resistance to what *is,* and for overcoming existing social forms through domination-free (nonrepressive) communication.

Presented defensively, this demand necessarily bears an elitist character. Resistance against solidified conditions is historically the concern of the few.

It is therefore not misleading to assert that critical theory, during the reconstruction phase of West German society, necessarily had to fall into dual isolation: It was isolated from scientific inquiry as well as from politics. As for political isolation, this lasted only as long as the political public reacted to critical theory, which was largely a critique of culture, less with irritation (i.e., less with direct concern) than with flexible acceptance. The theoretical premises wmre absorbed into the literary and artistic culture-industry, which not merely endured this critique but utilized it for the purpose of self-sensitization. Adorno and his followers particularly were placed in a position of an involuntary, yet accepted, elitism which dulled the edge of their political thought. On the other hand, the spontaneity that the Frankfurt School had confined to the realm of art predictably extended during the early 1960s into the realm of educational institutions and hence into the political sphere. And here this spontaneity became virulent. As Adorno later observed, the choking-off of spontaneity did not turn out to be the placid process hoped for by bureaucratic functionaries. "Do it yourself! Liberate yourself!" With this slogan, the dissidents did not just rap the knuckles of the dominating powers; they stepped on their toes. Such action necessarily contradicted the theoretical premise of the Frankfurt School. Adorno, however esoteric, always knew how to fit his formulations to the most concrete conditions of the moment. At that time, he wrote: "Spontaneity cannot be absolutized. It can no more be split off from objective situations and idealized than the administered world itself. Otherwise the hammer, which never replaces the carpenter, does more damage than repair."[4]

Above all, Adorno saw the element of theatricality, of pseudo-activity inherent in direct action. Others, by contrast, quickly recognized the throwback to the fascist tradition now embraced by the Left. In contrast to Adorno, Marcuse, at least for a time, placed his hopes rather casually, although not uncritically, in spontaneity. This initial constellation not only filled the shelves of bookshops but also had a salutary practical consequence. Seemingly unshakable institutions were shaken, notably the mummy crypts of the universities. They were shaken and changed at a tumultuous pace that exacerbated mutual embitterment. Critical theory was discussed more widely than its originators might have liked. Their isolation was thus repeated, but now on another plane.

Wellmer later recounted these developments:

> Habermas attempted to break through the dual isolation of
> critical theory [the political and the scientific]. He con-
> cluded from the failure of the revolutionary movement in
> Europe that critical theory must become critical toward
> itself if it is to regain the lost connection with political
> praxis.[5]

As I shall attempt to show, this claim implies a dilemma immi-
nent in critical theory. The theory attempts to connect anticipatory speculation, expressed as a scientifically controllable utopia,
with the methodological assumptions of a concrete discipline.
Yet it is precisely for this reason that self-reflection as "Knowledge for the sake of knowledge" (Habermas) is ideologically in-
fected in exactly the same way as critical theory's critique of
scientism. If critical theory is to connect with the attainments of
analytically oriented inquiries, it cannot soar above its subject.
Thus, the metacritique must remain almost distinct from its epistemological premises. Otherwise, its claim to be pure reflection
is in vain. The really decisive question is: "What problem areas
are taken up by the alleged radicalization of the critique of knowledge—what problem areas are isolated or even eliminated?" In
dealing with this question in this essay, I propose that Habermas'
conception focuses on precisely the very element that renders a
reconstruction of the Marxian premise impossible. This is not a
priori negative.

Let us define the frame of inquiry more precisely. Habermas
strives to eliminate the speculative remnant in the Marxian
theory of revolution. Since the power indirectly exercised over
the process of exchange is now controlled by a system of domination organized prior to its incorporation into the state and then
institutionalized by the state, it is no longer possible to derive
legitimization, as did Marx, from an apolitical order of the relations of production.[6] Intent on stability and economic growth, the
action of the state assumes a negative character in politics: it is
oriented toward the solution of technical problems.[7] In my view,
this was first made clear in Habermas' essay "Technology and
Science as 'Ideology.'" He takes his departure from Max Weber's
theory of rationalization, which demonstrated how rationality expands those areas of society that are susceptible to the criteria of
rational decision making. Habermas then arrives at a new
postulate: to the extent that technology and science penetrate

the institutions of society, these institutions themselves are
changed, and the old legitimizing devices are no longer ap-
plicable. This argument still runs parallel to Marcuse, who also
makes "the political content of technologic reason" the point of
analytic departure for a theory of advanced industrial society.
Habermas extends beyond this, however, in connection with a
criticism of Marx, which pulls the earlier premises of critical
theory out from under it. His starting point is this:

> Since the last quarter of the 19th century, two *developmental
> trends* have become noticeable in advanced industrial coun-
> tries. 1. An increase in state intervention aimed at assuring
> the stability of the system, and 2, an increasing indepen-
> dence of research and technology, which has made the
> (physical) sciences the primary productive force.[8]

State intervention was necessitated by the need for counteract-
ing dysfunctions endangering the system by means of a permanent regulation of the economic process. This has destroyed the
concept of bourgeois society. Its basic ideology of a just equivalence in exchange, which Marx had already exposed as a decep-
tion at the theoretical level, now also collapsed at the practical
level:

> Since the form of private capital investment could only be
> maintained by the corrective governmental stabilization of
> economic cycles and related sociological changes, the in-
> stitutional frame of society was thus re-politicized. As a
> result, politics is no longer a *purely* superstructural
> phenomenon.[9]

Habermas is hardly justified in his assertion that Marx had isolated the economic laws of societal change; moreover Marx did
not regard politics as a purely superstructural phenomenon. The
"negative" character—or to put it more precisely—the *defensive*
character of state intervention, defined by Habermas as aimed
at the stabilization of economic growth and at the avoidance
of system-endangering risks, is attained at the cost of restricting
the private sector.[10] Yet he perceives that this restriction nevertheless serves to secure private investment and to bind the loyalty of the masses to the capitalist form of social organization. But
this entails a concept almost wholly avoided by Habermas, whose

main interest lies in the problems of legitimization as ideological factors: one would have to investigate to what extent "defensive" state intervention is aggressively predetermined by economic interest groups. The basic ideology of equivalence exchange, debunked by Marx, is today no longer the central problem, although its basic mechanism of use value, exchange value, and surplus value still operates in the background. What is important now is the new interlinking of the state with the private economic sector (including the labor unions); this interlinking does not—as Habermas assumes—hinder state intervention in the realization of practical aims but rather assures in advance their realization in the context of the prevailing system. One must clarify the consequences: the "pseudoprograms" of state intervention, constantly emphasized by Habermas, are aimed exclusively at the functioning of the controlled system, and become a form of state dependence on its main industries. In this relationship, politics has been displaced from the locus assigned to it by the theory of democratic agreement. Politics is no longer made by parliaments. Neither is politics made primarily by an administrative bureaucracy of experts.

It is not the "pseudoprograms" that preclude practical questions and hence discussions of the "assumption of standards," which alone could produce a democratic consensus. Such discussions are, to put it bluntly, rendered impossible by capitalist interests.

In practice, the so-called arbitration function of government systematically favors the economically stronger against the weaker contestant in a conflict of interest. Its tendency is to strengthen those who already have power. Only *because* Habermas sets aside the economic base and one-sidedly links stabilizing state activity exclusively to the empirically ascertainable loyalty of the citizens is he able to ignore conditions of exploitation and repression and to base his argument on the "virtualization" of class conflict. Hence, the other contradictions inherent in the social structure also are perceived merely as marginal or as verifying phenomena. The concept of growth, particularly the concept of growing gross national product so proudly emphasized by the defenders of capitalism, has a deceptive—or rather a fraudulent—character inasmuch as it systematically obscures what Gorz calls "the actual social costs that accrue in the social reproduction of the labor force under changing conditions of life."[11] This includes, among other factors, the rising cost of sustenance, and education. Within the range of problems outlined here, Habermas' primary interest centers only on large-scale industrial research, an admittedly important area that combines science, technology, and investment into an interlinked system. Yet this theory of technology separates reflection on the relation between science and technology from the political-economic context and presents reflection as an independent area.

This is a decisive shift of emphasis. Another element of Marxist theory is thereby canceled by a stroke of the pen. Seen as the primary forces of production, technology and science thus supposedly obviate the applicability of the labor theory of value: "It no longer makes sense to calculate capital investment in research and development on the basis of the value of unqualified, simple labor force; institutionalized scientific-technological progress has become an independent source of value, relatively more important than the labor input of the immediate producers, which for Marx constituted the only source of surplus value."[12] Seen separately, the concentration on technology necessarily distorts the theoretical view of labor. The consequence is a perspective in which the "development of societal systems *appears* to be determined by the logic of scientific-technical progress. The immanent laws of this progress create the objective constraints for a politics responsive to functional needs. Once this appearance is effectively accepted, then propagandistic reference to the role of science and technology can explain and legitimate the reasons why in modern societies democratic consensus no longer applies to practical problems and 'must' be replaced by plebiscite-decisions about alternative leadership groups in the administrative *"personnel."*[13]

Habermas is not chiefly concerned with raising serious questions about this pseudolegitimization. His stress is on the fact that this technocracy thesis enters into the consciousness of the depoliticized majority of the population in the form of "background ideology" and thus acts as a legitimizing force.[14] He only marginally mentions that this is inextricably linked to the form of private capital investment. However, Habermas does not deny "the ideological force of technocratic consciousness." Here lies the possible departure point for a new interpretation of the critique of political economy *as* a critique of ideology. To clarify the relations of production (and thereby the social relations), it would be necessary to uncover the immanent structure of the given society rather than analyze this society in terms of a categorical framework. This is not a matter of merely studying historically succeeding modes of production or the various technologies of production—an approach that might justly be termed "economics" or even "technologism." Marx has already criticized this in concrete terms at a time when the logic of this process was by no means clearly evident. "If in a perfected bourgeois system every economic relation presupposes the other(s) within the bourgeois-economic form, and thus everything given is at the same time presupposition, then it is like any other organic system. The organic system itself, as totality, as its presuppositions and its development into a totality, consists in the system's ability to subordinate all elements of society to its own design as well as creating within society the apparatus that is still lacking for its own completion."[15] "Bourgeois society" (the individualistic economy and its ideological sources) is thus dissolved—even for Habermas, who deplores the passing of the old conditions inasmuch as they still rested on the basic concept of just and domination-free interaction; today the requirements for system preservation primarily define social structure. This view correctly assumed that bourgeois ideology, as Marx demonstrated, remained based on political and ideological phenomena and thus projected and secured its own world order. This order always claimed an ideational and hence ideological program. At one time, these supposedly scientific explanations had to be unmasked as ideology; similarly, today technocratic consciousness remains as ideology. To gain certainty about the institutionalized relations of coercion, one must first gain certainty about the relations of production. Where Marx attempted to show the "anatomy" of society in terms of the level of development of its productive forces and its particular relations of production, Habermas posits a more particularized premise based on empirical data that are unreservedly considered as absolute fact. According to Habermas, capitalist society has so changed that two key categories of Marxian theory—class struggle and class ideology—can no longer be directly applied. The conflict of social classes emerged as such only on the basis of the capitalist mode of production and thus created an objective situation in which the class structure of the politically constituted traditional society could be recognized. State-regulated capitalism, which grew from the dangers to the system posed by open class antagonism, is interpreted by Habermas as the end of class conflict. Then it naturally follows that science itself is declared to be the "life form" of industrial society (Wellmer) and that enlightenment seems possible only as the enlightenment of those directly or indirectly participating in the scientific enterprise. If this alone is perceived as the unity of critical theory and emancipatory praxis, then it emerges as a central moment in the developmental history of critical theory.

Let us take one step into the past: critical theory attempted to show that the subject is inseparable from its object. There is no totality if the subject does not experience the totality. On this point, Wellmer is a trustworthy chronicler: as long as the fear and misery of the masses were as concrete and real as the hope for a revolutionary resolution of class conflict, Marxist theoreticians could conceive their theoretical work as an immediate part of a revolutionary struggle. Not the judgment of professional colleagues, but the agreement of the masses, whose interests they attempted to articulate, was their touchstone. This has changed. Why?

Partly because critical theory during the 1930s regarded itself as a form of resistance against nascent fascism, its theoreticians formulated their thought with a global perspective. After the war, things were different. Dismayed by the distortions developing in the "formation of communism" after World War II, the adherents of critical theory attempted to draw a line of demarcation between true and false ideas. The heart of critique was no longer primarily the agreement of that group whose interests had to be articulated and served; now the theoreticians addressed themselves mainly to their professional colleagues. Wellmer's *Critical Theory*, as well as Habermas' essay "Bedingungen für eine Revolutionierung Spätkapitalistischer Gesellschaftssysteme," shows how the reality of revolutionary class conflict—which still persists as a praxis on a global scale—has been confined within a Eurocentric perspective and thereby negated. Moreover, this negation of class conflict has been declared globally valid.

As late as 1962, Habermas recognized correctly that sociology, understood as a purely empirical science, must remain neutral in its logical structure and methodology vis-a-vis the possible consequences of its own results as these are transmuted into praxis. Within this particular and obvious methodological requirement, room still remains for the double role of scientist and citizen. In other words, science can bring about change only where it is conscious of itself as a political praxis. However, the beginning schism was already prepared. Habermas' argument, still based on praxis in its genuine sense, conceived society as an action-consensus of speaking persons who enter social action in the context of deliberate communication and thereby must form themselves into a collective subject capable of action.[16] Work and communication were separated here for the first time, if only by implication. Still, the wish for a change of the "given" remained continuous and naive. "Critical sociology," Habermas wrote at that time,

> is capable of remembering what was once intended with what today has been concretized and actually attained. It takes account of the pretensive element in existing institutions, for where the utopian factor persists, it reveals—if realistically understood—within the existent that which it is *not.* The false identification of that-which-should-be with that-which-has-been attained is similarly, though not equally, dangerous and deceptive—regardless of whether this mis-identification has been terroristically enforced or manipulatively engineered. If critical sociology shows without either accusation or justification that security bought at the price of increased risk is not security; that emancipation at the price of increased regimentation is not freedom; that property at the price of reified pleasure is not abundance; then this necessarily bitter control of success will be sociology's contribution to the defense of society against the Huxleyan nightmare and the Orwellian horror.[17]

No doubt, Habermas' later, scientifically adumbrated idealism appears here still clothed in the diction of the "classical" Frankfurt School. Yet the economic fundamentals that, as Bloch observes, must never be thrown overboard as mere ballast, but must be retained as the basic discovery supporting and activating the Hegelian dialectic, had already been abandoned by Habermas. Even the early Habermas was noncommittal on the problem of revolution. Granted, he approvingly cites Joachim Ritter, who maintains that there is no other philosophy "so strongly and so wholly in its innermost attributes the philosophy of revolution as that of Hegel."[18] Habermas augments this thesis by adding that Hegel had elevated the revolution to a constitutive principle of his philosophy in order to avoid sacrificing his philosophy to the challenge of revolution. Hegel's philosophy of revolution, according to Habermas, transcends revolution as such. "Hegel places revolution at the core of his philosophy in order to prevent his philosophy from becoming the pimp of revolution. Thereby he has once again preserved dialectics as ontology, has once again secured for philosophy its provenance in theory, and has removed theory from mediation by historic consciousness and social praxis. . . ."[19] Later, Habermas seeks a similar "preservation" in his own philosophy. First, he accuses Marx of having sublated epistemology in favor of a universal history freed from its shackles. "If Marx had not thrown together interaction and work under the rubric of social praxis, if he had instead referred the materialist concept of synthesis equally to instrumental action and its linkage to communicative action, then the idea of human sciences would not have been obscured by identification with the natural sciences."[20] Habermas postulates that a radicalized critique of knowledge could ultimately be accomplished only in the form of a reconstruction of the history of the species. Conversely, a theory of society based on the assumption of human self-formation within the medium of social labor and class struggle is possible only as self-reflection of cognitive consciousness. Yet Marx had in fact never opposed "production" and "reflection"—and rightly so. He certainly never posited production as an independent category. Otherwise, he would not have been able to derive his doctrine of the deformation of man under the coercion of the relations of production. Yet Habermas insists on this formulation. Further, he insists that the objectivistically formulated Marxian crisis theory tended to neglect the human subject. It never even took account of the fact that its predictions incited not merely the proletariat in his revolutionary impetus but also the capitalist in his resolve to prevent that revolution. According to Habermas, Marx failed to see that economic process would become increasingly manipulated by will and consciousness, and that this would introduce into capitalism, for the purpose of its own self-preservation, precisely those elements of rationalization that Marx believed to be the exclusive characteristic of a socialist society.[21] Yet the Marxian "design of history" is not objectivistic. Nor did Marx misjudge the rationalizing potential of the capitalist system. True, he did not and could not foresee that the capitalist order and the bourgeoisie would survive the collapse of free competition in the particular manner in which they did survive. From this, Habermas draws the partly justified, if by no means original, conclusion that the inevitability of system-endangering "disproportions" is today no longer demonstrable on a short-term basis. Nevertheless, what does disproportion mean? This concept, which masks class antagonism, severs the link between capital and wage labor and transposes the conflict to the level of communication. Here, self-reflection as "critique of ideology engaged in emancipatory purpose" and functioning as a pure theory of knowledge can no longer find direct access to material problems. The praxis-deprived activity of the theoretician is absolutized, losing reference to material contexts. Theoretical work is presumed to reveal, almost as a signal, the possibility of a domination-free sphere. Science becomes its own cause. This also obviates the question as to why the radical demands, which even Habermas still considers necessary, can no longer be expressed by those whose interests are concerned. This context merely permits superficial explanations, such as the already mentioned loyalty of the masses to the system—a loyalty attained and secured by means of compensatory benefits relating to privatized needs. This neutralization of conflict, which Habermas can at first only impute to "reality," then leads to further conclusions: "Nobody may presumptuously identify himself with a consciousness to be engendered in the future by enlightened masses so as to act already today as a deputy in their behalf."[22] This leads us directly back to the question about the revolutionary subject and indirectly to the question about the means of change, that is, the question of "power." Sociology usually has a diffuse and abridged view of "power," and Habermas also sees it in an undifferentiated manner: "Marx presented dialectical sociology with the critical task of becoming a practical power; we know today, that in this course sociology has itself become enmeshed in an unforeseen dialectic: the dialectic between revolutionary humanism and Stalinist terror."[23] Habermas here presents a less dialectical variation on a thought that Maurice Merleau-Ponty developed in a more precise and differentiated manner:

> It will be the essential task of Marxism to seek a form of power which is self-transcendent in the direction of a human future. Marx believed to have found it in proletarian power, i.e., in the rule of that class of men who society has robbed of their work and their lives and who are therefore able to extend recognition to each other beyond all peculiarities and thus to found a humanity. Cunning, lies, spilled blood and dictatorship are justified, inasmuch as they facilitate the rule of the proletariat—and only then. Marxian politics are in their form dictatorial and totalitarian. But this dictatorship is the dictatorship of the men who are most purely human; this totalitarianism is the totalitarianism of all workers taking possession of the state and the means of production. The dictatorship of the proletariat is not the will of a few functionaries who, like Hegel's state bureaucrats, are

the only initiates to the secret of history; rather the dictatorship obeys the spontaneous movement of proletarians of all
lands and rests upon the "instinct" of the masses.[24]

While Merleau-Ponty dogmatizes Marx in certain aspects, he retains the assumption that class struggle necessarily leads to the
dictatorship of the proletariat and that this signals the transition
to the classless society.

Our discussion cannot concern itself with an investigation of
whether or not Communism sticks to the rules of liberal thinking.
(All too obviously, Communism does not often lean toward
classical liberalism. The point is whether or not power is "revolutionary" and capable of establishing adequate human 'relations
between individuals.[25]) Habermas ignores this critical point. He
reverts to a position that can attribute to Marxism only a dual
function: as a political reality and as a theory that aims to
transform the total reality. Merleau-Ponty has been justifiably
criticized for never having furnished sociologically acceptable
proof that the proletariat does in fact possess the qualities re-
quisite for its revolutionary role. Habermas himself answers this
question by pointing out that he does indeed see the deprived
wage laborers of the nineteenth century as an exploited class. Yet
he believes that in advanced capitalism, privileged and deprived
groups no longer confront each other *as* socioeconomic classes.
According to his assumption, the barriers "cut across the population strata."[26] However, he fails to indicate *how* these barriers
transect the population strata and why there supposedly are no
more fixed socioeconomic classes. He merely postulates that the
two fundamental premises of Marx, which facilitate the revolu-
tionizing of the system, no longer apply:

1. The antagonism between the owners of the means of production and wage laborers no longer manifests itself as class struggle; the concerned subjects themselves no longer see themselves
as opponents, which is why conflict can no longer be politically
organized.
2. The institutional requirement for capital investment in
private form no longer presents the economic system with permanently insoluble problems.[27]

Again, these theses are in no way empirically documented. Nor
are they fortified with adequate theoretical support: they remain
assertions. This much is apparent: the asserted latency of class
conflict presupposes the stagnation of social forms under ad-

vanced capitalism (even though an internal dynamism prevails within). Its cohesion can be only vaguely subverted, and that only because of the weakness of capitalist legitimization, namely, the very depoliticization of public life necessary to the survival of the system. This depoliticization forestalls the democratic formation of consensus. By unmasking this fact, Habermas' thesis claims to reveal the system's points of strategic "vulnerability." Yet this can only be derived from the underlying assumption that the only possible "basis" for change is no longer the mode of production but rather the humans who are subjected to the coercive power of large organizations. What is lacking is the purposive groups whose position within the production process marks them as bearers of a possible enlightenment. Revolutionary consciousness can awaken only at the margins of the system.[28]

The bearers of revolutionary consciousness, writes Habermas, are the students. But they do not constitute a class. Moreover, in our geographic latitudes, they do not even form the avant-garde of a class, and nothing lies farther from their life-styles than true revolutionary struggle. On the other hand, Habermas sees certain portents that they might form the kernel of a "New Sensibility," that they might generate a "passion for practical reason" that might spread with the potential growth of the youth movement. In this way, Habermas paradoxically resorts, after all, to the "rational core of the new anarchism." Like Marcuse on some occasions, he develops the theory of the closed society into a thesis postulating the revolt of the pleasure principle against the reality principle. Along this path, he camouflages the fact that this sociopsychological situation inevitably rests on a socioeconomic basis.

In support of Habermas, one must certainly admit that no socialist revolution of a capitalist society has occurred as a result of a completed maturation process. (The resistive power of "mature" advanced capitalist societies against attempts at fundamental change must not be underrated.) Yet only blindness to economic conditions can lead to the thesis that self-regulation and the increasingly conscious-directive management can in the long run assimilate and socially transform rationality per se. And again, only blindness to economic conditions can ultimately arrive even at the assumption that the exploitive relations between countries of the First and Third Worlds can be gradually replaced by relations of strategic dependence and growing disparity. Again, we must ask: "What is meant by 'growing disparity' especially if it is no longer economically grounded?" Habermas does not support his assertion with precise data. He builds on the supposition that even at the international level, underprivilege would increasingly signify an "intolerable deprivation of rights," which would be less and less synonymous with exploitation. This, by the way, would imply a shift from the economic to the moral sphere of demands by the formerly exploited. But this also implies that they would have to bring the injustice of a *past* phase convincingly to the attention of the erstwhile colonial powers.

As a result, Habermas is certain that—first of all—no revolutionary situation exists, at least not in terms of a situation that might develop into revolutionary change. Furthermore, he assumes this to be the case on a global scale. Every single sign customarily accepted as portending revolutionary change is lacking. He arrives at this conclusion because he places a one-sided emphasis on developments, interpreting them from the perspective of the advanced capitalist countries of Europe (at the same time relating the stability of these systems to the stability of the East European communist countries, which on their part have not been able to engender alternatives). Second, for members of the Third World, he counters the concept of "exploitation," which he regards as too narrowly economic, with the psychological concept of "underprivilege" and "just indignation." This also is a Eurocentric viewpoint that denies and misapprehends the fact that the "underdeveloped," unlike ourselves, are not the inheritors of a frustrated revolution. "For us, revolution still remains a task," Latin American sociologist Darcy Ribero says rightly. "At bottom, the only task we face, for only the revolution can destroy existing structures. Furthermore, the revolution, and hence the critical theory of ourselves, of our history and our present, is for us not the result of mature conditions but the only possibility to bring about 'mature conditions', i.e., a higher stage of development of our society."[29] This has nothing to do with moralism. Third, it is decisive that Habermas can only verbalize the totality claim of his theory through self-reflection. He cannot fix it concretely precisely because he also sees in social science the social forces of production that maintain and propagate the totality of the given system and because he demands critical distance to reduce the "praxis-proximity" to the status of ad hoc knowledge. This makes pertinent questions problematic but avoids all effective influence on the political discussion of strategies and organization. "Truth" becomes the memory of an historic process and remains neutral toward political development.[30] Truth and objectivity revert upon themselves within dialogue and polemics. The participant assumes the obligation to defend what he tries to prove. He gives true utterance if the intentions signified in the act of speaking are not merely feigned but actually meant. Self-reflection, which for Habermas included the competent communicative partner, remains dialogue within one's own ranks.

Since Marx and Lenin, socially productive fear of the stability and adaptability of capitalism has been a necessary element of every realistic strategy of revolutionary social change. Yet this productive fear changes into an irrational fixation on the counter-revolutionary techniques of repression when it is removed from the context of political perspectives and the formulation of an explicit theory.[31] After the radical separation of work and language, which now remain only in a vague dialectic relationship, it becomes difficult to see how Habermas might reconstruct "the repressed elements and motifs within society from the historical traces of the repressed dialogue." If it remains at this level, the intended domination-free dialogue embodies at first a purely rhetorical function. It follows an idealistic demand—or to put it in more congenial terms—an emancipatory demand. But what is this demand, and how is it pursued? At first, man runs the risk of confining himself exclusively to external, instrumental action and of enveloping all men, including himself, into this purely instrumental action system. This is obvious and was so noted long ago by conservative social critics: the "new self-alienation of man, which can deprive him of his own identity and that of others is the danger that the creator loses himself in his creation, the constructor in his construction" (Schelsky). This danger cannot be denied. Yet under these conditions, the project of "a thorough analysis of historic process, guided by the interest of the future" (Habermas) becomes utopian consciousness and, as such, penetratingly ahistorical. It becomes pragmatic and programmatic. Class analysis and the concept of labor are not newly assessed by a reformulated critique of political economy. Rather, the concepts of class and labor are displaced in favor of a new anthropology (domination-free dialogue based on language as an anticipative instrument of emancipation). In contrast to Marx, Habermas construes the revolution as a purely subjective act. This subjectivization attempts to bridge the gap between praxis and critical theory, as well as supply the kind of praxis envisioned by critical theory. Yet self-reflection, as means and end, obliterates the historic process itself. Within the model of advanced capitalist society, historic process becomes a fixed absolute. It is assumed that what happens in advanced capitalist countries soon will happen in the Third World. The underprivileged of the advanced countries and the oppressed of the Third World merely have to wait. Meanwhile their moral indignation is appropriate and legitimate.

Revolution reduced to such terms contains a moralistic-philosophical ring that renders it amenable to discussion even in the salons of the well-meaning bourgeoisie. The concept of "domination-free communication" calls for conciliation that must occur within the framework of individual relationships even before, under the prevailing objective conditions, it *can* occur. A new definition of "revolution" would first have to delimit precisely what could be designated as revolution under present conditions, and such a definition would have to be differentiated according to the various dispositions of contemporary societies. For example, it must take account of the fact that the capitalist system, despite its aggravating crises and contradictions, is not yet discredited but may still, without seeming ridiculous, boast of concrete accomplishments. Two factors have touched on the original Marxian concept:

1. differentiation in the constitutive grouping of the laboring class;

2. the empirically ascertainable "inertia" of the laboring class.

There is no doubt that the equation "working class = proletariat, working class = revolution" propounded in vulgar Marxism is a myth. Habermas blames the scientism of advanced capitalist society, attained through technology, for the "virtualization of class struggle." Ernest Mandel, on the other hand, ascribes this development mainly to the bureaucratization of workers' organizations.

But here, too, the search seems to be for some initial spark from the outside. Students supposedly might form the initiating group whose political contagion might spread to the workers, especially to the young ones.[32] However, one should not overlook the fact that the "traditional" working class forms a relatively coherent block within the decompositional phenomena of this society. Absorption into the bourgeoisie (*embourgeoisement*) is not the primary problem so long as the possibilities of change remain virulent in the consciousness of the workers. Once society has succeeded in stabilizing the working class until it no longer pursues the aims originally attributed to it, society is itself stabilized by precisely that group. In other words, the working class may not have unconditionally integrated major portions of the bourgeois system of values even though it has provisionally accepted its values while retaining the option of systematic change under more favorable conditions. At any rate, one may cautiously conclude that the revolutionary role of the working class (as manifest in such events as the French uprising in May 1968 or the various wildcat strikes) is not so much a structural factor as a conjunctural possibility. The action of the working class is limited because the class, for understandable reasons, has limited itself. This process is by no means new. Lenin clearly perceived this. The revolutionary potential of this class becomes effective only if actualized within the frame of an historically concrete situation and when it is supported by political initiative, which does not have to originate entirely within the working class. In this sense, Habermas, and Marcuse's theory of marginal groups as revolutionary elements derives from Lenin's theory of revolution. They also adhere ultimately to Lenin's global definition: "When the 'lower strata' no longer want the old forms and the 'upper strata' no longer can function in the old way." But Habermas reflects this conflict only at the psychological level:

1. Within the framework of advanced industrial society: Only the psychology of affluence enables the status-favored segments of the student population to question the legitimacy of domination (putting themselves in the place of the non-conscious groups).

2. Within the global framework: The underprivileged of the Third World do not rebel because of economic deprivation (theory of imperialism); their rebellion arises from the inability of the established systems to equalize disparities quickly enough. Their protest is directed against a "morally intolerable deprivation of rights" (*"empörende Entrechtung"*/Habermas).

If we overlook their blindness to economic structures (although this is impermissible), what conclusions can be drawn from these premises?

Educational institutions, chiefly the universities, are no doubt important, but not because they enable privileged groups to develop and adopt temporary life-styles. Rather, it must be realized that at the universities, as an integral part of education itself, social conventions (and the "rationality" of the system) are severely questioned. Moreover, the insights thereby gained are integrated—even if partially—into later vocational life. This shift of orientation touches everyday life in both the social and the political sphere. A new understanding of technology becomes important. What matters is that the bearers of critical consciousness establish themselves in those sciences that produce instrumental knowledge. However, this cannot be attained by means of the precluded "domination-free discourse." This discourse remains obsolete as long as the particular science that propagates this idea, that is, philosophy, remains contemplative. The repolitization and hence the delegitimization of the existing system of domination cannot be accomplished by those students and student groups who do not represent an interest (Habermas) arising directly from their social situation. The rapid collapse of the antiauthoritarian movement has clearly shown this. Conversely, it appears far more likely that highly qualified graduates, along with politically conscious wage earners, will protest against the existing social structure and thereby also against the relations of production. In this sense, the abolition of poverty and the expansion of educative potential in developed capitalist countries are actually preconditions for change. This betokens a modification of the "classical" schema propounded by Marx. The dispossessed class, which does not know the nature of society and can gain this knowledge only through taking political power, is not the bearer of revolutionary consciousness. On the contrary, the necessary lever may be formed by groups with a relatively favorable position in society but who are frustrated in their work. In this way, the bourgeois revolution may be repeated in accordance with Lenin's thesis:

> The consciousness of the working class cannot be truly socialistic if the workers have not learned to stand up against *each* and *every* case of arbitrariness, oppression, violence, and abuse, no matter *which class* is involved in each instance. The consciousness of the workers cannot be true class consciousness if the workers do not learn from concrete and immediate political facts and events to observe *all* the manifestations of their intellectual, moral, and political life.[33]

A critical theory of revolution, which included both objective and subjective factors, may not ignore this view. Habermas and Wellmer polemicize against interpretations that one-sidedly absolutize the "natural" effective tendencies that necessarily actualize change of the capitalist order. This would not be objectionable if it were directed only against dogma and not against the premise per se. Under the pretext that emancipatory potentials are becoming more difficult to isolate and analyze in terms of a critique of political economy, the basic economic preconditions are entirely set aside. What remains are "plausible" explanations, unsystematically tied together. What remains is the thesis that modifications of the "superstructure" can lend a new and decisive impetus to the emancipatory movement. Thus continues the impotence of thought that remains thought.[34]

Although I do not wish to disparage the virtues of thought, it is necessary to destroy the illusion that discourse alone creates praxis. Seen in this perspective, critical theory, in the shade of Adorno, remains linked with the resignations of negativity. Social scientists talk with social scientists and call it domination-free dialogue. This may indeed be nonrepressive communication—as long as nobody asks who benefits from the dialogue. The intelligentsia as avant-garde? Or the enlightened group of social scientists who already take advantage of emancipatory possibilities on behalf of segments of the population who still remain mute? This claim becomes ultimately questionable when Habermas presents the ensuing communicative process between social scientists and politicians as a possibility for radical reform. In this area, critical theory in its search for undistorted communication no longer remains merely a critique of ideology. Legitimated as an emancipatory agent, it may here easily venture into the vicinity of instruments of domination (*"Herrschaftswissen"*). We must remember: in the 1930s, Adorno's and Horkheimer's partners in dialogue were not the representatives of specialized knowledge (not the social scientists) but were the working class. Now the motto is the "scientizing" of critique. As Wellmer puts it:

> Critical theory must admit to itself that the relentless investigation of a perverted rationality in all manifestations of society does not in itself conceptualize that society. Consequently, critical theory must seriously incorporate those intentions of Marxian and Freudian theory which had been employed in the empirical analysis of the mechanisms of social reproduction in such a way that concrete individuals and social groups could partially clarify their concrete sociohistoric position so as to give rise to practical consequences. Like Marxian theory, critical theory must attempt to analyze the developmental tendencies and origin of politically significant conflicts and problems inherent in the system; and finally it must reveal the objective means for

dissolving domination and false "circumstantial coercions". Yet a critical theory of society combining in this sense the critique of instrumental reason with enlightenment about the changes reproductive of mechanisms of domination under conditions of organized capitalism exists today only in its premises.[35]

How true! It indeed exists only in premises, and critical theory enmeshed in the idea of the "domination free discourse with all" (Habermas) buries again what once—always with high-styled prolixity—it attempted to unearth. Because the actual limits for this domination-free discourse are no longer seen as class barriers, emancipation has been turned into an empty word that remains empty. In this context, one must consider the following point: the oppressed class not only doubts the communicative competence of the dominant class but also has reasons to assume that its attempts to enter into dialogue with the dominant class will only provide the latter with opportunities to secure its domination.[36]

Despite its own pessimistic background, critical theory has recently presented frankly optimistic arguments. In its misperception of events outside Germany and Europe, critical theory touched on the Here and Now with precipitous and uncertain theses. This invites the suspicion that there is no critical theory at all, but only a classical theory. Thus, *la misère de la philosophie* becomes *la misère de la sociologie*.

A NECESSARY POSTSCRIPT

Since the writing of this essay in 1970 and its revision in 1972, the political situation in West Germany, which provides the context for these observations, has undergone further development.

In the first place, the liberal social-democratic government unsuccessfully tried to find ways of dealing with unpredictable structural economic crises. Habermas and Claus Offe correctly recognized this failure as part of the legitimization problem in late capitalist societies and attempted to systematize this inquiry. Habermas, in particular, has furnished a general formulation:

If world views disintegrate due to the separation of their cognitive and socially-integrative components; if today any

world-stabilizing meaning structures are irrevocably con-
signed to the past, what will then fulfill the moral and practical task of constituting the identity of individuals and
groups?[37]

Secondly, critical theory has responded to societal change, primarily by widening its own schism. The so-called Frankfurt
School, which had hitherto retained a central coherence despite
divergent trends, has itself become fragmented. To cite examples: In his recent work, Oskar Negt concerns himself with
"The Dialectic between Bourgeois and Proletarian Concepts of
the Public Realm." His plausible conclusion: Under established
capitalist domination, proletarian characteristics are seen as
logically dependent on the perspective of nonemancipation. Yet
from an emancipatory viewpoint, proletarian characteristics appear as inconsequential.[38]

In contrast to the critical theory criticized in my essay, this further development restores to critical theory a revolutionary
momentum, at least until one questions how the participants in
such a movement may be practically organized. Habermas, on
the other hand, is concerned with the theoretical reconstruction
of historical materialism.

However, Habermas has *not* altered his fundamental contention that advanced capitalism has managed to contain and keep
latent the class conflict. He maintains that capitalism prolonged
the favorable phases of the economic cycle and converted
periods of capital devaluation into permanent crises of inflation
with only moderate economic swings. "The class compromise inherent in the structure of late capitalism unifies [almost] everyone into a single body of participants."[39] For the present, this
does not describe actual conditions, at least not in Germany or
the United States.

In keeping with his own intellectual development, Habermas
refers his materialistic thesis to the realm of theory. Reconstruction of historical materialism means "taking apart my theory and
goal: This is the normal way (even for Marxists) to deal with a
theory in need of partial revision but whose motivating potential
is still not yet exhausted."[40]

Given this stance, Habermas' interest in Marx and Engels *cannot* be dogmatic or, for that matter, purely historical.[41] His attention focuses on "hidden" formulations in the realms of ego-
development and world views as well as in ego-identity and group
identity.[42] He states his positions as follows:

> We may . . . regard the development of productive forces as
> a mechanism for creating problems, which prompts change
> of the relations of production and an evolutionary renewal
> of production methods *without actually realizing such change.*
> . . . Several instances are known where an increase of pro-
> ductive forces caused problems within the system, which
> made excessive demands on the control capacity of simi-
> larly organized societies and thus have shaken the basic
> structure of the community. . . . But the great, endogenous
> developments culminating in the first periods of high cul-
> ture or the rise of European capitalism, did not spring from
> a notable expansion of productive power; rather, they
> brought about such productive expansion as their result.[43]

Habermas concluded that humans generate not merely the
technical knowledge necessary for developing productive forces
but also the moral-practical consciousness necessary for
developing appropriate structures of interaction. The rules of
communicative behavior may well derive from a reaction to
changes in the realm of instrumental and strategic action, but the
development of communicative rules then follows its *own* logic.

My essay pointed to the untenability of such a strict separation
between instrumental and communicative behavior. Such
separation implies that individuals within a society cooperate only apart from instrumental action. Yet despite this, one must admit that some of the partial conclusions Habermas draws from
this postulated separation are well worth considering. Within the
sphere of instrumental action, we deal mainly with objects,
events, and conditions that can be manipulated. Within the
sphere of communicative behavior, we deal with persons, expressions, and conditions that are symbolically structured and
understandable. And it is here that Habermas, with some
justification, unifies information theory and linguistics to a
materialist theory of evolution, a theory that I can only allude to
here.

The question remains: "What has changed within critical
theory?" It has, at least with Habermas, increasingly developed
its philosophical discourse along scientistic lines without abandoning its original position. *La misere de la sociologie,* which I had
equated to *la misere de la philosophie,* still can be only negatively
regarded if one is searching for ultimate solutions. If, however,
we admit the right to error, which I consider essential in order to
explore cul-de-sacs and aim toward possible rather than ultimate

solutions, then we must respect Habermas' coherence and persistence. Moreover, I regard as highly important his main thesis that historical materialism must not confine itself merely to instrumental action in the technical and organizational sphere. The dimensions of moral insight, "practical" knowledge, communicative behavior, and social integration must be merged. The attempt to arrive at a normative scientific basis for a—still—materialistic theory of society may be ultimately—and certainly is for the present—frustrating as well as desperate. Yet such an attempt is justified and cannot be dismissed with glib arguments.

NOTES

1. Ernst Bloch, *Padagogica* (Frankfurt/M.: 1971), p. 60.
2. Albrecht Wellmer, *Kritische Gesellschaftstheorie und Positivismus* (Frankfurt: 1969),p. 41.
3. Ibid., p. 42.
4. T. W. Adorno, *Kritik. Kleine Schriften zur Gesellschaft* (Frankfurt/M.: 1971), pp. 148-149.
5. Wellmer, *Kritische Gesellschaftstheorie*, p. 55.
6. Jurgen Habermas, *Marx und die Revolution* (Frankfurt/M.:1970), p. 26.
7. Ibid., p. 27
8. Jurgen Habermas, *Technik und Wissenschaft als Ideologie* (Frankfurt/M.: 1968), p. 74.
9. Ibid., p. 75.
10. Habermas, *Marx und die Revolution*, p. 27.
11. Claus Offe, *Burgerinitiative*, ed. H. Grossmann (Frankfurt/M.: 1971), p. 154.
12. Habermas, *Marx und die Revolution*, pp. 29 ff.
13. Habermas, *Technik und Wissenschaft als Ideologie*, p. 81.
14. Ibid.
15. Karl Marx, *Grundrisse* (Berlin: 1953), p. 189.
16. Jurgen Habermas, *Theorie und Praxis*, Neuwied 2nd. ed. 1967, Tome 11, p. 233.
17. Ibid. p. 230.
18. Joachim Ritter, *Hegel und die Franzosische Revolution, Veroffentlichung der Arbeitsgemeinschaft fur Forschung des Landes Nordrhein-Westfalen*, Heft 63, Koln/Opladen, 1957.
19. Habermas, *Theorie und Praxis*, p. 106.
20. Jurgen Habermas, *Erkenntnis und Interesse* (Frankfurt/M.: 1968), p. 85 (English translation: *Knowledge and Human Interest* (Boston: 1972).
21. Habermas, *Theorie und Praxis*, pp. 330 ff.
22. Jurgen Habermas, *Die Scheinrevolte und ihre Kinder*, in, *Die Linke antwortet Habermas* (Frankfurt/M.: 1968.)
23. Habermas, *Theorie und Praxis*, p. 223.
24. Merleau-Ponty, M. *Humanismus und Terror*, Vol. 1 (Frankfurt/M.: 1966), pp. 12 ff.
25. Merleau-Ponty, *Humanismus*, p. 11.
26. Habermas, *Marx und die Revolution*, pp. 34 ff.
27. Ibid., p. 24.
28. Jurgen Habermas, *Protestbewegung und Hochschulreform* (Frankfurt/M.: 1969), p. 20.

29. Darcy Ribero, *Der Zivlisatorische Prozess* (Frankfurt/M.: 1971).
30. Jurgen Ritsert and Claus Rolshausen, *Der Konservatismus der kritischen Theorie* (Frankfurt/M.: 1971). p. 98.
31. Oskar Negt, *Die Linke antwortet Habermas* (Frankfurt/M.: 1968), p. 21.
32. Ernest Mandel, *The New Vanguard,* in *The New Revolutionaries* (New York: 1970), p. 50.
33. W. I. Lenin, *Was tun?* in *Werke Tome 5* (Berlin: 1959), p. 426.
34. Ritsert and Rolshausen, *Der Konservatismus,* p. 101.
35. Wellmer, *Kritische Gesellschaftstheorie,* p. 145.   .
36. Hans Joachim Giegel, *Reflexion und Emanzipation,* in *Hermeneutik und Ideologiekritik* (Frankfurt: 1971), p. 279.
37. Jurgen Habermas, *Legitimationsprobleme im Spatkapitalismus* (Frankfurt: 1963).
38. Oskar Negt and Alexander Kluge, *Offentlichkeit und Erfahrung* (Frankfurt/M.: 1972), p. 485.
39. Jurgen Habermas, *Zur Rekonstruktion des Historischen Materialismus* (Frankfurt/M.: 1976), p. 311.
40. Ibid., p. 9.
41. Ibid.
42. Ibid., p. 13.
43. Ibid., p. 161.

4.
IDEALISM AND MATERIALISM IN SOCIOLOGICAL THEORY

MICHAEL MANN

No one needs to be convinced of the importance of the controversy between idealism and materialism in sociological theory. Virtually everyone who has theorized about societies has felt it necessary to situate himself in relation to this controversy. Most have fallen into two broad camps: Marx, Engels, and subsequent Marxists, who label themselves and are so labeled by others as materialists; and Weber, Durkheim, and Parsons, who are called "idealist" and who have indeed emphasized the role of "ideas," which they assert are neglected by materialists. Actually, their position is complicated by their also espousing a "multifactor" approach, which generally restrains them from simply asserting the *primacy* of ideas.[1] Nevertheless, both sides agree that they are worlds apart in their view of the importance of "ideas" in societies.

I maintain that this controversy is of no use to sociology, and, indeed, that it has hindered the development of sociological theory. The dualism of "ideas" versus "material reality" or "material practice" is unacceptable. It has obstructed scholarship into the work of the classical theorists, especially that of Marx and Weber, by artificially separating them. It also has handicapped the emergence of more recent, original sociological theory by forcing writers into one or the other mold. This essay contributes at both levels, that of scholasticism and that of original theoretical inquiry. Naturally, an essay of this length cannot be comprehensive; moreover, it does not address itself to the philosophical materialist/idealist debate about the relationship between matter and mind. It makes no contribution to philosophy but claims that the contribution made by philosophy . . . to sociology has, in this respect at least, been distinctly unhelpful.

The sociological controversy has not proceeded in a very satisfactory manner. If we arbitrarily start with Marx, we find that his historical "materialism" was framed as a polemic against *particular* idealist philosophies, and (as we shall see), like all polemic, it obscures as much as it reveals. Then Weber attacked materialism of the Marxian variety, not at its strongest point, Marx himself, but at its weakest, the German Marxism of his own time, which expressed very mechanistic, deterministic theories.[2] This neglect of Marx continues into the writings of Parsons, who formulates an "antimaterialist" position without referring directly to actual materialist arguments. Marxists usually reciprocate by using the term "idealist" as a nonspecific term of abuse. The relatively hermetic quality of much contemporary writing emanating from the two schools is evident from the paucity of their cross-referencing.

Blindfolded polemic does not make for theoretical progress. At its worst, it is mere ritual. I will not waste much space arguing that Marx was not a determinist or that Weber did not ignore material interests, for even at its best, the debate is somewhat stagnant. Having conceded, for example, that Marx recognized that "consciousness" and "ideas" were more than mere epiphenomena, what point remains at issue? As far as I can ascertain, no one has sought to understand both traditions in order to locate the precise nature of the disagreement. This essay attempts to do just this, concentrating on the work of Marx, Engels, Weber, Durkheim, and Parsons, although it does not aim at a comprehensive coverage of their views.

My overall argument is that so-called materialists and idealists are not divided by a single, sweeping divergence on the general role of ideas in society. On the contrary, they both regard that role as problematic, ambiguous, and perhaps insoluble. The most general clear-cut disagreement is between Marx and Weber regarding the possibilities of attaining objective knowledge of the world. Marx and Engels regard this as possible, although not yet attained; Weber does not. This difference has been noted by Giddens,[3] and I wish here to expand his point. As we shall see, Weber's "idealism" allows for a larger and more independent role of certain ideals—"nonempirical existential ideas," to use Parsons' term, "ideologies," to use the Marxist term (see my later note on the problem of nonequivalent terminology). Specifically, this gives greater structural autonomy to intellectuals and to intellectual institutions, of which the most important are religiious. This enables us to see that the argument is not over the relations of "ideas" to "reality" or "practice" but that between "ideas-and-practice combined" in two different spheres of society, the economic and the ideological. Marx gives us a clear conception of the former, Weber of the latter. Once arrived at this position, however, we can see that other social spheres must be introduced into the argument, and we are out of the dualist terrain.

A second specific controversy does not involve Weber but ranges normative functionalists, such as Durkheim and Parsons, against those who have a more "materialist"—or at least a realpolitik—view of the origin of social authority. Durkheim and Parsons give an ontological primacy to social norms, specifically to those norms legitimating society's central power structures. These shared ideas are given a different origin by most other theorists: the factual power domination of one group by another. I support this view.

THE ATTACKS ON MARXIST MATERIALISM

Let us start with the most formidable sociological critic of "materialism": Max Weber. In *The Protestant Ethic and the Spirit of Capitalism,* he says he is countering the so-called materialistic conception of history, which he claims is a one-sided explanation of the determination of history by economic forces. By contrast, "The following study may [contribute] to the understanding of the manner in which ideas become effective forces in history." Weber was careful to add, of course, that he was not producing an equally one-sided idealist theory, but this very statement and the footnote that accompanies it indicate a dualism between "ideas" and "material reality."[4] Parsons endorses this dualism, claiming that Weber perceived the inadequacies of Marxian theory when he became "convinced of the indispensability of an important

role of 'ideas' in the explanation of great historical processes."[5] Many subsequent sociologists have agreed with this attack on Marxism. Here is a typical textbook dismissal of Marxism: "Economic man must eat, but the whole man needs also to
love and think and create and understand."[6] How one can
disagree with this last statement? If Marxism really did neglect
"loving, thinking, creating, and understanding," it would be a
pitiful theory indeed! I shall show that this is not the case.

Parsons mounted a far more interesting, because more
precise, attack. His essay "The Role of Ideas in Social Action"
contains a useful summary of an argument he scattered throughout
his work. Here he attempts to go beyond the arguments that
"Ideas *in general* have been held either to have or not to have an
important role in the determination of action."[7] Instead, he identifies three specific types of ideas and proceeds to contrast
Weber's analysis of these favorably to that of materialists.
Although I disagree with some of his arguments, I find this
typology useful. The three types are:

1. *Empirical existential.* These are verifiable perceptions of
reality. That they influence a person's choice of action are
evidenced by our recognition that a person would have
acted differently "if he had known the real facts." Parsons
considers Weber's account of formal rationality an exemplary treatment of this type of idea and considers
economic theory and technology its main social-structural
embodiments. He argues that materialism cannot analyze
this properly because ideas are classified in the superstructure while technology goes into the base. This is not correct,
and as we will see, a real disagreement does not exist here.
2. *Nonempirical existential.* These are perceptions of reality
that, although not demonstrably erroneous, "surpass experience." Ultimate ends and cosmological beliefs are included here, and religions are their main social-structural
embodiment.[8] Parsons again refers to Weber as the exemplary theorist here, this time to his sociology of religion.
According to Parsons, Weber demonstrated that the
economic structure of early Western Europe did not favor
the emergence of capitalistic development when compared
to that of ancient India and China (if anything, the reverse
was true). The decisive difference between them, and thus

the crucial impetus toward capitalism, lay in the content of the West's religious beliefs.[9] Thus, the content of nonempirical existential ideas ultimately was the determining cause of the development of capitalism. Obviously, this is opposed to Marxist materialist theories of the same development and involves at a theoretical level one of the real disagreements I mentioned earlier, the problem of objective knowledge and the role of intellectuals and their institutions.

3. *Normative.* These are evaluative ideas, "ought" statements about right and wrong. Parsons' *Structure of Social Action,* a better source for this type of idea, gives a place of importance in sociology to Durkheim's attack on utilitarian social contract theory. According to Durkheim, the trouble with a theory that predicates social order on self-interested individuals rationally entering into contracts with each other is that

> . . . if interest relates men, it is never for more than some few moments. . . . There is nothing less constant than interest. Today it unites me to you; tomorrow it will make me your enemy. . . . Everything in the contract is not contractual . . . wherever a contract exists, it is submitted to regulation which is the work of society and not that of individuals.[10]

Durkheim and Parsons argue that exchange presupposes norms, and that contracts are normatively regulated. And although the main attack is directed against Herbert Spencer and the utilitarians, it also applies to materialists like Marx. For Parsons, Marxism is a theory of "interests" and so neglects norms. This criticism often is made by commentators on Marx when dealing with the base-superstructure distinction. They argue that property relations, which are in the base, presuppose legal norms, which are in the superstructure.[11] In this view, therefore, materialists and others differ over the relative force of material interests and social norms. Yet this version of the difference is confusing. These writers neglect the fact that Marxists do not ignore norms but give a different account of their origin. I will return to this later.

Parsons' account is a detailed attack on Marxist materialism. The distinctions he makes are of the utmost importance, for eventually they lead us beyond dualism. However, unfortunately he echoes the argument that Marx neglects "ideas in general" by placing them in the superstructure. Although this is wrong, it is an excusable reading of Marx's more polemic works, as we shall now see.

AMBIGUITIES IN MARX: THREE READINGS OF
THE GERMAN IDEOLOGY

When we interpret Marx's writings on ideology, our main difficulty is that most of them are polemics against particular targets, German idealist philosophers of his time. As sociology can safely ignore the works of the actual butts of his polemic (Bruno Von Bauer, Max Stirner, and the rest of the Young Hegelians), I will instead later quote a rather more important opponent and influence: Kant.

Polemic is an inadequate way of establishing one's own argument, and Marx does not avoid this trap. I will quote two passages from Marx and Engels' *The German Ideology* to illustrate:

> As individuals express their life, so they are. What they are, therefore, coincides with their production, both with *what* they produce and with *how* they produce. The nature of individuals thus depends on the material conditions determining their production.

> Men are the producers of their conceptions, ideas, etc.—real, active men, as they are conditioned by a definite development of their productive forces and of the intercourse corresponding to these, up to its furthest forms. Consciousness can never be anything else than conscious existence, and the existence of men is their actual life-process. If in all ideology men and their circumstances appear upside-down as in a *camera obscura,* this phenomenon arises just as much from their historical life-process as the inversion of objects on the retina does from their physical life-process.
>
> In direct contrast to German philosophy which descends from heaven to earth, here we ascend from earth to heaven. That is to say, we do not set out from what men say, imagine, conceive, nor from men as narrated, thought of, imagined, conceived, in order to arrive at men in the flesh. We

set out from real, active men, and on the basis of their real life-process we demonstrate the development of the ideological reflexes and echoes of this life-process. The phantoms formed in the human brain are also, necessarily, sublimates of their material life-process, which is empirically verifiable and bound to material premises. Morality, religion, metaphysics, all the rest of ideology and their corresponding forms of consciousness, thus no longer retain the semblance of independence. They have no history, no development; but men, developing their material production and their material intercourse, alter, along with this their real existence, their thinking and the products of their thinking. Life is not determined by consciousness, but consciousness by life.[12]

Mixed up in these passages are no less than *three* contrasts used as explanations of "materialism" and "idealism." They are:

Materialism		*Idealism*
"life"	versus	"consciousness"
"material production"	versus	"morality, religion, metaphysics, all the rest of ideology"
"real, active men"	versus	"German philosophy"

Different in meaning, these contrasts are nonetheless used interchangeably. The confusion goes on to bedevil the whole idealist-materialist debate. The charge that Marx neglects "ideas in general" and relegates them to the superstructure comes from only the first contrast. Let us consider it.

LIFE VERSUS CONSCIOUSNESS

Marx frequently uses the contrast between "life" and "consciousness." It is found mostly in his early works, although it later reappears occasionally, most notably in the definitive 1859 *Preface to the Critique of Political Economy*: "It is not the consciousness of men that determines their being, but, on the contrary, their social being that determines their consciousness."[13] Marx often phrases such statements in the language of "reflection" and "inversion"—ideas merely reflect reality in a distorted way, as in the *"camera obscura"* image used in *The German Ideology*. Placing ideas in a superstructural role is truly determinist. Many Marxists doubly dissociate themselves from this theory by calling it "mechanical determinism." It is based on a mere polemical trick—*of course,* "life," that is, the *whole* of the human situation, is superior to "consciousness," that is, only a *part* of the human situation. No one, not even Hegel, would dispute that (if he recognized the terms).

We could simply ignore the trickery and interpret "life" as meaning a kind of "unthinking, instinctual beingness," a "biologism." But we would see at once that the contrast would be both incorrect and quite foreign to Marx's purposes. The mind is not a passive receptor of external stimuli: at the very least, it selects from among stimuli according to preexisting mental constructs and concepts, more probably it actively molds and changes them. Marx himself was emphatic on this point in the first of his *Theses on Feuerbach:* "The chief defect of all hitherto existing materialism is that the thing, reality, sensuousness is conceived only in the form of the *object or of contemplation* but not as *sensuous human activity, practice,* not subjectively."[14] Or again, when engaged in the very traditional practice of distinguishing human beings from animals, he says, "what distinguishes the worst architect from the best of bees is this, that the architect raises his structure in imagination before he erects it in reality."[15] In his political life (which cannot be forgotten when dealing with his ideas), Marx adopted a similar emphasis. We have, for example, Annenkov's graphic eyewitness account of the political debate in London between Marx and the "spontaneist" revolutionary, Weitling. Marx's temper rose steadily as he argued: "To call to the worker without any strictly scientific ideas on constructive doctrine was equivalent to vain dishonest play at preaching which assumed on the one side an inspired prophet and on the other only gaping asses." Annenkov continues: "Marx finally lost control of himself and thumped so hard with his fist on the table that the lamp on it rung and shook. He jumped up saying 'ignorance never yet helped anyone.'"[16] All this shows that Marx did not separate "ideas" from "material practice"; the former are necessarily contained in the latter.

The "natural materialism" that Marx rejects also would be deterministic, but deterministic strands run through Marxism. Two in particular emanate both from Marx and Engels' admiration for Darwin and from the political power of the "history-is-on-our-side" type of argument. Both have continuously reappeared in the Marxist movement. Marxism at all times has contained relatively deterministic and voluntaristic camps. In the former, we would place Lenin, Stalin, and Plekhanov; in the latter, Georg Lukacs, Rosa Luxemburg, and Antonio Gramsci. But in general, it would be more apt to label the so-called Marxist determinants, whether natural or social, as limits to human action. As Marx expresses it in *The 18th Brumaire of Louis Bonaparte:* "Men make their own history, but they do not make it just as they please: they do not make it under circumstances chosen by themselves, but under circumstances directly encountered, given and transmitted from the past."[17]

This statement is surely orthodox sociology—indeed, it could be taken from as modern a work as Berger and Luckmann's *Social Construction of Reality*—but it does not take us very far. In what circumstances did Marx believe that men make their own history? And where does their consciousness come from? These scholastic questions are best answered by briefly considering Marxist theories of the class consciousness of the modern proletariat.

The "reflectionist," determinist argument would run as follows: the objective contradictions of capitalism are experienced by the proletariat and then as automatic response generate revolutionary consciousness. This is the inevitable outcome of capitalism; yet if we search twentieth-century Marxism for "inevitabilist" statements, we do not find them taking this form. In the Leninist, and Stalinist, tradition, statements about the inevitable victory of the proletariat are linked to a theory about "the vanguard role" of the Communist party. There will be no revolution without "the leading role of the party" and therefore of the bourgeois intellectuals who, along with the most advanced sections of the working class, dominate it. The more cautious Marxists, whether of this tradition (like Lukacs) or outside it (like Rosa Luxemburg), tend to be more explicit about what is and is not inevitable. According to them, capitalism's objective contradictions *must* lead to ever-worsening economic crises, but the revolutionary response of the proletariat is not guaranteed.

That depends on its "maturity," its ability to understand its "historical role" as explained, perhaps, by the party. In all of these formulations, the consciousness of both the proletariat and the party is problematical. In the Leninist version, concessions are made toward idealism, in the sense that an historical outcome is based partially on the consciousness of professional intellectuals. The Leninist party can indeed be treated as a Durkheimian "sacred" institution, as for example, in Lockwood's tongue-in-cheek analysis.[18] But my criticism here is not about the ambiguity with which most Marxists treat consciousness in general, nor of the tentative moves made, because of historical complexity and uncertainty, toward "idealism." These seem necessary. Rather, my criticism is directed against Marxists who insist on regarding historical materialism as a distinct historical method that has "nothing in common with idealism," whose polemic against idealism cannot be sustained until they *do* develop an explicit materialist theory of consciousness in general. Because nearly all modern Marxists use the polemic form when dealing with this problem, the criticism may be widely applied.

Yet similar criticisms can be applied to so-called idealists, those who assert that ideas in general have an autonomous role in history. Ideas are not "free-floating," available in all situations to all persons. They have definite social and historical correlates. Weber, of course, recognized this, and in practice, his "idealism" is always severely qualified. For example, his voluntaristic theory of action makes several concessions to determinism. Weber always tries to start from a "subjectivist" point by defining his basic concepts according to the "meaning" given to phenomena by human subjects, but sooner or later he recognizes limits to voluntarism. He notes that not all action is "meaningful" and that constraint is exercised by external forces with or without the knowledge of the actor.[19] Several of his most important analyses concern reification processes—the way in which the social creations of men attain an objective existence and thus constrain men. Thus, capitalism becomes an "iron cage" that determines the lives of men "with irresistible force,"[20] and bureaucracy becomes inevitable and rigid.[21] Moreover, his repeated observation that capitalism, bureaucracy, the expropriation of the workers from the means of production, and many other phenomena are "formally rational" but "substantively irrational" implies a considerable experience of external constraint by the persons concerned. Unlike Marx, Weber cannot be criticized for failing to live up to his philosophy, for he does not claim to be an idealist. We can, nevertheless, criticize Weber and his followers for their overgeneral remarks about materialism and the role of ideas. This is not to minimize the great difference in *emphasis* between Weberians and Marxists in these matters, but neither side actually has propounded a distinct theory of the role of ideas in general or has proposed a solution to the determinist-voluntarist dilemma.

This is not surprising, however, because the dilemma is not soluble and the theory does not exist. Just as the concept of "idealess" instinctual activity does not help to analyze human behavior, an "immaterial" ideal also is not helpful. The process of thinking is observably different from that of action, but human life requires their interaction. A theory of ideas ("a theory of theory") can have a physiological, even a psychological, basis but not a sociological one. The human brain may have certain capacities and thought may have certain qualities, but *what* is thought depends on human experience. Ideas in general do not exist *sui generis* in society. The distinction between "ideas" and "materiality" thus has no sociological utility. The useful distinctions that can be made, that derive from the idealist-materialist controversy, involve distinctions between "ideas and practice combined" in the sphere where man intervenes in nature for the purpose (originally) of satisfying subsistence needs. This is in fact *material or economic production,* the second of *The German Ideology*'s definitions of materialism, the one most in keeping with the whole spirit of that work and the one I will use.

The distinction between voluntarism and determinism also is not useful, although for a different reason. Sociological methodology presupposes that regularity exists in social life, and it uncovers that regularity (although in the most rigorously undertaken statistical investigations it is comparatively rare to explain as much as 50 percent of the perceived variation). However, as social actors, we characteristically represent our actions as deriving from "choice." This choice may not appear to us as *free,* but it generally appears as the choice between alternative courses of action. It is often stated that the actor can confound the sociologists and choose an unexpected course of action, but this does not happen often enough to vitiate the sociological enterprise. More than this we cannot say. The difficulty is that lack of predictive success, lack of correlation, does not necessarily indicate "free will," not is it ever likely to, for the dyed-in-the-wool behaviorist determinist knows that social causation is extremely complex. He believes that previous research has uncovered a whole host of "determinants" of behavior—origin, birth order, sex, age, health, religion, nationality, and so forth. Thus, each individual in effect may be a unique combination of social characteristics, each of which may have a known effect on whatever dependent variable is under discussion. One reader of this might be the only forty-year-old, downwardly mobile, eldest son, Catholic, Welsh, alcoholic social worker in the world. The determinist would expect his behavior to be as unique as the voluntarist would. He may (or may not) represent his own behavior as "free" and "willed," and he may be wrong (people often are). We have no means of discovering whether he is free or whether he is the recipient of complex social forces. We cannot therefore decide whether "ideas" are independent of "materiality" or "practice." Moreover, to be a determinist or voluntarist is an act of faith, a Pascalian wager.

This has severe consequences for Parsons' arguments about his first and third types of ideas: "empirical existential" and "normative." Parsons claims that Marxian materialism neglects both of these because it classified all ideas in the superstructure. However, we have seen that this is not so. If we retain the base-superstructure division, then the base contains "ideas and practices combined" relevant to man's intervention in nature. Therefore, the base contains some, although not all, empirical existential ideas (i.e., means-ends calculations) and some norms. Thus, Marxism is only confused about where to "place" ideas if one has a prior conception that "ideas in general" exist *sui generis* with certain sociological properties. This is Parsons' conception, and it also is that of many Marxist polemics, but it is erroneous. By abandoning it, we also can perceive more interesting versions of both Marxian materialism and Weberian idealism. The crucial question is not whether some ideas are in the base and some in the superstructure, but whether ideas and practices that are important for man's intervention in nature originate outside of this sphere of life. If they do, then the whole distinction between base and superstructure breaks down, and the primacy of material production vanishes. Parsons' second category of idea, "nonempirical existential" (ideology), does *prima facie* pose this kind of threat, as we shall see later. But his other two categories do not.

First, let us consider "empirical existential" ideas. Parsons' argument is puzzling. Every social theory makes two assumptions about the kind of "technical reason" implied in this category. It has to assume that human beings can reason, that is, can systematically and correctly weigh alternative means of attaining desired ends. And it has to assume that they sometimes make mistakes. Without the first, there would be no social regularity; without the second, there would be no need of human sciences. If we exclusively adopt the "reflectionist" language often used by Marx to talk about ideas, the possibility that people could make mistakes would not arise, and hence, Marxism would have no reason for existing. This is a criticism that has been made before, for example, by Lichtman, who concludes, as I do, that it is truer to Marx's theory as a whole to ignore "reflectionism."[22] Thus, Marx and Weber do not differ on this issue. It would be nice, of course, if they had given us a theory of the circumstances in which people do make mistakes!

Second, we must consider norms. Parsons, Plamenatz, and others argue that production relations, specifically property, imply the prior existence of normative regulation, whether by law or custom, that originate outside the sphere of material production. It is rather unclear where, in their view, norms do originate; we must presume that they follow Durkheim in elevating the moral, normative aspects of society to a kind of ontological primacy. Unfortunately, this position ignores the fact that norms can and often do originate from situations of unregulated power. This is the model of norms that is implicit in Marxism. Poggi has begun the task of making this explicit.[23] He notes that Marxism is not an "interest" theory of the utilitarian type, for it argues that the atomized, free individual motivated by self-interest is not the reality of bourgeois society, but its ideology. Market exchange is thus not equalitarian but is maintained by exploitative, asymmetric relations embodied in the market itself—not imposed from outside by a Hobbesian state, which is what Parsons regards as implicit in Marxism.

Marx never starts with the individual but with *social* production. Therefore, if we do consider the individual, his "interests" are already defined and regulated by processes of social cooperation and exploitation. These processes involve norms (among other things), but those norms are not "givens."

Rather, they derive from a prior *factual* domination. Consider the example of the worker's acceptance of the norms regulating market exchange and commodity production, including the exchange of his labor for a wage. Simplifying somewhat, we can see that in the course of industrialization many millions of workers came into this relationship for the first time. Their inclination to accept it was partly determined, of course, by habits of obedience, norms of deference, and so forth, instilled in their prior "feudal" experience, but important elements of this relationship were new to them (the narrowness of the cash nexus, freedom on the labor market, the idea that this freedom was equivalent to the capitalist's freedom, etc.). Therefore, norms regulating these elements were not already in existence. Alternatives to acceptance were available (return to the countryside, unemployment in the town, revolution), but they were not attractive. Therefore, the existence of the situation was accepted as the bounds of attainable reality. As even Durkheim recognized, given the passage of enough time, stable relations become moral ones.[24] Indeed, enough empirical evidence is available on the contemporary working class to confirm that the difference between *facticity* and *norm* is extremely blurred and that compliance results from a "pragmatic acceptance," based not on conscious calculation but on a relatively unquestioned belief that this reality is the only one attainable.[25]

Thus, I am arguing not only that Marxism has a theory of the derivations of norms but that, when applied to norms regulating interclass relations, it is essentially correct. (Marxism also has a theory of the disintegration of those norms, but that is more controversial.) However, not all norms can be so explained. In the example just given, the new working class had already accepted normative elements of cooperation with superior classes, perhaps including the legitimacy of property itself. But why should we regard these norms as "original" rather than as derivative of factual power relations at an earlier phase of history? Modern normative functionalism has lost that sense of the precariousness of norms so characteristic of its conservative predecessors. Here, for example, is what David Hume says about authority:

> If the reason be asked of that obedience, which we are bound to pay government, I readily answer, *Because society could not otherwise subsist;* and this answer is clear and intelligible to all Mankind. . . .
>
> But *to whom is allegiance due? And who is our lawful sovereign?* This question is often the most difficult of any, and liable to infinite discussions. When people are so happy that they can answer, *Our present sovereign, who inherits in a Direct line from ancestors that have governed us for many ages,* this answer admits of no reply, even though . . . its first authority was derived from usurpation and violence. It is confessed that private justice, or the abstinence from the properties of others, is a most cardinal virtue. Yet reason tells us that there is no property . . . but must in some period, have been founded on fraud and injustice.[26]

Hume has clearly distinguished between the necessity for social cooperation and submission to authority, on the one hand, and submission to any *particular* authority or institution, on the other. Although he believes that we should obey our parent sovereign and respect property, he recognizes that they are historically contingent and artificially imposed institutions.[27] So too did Weber, Pareto, Mosca, and many other theorists. Particular forms of authority, including property, are historically created products of a mixture of force, exchange, interest, and norms derived from prior social arrangements. The precise mixture is a matter of empirical inquiry. Marxism's historical analysis of the rise of authority institutions may well understate the degree of normative carry-over. This will not be considered here, although I will later briefly return to the problem of distinguishing between "enduring" and "created" norms. There is, however, no *conceptual* blockage in Marxism as there is in normative functionalism.

MATERIAL PRODUCTION VERSUS IDEOLOGY

The second distinction found in *The German Ideology*, that between "material production" and "ideology," brings us to the most important and fruitful disagreement between the materialist and idealist schools of sociology. However, even the term "material production" needs clarification. Marx and Engels use "material" in connection with two separate arguments. First, they assert that the theories merely reflect the actual life experience of men in society (and hence that truth is socially specific). Second, they observe that idealist experience—as embodied in religious, educational, and political institutions—is far less important in determining the course of history (and therefore the nature of ideas themselves) than is experience in the economic sphere of material production. Thus, "material" means either *practice* in general, as opposed to ideas, or *economic* practice in particular. At times, Marx and Engels confuse arguments related to the first meaning of material to deal with the second. In their quotations given earlier, they equate "the expression of life" with "production" and argue that the primacy of the latter derives from the former.

Yet this is not so. These statements do not necessarily imply *homo faber,* man the craftsman or artisan, as Schlomo Avineri believes.[28] For why should one not also regard ideology as "active production"? In practice, politics, religion, and science are as "material," in the first sense of activity, as economic production. Perhaps this assertion does not seem self-evident, for, after all, we immediately recognize that the productive lives of ordinary people are more "material" than the philosophizing of the Young Hegelians. Yet we can find more "material" instances of intellectual activity than this. Applied science is the obvious example and is often used to produce distinctively non-Marxian substantive theory.

Parsons claims that science is autonomous vis-a-vis material production. I will not discuss this claim here; for the moment, I am concerned only with the conceptual blurring. Marx sometimes blurred "material" and "intellectual" activity rather disastrously. For example, he regards the production of Milton's *Paradise Lost* and the art of singing as "work" and "activity,"[29] and "religion, family, state, law, morality, science, art, etc.," are "particular modes of production."[30] As Ollman has observed, there is no clear distinction in Marx's writings between the concepts of "activity," "work," and "creativity."[31]

We must remedy this. As already noted, "material" here denotes only that which in the social sphere is concerned with man's intervention in nature, that is, the "economic" sphere. And in keeping with the conclusion of the previous section, it involves ideas and actions combined. It also follows that the concept of ideology, or ideological practice, cannot refer solely to "pure ideas." What, then, are the ideas and actions that belong to the ideological sphere? What do "morality, religion, metaphysics, all the rest of ideology"—Marx's second definition of idealism in *The German Ideology?*—have in common?

Weber answers that question more clearly than Marx, especially with his pivotal concept of *meaning*. It is implicit in Weber's *verstehende Soziologie* that the quest to find "meaning" in the world is as basic to human nature as is the satisfaction of material wants. The essence of a meaning system is that it goes beyond what is empirically given and empirically provable.[32] The typical meaning system involves three elements, all nonverifiable (and nonrefutable): statements of fact, purpose, and norms. Most religions, for example, claim that (1) God created the world and man (2) for a purpose that requires (3) a demonstration of morality by man. None of this is scientifically *testable,* but it constitutes "the meaning of life," which, according to Weber, human beings have a need to create. This sociological/psychological axiom is closely connected to his philosophical stand against positivism. The "facts," or rather our experiences of them, do not stand on their own but are given "meaning" by broader mental constructs and values.

Stated this simply, Weber's position is hardly controversial. It is not immediately apparent how it differs from Marx's (implicit) position. Furthermore, when we examine Weber's writings on the origin of meaning systems we are in for a surprise. For religion, according to him, is originally an attempt to give meaning to material experience (although he is as variable as Marx in his use of the term "material"): "The most elementary forms of behavior motivated by religious or magical factors are oriented to *this* world." This primitive religion is "relatively rational"; it "follows rules of experience," and it often involves sacrifices "without any other-worldly expectations whatsoever" . . . "even the ends of the religious and magical actions are predominantly economic."[33] This loosely materialist explanation of religion does not conflict with Marxism. Although we have no Marxist accounts of the origin of religion, its continuance, according to both Marx and Kautsky, is due to the need of the masses to give meaning to a class exploitation that is objectively irremovable at this stage in history. This should be stated very clearly because the famous "opium of the people" quotation is normally misinterpreted to indicate that religion is a trick used by the ruling classes to subjugate the masses. On the contrary, Marx makes it clear that the masses have created their own opium as a way of explaining their alienation.[34] So where does the difference lie, and why is Weber more of an "idealist" concerning meaning systems than Marx? There are actually two differences.

The first difference lies in their respective epistemological positions. Weber did not believe in the possibility of establishing objective knowledge. Nonempirical constructs and values would *always* enter into scientific explanations because there is always a gap between empirical experience and systematic knowledge, a gap that has been filled throughout human history by meaning systems, by ideologies. Marx, on the other hand, is a "developmental positivist." With human progress, material experience—or rather the experience of each revolutionary class—comes closer to generating objective knowledge. This process culminates with the proletariat, the first "universal class" in history whose material experience can generate true science. This epistemological position is spelled out most clearly by Lukacs in his essay "Class Consciousness."[35] This also enables mankind to perceive the process of history. Thus, sometime in the future, mankind will see that religion was the product of certain material conditions and, moreover, that it was an *inadequate* explanation of them. God does not and did not exist, he was created to explain alienation that *actually* resulted from class exploitation. Religion, and indeed every system of ideas that goes beyond empirical experience, is scientifically worthless and probably false. Weber, as a relativist, could not make this statement, and although he clearly believed in scientific progress, his account of the development of rationality is deeply ambiguous, as it avoids the issue of whether or not this was the development of substantive, as well as formal, rationality. This ambiguity allows greater social force to "ideology" in Weber's theory than it does in Marx's.

The epistemological difference carries over into their accounts of historical forces. As knowledge can never be certain, according to Weber, its creation is always problematic. The gap between empirical experience and systematic knowledge allows for the social autonomy of ideology vis-a-vis material practice. The latter can never fully *correct* the former, and although Weber apparently explained the origin of ideology in material practice, its subsequent development has a substantial *immanence.* The religious sphere becomes characterized by qualities that are removed from the ordinary routine of living. The gulf between these qualities (called "charisma" by Weber) and material life resembles Durkheim's famous definition of the sacred as "things set apart."[36] Once set apart, so they remain. In *Sociology of Religion,* Weber emphasizes the immanence of religious development, the tendency of religious ideas and actions to generate their own contradictions and their own dialectic (although these are not Weber's terms). This has both doctrinal and institutional aspects, and—especially in the more complex societies—Weber notes the specific group interests and social organizations of priests, magicians, prophets, churches, and so forth, that is, *intellectuals* whose social calling is to explore overarching problems of meaning. The ideologies they create are ultimately untestable and so have a certain independence from material practice. Moreover, by virtue of the human need to finding meaning in the world, the intellectuals have a certain power over those engaged in material production.

Thus, for Weber, "ideas and practices combined" in the ideological ("meaning system") sphere of society have both a structural autonomy from and a certain determinancy over those in the sphere of economic production. This is the only useful definition of sociological idealism. Weber was cautious in his ad-

vocacy of this position, noting at every stage the reverse influence of economic factors on ideology. Furthermore, he often
abandoned even this dualism, admitting into particular historical
analyses important military, political, and other influences.
Nevertheless, Parsons' overall "idealist" interpretation of his
Sociology of Religion, which I noted earlier, is essentially correct,
and a substantial difference does exist between this type of
idealist sociology and materialism. To see the precise nature of
this difference, it is helpful to turn to the third contrast of *The
German Ideology,* that between "real, active men" and "German
philosophers."

REAL, ACTIVE MEN VERSUS GERMAN PHILOSOPHERS

Marx and Engels were producing an essentially democratic
theory of history. By contrast, "German philosophers" received
from the eighteenth century Enlightenment a belief not only in
the autonomy of intellectuals but also in their determining role in
history. In general, they saw the possibility of major social progress coming from their own efforts to enlighten the mass of the
people. Kant epitomized this belief in his essay "What Is Enlightenment?" which begins:

> Enlightenment is man's release from his self-incurred tute-
> lage. Tutelage is man's inability to make use of his under-
> standing without direction from another. Self-incurred is
> this tutelage when its cause lies not in lack of reason but in
> lack of resolution and courage to use it without direction
> from another *Sapere aude!* "Have courage to use your own
> reason!"—that is the motto of enlightenment.
>   Laziness and cowardice are the reasons why so great a
> portion of mankind, after nature has long since discharged
> them from external direction . . . nevertheless remains un-
> der lifelong tutelage and why it is so easy for others to set
> themselves up as their guardians. It is so easy not to be of
> age. . . .
>   After the guardians have first made their domestic cattle
> dumb and have made sure that these placid creatures will
> not dare take a single step without the harness of the cart to
> which they are tethered. . . ."[37]

and so the text continues. What is extraordinary about this is the tone as well as the content. The people lack courage, they are frightened to become of age, they are dumb and placid creatures. The patronizing tone was common among the Enlightenment philosophers: it was a political manifestation of their lack of any concept of interaction between the ideas of the intellectuals and the practices of the mass of the people. If we add the distinctively mystical style of the Hegelians, we can perhaps sympathize with Marx and Engels' polemic, for German philosophers *did* overrate their own importance.

Weber had no such personal delusions. He also possessed a concept of interaction between different spheres of society. But it was "open ended." That is, the interaction could take any form: "No significant generalization can be made as to when and how this will occur."[38] Marx and Engels produced such a generalization, a democratic one. They believed that ideology *is* ultimately tested and corrected, that is, determined by the material practice of the mass of the people, and they stated when this occurs. No ideological system survives a change in the mode of economic production. In the words of the *1859 Preface*, "with the change of the economic foundation, the entire immense superstructure is more or less rapidly transformed."[39] Thus, ideology, whatever its force and autonomy within the mode of production (and this might be large), is not influential in the transition from one mode of production to another—and such revolutionary transitions define in the last instance the historical process.[40]

This distinction also applies to the normative sphere discussed earlier. All societies require social cooperation and an authoritative allocation of rights and duties, and norms legitimating authority are universal. However, norms legitimating specific forms of authority—say, the state or private property, feudalism or capitalism—are historically contingent on, not deducible from, prior normative arrangements and require the use of force and a manipulation of interests. Marx gives us a model of the balance between "enduring" and "created" norms, arguing that each revolutionary class transfers to itself the legitimacy of enduring norms by demonstrating that its interests are the interests of society as a whole, of social cooperation itself. This is not unique to Marxism, of course: Mosca expressed this theory more succinctly with his notion of the *political formula* of the rising elite.[41] The difference between them lies in Marx's assertion that the revolutionary group arises from within the mode of economic production.

We can now summarize the argument of this section. *Ideology is most usefully defined as the "ideas and practice combined" of the ideological sphere of society, which, in turn, is that portion of human activity concerned with man's need to find meaning in the world.* Marxist materialists agree with idealists that this is a basic human need that has two social consequences: first, all men have "ideological interests" that are relatively autonomous from their material (i.e., economic) practice because the latter cannot *normally* test any overall meaning system they might possess; second, intellectuals and institutions concerned with meaning systems enjoy a relative autonomy from the economic institutions of society. Now we come to the differences. Weber saw no *necessary* relationship between ideological and material practice. That is, in one empirical case, ideological factors might be dominant, in another material factors. There is no overall pattern in history between these factors, and so we cannot have a theory of their interrelations.

There is no pattern in this specific case of ideology and material practice because the latter can never fully test the former. Marx, by contrast, sees a necessary relationship, one in which material practice plays the ultimately determining role precisely because material practice does offer a test of ideology, through revolutionary praxis.

In evaluating materialist theories, which are the most influential of modern sociology, we therefore have two problems; the philosophical problem concerns the possibility and the methodology of attaining objective truth. The sociological-historical problem concerns whether or not the ideological sphere of society retains its autonomy and social force through transitions from one mode of economic production to another. The first of these is outside the competence of sociology (and indeed of this author); however, an answer to the second might also solve the first problem. But it must be answered in a wider context. Having argued that the issue does not lie between "ideas in general" versus "material practice" but between "ideas and practice combined" in different social spheres, we must consider the sociological-historical roles of spheres other than the ideological and the economic. In particular, the political and military spheres suggest themselves. But this is a problem to be considered elsewhere. Social theory wil not progress until it abandons the debate of "ideas" versus "material practice."

NOTES

1. T. Parsons has thoroughly impaled himself on the horns of this dilemma. In his "cybernetic hierarchy," values are placed higher than material conditions, and therefore, Parsons calls himself (albeit with reservations) a "cultural determinist," yet as he regards values and material conditions as both necessary and independent factors for social change, he cannot logically elevate one above the other. See T. Parsons, *Societies: Evolutionary and Comparative Perspectives* (Englewood Cliffs, N.J.: Prentice-Hall, 1966).
2. A. Giddens, *Capitalism and Modern Social Theory* (Cambridge: Cambridge University Press, 1971).
3. Ibid., pp. 212-213.
4. M. Weber, *The Protestant Ethic and the Spirit of Capitalism* (London: Unwin, 1930), pp. 90, 183, 283-284.
5. M. Weber, *The Theory of Social and Economic Organization,* ed. T. Parsons (New York: The Free Press, 1964), p. 6.
6. R. Bierstedt, *The Social Order* (New York: McGraw-Hill, 1963), p. 547.
7. T. Parsons, *Essays in Sociological Theory* (New York: The Free Press, 1949), p. 19.
8. I shall use the rather clumsy term "nonempirical existential idea" sparingly, replacing it generally with "ideology." However, it should be noted that the Marxist concept of ideology denotes knowledge that is *false*. Empirically, the same type of knowledge is included as in Parsons' concept, that is, religious and other total meaning systems, but a different epistemology is then added. This will be discussed later.
9. Cf. T. Parsons, *The Structure of Social Action* (New York: The Free Press, 1968), pp. 500-578.
10. Emile Durkheim, *The Division of Labor in Society* (New York: The Free Press, 1964), pp. 204, 211; see also Parsons, *The Structure of Social Action,* pp. 311-316.
11. J. Plamenatz, *Man and Society,* Vol. 1 (London: Longmans, 1963), pp. 274-290; H. B. Acton, *The Illusion of the Epoch* (London: Routledge & Kegan Paul, 1955).
12. K. Marx and F. Engels, *The German Ideology* (Moscow: Progress Publishers, 1964) pp. 32, 37-38.
13. K. Marx and F. Engels, *Selected Works* (Moscow: Progress Publishers, 1968), p. 181.
14. Marx and Engels, *The German Ideology,* p. 645.
15. K. Marx and F. Engels, *Capital, Vol. 1* (Moscow: Progress Publishers, 1965), p. 178.
16. D. McLellan, *Karl Marx: His Life and Thought* (London: Macmillan, 1973), pp. 156-157.
17. Marx and Engels, *Selected Works,* p. 96.
18. D. Lockwood, *Solidity and Schism,* Unpublished ms. (University of Essex: 1975), Chap. 4.
19. M. Weber, *Economy and Society* (New York: Bedminster Press, 1968), pp. 7, 14, 21-22.
20. Weber, *The Protestant Ethic,* p. 181.
21. Weber, *Economy and Society,* pp. 223-224.
22. R. Lichtman, "Marx's Theory of Ideology," *Socialist Revolution,* Vol. 23 (1975): 45-76.
23. G. Poggi, *Images of Society* (London: Oxford University Press, 1972), pp. 137-151.
24. Durkheim, *The Division of Labor in Society,* p. 366.
25. M. Mann, "The Social Cohesion of Liberal Democracy," *American Sociological Review,* Vol. 35 (1970): 423-439, and *Consciousness and Action in the Western Working Class* (London: Macmillan, 1973).

26. David Hume, "Of the Original Contract," in *Social Contract,* ed. E. Barker (London: Oxford University Press, 1947), pp. 229–230.
27. Of course, if property is imposed by military force and force is contained in the "superstructure," Marxism might still be in trouble. For the moment, I am considering only the relations between material production and ideology.
28. S. Avineri, *The Social and Political Thought of Karl Marx* (Cambridge: Cambridge University Press, 1968).
29. K. Marx, *Theories of Surplus Value* (New York: International Publishers, 1951), pp. 186, 190.
30. K. Marx, *Economic and Philosophic Manuscripts of 1844* (London: Lawrence and Wishart, 1970), p. 103.
31. B. Ollman, *Alienation: Marx's Conception of Man in Capitalist Society* (Cambridge: Cambridge University Press, 1971), p. 104.
32. Thus, it includes Parsons' second category of ideas, "nonempirical existential," as well as a fourth category, mentioned but not analyzed by him, "nonempirical normative ideas."
33. M. Weber, *The Sociology of Religion* (London: Metheun, 1966), p. 1.
34. K. Marx, *Writings of the Young Marx on Philosophy and Society,* ed. L. D. Easton and K. H. Guddar (Garden City, N.Y.: Doubleday, 1967), p. 250; cf. K. Kautsky, *Foundations of Christianity* (London: Orbach and Chambers, 1925).
35. G. Lukacs, *History and Class Consciousness* (London: Merlin Press, 1971), pp. 46–82.
36. Although, as Parsons has noted, Durkheim's position, unlike that of Weber, contradicts his avowed epistemology (positivism); Parsons, *The Structure of Social Action,* pp. 409–450.
37. I. Kant, *On History,* (Indianapolis: Bobbs-Merrill, 1963), p. 3.
38. Weber, *Economy and Society,* p. 340.
39. Marx and Engels, *Selected Works,* p. 182.
40. Actually, the *1859 Preface* and the concept of mode of production are highly controversial within Marxism. I do not have the space to enter into this controversy here.
41. G. Mosca, *The Ruling Class* (New York: McGraw-Hill, 1939), pp. 70–72.

5.
FOR MARX AGAINST ALTHUSSER*

JOHN O'NEILL

Nowadays everybody reads Marx. Or at any rate, many people are ready to read books about Marx, preparatory to reading Marx himself. Everyone admits that it is not easy to read Marx. Marx did not always write very well, much of his writing is polemical in the worst sense and his *magnum opus, Capital,* apart from being unfinished except for the first volume, is not readable for most people unfamiliar with the categories of Hegelian logic. At best *Capital* influences the consciousness of the proletariat only in as much as it is read sentimentally, as the history of their misery. Beyond that it is a tissue of conceptual and logical errors that make it the bastard child of economic philosophy or, worse still, of philosophical economy. Nevertheless, despite the increasing disenchantment with socialist reality in the East, and the apparent containment of Marxism in the West, Marx continues to be read. We have Marx in our bones. 'Of course', as Althusser remarks,

*Originally published in *The Human Context*, Vol VI, No. 2, 1974, 385–398. Reprinted by permission. Copyright © 1974.

. . . we have all read, all do read *Capital*. For almost a century, we have been able to read it every day, transparently,
in the dramas and dreams of our history, in its disputes and
conflicts, in the defeats and victories of the workers' movement which is our only hope and our destiny. Since we
'came into the world,' we have read *Capital* constantly in the
writings and speeches of those who have read it for us, well
or ill, both the dead and the living, Engels, Kautsky, Plekhanov, Lenin, Rosa Luxemburg, Trotsky, Stalin, Gramsci,
the leaders of the workers' organizations, their supporters
and opponents; philosophers, economists, politicians. We
have read bits of it, the 'fragments' which the conjuncture
had 'selected' for us. We have even all, more or less, read
Volume One, from 'commodities' to the 'expropriation of
the expropriators.'[1]

Capital, then, is not merely a piece of crabbed economic
analysis. It is an ethnography of our daily lives in which the texture of experience is interwoven with the realities of property,
power and money that determine for us the rhythms of ease and
misery, not just in our daily schedules but in the division of the
earth into dominions and colonies. In such a world, to think at all
is to presuppose the pain and exploitation of one's fellow men,
and to do so responsibly is to subscribe to a tradition of thought
in which reason thirsts for justice. It is to draw one's substance
from the legacy of the Enlightenment, to experience the bondage
of reason without revolution, to join the struggle of men
everywhere who believe in the Utopian service of knowledge to
justice. For this reason, then, *Capital* fixes in the Marxist mind as
a monumental effort to tie together the misery of the day's labor
with a vision of science and justice. And this is the peculiar
burden of the Marxist mind—to analyse appearances and yet to
submit to the palpable and everyday vision of social justice.

At first sight it looks as though Althusser's project is to understand the Marxist mind, to enter into its vision, perhaps to sit with
Marx in the museum, to try to understand this persistent effort
within the very storm of history, to read history and politics as a
story of reason and the emancipation of the masses. Only such an
approach is adequate to the hermeneutic task of the Marxist
mind confronted with the history and politics of its own revolutionary intervention, which has itself separated reason and
freedom in ways it could not foresee. Marxists are inveterate
readers not because they belong, as some argue, to a stranded

sect of millenarian and chiliastic believers, but because *Marxists are humanists*. That is why Marxists read all history as the history of class struggle. That is why, à la Hegel, they believe that there are times when universal history passes through the eye of the needle, when the proletarian revolution concretizes the 'future-philosophy of the world' into the 'world-future of philosophy'. It is for the same reason that in the midst of these world-shaking events Marxists continue to read and to write.

But in the next breath Althusser means to put an end to so much reading and writing, by reading *Capital, once and for all,* line by line, in the original German(!), while pretending that this is only an exercise in ambiguity, embracing the existential responsibilities of its own interpretative effort. Each of us must read Marx, because of our times, just as we look at the sky for tomorrow's weather. But, Althusser continues:

> some say it is essential to read *Capital* to the letter. To read the text itself, complete, all four volumes, line by line, to return ten times to the first chapters, or to the schemes of simple reproduction and reproduction on an enlarged scale, before coming down from the arid table-lands and plateaux of Volume Two into the promised land of profit, interest and rent. And it is essential to read *Capital* not only in its French translation (even Volume One in Roy's translation, which Marx revised, or rather, rewrote), but also in the German original, at least for the fundamental theoretical chapters and all the passages where Marx's key concepts come to the surface.[2]

Thus, what the very history of *Capital* shows to be impossible, indeed even more impossible than Marx's own efforts to put *Capital* into a finished form, is now to be settled by Althusser and his associates. Together this small band feels confident enough of its place in history to provide a reading of *Capital* that will reduce the readings of Lenin, Lukacs, Luxemburg and Gramsci to the abortive wastes of premature theorizing.

I

Althusser's method is to destroy the unity of Marx's theoretical initiative by raising the question of whether the 'object' of *Capital* is economics or history, and thus to rediscover Marx's own philosophy behind his back, so to speak, in order to reduce it to the science of dialectical materialism. But this is a conclusion that we must reach more slowly and in pace with Althusser's own reflections upon 'reading' *Capital*. For what is curious in Althusser's enterprise is the way he manages to reach positivist conclusions from what is an apparently phenomenological starting-point sensitive to the issues that we have raised so far.

Ours is an age, says Althusser, in which we have discovered that silent being that underlies our expressive deeds of looking, talking, writing, and reading:

> However paradoxical it may seem, I venture to suggest that our age threatens one day to appear in the history of human culture as marked by the most dramatic and difficult trial of all, the discovery of and training in the meaning of the 'simplest' acts of existence: seeing, listening, speaking, reading—the acts which relate men to their works, and to those works thrown in their faces, their 'absences of works.'[3]

We owe it to Marx, Nietzsche and Freud that we now comprehend a work, a culture or a period through the 'absence of its concept', by which it accomplishes something more and something less than its agents intended. A structuralist reading, Althusser argues, is not the 'innocent reading' of the young Marx, sweeping away 'concrete' appearances in order to reveal the 'abstract' essence of economics, politics and history guided by a scriptural reading of Hegel's Absolute Knowledge and Marx's own eschatology. The young Marx is still trapped in the religious myth of reading the book of nature as the revelation of an alienated human essence. His philosophy of history remains a theodicy, an ideological reading that has still to become a science of history, and this is the shift that occurs in *Capital:* 'By discovering that the truth of history cannot be read in its manifest discourse, because the text of history is not a text in which a voice (the *Logos)* speaks, but the inaudible and illegible notation of the effects of a structure of structures.'[4]

Already we are enmeshed in Althusser's own reading of texts, in his own way of deciding the presences and absences in Marx's work. I shall argue that Althusser's reading of *Capital* is from the very beginning[5] determined by a method of exorcism that expels what is there in the name of what is not there, to make room for what is not there in the name of Marx's 'object'. It is therefore necessary to intercept Althusser at the very beginning, i.e., the question of what is absent and what is present in an author's work must determine the responsibility of our reading. Thus we must be conscious that Althusser's reading of *Capital* first of all suppresses its humanistic impulse. This, however, is tantamount to a political reading of Marx since it separates in the name of theoretical autonomy the unity of Marxist praxis that has become troublesome to the Soviet bloc. In other words, we need to be aware of the organization of background and foreground that determines our reading of the text and the 'context' of *Capital*. It is the 'break' between Hegel and Marx that makes Althusser conscious of what he calls his 'culpable reading' of Marx. Although he presents this 'break' as the fulfilment of Marx's Promethean critique of philosophy, whose death is the birth of Marxist science, Althusser disavows the humanist intentions that justified the revolt of Prometheus and the pathos of his interminable suffering. Althusser wants no more caricatures of the Promethean Marx chained to a suffering mankind: Marx is to be a scientist, despite himself: 'To break with the religious myth of reading: with Marx this theoretical necessity took precisely the form of a rupture with the Hegelian conception of the whole as a "spiritual" totality, to be precise, as an expressive totality.'[6] Once Marx had broken with Hegel's spiritualization of history he was free from the religious myth of history as the expression of the human senses, of the voice of the heart, of the ear of man that discerns in Being a Logos and a Truth.

But this is surely an unmusical reading of Marx. Marx did not argue that religion is simply an illusion, a distorted way of seeing what science produces as knowledge. Religion is the expression of man's generic nature, which cannot be reduced to an object except through another, a master of a class, just as it can only achieve selfhood through others in recognition and community. Religion is the expression of man's generic being under social and historical conditions that alienate man from his own legacy. Religion is not a simple failure to see things; it is the vision of the failure of things where man is concerned.

> *Religious* suffering is at the same time an *expression* of real suffering and a *protest* against real suffering. Religion is the sign of the oppressed creature, the sentiment of a heartless world, and the soul of soulless conditions. It is the *opium* of the people.
>
> The abolition of religion as the *illusory* happiness of men, is a demand for their *real* happiness. The call to abandon their illusions about their conditions is a *call to abandon a*

condition which requires illusions. The criticism of religion is, therefore, the *embryonic criticism of this vale of tears* of which religion is the halo.[7]

It is not a question of reducing religion to economic causes but of being able to see that the expressive being of man, in other words man's *metaphysical* nature, is such that the domains of religion, politics, economics and art resonate in each other, even though each has a distinctive valence in the social structure of any given historical period. What Marx understands by the critique of ideology is the effort to situate each of the praxes of economics, politics and philosophy within a historical milieu from which they cannot be abstracted, but to which they are not simply reducible. This is, of course, what Marx established in his 'Theses on Feuerbach' and the *German Ideology,* which Althusser treats, however, as pre-scientific efforts in Marx's theoretical development.

Again we must not overlook the way Althusser reduces the problem of the historical vision of critical reason which occupied Marx throughout his early and later works to an epistemological critique of naive realism and its simple-minded logic of vision. In terms of this argument Marx failed to understand the scientific departure in his own reading of classical economics, because he treated those texts as a given in which it remained only for him to correct certain theoretical gaps as *failures of vision,* without being able to present an adequate account of his own implicit theoretical advance.

> This single logic of sighting and oversight thus reveals itself to us as what it is: the logic of a conception of knowledge in which all the work of knowledge is reduced in principle to the recognition of the mere relation of *vision;* in which the whole nature of its object is reduced to the mere condition of a *given.* What Smith did not see, through a weakness of vision, Marx sees: what Smith did not see was perfectly visible, and it was because it was visible that Smith could fail to see it while Marx could see it. We are in a circle—we have relapsed into the mirror myth of knowledge as the vision of a given object or the reading of an established text, neither of which is ever anything but transparency itself—the sin of blindness belonging by right to vision as much as the virtue of clear-sightedness—to the eye of man.[8]

Althusser's reading of Marx's theoretical departure with respect to classical economics, whose significance allegedly escaped Marx himself, must be understood as the departure Althusser himself seeks to introduce into the Party's own history of naive realist determinations of socialist theory. It is, I would argue, the absence of Althusser's own object that veils his efforts to clarify the theoretical autonomy of the domains of history, economics and politics in terms of his critique of realist epistemology and Hegelian idealism. Having raised the ghost of naive realism, Althusser proceeds to give an account of the nature of theoretical abstraction or concept formation which reduced the literal notion of abstraction from concrete particulars to a permanent absurdity. This is an exercise that may be therapeutic for the Party mind bulldozed by socialist realism. But it is hardly a serious epistemological issue in Marx, who considered it a good part of 'la misère de la philosophie' to which idealists and realists may both contribute, in as much as they overlook the genesis of ideas within specific historical praxis.

> Monsieur Proudhon has very well grasped the fact that men produce cloth, linen, silks, and it is a great merit on his part to have grasped this small amount. What he has not grasped is that those men, according to their powers, also produce the social relations amid which they prepare cloth and linen. Still less has he understood that men, who fashion their *social relations* in accordance with their material mode of production, also fashion *ideas* and *categories,* that is to say the abstract, ideal expression of these same social relations. Thus the categories are no more eternal than the relations they express. They are historic and transitory products. For M. Proudhon, on the contrary, abstractions and categories are the primordial cause. According to him, they, and not men, make history. The *abstraction,* the *category taken as such,* i.e., apart from men and their material activities, is of course immortal, unmoved, unchangeable, it is only one form of the being of pure reason; which is only another way of saying that the abstraction as such is abstract. *An admirable tautology!*
>
> Thus, regarded as categories, economic relations for M. Proudhon are eternal formulae without origin or progress.[9]

This early text is resonant with what Althusser calls 'a second and quite different reading' in which, as he says himself, the argument in terms of the logic of vision yields to a critique, not of the failures of vision in Marx's predecessors, but of their failure to perceive what they *did* see, namely, *the field of production*. The notion of the 'production' of theory constitutes a problematic that it is the task of critical theory to comprehend. Althusser argues, however, that Marx himself, although he unwittingly provided the answer to this problematic, was unable to pose its question explicitly because he remained tied to the field of classical economics:

> This restoration of an utterance containing emptinesses and this production of *its* question out of the answer enable us to bring to light the reasons why classical economics was blind to what it nevertheless saw, and thus to explain the non-vision inside its vision. Moreover, it is clear that the mechanism whereby Marx is able to see what classical economics did not see while seeing it, is identical with the mechanism whereby Marx saw what classical economics did not see at all—and also, at least in principle, identical with the mechanism whereby we are at this moment reflecting this operation of the sighting of a non-sight of the seen, by *reading* a text by Marx which is itself a reading of a text of classical economics.[10]

II

We must ask, therefore, what is the question to which Althusser's own symptomatic epistemology is an answer? For there is surely something backward looking in Althusser's lengthy *reductio ad absurdum* of naive realism, as well as his insistence upon an epistemological break between Hegel and Marx. Indeed it is the latter effort that increases the relentlessness of Althusser's critique of naive realism—which is otherwise not a serious issue for Marx, supposing we derive any sense from the *Theses on Feuerbach*. Moreover, since the yield of Althusser's reading of *Capital* is simply the apparent recovery of the theoretical autonomy of the domains of economics and politics, but at the expense of Marxist humanism and historicism which provided a principle for the *ordering* of these domains, we can only conclude that Althusser's epistemology ultimately answer the question of theoretical

autonomy in terms of a *parti pris*, or a *jeu de mots*, in which the
Party is the unconscious method of the 'production' of socialist
theory. In other words, Althusser reduces the autonomy of socialist theorizing to the 'savage practice' of Party praxis, while appearing to save its autonomy as a productive effort, irreducible to
other productions, such as the imperative of politics and economics. In this way Althusser succeeds in barbarizing Marx's
Theses on Feuerbach with a gloss on Lenin's political praxis:

> That is how Lenin responded to the prophecy in the XI
> Thesis, and he was the first to do so, for no one had done it
> before him, not even Engels. He himself responded in the
> 'style' of his philosophical practice. A wild practice *[une
> pratique sauvage]* in the sense in which Freud spoke of a wild
> analysis, one which does not provide the theoretical creden-
> tials for its operations and which raises screams from the
> philosophy of 'interpretation' of the world, which might be
> called the philosophy of *denegation*. A wild practice, if you
> will, but what did not begin by being wild.[11]

Let us be clear about what is at issue in Althusser's attempt to
sever the connection between the synchronic and diachronic
structures contained in the theory of historical materialism. If
'Marxism is not a species of historicism' then we may neglect
Lenin's reading of Hegel in order to orient himself at a critical
juncture in the history of imperialism and nationalist revolutions.
But the theoretical brilliance of Lenin's analysis of imperialism
lies in his grasp of national liberation movements as products of
the world economy created by monopoly capitalism which, provided the proletariat can transform imperialist wars into civil
wars, becomes a genuinely revolutionary period. Thus Lenin was
able to reject the Revisionists and Opportunists in the International because they failed to understand how the class implications of imperialism, when grasped in their specific dialectical
implications, were favourable by means of civil war to the proletarian revolution, in Russia and elsewhere. Lukacs has the same
view as Merleau-Ponty of Lenin's political practice, separating it
entirely from what others might regard as *Realpolitik:*

> Above all, when defining the concept of compromise, any
> suggestion that it is a question of knack, of cleverness, of an
> astute fraud, must be rejected. 'We must,' said Lenin, 'deci-

sively reject those who think that politics consists of little tricks, sometimes bordering on deceit. *Classes cannot be deceived.* For Lenin, therefore, compromise means *that the true developmental tendencies of classes* (and possibly of nations—for instance, where an oppressed people is concerned), which under specific circumstances and for a certain period run parallel in determinate areas with the interests of the proletariat, are exploited to the advantage of *both.* [12]

In the postscript to his essay on Lenin, Lukacs repeats the argument for the unity of Lenin's theoretical grasp of the political nature of the imperialist epoch and his practical sense of proletarian politics. In trying to express the living nature of that unity in Lenin's own life, he describes how Lenin would learn from experience or from Hegel's *Logic* according to the situation, preserving in himself the dialectical tension between particulars and a theoretical totality. What Althusser fails to make clear is how by turning to Hegel Lenin sought to find a way to avoid making theory the mere appendage of State practice, while reserving a more creative political role to practice than the retroactive determination or revision of ideology. But this means that Marxist materialism can never be the simple enforcement of political will, any more than political will can be exercised without a theoretical understanding of the specific class relations it presupposes. Thus Lenin remarks:

> The standpoint of life, of practice, should be first and fundamental in the theory of knowledge. . . . Of course, we must not forget that the criterion of practice can never, in the nature of things, either confirm or refute any idea *completely.* This criterion too is sufficiently 'indefinite' not to allow human knowledge to become 'absolute,' but at the same time it is sufficiently definite to wage a ruthless fight against all varieties of idealism and agnosticism. [13]

Of course in these later Hegelian formulations Lenin is modifying his own revision of Engel's dialectical materialism as set forth in *Materialism and Empirio-Criticism,* thereby rejoining the challenge set to this work by Lukacs's own *History and Class Con-*

sciousness, as well as Karl Korsch's *Marxism and Philosophy,* both published in 1923. Lukacs's essay on Lenin was published on the occasion of the latter's death in 1924. What died with Lenin was orthodox Marxism, although its dead hand was to be upon social-ism for another thirty years or more. Orthodox scientific Marxism was completely undermined with Lukacs's insight into the histor-ically determined praxis of science. But while it is clear that sci-entific socialism was unready for Lukacs, the same must be said of the West, where only today is the critique of scientific praxis entering into a properly reflexive or critical social science. In *His-tory and Class Consciousness* Lukacs made it clear that living Marx-ism is inseparable from its idealist and Hegelian legacy. This split Russian and Central European Marxism. Today it is the core of neo-Marxist critical theory as developed by Horkheimer, Marcuse and Adorno. What emerges from these developments is that the Hegelian concept of totality furnishes a matrix for the integration of ethics and politics through the restless dynamics of man's at-tempt to measure his existential circumstances against the ideal of his human essence, which he achieves through the struggle against self and institutional alienations. The Hegelian Marxist totality is thus the basis for the integral humanism of Marxist social science.[14]

These developments, whose complexity we can hardly pretend to have raised in any historical depth, are effectively 'purged' by Althusser's notions of an 'implicit' reading. That is to say, in tak-ing account of Lenin's reading of Hegel between 1914 and 1916 Althusser argues that in effect Lenin stripped the *Logic* to its *sci-entific* core already arrived at in *Materialism and Empiro-Criticism* without the benefit of Hegel, except in as much as he had *already* read him in reading the first chapter of *Capital!* Furthermore, the ultimate theoretical gain from this scientific 'purge' of the *Logic* is that the subject of *Capital is a process without a subject,* namely, a structure and not a historical process of alienation.[15] Thus Althusser concludes by reversing Lenin's judgement that an un-derstanding of *Capital* is impossible without Hegel's *Logic* with the verdict: 'For a hundred and fifty years no one has understood Hegel! To understand Hegel one must have thoroughly studied and understood Marx's *Capital.'*

According to Althusser, though this is hardly news and is cer-tainly more Hegelian than he seems to think, the specificity of scientific Marxism lies in its theory of the overdetermination of social structures, which accounts for their features of simultane-ous complexity and unity. Such 'structures' in dominance are the

only proper referents of the notion of unity or totality in Marxist
theory. The theory of the overdetermination of social structures,
he argues, has nothing in common either with the Hegelian unity
of essence and its alienated appearances or with the monistic
causality of material determinism. The Hegelian unity relent-
lessly negates the differences that never exist-for-themselves and
therefore can never determine any practical policy that could
materially affect the development of the spiritual unity of its
essence.

> My claim is that the Hegelian totality: (1) is not really, but
> only apparently, articulated in 'spheres'; (2) that its unity is
> not its complexity itself, that is, the structure of this com-
> plexity; (3) that it is therefore deprived of the structure in
> dominance which is the absolute precondition for a real
> complexity to be a unity and really the object of a *prac-
> tice* that proposes to transform this structure: political prac-
> tice. It is no accident that the Hegelian theory of the social
> totality has never provided the basis for a policy, that there
> is not and cannot be a Hegelian politics.[16]

Thus Althusser's structuralist redefinition of the theory of historical materialism, severed from its roots in Hegel and Feuerbach, serves to suppress the history of socialist theory that continuously reconnects in revolutionary ways with a Hegelian politics pitted against the alienation of socialist and capitalist rationality. The new context of socialist theory is the convergence of
the processes of technical rationality and bureaucratic relations
of production in industrial societies, capitalist or socialist. In this
context the social sciences adopt cybernetics or synchronic models of social structure, on the analogue of the information processes that are the typical output, as well as input, of such systems. In other words, it is the production process of advanced industrial societies that, as Marcuse has argued, is thoroughly
'ideological'. The industrial ideology of both capitalist and socialist societies is predicated upon a technological rationality that
ignores the substantive values of humanist reason. The technique
of this denial is the suppression of history and the denial of
Utopia. But history and Utopia are the roots of critical reason.

Althusser's reading of *Capital* ignores the way Marx's meta-eco-
nomics structure *Capital* as a *critique*. This means that *Capital* is
not simply a scientific work produced by the distinction between

essences and appearances. This would serve only to separate it
from common sense knowledge, but not from classical economics. Nor is the distinction between essence and appearance reducible to Marx's distinction between the ideological superstructure
and its economic substructures. This again is a feature of historical materialism that does not distinguish it from classical sociology. The *critical question* in *Capital*, but also in every work of
Marx, is how is it possible that the being who produces everything
should produce his own non-being? How is it that the presence of
man is the history of the absence of man? This question is raised
in *Capital* as a question about the nature of the historical and
social distance between the absence of man and the presence of
man. Marx's method is clearly structuralist in his analysis of the
socioeconomic conditions of the absence of man, i.e. the historical structure of surplus-value. But what makes his theoretical
grasp of the structures of surplus-value critical is precisely its *historicist confrontation* between the order of scientific *theory* and the
social *praxis*, which produces scientific knowledge in the course
of its own dynamics.[17]

> While it may be said, therefore, that the categories of bour-
> geois economy contain what is true of all other forms of
> society, the statement is to be taken *cum grano salis*. They
> may contain these in a developed or crippled or caricatured
> form, but always essentially different. The so-called histor-
> ical development amounts in the last analysis to this, that
> the last form considers its predecessors as stages leading up
> to itself and always perceives them from a single point of
> view, since it is very seldom and only under certain condi-
> tions that it is capable of self-criticism; of course, we do not
> speak here of such historical periods as appear to their own
> contemporaries to be periods of decay. The Christian reli-
> gion became capable of assisting us to an objective view of
> past mythologies as soon as it was ready for self-criticism to
> a certain extent, *dynamei*, so to speak. In the same way bour-
> geois political economy first came to understand the feudal,
> the ancient and the oriental societies as soon as the self-crit-
> icism of bourgeois society had commenced. In as far as
> bourgeois political economy has not gone into the myth-
> ology of identifying the bourgeois system purely with the
> past, its criticism of the feudal system against which it still
> had to wage war resembled Christian criticism of the
> heathen religions or Protestant criticism of Catholicism.[18]

In this passage from Marx's discussion in the *Grundrisse* of the method of political economy, we see that the notion of critique rests upon the transformation of a social order in which the new social system, for example capitalism, is the absent concept in the horizon of the mercantile practices still embedded in feudalism but seeking outlets in the towns, the nation-state and Protestantism.[19] The absence of man in the feudal world is framed in terms of the rationalist critique of authority and tradition that opens up the realm of individual conscience to gear with the new experience of society as a field of individual interest, subject only to market forces. Under capitalism, the presence of man is the emergence of the individual and the absence of divinely ordained states. It is just here, however, that the critique contained in *Capital* reveals its full force by showing that the *class* structure of bourgeois individualism is precisely the absence of man as a *human* being. Classical economics is therefore the direct expression of the absence of true humanism under capitalist conditions. The impersonal laws of commodity production and exchange relationships conceal the specific class relations of production that make possible the simultaneity of exchange and exploitation, i.e. the expropriation of labor by capital. Marx's critique of classical political economy, however, is not contained as such in the elaboration of the concepts of labor-value, exploitation and surplus-value. Nor is it wholly exhausted in the revelation of the specific historical and constitutional preconditions of the economic exchange between labor and capital as commodities. Marx's critique of political economy is essentially a humanist critique of *the absence of man* and his world-alienation produced through the subjectivization of the principle of property.

> Under the guise of recognizing man, political economy, whose principle is labor, carries to its logical conclusion the denial of man. Man himself is no longer in a condition of external tension with the external substance of private property; he has himself become the tension-ridden being of private property. What was previously a phenomenon of *being external to oneself,* a real manifestation of man, has now become the art of objectification, of alienation. This political economy seems at first, therefore, to recognize man with his independence, his personal activity, etc. It incorporates private property in the very essence of man, and it is no longer, therefore, conditioned by the local or na-

tional *characteristics of private property* regarded as existing outside itself. It manifests a cosmopolitan, universal activity which is destructive of every limit and every bond, and substitutes itself as the *only* policy, the *only* universality, the *only* limit and the *only* bond. But in its further development it is obliged to discard this hypocrisy and to show itself in all its cynicism. It does this, without any regard for the apparent contradictions to which its doctrine leads, by showing in a more one-sided fashion, and thus with greater logic and clarity, that *labor* is the sole *essence of wealth,* and by demonstrating that this doctrine, in contrast with the original conception, has consequences which are *inimical to man.* Finally, it gives the death-blow to *ground rent;* that last individual and natural form of private property and source of wealth existing independently of the movement of labor, which was the expression of feudal property but has become entirely its economic expression and is no longer able to put up any resistance to political economy. (The Ricardo School.)[20]

III

Every reading of history stands to be judged by history. This is not the conclusion of a historical determinism, as it might seem, but is rather a statement of the problematic of the philosophy of history. It calls for an account of the relation between knowledge and action in which we must avoid both the scientism of simplistic realism and the nihilism of subjective relativism, which equally destroy the hermeneutic of reason in history. Marxist rationalism is more than an epistemology because it is concerned with the human meaning of knowledge, and is therefore always critical with respect to the uses of science. At the same time Marxism does not reduce knowledge to a class practice because this would barbarize its humanist aims. We must avoid altogether the idea that history is governed either by scientific laws or by an occult logic that makes human events rational, whatever the appearances. But this means we need a proper conception of human knowledge and the historical space in which it unfolds. Hegel and Marx between them have taught us that the human spirit does not exist outside of history, any more than history itself can unfold except as the externalization *(Entäusserung)* of human subjectivity. Idealism and materialism are false alternatives. They fail to describe the constitution of historical space as a praxis determined by the affinity of choices *(Wahlverwandt-schaft)* men make in their economic, political and religious lives. This is how we read Marx's conception of the subjectivization of the productive forces of nature into the master concepts of *labor* in classical economics and of *faith* in the Protestant religion.

> Engels is right, therefore, in calling Adam Smith the *Luther of political economy. Just as Luther recognized religion and faith* as the essence of the real *world* and for that reason took up a position against Catholic paganism; just as he annulled *external* religiosity while making religiosity the *inner* essence of man; just as he negated the distinction between priest and layman because he transferred the priest into the heart of the layman; so wealth external to man and indepen-dent of him (and thus only to be acquired and conserved from outside) is annulled. That is to say, its *external* and *mindless objectivity* is annulled by the fact that private prop-erty is incorporated in man himself, and man himself is rec-ognized as its essence. But as a result, man himself is brought into the sphere of private property, just as, with Luther, he is brought into the sphere of religion.[21]

Thus the cultural pluralism that Althusser seeks to establish through his 'culpable reading' of Marx lies there for any innocent reader who has not burdened himself with Althusser's 'epistemological break' and its spurious separation of Marxist humanism from Marxist science. The pluralism inherent in Marx's economic and philosophical conception of capitalism is not the opposite of a unified interpretation of history sought by Marxist social science. But neither is it a covert appeal to the political independence of the ideological superstructure that now determines socialist history. On the contrary, the methodological pluralism in historical materialism attest the solidarity of the realms of economics, politics, law and religion within a praxis that is a qualitative relation between man, society and nature. Thus a Marxist reading of history is an initiation into the whole of human history and all of its facets; it is, in short, a humanist edu-cation *(Bildung)*.

The problematic of Marxist theory is *not* the role of humanism in Marxist science. On the contrary it is the role of Marxist science in humanism. For humanism is not a science but a form of conduct. It is 'a reason *within* unreason', as Merleau-Ponty says. Of course humanism remains an idle wish, a palace surrounded by hovels, unless it joins with science and politics. But as we have learned from Weber, these are uneasy vocations for which science may teach us responsibility in the place of faith, but neither certainty nor the abandonment of hope, because the question of the meaning of human experience continuously transforms our history. Thus there can never be a science of history, but only a series of 'responsible readings' that are not entirely disjunctive because the human present does not leap out of the past any more than it faces the future as a void.

> There is no history where the course of events is a series of episodes without unity, or where it is a struggle already decided in the heaven of ideas. History is there where there is a logic *within* contingence, a reason *within* unreason, where there is a historical perception which, like perception in general, leaves in the background what cannot enter the foreground but seizes the lines of force as they are generated and actively leads their traces to a conclusion. This analogy should not be interpreted as a shameful organicism or finalism, but as a reference to the fact that all symbolic systems—perception, language and history—only become what they were although in order to do so they need to be taken up into human initiative.[22]

Thus Marx himself understood that the 'mathematical' reading in the method of classical economics is dependent upon the axioms of continuity and exchangeability, or the algebra of money, which imposes an objective unity upon the subjective and social processes of alienation. The objectivism of classical economics is the truly 'culpable' reading of a historical and social system that Marx reads 'innocently' as the absence of man. But this means that Marx's critique of political economy is not based upon a literal reading in anything like the positivistic sense that Althusser intends with respect to *Capital*. Marx's reading of classical economics, like Hegel's reading of the history of philosophy, is a phenomenology of the tradition of rationality, of the history of reason *and* unreason. Therefore the object of *Capital* is not its *topic*, i.e, the analysis of the structures of surplus-value formation, but its *objective*, namely, the recovery of the subjective axioms of objectification in alienated and non-alienated modes of expression. That is to say, Marx's theoretical enterprise is governed by a rationalist philosophy of history which determines positively and negatively the critical stages of human development. Thus the Marxist reading of history is essentially a violent reading in contrast to the mathematical reading of classical economics, whose vision is ultimately that of the stationary state in a world of surrounding misery and poverty. The violence of Marxism is the violence of the turning-points in human history. For the same reason, *Capital* is not what Marx is writing *about,* because the sense of its analysis feeds off the next stage of human development. This only haunts the text in the language of moral criticism, but is essential to it, if we are to 'see through' the analysis to the form of life that socialism inscribes in the grammar of history through the vocabulary of revolution. The question that *Capital* seeks to answer is: What is the human meaning of capitalism? It then proceeds to unfold this question in the grammar of structuralist economics. Through this procedure Marx uncovers the absence of man's human presence in the asceticism of the labor/capital exchange system that is implicitly made the unreal inversion of the ideal value of man for man.

Habermas has argued that Marx's phenomenology is inadequate because he reduced the synthesis of the moral and political grammar of the human ideal to the materialist synthesis of species reproduction.[23] But this, of course, is the product of Habermas' own reduction of historical materialism, which creates the need to recover the absence of men by turning in part to Hegel and Freud. The failure to read the absence of man in Marx's texts is itself a historical and political failure.[24] This mode of reading is the method that is truly the enemy of the open society. It is the weapon of the Party with its back to history and the education of mankind. It destroys the myth of humanity that cannot be made a science, because science itself is dependent upon the humanist faith in Reason, however much science forgets its own history. Thus Althusser's scientism is the ultimate violence of an unhistorical reading of Marx in place of the authentic violence of a reading that is the necessity of the orientation of reason amid unreason.

NOTES

1. Louis Althusser and Etienne Balibar, *Reading Capital,* transl. Ben Brewster (New York: Pantheon Books, 1970), p. 13.
2. Ibid., pp. 13–14.

FOR MARX AGAINST ALTHUSSER

139

3. Ibid., pp. 15-16.
4. Ibid., p. 17.
5. *Lire le Capital* presupposes the exercise undertaken in *Pour Marx* (Paris: Fran-çois Maspéro, 1966). I have already dealt with this argument in my essay, "On Theory and Criticism in Marx", in John O'Neill, *Sociology as a Skin Trade, Essays Towards a Reflexive Sociology* (London: Heinemann, 1972), and in *Situating Marx*, ed. Walton C. Hall (London: Chaucer, 1972).
6. Ibid., p. 17.
7. Karl Marx, "Contribution to the Critique of Hegel's Philosophy of Right," in *Early Writings*, transl. and ed. T. B. Bottomore (New York: McGraw-Hill, 1964), p. 43.
8. Althusser and Balibar, *Reading Capital*, p. 19.
9. Marx to P. V. Annenkov, Brussels (28 December 1846), in K. Marx and F. Engels, *Selected Correspondence* 1846-1895 (New York: International Publishers, 1934), pp. 14-15.
10. Althusser and Balibar, *Reading Capital*, pp. 23-24.
11. Louis Althusser, *Lenin and Philosophy and Other Essays*, transl. Ben Brewster (New York: Monthly Review Press, 1971), p. 66.
12. Georg Lukacs, *Lenin: A Study on the Unity of His Thought*, transl. Nicholas Jacobs (London: NLB, 1970), p. 79.
13. Quoted in Alfred Schmidt, *The Concept of Nature in Marx*, transl. Ben Fowkes (London: NLB, 1971), pp. 118-119.
14. O'Neill, "History as Human History in Hegel and Marx", in Jean Hyppolite, *Studies on Marx and Hegel*, transl. with notes and bibliography John O'Neill (New York: Basic Books, 1969).
15. Louis Althusser, "Lenine devant Hegel," *Lenine et la philosophie suivi de Marx et Lenine devant Hegel* (Paris: Francois Maspero, 1972).
16. Louis Althusser, *For Marx*, transl. Ben Brewster (New York: Vintage Books, 1970), p. 204.
17. My conception of Marx's structuralism is similar to Godelier's view, although not sharing either his agreement with Althusser of his view that the diachronic shift between social structures is a matter only of scientific analysis without benefit of Marx's humanism and historicism. Cf. Maurice Godelier, "Remarques sur les concepts de structure et de contradiction," *Aletheia*, 4 (May 1966): 228-236.
18. Marx, *The Grundrisse*, transl. and ed. David McLellan (New York: Harper & Row, 1971), p. 40.
19. K. Marx and F. Engels, *The German Ideology* (Moscow: Progress Publishers, 1964), Part I.
20. K. Marx, "Economic and Philosophical Manuscripts," in *Early Writings*, (New York: International Publishers, 1964), p. 148.
21. Ibid., pp. 147-148.
22. Maurice Merleau-Ponty, "Materials for a Theory of History," *Themes from the Lectures at the College de France 1952-1960*, transl. John O'Neill (Evanston, Ill.: Northwestern University Press, 1970), pp. 29-30.
23. Jurgen Habermas, *Knowledge and Human Interests*, transl. Jeremy Shapiro (Boston: Beacon Press, 1971), p. 42. I have considered Habermas' argument on the materialist synthesis in Marx in my essay referred to in note 5 above. Although I disagree with the derivation of Habermas' argument, I believe it bears upon Althusser's procedure.
24. Habermas himself provides for this conclusion in his essay, "Toward a Theory of Communicative Competence," in *Recent Sociology No. 2, Patterns of Communicative Behavior*, ed. Hans Peter Dreitzel (New York: Macmillan, 1970). This essay in fact makes it necessary to remark that my specific criticism of *Knowledge and Human Interests* is that it fails to recognize that the interest in autonomy and responsibility (*Mundigkeit*), which Habermas treats as the foundation of social and political dialogue, is a principle determined by a rationalist philosophy of history, as I have argued in this essay.

6.
SOCIAL PRACTICE, SOCIAL ACTION, SOCIAL MAGIC*

GÖRAN THERBORN

The so-called "theory of action" is one of the most grandiose theoretical schemes of 20th century social thought. Developed in sociology it pretends to provide a frame of reference not only for all the social sciences, but also for the sciences of culture and for psychology and to provide a link to biology, as dealing with the human organism. The organism, the personality, the social system, and the cultural system are presented as subsystems of action, cybernetically related in hierarchies of conditioning and control.[1] The theory of action has been worked out over a third of the century, by Talcott Parsons,[2] but the theory and its influence is much more than a one man affair. Some of its most basic statements have been collective efforts.[3] Also among the critics of Parsons, tribute has been paid to the theory of action, e.g., by Homans.[4] It has a central place in all the different sociologies falling back on Max Weber.

*Originally published in *Acta Sociologica*, Vol. 16, No. 3, 1973. Reprinted by permission. Copyright © 1973.

The Greek noun "praxis" means doing, or action. Praxis or practice is a central concept in another wide-encompassing social theory, Marxism. In his first *Thesis on Feuerbach* the young Karl Marx wrote in 1845: "The chief defect of all previous materialism is that things, reality, the sensible world, are conceived only in the form of objects of observation, but not as *human sense activity, praxis,* not subjectively."[5]

How do the concepts of social action and social practice (praxis) relate to each other? That is the first problem this paper will deal with.

In the Feuerbach Theses Marx contrasted the conception of human life as human practice with a contemplative materialism. When Parsons first launched his theory of action, he emphasized that it was a "voluntaristic theory of action."[6] Here an important theme of modern sociological discussion seems to be involved. It is being said, recently, e.g., by Joachim Israel, that "one of the main division lines in contemporary social science, psychology as well as sociology, concerns the position taken with regard to the problem of man as an agent."[7] Israel distinguishes a conception of man "mainly as a passive object subjected to environmental influences" with one of man as "an active, creative subject." This theme has been developed by, among others, Wrong, Gouldner, Buckley, and Etzioni.[8] (The latter two are, however, more concerned with the activeness of human societies or social systems.) How are the theories of action and practice related to that discussion?

The last point is closely connected with a third, and more general question, i.e., the relationship between social theory and "background assumptions"[9] or normative statements about the nature of man and society.[10] What is the fruitfulness and significance of analyzing the former in terms of the latter? That question will also be briefly touched.

ACTION AND WILL IN THE THEORY OF ACTION

"The theory of action is a conceptual scheme for the analysis of the behavior of living organisms. It conceives of this behavior as oriented to the attainment of ends in situations, by means of the normatively regulated expenditure of energy," Parsons-Shils have said.[11] In this context the intention is not to go into all the elaborations of the Parsonsian action "frame of reference."[12] What we shall do is to point to its most decisive aspects. These aspects are twofold, one of them separates the theory of action from other ways of treating "the behavior of living organisms," the other characterizes Parsons' own brand of action theory as distinct from other variants.

Action theory is primarily a theory that looks at behavior "from the subjective point of view," i.e., the point of view of the actor. "It is evident that these categories of the theory of action, i.e., end, situation, and a selective standard relating the first two have meaning only in terms which include the subjective point of view, i.e., that of the actor. A theory which, like behaviorism, insists on treating human beings in terms which exclude the subjective aspect, is not a theory of action in the sense of this study."[13] Though Parsons after the war became more soft on behaviorism,[14] the subjective point of view has all the time remained crucial to his scheme of action.[15]

This very special definition of action was explicitly put forward, before Parsons, by Max Weber:

"In action is included all human behavior when and in so far as the acting individual attaches a subjective meaning to it."[16]

The opposite to action, in this sense, is thus not passivity but merely reactive behavior or behavior studied only objectively without trying to understand (Verstehen) the point of view of the actor. Weber continues the above quotation: "Action in this sense may be either overt or purely inward or subjective; it may consist of positive intervention in a situation or of deliberately refraining from such intervention or passively acquiescing in the situation."

This is essential to Parsons too. He is at pains to point out that the theory of action is concerned with the analysis of certain aspects of the behavior of the organism, "particularly that phase which involves the control and direction of such behavior through culture-level symbolic systems and the organization through which that control is implemented. There are two points at which this assumption becomes essential. The first is that it establishes basic continuity with the biological world. . . . The second point is to *draw the line vis-a-vis physical behavior. This is not, as such, action,* in the analytical sense, but is controlled by action processes."[17]

Parsonian action is not concerned with the sordid trivialities of physical behavior, but with the *actors' orientation* to and control of such behavior. Therefore, Parsons concludes, those who complain that there is no action in action theory have simply misunderstood what the theory is all about.[18]

After the war Parsons has felt sufficiently secure of his own influence to speak only of the theory of action, or of the "general" theory of action. In 1937 the theory was presented as a specific theory of action, as an alternative to and as a victor over other theories of action. At that time Parsons talked of the "voluntaristic" theory of action. The crucial thing about the latter is that it includes, in a systematic way, normative elements in the scheme of action. A normative element means here that something is held by the actor as desirable in itself. Parsons says that: "The logical starting point for analysis of normative elements in human action is the fact of experience that men not only respond to stimuli but in some sense try to conform their action to patterns which are, by the actor and other members of the same collectivity, deemed desirable."[19]

The differentia specifica of the voluntaristic theory of action is the inclusion of both non-random normative elements and objective conditions in the means-end schema.[20] The former distinguishes it from all forms of positivism; the latter separates it from purely idealist-emanationist theories. Since the latter type of theory has played a limited role in the Anglo-Saxon world, Parsons' main thrust is against utilitarianism and radical positivism.

The meaning of the word "voluntaristic" in Parsonsian theory is thus as peculiar as its meaning of action. Voluntaristic is not conceived of as the opposite to deterministic. The utilitarian world was anything but deterministic, and utilitarian man was no will-less object. The fundamental problem of utilitarianism, as Parsons saw it, was that it did not say anything about how the various ends that individuals were striving for were related to each other. Every individual was looked at as pursuing his own self-interest. This was an untenable position, because in this way, Parsons argued, the fact of social order could not be accounted for. How could there become a society, and not a war of all against all, out of a myriad of individuals, each striving for his own ends?

Utilitarianism therefore tended to break down either in "radical rationalistic positivism" or in "radical anti-intellectualistic positivism." In both these accounts for human behavior the normative element was deleted, and scientifically valid knowledge was the only significant orientation to action. In the former the actor himself acted according to his scientific knowledge of the situation, in the latter the actor acted in ignorance and error but the result of this ignorance and error could be stated by the scientific observer (as in instinct psychology and Social Darwinism). Neither variant of radical positivism could, in Parsons' view, solve the utilitarian dilemma of treating human ends either as random or as assimilable into the conditions of the situation of action, into either heredity or environment.[21]

By way of conclusion, in relation to utilitarianism—liberal economics as well as the social philosophy of Hobbes and Locke and their successors—Parsons' "voluntarism" means determinism: the ends individuals strive for are determined by the common values of the society they live in. In relation to the radical rationalistic anarchism of Godwin or the radical anti-intellectualism of biologistic social theories, the voluntaristic theory of action is a normative theory of action.

So, Parsons' "voluntaristic theory of action" is neither voluntaristic nor about action in the ordinary sense of these words. That many of Professor Parsons' colleagues deny his work the status of "theory" needs not concern us here. But what is it then? In an attempt to throw some new light on this question we shall start from a quotation in *The Structure of Social Action* that seems to contradict the just-mentioned conclusion. "The active element of the relation of men to norms, the creative or voluntaristic side of it, is precisely what the positivistic approach tends to minimize—for it thinks in terms of the passive, adaptive, receptive attitude embodied in the ideal of an empirical scientist."[22] Parsons here expresses the very different view of the role of science in society between positivism on the one hand, and historicism on the other, to which Parsons, through Weber, is related. A crucial part of this role, in the positivist conception, is to quiet the passions of men.[23] There is, however, much more than this that Parsons wants to say here. The context is a discussion of Durkheim and of the problem that the identification of the moral and the social seems in danger of elevating social conformity into the supreme moral virtue.[24] Parsons readily admits that there is such a danger, and he is not praising conformity as such. On the other hand he is adamant on the necessity and desirability of a moral consensus in a society.[25] His answer to the criticisms of Durkheim mainly stresses two things. First of all he emphasizes that norms are not only facts of social life, they are ideals which people strive to actualize. Second, he points to the internalization of norms: "But if the social becomes a constitutive element in the individual's own concrete personality, then his relation to society must be thought of in quite different terms than in positivism. He is not placed in a social environment so much as he *participates* in a common social life."[26]

I would suggest that Parsons' answer here as well as the aim of the theory of action boils down to *stating the positive value of collective value commitment*. That is of value commitment *as such* with no or little concern for practical activity for the realization of values. This has both a theoretical and a more immediately ideological aspect. Theoretically it can account for the "problem of order" and provide more satisfactory non-Marxist social theory than the old utilitarianism and thus an acceptable solution to the "individualism-socialism dilemma" to uneasy bourgeois intellectuals of the American 1930's.[27]

Parsons is not using an explicit, concrete specimen of value commitment. The background of his commitment to value commitment is, however, fairly obvious. The extreme importance Parsons attaches to religion in tracing the development of economic and political as well as ideological phenomena is striking, and has been rightly stressed by Gouldner.[28]

Talcott Parsons is the son of a Congregational clergyman,[29] and he has himself pointed to the importance of this religious background and to the great impact upon him of Weber's *The Protestant Ethic and the Spirit of Capitalism.*[30] This background is essential to Parsons' critique of the limitations of liberal conceptions of "economic rationality" and "rational self-interest." And that critique is the theoretical aspect of the "voluntaristic theory of action." Parsons says: "In a variety of ways, problems of religion have been prominent for me almost from the beginning. . . . This concern with religion—in the role not of a *dis-* but more of an *un*believer, in the terminology of a recent Vatican conference—has been a major orientation point in my intellectual career. It was already a major aspect of my early rejection of 'positivism' but at the same time has been a focus of a continuing attempt to understand the balance of the roles of rational and nonrational components in human action. Clearly, however, such a focus of intellectual concern leads one beyond the more purely cognitive problems of religion into those of moral commitment, affective engagement, and practical action."[31]

The voluntaristic theory of action can be said to be a religiously inspired affirmation of the necessity and desirability of collective value commitment. Not even in its pre-war formulation was Parsons' theory a theory of action, will and active man.[32] A more adequate title for Parsons' great and brilliant book of the 1930's would have been *The Value of Social Values.*

THREE ASPECTS OF MARXIST PRACTICE

The concept of practice or praxis is certainly central to Marxism. This is stressed by the great leaders of the Marxist labor movement, like Lenin,[33] Gramsci,[34] and Mao Tse-tung,[35] as well as by Marxist scholars, like, e.g., Althusser,[36] Cornu,[37] and Lefebvre.[38] According to Auguste Cornu,[39] the author of the monumental biography of Marx and Engels which by its fourth volume has only reached *The German Ideology* and the years 1845–46, praxis replaces alienation as the central notion of Marx's thought, the notion from which the fundamental principles of dialectical and historical materialism are developed.

To Lefebvre,[40] praxis "is the point of departure and the point of arrival of dialectical materialism." Althusser says that the theory of practice in general is dialectical materialism.[41] The aim of this paper is not to make a thorough analysis of the concept of practice in Marxism. The intention is limited to laying bare its fundamental meaning and strategic role in Marx's work. Usually Marx's Theses on Feuerbach are regarded as the key text of the Marxist conception of practice. To be understandable, this short aphorismal fragment, never intended for publication—it was published posthumously by Engels more than forty years later—must however, be located in a wider context.[42]

What is this context? It is a process of rupture with speculative German philosophy, the "German Ideology," and a process of transition from left-wing liberalism and democratic radicalism to communism and proletarian revolution. Let us remind ourselves of some basic data. The Theses on Feuerbach were written in spring 1845. A year before Engels had written and published a critique of bourgeois economics, *Umrisse zu einer Kritik der Nationalökonomie,* after which Marx and Engels entered into correspondence. In June, 1844 occurred the rebellion of the Silesian weavers, the first proletarian uprising in Germany. Marx emphasizes the enormous significance of this event and contrasts both the theoretically advanced character of the proletariat and its audacity with the backwardness and the timidity of the bourgeoisie. On these points Marx breaks with Arnold Ruge, the radical with whom Marx had edited the *Deutsch-Französiche Jahrbücher.* In the summer of 1844 Marx was working on the *Economical-Philosophical Manuscripts,* where he for the first time declares himself a communist and where he states that "my conclusions are the fruit of an entirely empirical analysis, based upon a careful critical study of political economy."[43] Engels and Marx meet in Paris in August-September 1844 and begin their Critique of the Critical Critique against Bruno Bauer and the Young Hegelians, a work published the following year under the title *The Holy Family.* In the autumn of 1844 Engels writes *The Condition of the Working Classes in England.* This is a book not only about the misery of the working classes but also about their resistance, their movement, their struggle. Engels predicts: "The revolution *must* come, it is already too late to bring a peaceful solution to the question..."[44] In September 1845 Marx and Engels start working on a full-scale critique of *The German Ideology.*

Compared to England and France, Germany in the 1840's was an underdeveloped country, economically and politically. Philosophically, on the other hand, Germany, the country of the great philosophical systems of Kant and Hegel, was rather overdeveloped. What in Germany corresponded to the real—politically and economically acting—liberalism and socialism of England and France, was philosophizing about liberalism and socialism. That was what characterized The German Ideology, according to Marx and Engels.[45]

Here we have the context, where the Marxian notion of practice emerges. It refers to the real social life of human beings in contrast to the categories of consciousness, Idea, critique etc., of German idealistic philosophy. Praxis or practice is the opposite of Theory as pure thought, as abstract speculation. In a fragment on Feuerbach (other than the Theses) Marx speaks of "from thinking distinguished sensual *action, praxis,* and *real activity.*"[46] In this opposition the word praxis is used throughout *The Holy Family* and *The German Ideology.*[47] *Praxis is for Marx and Engels a concept for the break with all philosophical speculation.* This is very important, because it shows the chasm between Marx, Engels and the Marxist tradition of Lenin, Gramsci, Mao etc. on one hand, and on the other hand the *Marxisant* philosophers, like Sartre[48] and not to speak of various Eastern Europeans like Kosik[49] and the Yugoslav writers around the journal *Praxis.* What the latter have done is to build a philosophical speculation about praxis! In that project the esoteric connotation of the Greek word Praxis—as different from the more everyday 'practice'—has an obvious function. With the prosaic Marxist orientation of this paper the words 'praxis' and 'practice' are here used simply as synonyms.

But the Marxian meaning of praxis must be specified. "The standpoint of life, of practice, should be first and fundamental in a theory of knowledge,"[50] says Lenin, basing himself on Marx and

Engels. The standpoint of practice does not mean a pragmatic, empiricist conception of knowledge. What Marx and Engels broke with was not theoretical activity—they devoted most of their remaining life to it—but metaphysical speculation. And Lenin emphasized: "Without a revolutionary theory, there can be no revolutionary movement." Therefore, Althusser can speak of theoretical practice in a clearly determined sense,[51] and Mao can list scientific experiment as one kind of social practice.[52] What Marx and Engels pointed to in the middle of the 1840's was *a different object of theoretical practice*—and therefore a different kind of theory—than that of the German ideologists to *the historical, social practice of men.*

Before Marx, Ludwig Feuerbach, the leading radical German philosopher of the early 1840's, had developed the view that religion and philosophy were abstract expressions of the real human situation and that they constituted modes of existence of human alienation. But what characterized this real human situation? What was the practical as opposed to the abstractly philosophical? In the Economic-Philosophical Manuscripts, Marx had dealt with the alienation of labor. This was, however, still a kind of philosophical economics in a synthesized Hegelian-Feuerbachian framework. *The Holy Family* contains no critique of Feuerbach, who is there, on the contrary, regarded as having achieved theoretically what the English and French communists have achieved in practice, the *Darstellung* of the with humanism coinciding materialism, Marx-Engels.[53] It is only in the *Theses on Feuerbach* and in *The German Ideology* that Marx and Engels break with the most advanced of the German philosophers.

In the "falsely transparent"[54] Theses Marx contrasts Feuerbach's contemplative view of the sensual world with a conception of this world as praxis. What this means becomes fully clear in *The German Ideology,* where the authors say of Feuerbach: "He does not see how the sensual world around him is not an immediate given from eternity and always the same thing, but the product of industry and the state of society, and this in the sense, that it is a historical product. . . ."[55] To the founders of historical materialism *"human sensual activity, praxis," is above all changing modes of production.* Feuerbach, on the other hand, "knows no other 'human relationships' 'of man to man' than love and friendship, and only in an idealized way at that."[56]

There is a third specification of praxis, which it is absolutely necessary to make, to grasp its role in Marxist theory. We have to clarify the meaning of the third Thesis on Feuerbach: "The materialist doctrine concerning the changing of circumstances and education, forgets that circumstances are changed by men and that the educator must himself be educated. The doctrine has therefore to divide society into two parts, one of which is superior to society. The coincidence of the changing of circumstances and of human activity can only be grasped and rationally understood as revolutionary *praxis*.[57] The conception of revolutionary praxis is not to be understood in any philosophizing way. In his later publication of Marx's theses Engels inserted after the second sentence: "(E.g. with Robert Owen)."[58] And who was Robert Owen, to whom the thesis refers? He was one of those spoken of in the Communist Manifesto as critical-utopian socialists. In the Communist Manifesto it is said of Owen, Fourier, and the other utopians, among other things, that they saw no historical self-activity of the proletariat. Praxis here has a concrete political meaning. What is elliptically alluded to in the third Thesis on Feuerbach is somewhat elaborated in the German Ideology, where it is stated that: "for the creation on a mass scale of this communist consciousness, as well as for the success of the cause itself, it is necessary for men themselves to be changed on a large scale, and this change can only occur in a practical movement, in a *revolution;* that revolution is thus necessary not only because the ruling class cannot be overthrown in any other way, but also because only in a revolution can the *overthrowing* class rid itself of the accumulated rubbish of the past and become capable of reconstructing society."[59]

Revolutionary praxis is the revolutionary class struggle of the proletariat in distinction to the moral exhortations and colonizing examples of the utopian theoreticians.

The three aspects of practice—human sensual activity in general, material production, class struggle—are organically related in Marxist thought. This is clearly brought out in the German Ideology: "This [Marx-Engels'] conception of history, therefore, rests on the exposition of the real process of production, starting out from the simple material production of life, and on the comprehension of the form of intercourse connected with and created by this mode of production, i.e., of civil society in its various stages as the basis of all history . . . it does not explain practice from the idea but explains the formation of ideas from material practice, and accordingly comes to the conclusion that all the forms and products of consciousness can be dissolved, not by intellectual criticism, not by resolution into 'self-consciousness' . . . etc., but only by the practical overthrow of the actual social relations which gave rise to this idealist humbug; that not criticism but revolution is the driving force of history, as well as of religion, philosophy, and all other types of theory."[60]

ECONOMICS, PHILOSOPHY AND PRACTICE

Marx's concept of practice is developed in the works of the break with German philosophical speculation. In his later economic works it does not figure very prominently. We find here, however, an interesting use of it. Marx sometimes refers to practice or activity in discussions of the theory of value, relating it to the labor theory of value in contrast to subjectivist (or potentially subjectivist) theories. Thus about Adam Smith:

> Smith looks at labor psychologically, in relation to the fun or unhappiness, that it serves to the individual. But besides this *sentimental* [gemütlich] relationship to his activity it is also something else—firstly for others, as just the sacrifice of A would be of no utility to B; secondly; a certain behavior by himself to the thing, which he works and to his own powers for work. It is *positive, creative activity.* To the worker one hour of work may always be an equally big sacrifice. The value of the commodities, however, does not depend on his feelings; not the value of his hour of work either.[61]

The German economist Adolph Wagner had written: "It is a natural drive of man to bring the relation in which internal and external goods stand vis-à-vis his needs to a distinct consciousness and understanding. This is achieved by the estimation (evaluation) in which value is attributed to the goods, or respectively, the things of the external world, and this value itself is measured."[62]
Marx commented that among other things:

> But for a professorial schoolmaster, the relations of men to nature are not initially *practical,* i.e., relations established by deeds, but *theoretical.* But in no sense do men begin by "standing in this theoretical relation to the things of the ex-

ternal world." They begin, like every animal, by *eating,
drinking*, etc., not by "standing" in a relation, but by *actively
responding*, by mastering certain things of the external world
by deeds, and thus satisfying their needs (i.e., they begin
with production).[63]

Marx's view of work as human activity and not as sacrifice has
also certain effects on his view of the future socialist and communist society, which is characterized more by free activity than
by, say, affluent consumption, free communication or love.[64]
"What we want to do here, however," Marx says, "is not to go into
his [Smith's] view of labor, his philosophical one, but the economic moment."[65]

Even if it is not basically a philosophical category, the Marxist
concept of practice also occupies a central role in the philosophy
of Marxism, in dialectical materialism. Starting from Marx's
analysis of productive activity and the labor process, Althusser
has given us a definition of practice in general, a listing of the
basic social practices, and an extremely fruitful application of the
concept of (theoretical) practice to problems of epistemology.
Althusser's definition of practice is the following: "By *practice* in
general we understand every process of *transformation* of a determined given raw material into a determined product, a transformation effectuated by a determined human labor, utilizing
determined means (of 'production'). In every practice conceived
in this way the *determinant* moment (or element) of the process is
neither the raw material nor the product, but the practice in the
narrow sense: the moment of *transformation* work itself, which
puts into action /met en oeuvre/, in a specific structure, men,
means, and a technical method of utilizing the means."[66]

Next, we will compare this structure of social practice with
Parsons' structure of social action. But the crucial role of the
concept of practice in dialectical materialism primarily lies
elsewhere.

We have already seen that, referring to the revolutionary class
struggle, the view of praxis is what separated the old mechanical
materialism from the new dialectical materialism of Marx and
Engels. In Lenin's *Materialism and Empirio-Criticism* the "criterion
of practice" is used against the idealist philosophizing of Ernst
Mach and some other physicists around the turn of the century.
Lenin here also underlines that the struggle of parties in
philosophy, in which Lenin intervenes, "in the last analysis
reflects the tendencies and ideology of the antagonistic classes in
modern society."[67]

In Mao Tse-tung's *On Practice,* practice is given decisive importance. Its primary area of intervention is, however, different from that of Lenin's work. As the official Chinese committee for the publication of Mao's work points out, "*On Practice* was written in 1937 to expose within the party the dogmatic kind of subjectivism which belittles practice."

In these two works we find how the concept of practice is used both to represent politics, the class struggle in the domain of scientific theory and to represent scientificity in politics. Lenin attacks the conclusion of some physicists that with the new development of physics "matter has disappeared," that the notion of objective reality is meaningless etc. Against various ideological deviations Mao points to the scientificity of Marxism-Leninism: "Idealism and mechanical materialism, opportunism and adventurism, are all characterized by the breach between the subjective and the objective, by the separation of knowledge from practice. The Marxist-Leninist theory of knowledge, characterized as it is by a scientific social practice, cannot but resolutely oppose these wrong ideologies."[68] This double intervention in science and politics, representing the one in the other, is what according to Althusser[69]—revising his earlier conception[70]—constitutes the new Marxist practice of philosophy. Here the concept of practice becomes crucial.

SOCIAL PRACTICE AND SOCIAL ACTION

The threads can now be pulled together, and we can confront the first question of this paper: How do the sociological concept of action and the Marxist concept of practice relate to each other? If we compare Parsons' work on *The Structure of Social Action* with the Marxian works of rupture from 1845, at least two differences between the conceptions of action and practice are striking. It is true that Parsons as an American sociologist did not, as Marx had to, have to assert the necessity of empirical social science against philosophical speculation. But a reader of Parsons might have expected that a work written and published in the crisis of the 1930's and presented as being about social action would have had something to say about the empirical world of unemployment, misery, resistance, reform and revolution. Parsons has, however, nothing to say. Marx would certainly have regarded this as the opposite of a practical orientation.[71]

As Parsons himself has pointed out, *The Structure of Social Ac-*

tion was begun as a study of interpretations of capitalism.[72] One of the things Parsons was concerned with was the "in-dividualism–socialism dilemma" and with finding a path out.[73] Parsons was obviously of the opinion that he found one in the voluntaristic theory of action, which he dug out of the work of the European classics. "From Durkheim's point of view, as from that of Pareto and Weber, socialism and laissez-faire individualism are of the same piece—they both leave out of account certain basic social factors with which all three are concerned."[74] What is important about this, here, is that this finding is not related to any kind of social force and political programme.[75] It is a com-pletely contemplative position. In this respect, too, the theory of action is the opposite of a theory of praxis.

It might be added as a third obvious difference between Marx and Parsons that to the latter, economic action has not the fun-damental, determining role as economic practice has to the founder of historical materialism. This is of course true, but in this particular comparative context it is not as important as another aspect (and as the two above). The fact is that to Parsons, as well as to Weber and the later Homans, economic action is of central interest. Weber and Parsons have been interested in the understanding of capitalism. All three have given economic ac-tion in the sense of economic theory a strategic place in their theories and have started their theories of action to a great extent from the economic theory of action. So, the problem in this con-text is not so much economic versus non-economic as the mean-ing of 'economic' in economic action and economic practice.

Weber says: "If anything, the most essential aspect of economic action for practical purposes is the prudent choice be-tween alternative ends."[76] On the page before, Weber stated: "Economic action involves a conscious, primary orientation to economic consideration. It must be conscious, for what matters is not the objective necessity of making economic provision, but the belief that it is necessary." In a footnote Weber adds, in order to avoid all misunderstanding: "Robert Liefmann has rightly laid emphasis on the subjective character of the concept; that is, the fact that it is the subjectively understandable orientation of ac-tion which makes it economic action."

Parsons in his *The Structure of Social Action* points out that "'production' in the economic, as distinct from the technological, sense consists in the allocation of means to the satisfaction of wants."[77] Economic theory is concerned with this allocating ac-tion.[78]

Later, Parsons comes to regard economic exchange and the supply–demand schema as a special case of the performance-sanction schema of the general theory of social action and social systems, which is now analyzed in terms of exchange.[79]

Finally Homans, talking about elementary economics, from which, together with behavioral psychology, he has taken his mode of social exchange: "As for elementary economics, it is a set of propositions describing the behavior of men exchanging material goods for money in a so-called perfect market."[80]

Common to Weber, Parsons and Homans, in distinction to Marx, is that they consider as economic action not the productive activity, the work process—which is left aside as technology or merely "physical behavior"—but primarily the choices people make, the *attitudes* they take to various means and ends. Not the *production* of goods but the *exchange* of them is action of interest to the action theorists. Now we can see the difference between the structure of social action and the structure of social practice.

After having defined the theory of action (see above) Parsons-Shils spelled out the meaning of the definition: "There are four points to be noted in this conceptualization of behavior: (1) Behavior *is oriented* to the attainment of ends or goals or other anticipated states of affairs. (2) It *takes place* in situations. (3) It *is normatively regulated.* (4) It *involves* expenditure of energy or effort or motivation."[81] The peculiar sense of action in this scheme is well expressed by the authors' use of verbs to describe it: action is oriented, it takes place, it is regulated, it involves something. But nothing is being done. In a later formulation by Parsons this is even more blatant: "The unit act involves the *relationship of an actor to a situation composed of objects,* and is conceived as a choice (imputed by the theorist to the actor) among alternative ways of defining the situation."[82]

The structure of social practice—as clarified by Althusser—on the other hand, is characterized by: (1) a beginning, a given raw material, (2) a process of transformation affected by a certain type of work using certain means, (3) a result, a product.[83] Practice is not just "oriented" to something, it makes it. Therefore the theory of social practice is not primarily concerned with the subjective orientation of the actor but with the objective process of transformation. Economic practice is to Marxism not "the prudent choice between alternative ends" but a process of material transformation structured by determined forces and relations of production.

From what we have seen of Marx's opinion of Adam Smith and

Adolph Wagner, it is clear that the theory of action represents a non-practical view of social phenomena, that *as a theory the theory of an action is the opposite of a theory of practice.* From Marx's economic theory we also know that according tó Marx the processes of exchange are determined by the mode of production (in the strict sense of this word).[84] Marxists today take a similar position vis-à-vis the theories of social system and exchange.

Marx is not unaware of the "action" aspect of human behavior. In *Capital* we can read: "But what distinguishes the worst architect from the best of bees is this, that the architect raises his structure in imagination before he erects it in reality. At the end of every labor-process, we get a result that already existed in the imagination of the laborer at its commencement. He not only effects a change of form in the material on which he works, but he also realises a purpose of his own that constitutes the law of his modus operandi and to which he must subordinate his will."[85]

The point is that this awareness is in Marx's theory not developed into a subjective means-ends schema. When a few lines later he gives an enumeration of the "elementary moments of the labor process" he lists "the purposive activity or work itself, its object, and its means," but not any end in anticipation. The quotation above hints at the reason: the purpose of economic activity is nothing subjective, it is something which determines the mode of activity, and to which the individual has to subordinate his will. In the Marxist theory this objective purpose is not regarded as derived from a normative order but as manifested in objective forces and relations of production. It is the latter and not the actor's orientations to a normative order that Marxist theory puts into focus.

THE IMAGE OF MAN

A second question asked in the beginning of this paper was whether the contemporary sociological discussion of assumptions of man, as a creative subject or a passive object, had any bearing upon the theories of action and practice. After the analysis of the latter the answer will be obvious: No. When Parsons was drawing the dividing lines between his own "voluntaristic" theory of action and other, the active subject was of no use. Neither the utilitarianism of Hobbes, Locke, Bentham and the classical economists, nor the biologistic theory of Social Darwinism nor Godwinian anarchism thought of man as a passive object—nor did Parsons himself at that time.

But what about Marx then, flying the banner of praxis against the contemplative object view of "all previous materialism"? As a matter of fact, the earlier materialism was not a fatalistic environmentalism. It was a rebellious, or a least reformist creed. It was an ideology of the rising revolutionary bourgeoisie and after the French revolution an ideology turned against bourgeoisie society. The French materialism of the 18th century, Marx-Engels point out, was "a struggle against the prevailing political institutions" and it issued "directly into socialism."[86] The problem with the old pre-Marxist materialism was not that it saw man as a passive object, but that it saw a few men—legislators, teachers, writers or social ideals—as very active subjects and many men—the masses—as very passive. It was against this view that Marx wrote the third Thesis on Feuerbach.

From what has been said we can also conclude that Gouldner's arguing that "there was a convergence between his [Parsons'] voluntarism and that of at least the young [pre-1847] Marx, for both agree that man is and should be a goal-oriented striving creature whose history reflects his own efforts" is a completely misleading play with words.[87]

Parsons' view of the convergent voluntaristic theory of action and the development of Marx's thought can, contrary to what Gouldner pretends, neither be correctly analyzed as movements along a voluntarism–determinism axis nor can they be put on the same level at all.

To the extent that the above analysis of the theories of social action and social practice is correct it shows the danger of loose talk about normative assumptions of the nature of man and society in social theories. What makes these theories interesting and worth studying and discussing is that they are *more* than general assumptions, of man etc. If the analysis is focused on the latter there is a strong tendency to cheap, obscuring, and misleading analogies.

Of course, the study of the ideological background or context of science and of the ideological content of social theories can be a serious analysis and as such a very important contribution. Since Gouldner has been used as a negative example above, his showing of the roots of Erving Goffman's dramaturgical model of social life—in the "new middle class" of the service sector where "there is a keen sense of the irrationality of the relationship between individual achievement and the magnitude of reward" can be cited as an illuminating, though sketchy, example.[88]

The man-as-creative-subject-versus-man-as-passive-object discussion, however, does not seem to have contributed very much to rigorous scientific analysis, rather the contrary. On the other hand it has undeniably preoccupied sociologists very much. I would like to end this paper submitting a hypothesis of the reason for the phenomenon.

THE MAGICAL FUNCTION OF NORMATIVE SOCIOLOGY

We can start from a sentence of Buckley: "Much of current theoretical dialogue centers here: functional, consensus and equilibrium theories emphasize the structural constraints and minimize the play of the range of alternatives that are continually shifting the limits of those constraints, whereas their critics emphasize (and perhaps sometimes overemphasize) the openness and the fluidity."[89] It will not be controversial that, generally speaking, in this debate the functional, consensus, and equilibrium theorists are regarded as conservative by their critics, who view themselves as liberal, radical, committed to social change, etc.

Upon a moment's reflection the role-cast seems rather paradoxical. Would it not be at least as natural, and, perhaps, even rather more natural, that those committed to social change stressed the static, constraining character of the present society—that is, in this case the United States—and its strongly dominant value system. Then the need to change that coercive structure would seem obvious to those desirous of fluidity, free activity and a plurality of value systems. The criticism of the conservative functionalists would then have been more in terms of their grossly exaggerating the range of alternatives, the openness, the opportunities for creativity and so forth in the prevailing society.[90]

The reason why the overwhelming part of mainstream sociological criticism has taken the path it has is probably due to a great extent to *magical function of a great deal of liberal and radical sociology*. More blatantly, more honestly and frankly than most, this function is suggested by Joachim Israel[91] in a discussion of models of man. After questioning the scientific fruitfulness of a mechanical model, Israel goes on: "Finally one may ask: 'Do I wish man to behave as a mechanism?' Such a question implies questioning the ethical relevance of such a hypothesis (which is just another way of saying that values may partly be responsible for the selection of initial stipulations)." (Emphasis omitted.) In consonance with his view of how social scientific theories "bring about social facts which they study"—by wishful thinking—Israel suggests that economic theory, by considering water and air as utilities free of cost, has given rise to the behavior of capitalists in polluting air and water (as well as it has taken account of a fact of capitalism and has legitimized it).[92] A similar view has been put forward, a little more circumspectly, by Seeley (1963) in his "science-as-legislation theorem."[93]

Friedrichs has distinguished between a priestly (positivistic and value-free) and a prophetic mode among sociologists.[94] There is also a *magical* one. By uttering spells—like: man is a creative subject, society contains a wide range of values and other alternatives, social systems pull themselves up by their own bootstraps and change, and such like—the sociologist *makes* man active, society open and changing. In this perspective the sociologists with mechanistic, passivistic and other bad models are the black magicians, uttering evil spells on man and society.

As Malinowski long ago found among the Trobrianders and pointed out, magic on the one hand and technology and science (in the sense of "simple truth, drawn from observation of nature" at least) on the other are not incompatible.[95] They go along with each other, intertwined. This is also the case of the present-day sociological magicians, who are—the best of them—as busy with their sociological technology as the Trobrianders with their gardening, canoe-building and fishing activities. In the most reliable of their pursuits—as fishing by poison, "industrial" manufacturing—the Trobrianders used no magic. They did so only and increasingly in the risky and uncertain ones.[96] There is a parallel among the sociologists also in this respect. Magic has its place in works on general theory, metasociology, sociology of sociology and such like, but not in everyday empirical investigations. We should also remember what Malinowski said about the essence of magic: "it is essentially the assertion of man's intrinsic power over nature."[97] But in an imaginary way—and that is the point also with contemporary activistic sociology.

The theory of magic, I would suggest, throws some light on how a good deal of current sociological conceptions function. But a functional explanation is insufficient. We are also interested in why the sociology in question functions the way it does. Here one further hypothesis will be put forward.

The debate in later years about the sociologists' conception of man is very similar to the discussion of the 1950's triggered off by books like Riesman et al. *The Lonely Crowd* and Whyte's *The Organization Man.* The issue at that time was the over-socialized organization men, who, in the era of what Marxists call monopoly capitalism, were replacing the inner-directed individualists of competitive capitalism.

The hypothesis I would venture is that the active sociology is reflecting a malaise among parts of the new middle strata—those parts more directly tied to the classical bourgeoisie and its culture. e.g., the academic humanities—with the transition from competitive to monopoly capitalism. This malaise tends to take magical expressions because from a non-Marxist and non-socialist perspective there is no viable social force leading forward and capable of realizing social change, and the way back to competitive capitalism is closed. "Hence," with the words of Malinowski, magic, as the type of activity which satisfies this need of standardized optimism, is essential to the efficiency of human [read: left-wing liberal] behavior."[98]

NOTES

1. For recent succinct formulations of Parsons' theory of action, see T. Parsons, *Societies* (Englewood Cliffs, N.J.: Prentice-Hall, 1966), Chap. 2; *Sociological Theory and Modern Society* (New York: 1967), Chap. 7; "Some Problems of General Theory in Sociology," in *Theoretical Society*, ed. J. McKinney and E. Tiryakian (New York: 1970).
2. T. Parsons, *The Social System* (Glencoe, N.Y.: The Free Press, 1951); *Societies; Sociological Theory and Modern Society; The Structure of Social Action* (New York: 1968); "Some Problems of General Theory in Sociology."
3. T. Parsons, R. Bales, and E. Shils, *Working Papers in the Theory of Action* (Glencoe, N.Y.: The Free Press, 1953); T. Parsons and E. Shils, eds., *Toward a General Theory of Action* (New York: 1962).
4. G. Homans, "Bringing Men Back In," *American Sociological Review*, vol. 29 (December 1964).
5. K. Marx, *Thesen über Feuerbach*, in *K. Marx und F. Engels Werke*, vol. 3 (Berlin: 1962).
6. Parsons, *The Structure of Social Action;* see further the account of the early Parsons by J. F. Scott, "The Changing Foundations of the Parsonian Action Scheme," *ASR* (October 1963).
7. J. Israel, "Is a Non-Normative Science Possible?" *Acta Sociologica*, vol. 29 (December 1972): 79.
8. D. Wrong, "The Oversocialized Conception of Man in Modern Sociology," *ASR*, vol. 26 (April 1961); A. Gouldner, *The Coming Crisis of Western Sociology* (London: 1971); W. Buckley, *Sociology and Modern Systems Theory* (Englewood Cliffs, N.J.: Prentice-Hall, 1967); A. Etzioni, *The Active Society* (New York: 1968).

9. Gouldner, *The Coming Crisis of Western Sociology*, pp. 31 ff., 51 ff.
10. Israel, "Is a Non-Normative Science Possible?" p. 70.
11. Parsons and Shils, *Toward a General Theory of Action*, p. 53.
12. Important steps in the elaboration of the theory of action are Parsons, *The Structure of Social Action;* Parson and Shils, *Toward a General Theory of Action;* Parsons, Bales, and Shils, *Working Papers in the Theory of Action;* T. Parsons and N. Smelser, *Economy and Society* (London: 1956); and Parsons, *Sociological Theory and Modern Society.* Some relatively recent analysis of it are, among others, M. Black, (ed.), *The Social Theories of Talcott Parsons* (Englewood Cliffs, N.J.: Prentice-Hall, 1961); Scott, "The Changing Foundations of the Parsonian Action Scheme"; W. Mitchell, *Sociological Analysis and Politics* (Englewood Cliffs, N.J.: Prentice-Hall, 1967); and Gouldner, *The Coming Crisis of Western Sociology.*
13. Parsons, *The Structure of Social Action*, pp. 77 ff.
14. This is indicated by the collaboration with the rather behaviorist psychologist Edward Tolman in Parsons and Shils, *Toward a General Theory of Action.* This theme is developed by Scott, "The Changing Foundations of the Parsonian Action Scheme."
15. See, for example, T. Parsons, *"The Point of View of the Author,"* in Max Black, *The Social Theories of Talcott Parsons.*
16. M. Weber, *The Theory of Economic and Social Organization* (New York: 1964), p. 88.
17. Parsons, "The Point of View of the Author," pp. 326 f., emphasis added.
18. Ibid.
19. Parsons, *The Structure of Social Action*, p. 76.
20. Ibid., pp. 77 ff.
21. Ibid., Chaps. 2 and 3.
22. Ibid., pp. 396 f.
23. I have elaborated this somewhat in a paper presented at the VII Nordic Sociology Congress. "Vetenskap och ideologi i marxism och olika sociologier," mimeo, 1972.
24. Parsons, *The Structure of Social Action*, p. 390.
25. Ibid., pp. 395 f.
26. Ibid., p. 399.
27. Parsons himself has explicitly stated this "individualism-socialism dilemma," ibid., p. vi. See further below note 73.
28. Gouldner, *The Coming Crisis of Western Sociology*, pp. 255 ff.
29. Black, *The Social Theories of Talcott Parsons*, p. 4.
30. Parsons, "Some Problems of General Theory in Sociology," p. 837.
31. Ibid., pp. 872 f.
32. A contrary view is held by Buckley, *Sociology and Modern Systems Theory*, p. 106; Gouldner, *The Coming Crisis of Western Sociology;* and Scott, "The Changing Foundations of the Parsonian Action Scheme." The central role of common values and the extremely limited role for voluntarism in Parsons' postwar schemes is generally agreed upon. But for some writers, for example, Buckley, this means that Parsons' earlier voluntarism is being "reopened" in his elaborations of exchange models from the late fifties on.
33. V. I. Lenin, *Materialism and Empirio-Criticism* (Moscow: 1947).
34. A Gramsci, *Id materialismo storico: Quaderni del Carcere I* (Torino: 1964). When Gransci, in order to evade his not too intelligent jail censors, had to use a code name for Marxism in his notebook, he chose to call it "filosofia della prassi," the philosophy of practice, p. XXIII.
35. Mao Tse-tung, *On Practice* (Peking: 1965).
36. L. Althusser, *Pour Marx* (Paris: 1965).
37. A Cornu, *Karl Marx et Friedrich Engels*, vols. 3 and 4 (Paris: 1962).
38. H. Lefebvre, *Le materialisme dialectique* (Paris: 1962).
39. Cornu, *Karl Marx et Friedrich Engels*, pp. 25–29.

40. Lefebvre, *Le materialisme dialectique*, p. 95.

41. Althusser, *Pour Marx*, p. 169.

42. This context can be grasped by Marx's and Engels' works of the period and by excellent biographies, such as Cornu, *Karl Marx et Friedrich Engels;* and M. Lowy, *La théorie de la révolution chez le jeune Marx* (Paris: 1970).

43. K. Marx, *Economic & Philosophical Manuscripts*. (New York: International Publishers, 1961), p. 91.

44. F. Engels, *Die Lage der arbeitenden Klassen in England*, in Marx and Engels, *Werke*, vol. 2 (Berlin: 1962), p. 505.

45. See especially K. Marx and F. Engels, *The German Ideology*(New York: International Publishers, 1960), pp. 192 ff., 481 ff.

46. Published as appendix in Marx and Engels, *Werke*, vol. 3, p. 536.

47. Some examples are K. Marx and F. Engels, *Die heilige Familie*, MEW 2 (Berlin: 1962), pp. 12, 41, 56, 116, 132, 150, 161 f., 204; *Die deutsche Ideologie*, MEW 3 (Berlin: 1962), 31, 34, 38, 39, 178, 226, 528.

48. J.-P. Sartre, *Critique de la raison dialectique* (Paris: 1960).

49. K. Kosik, *Die Dialektik des Konkreten* (Frankfurt: 1967).

50. Lenin, *Materialism and Empirio-Criticism*, p. 142.

51. Althusser, *Pour Marx*.

52. Mao, *On Practice*.

53. Marx and Engels, *Die heilige Familie*, p. 132. Engels in a correspondence to the English paper *The New Moral World*, written February 2, 1845, Marx and Engels, *Werke*, vol. 2, p. 515.

54. Althusser, "The Theses on Feuerbach," in *Pour Marx*, p. 188.

55. Marx and Engels, *Die deutsche Ideologie*, p. 43.

56. Ibid., p. 44.

57. Ibid., pp. 5 f. When he published the Theses, Engels changed "revolutionäre" (revolutionary) into "umwälzende" (upheaving) Praxis. Cf. Lowy, *La theorie de la révolution chez le jeune Marx*, p. 122. Both versions are given in Marx and Engels, *Werke*, vol. 3.

58. Marx and Engels, *Die deutsche Ideologie*, p. 534.

59. Ibid., p. 70. In *The Holy Family* these utopian socialists are not only not attacked, but they are presented as those who made an incisive critique of the "*real* basis of contemporary society" and as those whose critique at the same time "practically corresponded to the movement of the *big mass*"—Marx and Engels, *Die heilige Familie*. There is no break with "all previous materialism" in *The Holy Family* where, on the contrary, the continuity between communism and 18th century French materialism is underlined. Directly opposite to the point of view of the Theses, the authors of *The Holy Family* held, unproblematically, that: "If out of the sensual world and the experience of the sensual world Man forms all cognition, perception, etc., then it leads up to [so kommt es darauf an] arranging the empirical world in such a way that he explains the really human in it, accommodates himself, that he experiences himself as Man—ibid., p. 138).

Together with what we found of the treatment of praxis as production in *The Holy Family*—the absence of a distinction from Feuerbach in this respect too—this shows important changes in the Marx's views from *The Holy Family* to the *Theses on Feuerbach*. The changes that have been relevant here pertain to the conception of praxis, virtually universally regarded as central to Marxist thought. Althusser has argued that there is a rupture in Marx's work of 1845, drawing the line between *The Holy Family*—as belonging to the youthful works—and the *Theses*, as constituting together with *The German Ideology* the works of rupture or break—*Pour Marx*, pp. 27 ff. Later Althusser has qualified his thesis of a definite rupture in 1845 by stating that "something really decisive does begin in 1845"—*Lenin and Philosophy and other Essays* (London: , 1971), p. 90. What we have found here strongly supports Althusser's basic view of the discontinuity in Marx.

60. Marx and Engels, *Die deutsche Ideologie*, pp. 37.f.

61. K. Marx, *Grundrisse der Kritik der politischen Ökonomie* (Berlin: 1959), pp. 509 f.

62. K. Marx, *Randglossen zu A. Wagners "Lehrbuch der politischen Ökonomie,"* *MEW* 19 (Berlin: , 1962), p. 362, emphasis omitted. English translation available in K. Marx, "Marginal Notes on Adolph Wagner's Lehrbuch der politischen Okonomie," *Theoretical Practice*, no. 5 (London: 1972), p. 45.

63. Marx, *Randglossen zu A. Wagners "Lehrbuch der politischen Ökonomie,"* pp. 362 f.; "Marginal Notes on Adolph Wagner's Lehrbuch der politischen Ökonomie," p. 46. This passage of the *Marginal Notes on Adolph Wagner* is not included in the Swedish edition of *Capital*, K. Marx, *Kapitalet I* (Staffanstorp: , 1969).

64. See, for example, K. Marx, *Selected Writings in Sociology and Social Philosophy*, ed., T. B. Bottomore and M. Rubel (London: , 1961), p. 243 ff.

65. Marx, *Grundrisse der Kritik der politischen Ökonomie*, p. 505.

66. Althusser, *Pour Marx*, p. 167.

67. Lenin, *Materialism and Empirio-Criticism*, p. 371.

68. Mao, *On Practice*, pp. 24 f.

69. Althusser, *Lenin and Philosophy and Other Essays*, pp. 64 f.

70. Althusser, *Pour Marx*.

71. See, for example, the first part of Marx and Engels, *Die Deutsche Ideologie*, pp. 13-77.

72. Parsons, *The Structure of Social Action*, p. xxii.

73. In the face of what Parsons himself many times has said and written, Rhoads's (1972) conservative defense of Parsons against Gouldner provides a fascinating case of either outright bluffing or ideological blindness—or both—J. Rhoads, "On Gouldner's Crisis of Western Sociology," *AJS*, vol. 78 (July 1972): 136-154. Parsons has said about his *The Structure of Social Action:* "It is important to the story of the book that it dealt empirically with some of the broadest questions of the nature of modern industrial society—notably the nature of capitalism. On the theoretical side, the book concentrated on the problem of the boundaries and limitations of economic theory. It did so in terms which did not follow the established lines of either the theory of 'economic individualism' or its socialist opponents, even the British democratic socialists to say nothing of the Marxists. Those orientations were probably of considerable importance in getting early attention for the book, since many intellectuals felt caught within the individualism-socialism dilemma, and economics seemed at the time to be the most important theoretical social science." Parsons, *The Structure of Social Action*, p. vi. One of the results of Parsons' investigation was that Durkheim, Weber, and Pareto had found that "socialist economics failed to meet the issues raised by the theory of laissez-faire individualism"—ibid., p. 341. As against all this, Rhoads (1972, 146) flatly asserts: "There is little evidence that the voluntaristic and systems theories [of Parsons] were developed as an anti-Marxist, procapitalist attempt"—Rhoads, "On Gouldner's Crisis of Western Sociology," p. 146.

74. Parsons, *The Structure of Social Action*, p. 341.

75. Parsons was soon to relate the path out of the "dilemma" to the phenomenon of the professions—ibid., p. xi; *Essays in Sociological Theory* (New York: 1964), Chaps. 2-3. But this social anchorage dealt not with any of the material problems of capitalism—inequality, poverty, unemployment, the agricultural crisis etc.—but with personal motivation, with the problem of self-interest. Self-interest in the utilitarian sense was not, Parsons came to think, the motivation of professionals. With the transference of the profit orientation from individual entrepreneurs to corporations, the business world was also becoming professionalized.

76. Weber, *The Theory of Economic and Social Organization*, p. 160.

77. Parsons, *The Structure of Social Action*, p. 132.
78. Ibid., pp. 266, 765 ff.
79. Parsons and Smelser, *Economy and Society;* Parsons, *Sociological Theory and Modern Society*, Part 3.
80. Homans, "Bringing Men Back In," p. 12.
81. Parsons and Shils, *Toward a General Theory of Action*, p. 53, emphasis added.
82. Parsons, *Sociological Theory and Modern Society*, p. 193.
83. Althusser, *Pour Marx*, p. 167.
84. For a succinct formulation, see Marx, *Grundrisse der Kritik der politischen Ökonomie*, pp. 19 f.
85. K. Marx, *Das Kapital*, vol. 1 (Hamburg: 1921), p. 140: *Kapitalet*, vol. 1, p. 154.
86. Marx and Engels, *Die heilige Familie*, p. 132.
87. Gouldner, *The Coming Crisis of Western Sociology*, pp. 185 ff., 189.
88. Ibid., pp. 378 ff.
89. Buckley, *Sociological and Modern Systems Theory*, pp. 132 f.
90. This type of criticism *is* put forward by writers outside the mainstream. A good and funny example is D. L. Smith "The Sunshine Boys: Toward a Sociology of Happiness," in *The Sociology of Sociology*, ed. L. Reynolds and J. Reynolds, (New York: 1964). Smith talks of the "Sunshine Guild," comprising "the Supreme Sunbeam, Seymour Martin Lipset; the Sustaining Sunbeam, Nathan Glazer; and the Subsidiary Sunbeam, Amitai Etzioni," the latter, author of *The Active Society.* Cf. also the important overview of P. Bandyophay, "One Sociology or Many: Some Issues in Radical Sociology," *Science and Society*, vol. 35 (1971): 1–26.
91. Israel, "Is a Non-Normative Science Possible?" p. 81.
92. Ibid., pp. 77 f.
93. J. Seeley, "Social Science? Some Probative Problems," in *Sociology on Trial*, ed. M. Stein and A. Vidich (Englewood Cliffs, N.J.: Prentice-Hall, 1963), pp. 53–65.
94. R. Friedrichs, *A Sociology of Sociology* (New York: 1970).
95. B. Malinowski, *Argonauts of the Western Pacific* (London: 1932), pp. 392 ff.; *Coral Gardens and Their Magic*, vol. 1 (London: 1935); *A Scientific Theory of Culture and Other Essays* (New York: 1960), pp. 196 ff.
96. Malinowski, *Coral Gardens and Their Magic*, pp. 435 ff.
97. Malinowski, *Argonauts of the Western Pacific*, p. 401.
98. Malinowski, *A Scientific Theory of Culture and Other Essays*, p. 202.

7.
EIGHT WAYS TO ELIMINATE
THE SOCIOLOGY OF ACTION*

ALAIN TOURAINE
Translated by J. W. Freiberg

All sociology is not the sociology of action, but all sociological analysis is based on a sociology of action. The object of sociology is to explain the conduct of actors by the social relations in which they engage. A social relation is defined by a field of interventions that a society makes upon itself; interventions which normatively orient the conduct of actors. Relation and action can never be separated.

If one considers the principles of sociological analysis, yet refuses a sociology of action, that is, an analysis of the systems of relations between social actors, then one is outside of, or working against, sociology. This is equally true of those who reduce the meaning of action to the consciousness of the actor as it is of those who explain the "situation" of the actor. Sociology has everything to lose if it lets itself be conceived as multiple and

*Originally published in *Neue Hefte für Philosophie*, No. 9, 1976, 134–160. Reprinted by permission. Copyright © 1976.

without an essential unity. On the contrary, to be distinguished from subjectivism and objectivism, sociology must affirm itself to be the study of "social relations."

Within these limits, the sociology of action is naturally the center of sociological analysis. Furthermore, it can explore other territories that are the obverse of "society," that is, positive patterns of social organization where the structure, given from above, is directly manifest, and thoroughly dominates social relations. That is the only limit a sociology of action must know. Insofar as it must rid itself of the antisociological opposition between objective determinants and subjective intentions, it must recognize that the systems of relations complement and oppose one another in situations of constant flux. There is no society that should not or cannot be analyzed as a system of social relations; likewise, no society should be analyzed as a system of political and ideological order. Sociology, like society, is always tenuous, fluctuating between one extreme, movement, and the other extreme, order. Movement is the realm of cultural innovations and social conflict; order is the realm of political power and ideological categories.

We must neither separate nor confound these realms. Because a sociology of movement that ignores the constraining force of social order gives in to the illusions of a purely liberal vision, it represents society as a market, reducing it to nothing but the ideology of dominant groups.

On the other hand, a sociology of order which forgets that order itself is limited, that order is a product of conflicts and transactions, suspends the analysis of society as a nonsocial principle, which can be called despotism or rationality, or a combination of the two, which can only make us see that a political philosophy is a detriment to sociology. Moving ahead from the categories of social and cultural order, the sociologists should search for the sites of conflict where power relations decide who will dominate in social relations. The sociology of action is the movement itself of sociological analysis, going deeper than ideologies and techniques in order to find the meaning of conduct in social relations. Sociology is the inverse of ideology: ideology understands social relations from the point of view of the actor; sociology understands the actor from the point of view of social relations. Sociology must never appeal to principles, to essences; it must not evoke Man, or History or Society.

Moving on from these preliminary remarks, I want to briefly describe my notion of a *sociology of action*. I have attempted to do this in several books (e.g., *The Self-Production of Society* [Chicago: University of Chicago Press, 1976]). However, although the sociology of action only takes form when it combats the illusions of order and the, reductionism of subjectivism, it also is necessary to separate it from what threatens it, to define it by what it rejects. That is the raison d'être for the polemical reflections that follow; each of which treats a distinct way in which the study of social relations is compromised:

I. BY EVALUATING A SITUATION OR A SOCIAL CONDUCT IN THE NAME OF A PRINCIPLE THAT IS NONSOCIO-LOGICALLY DEFINED

The oldest rule of sociology is to explain the social by the social. This is sometimes difficult to follow, however, because sociology is very often—and, I dare say, always should be—motivated by indignation. The categories and order must be broken by refinding the social relations that are concealed and masked by the rules. And how can this be done, if not by sensing arbitrariness, manipulation, exploitation?

But if this indignation always initiates the analysis, it also deviates toward a Protestant moralism. That is, the fatigue of production line workers, once realized, leads to the conclusion that production line work is inhumane; one can even consider cities with high production and traffic density to be "unnatural" places for mankind. Such conclusions, which are indeed devoid of all sociological meaning, impede the original indignation. This erroneous approach is very prevalent in historical situations, where the most fundamental social conflicts, class conflicts, are little organized, especially when a new type of society is creating itself. The ruling class hides behind the concept of the "natural"evolution of things, opposing any resistance as resistance to progress rather than admitting to its own desired form of modernization. On the other hand, the social categories that favor the dominated classes only oppose the principles and values of a society; they are not yet ready to combat them.

Sociology today, at least in the industrialized countries, is subjected to opposed and interconnected pressures. In the last two decades, it has been exposed to the ideology of a new ruling class that spoke only of adaptation and change, of modernization, and of the disappearance of ideological and social confrontation. More recently, it has been attracted by utopias that have combatted this interested optimism and have protested in the name of mankind or of nature against a destructive progress.

The present task of sociology, its perennial task, is to search for the new social relations and the new social conflicts that form themselves in a profoundly transformed cultural field. One must, however, carefully avoid slipping into a nonsocially defined modernity and presenting a global critique carried out in the name of a nonsocial principle.

Sociology has just passed a long period during which it was either rejected or deformed. The time has come for it to claim its rightful place and to learn to speak *sociologically* about our society. The naive beliefs in modernization, abundance and scientific or technical progress have become impossible, in the face of social and political conflicts. The world is transforming itself, a new culture is emerging and new centers of power are arising. How, in the midst of this upheaval, when real social forces attack daily, can one believe that the present order is stable or that it can be judged from the height of grand principles?

II. BY REDUCING A SOCIAL RELATION TO AN INTERACTION

The object of sociology is to explain the social conduct of actors by the social relations within which they find themselves. These social conducts, however, cannot be explained by the consciousness of the actors because the different pictures that individual actors form of their interaction are inescapable, for example, the image of the owner and the image of the worker in a conflict involving work. It is the relation, not the actor, that must be studied. Nothing removes sociology farther from its object than to reduce it to the study of interactions because this poses the actors before their social conduct is studied. Sociology should not underestimate the study of interactions, but neither should it separate it from the field of relations. Social actors are not buyers and sellers in a simple exchange relations that is reducible to a zero-sum game. They are engaged in a relation in respect to each other, which is itself defined by a certain field. Classical sociology demonstrated that roles were associated with statuses and that these in turn were defined by a mode of organization. This leads to a general affirmation. The field of an interaction is defined by the intervention of a society on itself, and consequently, all relations take place between unequal actors; in fact, all relations, directly or indirectly, are based on one actor directing this intervention and one actor submitting to it.

All social relations are composed of relations of power. No purely horizontal social relations exist.

At the most organizational level, the roles of the worker and the foreman are defined by a system of authority that they did not produce; it is imposed on them either by the owners, by collective bargaining, or even by a collective self-management. Authority, under whatever rubric, organizes the enterprise, and the foreman is situated in relation to the worker because he represents authority.

This type of intervention, and thus of social field and social relations, is not the only type, although it defines the organizational level of social life. A second level, which gives order to the first level, is that of political institutions. Here, the actors define themselves by their influence on legitimate decisions. Again, their position has been defined by the juridical, legislative, or constitutional rules of their social regime. The inequality between the actors comes from their link with the principles and the interests on which the political "rules of the game" are founded.

Finally, at the most elevated level are the relations between classes. These relations are conflictual because here classes fight for control of an entire cultural field, for the management of the means of productions, that is, economic accumulation, a model of knowledge, and the capacity to act on itself, which I call the "cultural model."

The opposition of classes is not separable from how society acts on itself, from its "historicity." The superior class identifies itself with its historicity, which in turn is identified with the interests of the superior class. The dominated class meanwhile protests this dual identification and fights for a collective reappropriation of the means by which a society acts on itself.

There are social interactions that do not fall into these three types. But these are intersocial relations, or partners not belonging to any common ensembles, for example, the realms of the market, war, or pure state diplomacy. Moreover, these societal interactions belong to a totally different order of analysis than we are here concerned with. Social and intersocial relations mix in the domain studied by political science.

In the proper domain of sociology, social relations and social actions are inseparable concepts. The actors are not defined by their place—central or marginal, high or low—in a stratified ensemble because this supposes that society is a sort of personality, which leads us back to an idealism incompatible with scientific analysis. Biologist F. Jacob wrote recently that biology was progressively ridding itself of the idea of *"life"* in order to define itself as the study of *living beings.* In the same manner, sociology must deliver itself from the notion of *"society"* in order to study *social relations.* It is only at this moment, when one refuses to refer to God, Prince, Mankind, Progress, and all other metasocial items, that sociology is obliged to differentiate several types of social relations and actions. Intersocial relations consider only interactions and "realist" strategies, that is, a conjuncture is given in the interest of the actor, without whom legitimacy, institutions, norms, and values had already been created. Inversely, historicity produces its own "meaning" and this orients its social conduct. The actors-in-relation-one-with-the-other is only the expression of society separated from itself, of its distanciation from its own historicity, and, most of all, of the symbolic action and management of organizational power. The actor as the "subject" exploded. Historicity is not exercised by an actor; it exercises itself through the conflict between the ruling class and the ruled class. Similarly, authority in an organization exercises itself through the opposition of those who command and those who are commanded. Therefore, all social relations carry for each actor a double orientation: on the one hand, the actors orient themselves in respect to a partner; on the other, they orient themselves in respect to the creative action of meaning that constitutes the field of the interaction. Each actor relates to culture through a social relation that manifests the rupture running through human society, which is not only a functioning system capable of reproducing itself (a system of adaptation and apprenticeship), but which also is capable of producing its own orientations and, therefore, its own practices, institutions, and organizations.

This conception of social relations is difficult to accept because we are constantly influenced by our life experience. Our relations establish themselves in a "situation." The rules, the norms, the social organization seem to preexist, as the scenery in a theater preexists when the actors enter. This image corresponds to the consciousness of the actor and is almost enough to describe the intersocial relations. But it is necessary to overturn it completely if we want to enter into sociological analysis, for, if situations are anterior to relations, where do they come from if not from a hidden god, a metasocial principle, or natural laws? And is this not only another way to limit our understanding? Sociological "realism" is only an illusion, and rapidly changing societies can no longer give in to this illusion. The rule is not prior to the act. It occurs at the same time and is modified and contested by each act. Order is neither intangible nor coherent. It is only a partial formalization of changes in the movement of social relations; transformations in culture; and conflicts of power, influence, and authority. From this partiality comes the importance of social movements that make the appearance of social relations rather than constituting a "state" of society that determines the social relations. We could sum up the preceding remarks by saying that the dangerously widespread notion of "institution" must be rejected. This notion was necessary insofar as the social order seemed given, "instituted" by a metasocial order. When we recognize the society "institutes" itself, is the product of its own action, the notion of institution becomes an obstacle to sociological knowledge.

III. BY SEPARATING THE SYSTEMS AND THE ACTORS

The separation of systems and actors is indispensable because, as I have already warned, social conduct must never be confounded with the consciousness of actors. Furthermore, the definition of sociology as the study of systems of social relations is just another way of affirming this separation. Any system of social relations is constructed by sociological analysis and does not directly correspond to any precise historical case, whereas an actor is always a particular person and his actions are always events. In order to understand the actor, we are obliged to mobilize a plurality of situations and thus of social relations. We can easily admit that sociological explanations cannot fall back on the idea of "human nature," to values and intangible principles, whereas the actor never ceases to explain his own conduct in terms of the "beautiful" or the "good," of "rights of man" or of "civilization." In this sense, all sociology is indeed antihumanist, but observers other than sociologists constantly remind a vast public of this, and no sociologist therefore needs to be on guard against doing so.

I. First, we can separate ourselves from the temptation to explain conduct by situations because this inevitably leads to confusion. How can we explain conduct by a level of salary, a type of housing, a state of technology? It is obvious, therefore, that "situations" must be transformed into social relations.

However, a more elaborate form of explanation of conduct by situation does exist, namely, that which defines the situation in terms of social relations, specifically, in terms of division of labor. Cannot a society be situated in the evolution of the simple to the complex, of the undifferentiated to the differentiated, of slow and discontinuous change to rapid and incessant transformations? Integration and deviance, consensus and conflict also can be explained by the characteristics of organizations and even, to take Durkheim's word, by social morphology.

But we can recognize this evolution and interpret it in an altogether different manner. That which at first seemed to be "natural" diversification is only the extension of the action of society on itself. A complex society more profoundly produces itself—and therefore reproduces itself—than a less complex society. Further, it is a society where the field of social relations and conflicts never ceases to extend itself, and this is what makes us remain in the domain of social relations, even at moments when we assume we could leave.

> 2. A system of social relations is a system of actors trying to control the field that defines their interaction. At the highest level, social classes fight, each brandishing the same cultural model. Capitalists and workers fight in part for control of what they call with the same voice "progress." This obliges us to speak of the sociology of action, which necessarily places a certain cultural field at the most fundamental level of the analysis, that is, the level where society rests not on a situation of "forces" but on a system of actions, on actors struggling to direct the means by which society produces itself.

Once again, I want to avoid being misunderstood. It is not a matter of pretending that society rests on "ideas"; it is produced by the work it exercises on itself. Historicity does not result from a decision; it is defined absolutely by a capacity of practical intervention on economic activity, more particularly on the relations of a society with its natural environment, and it completely determines social and cultural practices. Nothing must ever separate meaning and activity. If we wish to use the popular image of the infrastructure of a society, we see that it is permeated by a historicity that is encompassed investment, cultural model, and "paradigm" of knowledge and is therefore conjointly and inseparably economy and representation, in one word, culture.

If we reject such a conception, we create an impassable abyss between the situation and the actors, for example, between an analysis of the capitalist system and that of the workers' movement: structuralist objectivism on one side, identification of the revolutionary subjectivism on the other. This can only mean one thing: the significance of a social movement is subservient to the management and direction of the very system it is trying to change. In more concrete terms, a movement of a popular class manifests the crisis of the established order and serves as an instrument for forming a new economic system and thus a new ruling class. We must never forget that the theoretical debates about sociological analysis contain political and social preferences and consequently are submitted to the pressure of ideologies that serve the popular classes or the ruling elites.

It is absurd to accuse the sociology of action of being "humanist" since it particularly offers a means of transcending moral judgements or essences. How can we progress beyond proclaiming liberation, justice, equality except by representing society as a drama in which actors conflict for control over the direction of historicity and are therefore oriented in an antagonistic manner toward the same cultural orientations?

3. This version of society—a game of conflicts—can only appear after society itself takes charge of the ensemble of its own experience instead of limiting the field of social action to a narrow ban constricted between a metasocial order and a structure of order, presented at once as being both internal and surrounding.

Presociological images of society were dominated by dual concepts: that which gives meaning from above society and that which gives meaning to the inertia of private and arbitrary interests. Where conflict should have been situated at the center of analysis, the presociologist instead put contradiction: that between the continuous and the discontinuous, that between meaning and nonsense, that between the forces of production and the social relations of production. The presociologist was always constrained to give to an actor a central and inexplicable role that was capable of evading this contradiction. How was this accomplished? We can understand this easily enough when it involves explanations of the rise of a new ruling class, the bourgeoisie fighting obscurantism ir. the name of enlightenment, imposing, at the same time, its law on the proletariat. But once again, the action of popular classes becomes incomprehensible in historical situations where this thought is developed and where "history" works to encircle and restrain actors. When we consider the rise of the working-class movement, not that of the bourgeoisie, we see the rise of an actor who in principle cannot transform itself into a ruling class. The welding together of the critical and creative aspects of a social movement becomes more difficult to understand and to realize. From there came the central role of a new historical agent that liberated the people from their masters and that also directed its own movement, which is at once the expression and the overcoming of the popular movement: the nation-state.

It is not by accident that sociology developed when social movements first claimed the right to be the creators of their own meaning instead of being only the servants of the party of the intellectuals or the nation-state.

Sociology does not constitute itself only by its effort to learn. Societies only learn to know themselves sociologically when, first, they no longer accept the existence of a metasocial order—divine providence, the principles of political philosophy, economic laws—and when, second, they are thoroughly subject to the intervention of a new culture and to a generalized conflict for social control.

IV. BY ARGUING FOR A HIERARCHY OF CATEGORIES OF SOCIAL FACTS (ECONOMICS, POLITICS, IDEOLOGIES)

I. It is extremely difficult to discover the reason why social thought was led to utilize such categories, particularly, to speak about economic or political "factors" or, even more curiously, "social" facts. Economic, political, or cultural facts: are they not social? Moreover, where are the boundaries of these facts when they are reduced from the "social"? Should we say that such classifications really do not have great importance and instead only manifest the

major divisions of organized or governed social practice?
Perhaps, except that in modern states ministries of
economy, of political institutions, and so forth do exist.

These preceding observations refer to the arbitrary character
of these categories. If we can speak of agents of socialization,
culture obviously is not only the ensemble of the methods of in-
culcating norms that legitimize the social order, but is also the
creation of a relation between a society and its environment.
"Culture" is thus both an infrastructural and a superstructural
fact. In the same manner, the most cursory examination reveals
that what is called politics is composed of at least two very different aspects: the representation of interests in the formation of
decisions that are then imposed on all members of a territorial
collectivity, and the domain of the state, the power of the gover-
nor to conduct peace, wage war, and control change.

Finally, when the economy is spoken of, it is sometimes in
terms of the mobilization of material resources in respect to certain political objectives, which are themselves subordinated to
cultural values, and, on the contrary, sometimes in terms of the
social forms of collective work and the utilization of its product,
which are considered as the base of society. Therefore, each of
the terms has at least two principal and contradictory meanings.
One gives to the invoked factor a fundamental role; the other
gives an order of dependent facts. In the face of this confusion,
one usually invokes a hierarchy of needs, going from material
necessities to purely "arbitrary" forms of culture. *Primum vivere,*
the perspective of those who accept the general image of
historical evolution according to which the "primitives" would
have responded to the most elementary needs, whereas the progress of techniques and resources permits "civilization" to
remove itself from this. Prudence and decency demand that we
no longer mention this genre of ridiculous and odious argument.

Certain historians have more wisely opposed different tem-
poralities. The long-term perspective would be the time of relations between man and nature; the short-term perspective would
be that of political "events." This corresponds rather well to the
image that an industrial society has of itself; it is convinced that it
is its material work that is essential and that the political interventions, like the cultural "works," are determined by the state
of work. But it would be difficult to make Hitler, Stalin, Mao or
even Castro, Nasser, or Boumedienne admit that political events
are only short-term waves, that are carried forward by the pro-

found movement of economic situations, especially when it appears that it is the economic and social politics that determine the state of the forces of production rather than vice versa. More generally, one must reject the image of a superposition of the most "artificial" activities over those that are the most natural. Because these too are all culturally and socially determined, as are ideologies or works or art. Anthropology ought to protect us from rationalizations by which industrial societies have described their social experience.

These remarks obviate the fact that the economic, political, or cultural categories are inseparable and that such aggregates or rationalizations of a historically situated ideology must be dissolved.

2. We can therefore say that what we thought were categories of social facts are in reality only "metasocial" categories, images of a superior order that supposedly gives order to social facts. The weaker the capacity of a society to act on itself, the more this metasocial order is removed from society and the more it gives "meaning" to human conduct. The progress of historicity, of the capacity of societies to reproduce themselves and therefore to extend the field of actions recognized to be social, has led to the progress of secularization, a weakening of the metasocial guarantors of social order. Culture, politics, economy—opposed to society—are precisely the principle successive forms of the metasocial order.

Societies that act only in a process of simple reproduction or growth of their production of goods and consumption represent historicity essentially as a perfect copy of human activity, except that it is transcendent. This metasocial order can be called cultural and, more concretely, religious (on the condition that one remembers that other religions exist, albeit without transcendance). Societies that act on the distribution of goods, what we call trade societies, represent metasocial order as the guarantor of exchange. This is the order of rules, laws, and political order as imagined and codified by political philosophy.

An industrial society, that is, a society capable of action on the reproduction of and distribution of consumed goods and on the organization of work, recognizes that it is the economic facts that command the social order. Science and, more generally, technology applied to production now permit action not only on consumption, distribution, and organization but also on production itself; therefore, the separation of the social and the metasocial has lost all meaning. Only in vain can we debate the relative importance of economic or social factors because no barrier between the two domains any longer exists. The economy has become political. The hypothesis that our societies are commanded by the law of the maximization of profit cannot be proven. To begin with, such a hypothesis does not even depend on the priority of the economic "factor" since it is formulated in psychological terms, and this psychology is rejected by the observations of the sociology of organizations and decisions. Furthermore, such an explanation is so general as to be extremely weak. That the capitalist class does seek to maximize (a term difficult to define) its profits is certainly true, on the condition that we add that this goal is not its only one; it would not be a ruling class if it did not preoccupy itself with the social order in general. Thus, the categories of social facts are only the archeological remnants of metasocial orders that past societies invoked in order to represent both reality and the limits of their action on themselves.

It is therefore necessary to affirm strongly that all analysis based on situating "factors" or "instances" in respect to one another is presociological and intellectually archaic.

3. Sociology cannot use these categories. Instead it must destroy them and replace them by its own work, that is, by the categories of social relations. Although this seems similar, it is an altogether different approach. As I said above, a social relation is an interaction placed in a field that is itself defined by a mode of intervention of a society on itself. This leads us to an immediate recognition of organizational relations, defined as interior to an organization by the exercise of an authority that manifests its power, the source of which is exterior to the organization.

At a higher level of analysis are political relations, defined not at the level where organizations function but at the level where the rules that are applied in the organizations are formed. The field of political relations is itself defined by a social power that dominates it: the ruling class.

Finally, class relations are manifestations of the conflict between historicity and, particularly but not exclusively, investment. These relations are given order by the unity of a system of historical action, thus by an ensemble of cultural relations determined by a given type of historicity.

These class relations are at once economic, political, social, and cultural, and similarly, organizational relations are social and cultural. Therefore, a level of social relations must never be identified with a category of social facts.

V. BY REFERRING TO VALUES

1. The most general problem of sociological analysis is to understand how society can be both united and divided. We cannot avoid accepting these two propositions conjointly: society is one and it is plural.

Some see only the division, as if society were a battlefield or a marketplace where the actors follow individual goals of survival, enrichment, and conquest. This image, however, does not explain where "norms," come from, as Durkheim observed almost a century ago. In reality, the most important social conflicts cannot be reduced to the sharing of a cake. And I deliberately use this expression to show how a purely conflictual conception of society becomes in fact conservative. Revolutionary thought wishes both to destroy one order and to install another liberated order. Revolutionary thought does not defend a particular camp; it legitimates action in the name of general principles. In the same manner, a ruling class controls the ensemble of society, particularly the technical or economic rationality.

Conflict is not important and is not even social conflict except insofar as the actors aim to direct the field of their interaction. Revolts or forms of opposition do exist in which the actors reject the general type of society and culture in which they live. But this involves only relatively limited movements, important insofar as they are movements of cultural innovation more than of social conflict. Central social conflicts, on the other hand, involve the two or more adversaries who strongly sense themselves to belong to the same culture, which situates their conflict and defines the stakes. Working-class opposition to capitalism has not presented an entirely different society and culture; on the contrary, it has wanted a collective reappropriation of the forces of production and the idea of progress. Owners and workers struggle for the right to direct industrialization, which both consider an economic reality and a cultural project.

> 2. Another social thought insists especially on the unity of society. Society is considered a person; a father of a family; or the head of a business who sets goals and chooses means, who rules the relations between the members of his group, and who assures its integration and the maintenance of its values. In fact, the key word of this sociology of social order is values, for they become the general cultural orientations that give order to the collective life by specifying social norms that translate themselves in organizations as roles.

Nothing is gained from considering this concept further. It was predominant in university sociology until made unacceptable by the profound and lasting upheavals of the student movements and, more generally, by the moral crises linked to the Vietnam war and to the disorganization of the international monetary and economic systems. This image of society is as faulty as the one described before. Although it is true that conflict presupposes an agreement between the combatants as to the stakes involved, it is false to assume that the actors refer to the same norms and values. Many studies have shown how even, at the most elementary level, it is false to believe in the constant existence of a common social language. Social relations are built more on misunderstandings, calculations, strategies, negotiations, and transactions than on reciprocity or consensus.

> 3. Perhaps we can avoid this double impasse by dissipating a common confusion; then, by separating two falsely united terms. The confusion evidently begins with the nature of the principle of unity, which one could call more simply, culture.

If one perceives culture as the ensemble of ideology inculcated in the population to guarantee and legitimize the established order and principles, culture obviously does not contain social conflicts, but is merely an instrumental use of culture by the holders of social power. When functionalist sociology invokes values as the principle of social integration, it becomes vulnerable to the reproach, and it is a correct one, that it identifies itself with the point of view of the rulers. The unity of the system of historical action that I am speaking of must, therefore, be completely separated from this discourse of legitimation.

Furthermore, such a separation is assured only if the cultural orientations that constitute the system of historical action are separated from the social norms, which are, indeed, only used as instruments of reproduction and legitimation by the established order.

What must be broken is the concept: "When they are applied to specific domains of social life, cultural values transform themselves into social norms." There is no continuity between values and norms or, more exactly, between cultural orientations and ideologies. Class relations must be inserted between values and norms. Cultural orientations are the stakes of class relations; social norms manifest the control of the ruling class over the cultural orientations. Thus, the notion of values in fact masks both the hiatus between cultural stakes and social interests, and the place of class conflict. Although it is all to the good that an ideological critique uncovered the role of a notion apparently not found within social conflicts, this critique was insufficient because it did not, progressing from the values of legitimation, discover that cultural orientations were absolutely linked to the historicity of a society. These orientations are found, therefore, at the most profound level of social action, that is, the level of productive forces; however, one must concomitantly recognize that the issue is not material forces but cultural action. Society as a whole finds itself framed by cultural orientations and values, by the instruments of its self-production, and by the ideological instruments that reproduce inequalities and privileges.

VI. BY CONSIDERING SOCIETY AS THE DISCOURSE OF THE RULING CLASS

1. A class would not be ruling if it did not have the power to monopolize political institutions, the state apparatus, and cultural organizations in order to defend its interests and the reproduction of its privileges.

The ideology of the ruling class is not directly exposed to the ideology of the popular class: the former hides behind abstract principles or pretended technical constraints. Critique must therefore act against this ideological hold and against these false semblances.

But beyond the mere recognition of ruling class ideology is the idea that the ensemble of categories of social practice represents a coherent manifestation of a dominant ideology. Such an affirmation is not reconcilable with a recognition of class relations and class struggles: because how can one simultaneously proclaim a unity and integration of a social order dominated by the positivism of a power or an ideology and recognize that a society is fraught with fundamental social conflicts? Recently, the sociology of education in France has exemplified the inevitable opposition of these two points of view. Pierre Bourdieu and Raymond Passeron showed how the school integrates all children, each in his place, in a dominant ideology, whereas Christian Baudelot and Roger Establet showed that the scholastic system has two tracks, one for the popular classes, one for the bourgeoisie. Is there one or two school systems? Now the affirmation of the integrative role that Althusser called "ideological state apparatus" cannot be interpreted in terms of class relations. This ends up affirming a principle of unity, not a principle of conflict; and we therefore speak of social stratification and inequality, in analogous perspective to that of the Chicago School, and, consequently, speak of absolute power and despotism, in the Durkheimian vein, that is, the capacity to completely impose the will of political decision. To affirm, on the other hand, the central importance of class relations means that one must recognize the concrete marks of conflict in social organizations and a certain capacity of action of popular forces in political institutions. How can one speak of the working class and of capitalist exploitation in an industrial society if the working-class movement cannot form itself, if the workers are entirely "alienated," if the unions only accept the logic of the dominant system, if the political and judicial systems completely reject the union demands, denying to them all influence over the work situation?

It is strange and even paradoxical that the image of a society reduced to the reproduction of the power of the ruling class has been so frequently expressed in recent years in societies where the institutionalization of conflicts is the most developed and where the political, social, and ideological recognition of these conflicts is the most general. One could understand that in an

autocratic society, despotic or totalitarian, one would try to show
that all the categories of social practice lead back to a unified
project of domination. However, I repeat, this project cannot be
identified with class domination as such because it is only adjustable directly at an ideological and political level.

2. This representation of society as the ideological discourse of the ruling class is only a bad compromise
betweeen two intellectually opposed, but equally coherent,
positions. The first holds that social organization and social
change are directed by the interests of the ruling class and,
more precisely, by the laws of capitalist economy. The other
represents society as a fight between forces of social classes
for the control of historicity, thus of the general cultural
orientations of the society.

Let us consider the first. It is precise. It poses the existence of a
system that is socially definable by capitalist exploitation,
although economically adjustable, and by the internal logic of
the dominant system. This conception runs up against two objections, one quite different from the other. The first reminds us
that, if an internal logic to the economic domination of class exists, nothing obliges us to say that this logic entirely commands
the functioning of society. To recognize the existence of
capitalist power does not mean, *ipso facto*, that we affirm it to be
total, that the state is only the agent of the ruling class, or that the
workers cannot lead social movements that overthrow or limit
capitalist power. It is false to believe that a society functions
because diverse interests negotiate and concur. It is essential to
recall that there is a dominant order, that the political game has
limits because it is institutionalized. However, we do not have to
go further and say that the ensemble of capitalist societies live
under the dictatorship of the bourgeoisie. If it is true that the ruling class champions order—with which it identifies
itself—against deviance—those who oppose order—it is ·more true
that a society must be analyzed as the confrontation of classes
fighting for the direction of historicity. To affirm that a society is
only a system of domination negates the existence and the
possibility of social movements. This can only be the ideology of
a ruling elite, which is anxious to maintain its reign. For society
to be dominated by one class, that class must use total political
hegemony and absolute ideological control. This occurred at the

beginning of English industrialism. Afterward, the bourgeoisies, even in Europe, were less hegemonical, and the role of the state was therefore more considerable and more complex.

How can we today defend the ideal of a completely independent economic order when, historically, economic and political facts are linked? Even those who speak of monopoly state capitalism recognize the impossibility of defining a purely economic power since the state plays such an essential role. Defenders of the logic of pure economic domination do object, albeit rarely, to this idea. We see all around us that economic domination is associated with political power and ideological manipulation (propaganda, advertising, cultural inculcation). But why do we not also see that the further our analysis of economic domination progresses—and I hope we advance as rapidly and as far as possible—the more the ruling class is seen as an actor, not as a simple transmitter of the laws of the economic system? The ruling class, whether or not it is called "technocratic," creates policy and diffuses its ideology. It more or less controls the state apparatus, which presupposes the existence of social forces in opposition, themselves carriers of economic and ideological interest and political influence. The more the traces of the metasocial guarantors of social order disappear, the more society reveals itself to be a conflict between social movements fighting for control of the cultural and economic means by which it produces itself and that constitute its meanings and practices.

3. In the central capitalist countries, the image of a society as ideological discouse is so contrary to observable facts—discoverable daily—that one must look for the hidden reasons for putting forth this image. In reality, it is only a response to the utopia of the ruling class, identifying its interests to social evolution as a whole, especially when social struggles that correspond to the new forms of class domination are not yet developed. This identification of the social organization to a dominant ideology is important because it reveals the class nature of dominant ideology and denounces in particular its favorite mask, that of the "end of ideology." Historically, this ideological critique has been entirely positive after two triumphant decades of the ruling class ideology. But it is nonetheless necessary to critique the ideology because it is inappropriate when reducing social and cultural organizations to a discourse. On the contrary, the direct and indirect presence of social conflicts must be rediscovered.

At its beginning, American industrial sociology, although generally conservative, gave a good example of ideological critique in revealing that the conduct of workers did not conform to the image Taylor presented of workers' behavior, for in fact they responded to financial stimulants by slowing down, not speeding up their production. The same type of analysis can be usefully applied to education, among other sectors, in order to understand the dropout phenomenon. Revolts, refusals, retreats, flights, silences, aggressions, perversions, or misappropriations of social or cultural instruments: they are all manifestations of the forces of opposition, as are conflicts, ideologies, and negotiations. During a brief period it sufficed merely to bring up the subject of the control of the ruling class and the leading elites over the ensemble of social practices. But that critique very quickly risked becoming a prisoner of the illusions it combated. Society is not altogether unidimensional and integrative; it is not true that it cannot be combated except from the outside or from the extreme periphery. Social movements in the industrialized countries and attacks against the international organization of the capitalist economy have shown the fragility, the contradictions, and the conflicts present in this dominant order—an order that was once thought so powerful, so much in control, so assured of the reproduction of its profits and privileges.

Much of the recent Marxist-inspired sociology has only been a counterpart to American-inspired functionalist sociology. It has indeed critiqued the ideology, but like the ideology it critiqued, it has been a sociology of order. It has been content to see the Devil where Parsonians saw God, to call "dominant ideology" what the others called "values"; it has not questioned the integration of the social order, and the coherence of the social and cultural organization.

A sociology of action cannot compromise with this approach. Surely, mechanisms of reproduction of social domination do exist, but two points must be added. First, what is reproduced is never entirely reducible to a class domination. It is instead an imperfect reproduction of the power and privileges of a class, more or less directly supported by an antipopular state.

Second, this reproductive process never perfectly duplicates the system of the class relations and conflicts except in particular cases, such as in totalitarianism, on the one hand, or in reactionary decadence, on the other. Large capitalist countries currently belong to neither of these situations.

In these societies, one is always tempted to believe that the fundamental conflicts are in fact only rivalries between interest groups within a pluralist political system. That is why, "pedagogically," this institutionalism must be balanced with an ideological critique that reveals its limits. But such an analysis is only polemical. It must constantly return to the essential, to the class conflicts through which a society defines its modes of action on itself.

VII. BY TAKING SOCIAL CLASSES FOR PERSONAGES

I. Social classes are not merely categories having resources or unequal chances. The confusion between classes and strata has never been too dangerous, in Europe at least, thanks to the influence of Marxist thought, which defined classes not in terms of consumption but in terms of production. It is necessary to go further, however, if we are to see why a well-guarded border must be established between the two orders. In reality, no one defines a social class, especially if it is dominant, simply by its relations of production, for this class also has the capacity to manage the state, to impose its ideology, and to repress or alienate its adversaries.

The more we broaden our definition, however, the greater our risk of arriving at a general description of social inequality that says nothing precise about the causes of inequality. Class relations are not situated in the order of production (as if they represented those who direct production and those who execute their orders); instead, class relations are situated in the production of production, that is, in investment. Moreover, investment cannot be considered independently of other dimensions of historicity because it is an action, and like all social action, it cannot be reduced to forces or resources. Investment is culturally oriented, that is, it is given order by the cultural model of its society. It is split up, therefore, into productive investments, which transform a certain part of economic activity, and into cultural investments, which correspond to the metasocial order and to the image of creativity that dominates the society: investments in temples and tombs or in mansions and banks.

It is the ruling class that directs historicity, that is, the ensemble of means by which a society, instead of simply reproducing itself, produces its own existence and meaning. The societies that sociology considers have this capacity to remove themselves from their daily activity by means of knowledge, investment, and a representation of their own creativity. But it is artificial to continue to speak of a society acting on itself. This action presupposes the division of society; this action can only be managed by a part of society acting on the whole. A society endowed with historicity, with the capacity to transform itself, is necessarily divided into a superior class, which manages the accumulation, and a popular class, which experiences this division, a division that is managed and used by the ruling class. This popular class struggles for the collective reappropriation of historicity.

Historicity and class relations are absolutely inseparable, so much so that a society cannot be conceived without classes. One can have a classless society only in a society without historicity, a society of pure reproduction, in which the equality of production and consumption leave nothing for investment.

All "historical" societies are therefore dominated by historicity and class relations. And the sociology of action's most important task is to analyze their interdependence.

> 2. However, if class relations is an indispensable concept for the study of "nonprimitive" societies (i.e. prehistorical or ahistorical societies), the notion of class obviously has a particular historical signification. It appears in the social thought of the modern epoch, particularly in eighteenth-century Scotland. It spread throughout the Europe of capitalist industrialization and now permeates all regions of the world, where new forms of industrialization are directed by the national or foreign bourgeoisie.

Historical privilege arises from the fusion of capitalist industrialization and three facts. First, historical privilege comes from the class relations themselves as they existed, although under other forms, before industrial society; (class relations also will exist after industrial society).

Second, a metasocial order of an economic nature was formed during the industrial epoch. Social facts were considered as determined by economic facts or relations, whereas in preindustrial capitalism, this metasocial order was of a "political" nature; in postindustrial society, all metasocial guarantors of social order disappear, and social action has no foundation other than social relations themselves.

In trade societies, the class relations have an economic dimen-

sion, but classes also define themselves in terms of their antagonistic relations to a metasocial order, which in this case is
symbolized by the prince. The classes are therefore both agents
of civic or political struggles and economic categories. This
duality exists everywhere except in industrial societies, where the
metasocial order is an economic order.

Thus, only during the industrial epoch are the classes as
economic categories both social and metasocial. The proletariat
also is equated with work; it is identified with the very forces of
production and progress. Likewise, the bourgeoisie is affirmed by
its ideologies as the agent of the evolution of progress, as the
liberator of traditions and constraints.

Third, the industrialization of Western Europe, especially of
Great Britain, was directly by national bourgeoisies. This class
was able to appear both as an actor in class relations and as the
elite directing historical change. Class struggles per se are confused with the struggle for direction of the state. It is the
historically defined conjunction of these three privileges of
classes that has given to them the role of the central personages
of history, first proclaimed by bourgeois historians as Guizot and
de Tocqueville.

The present development of historicity has, in an apparent
paradox, enlarged the field of class relations and the utility of the
concept when the classes themselves have ceased to be the central personages of history. But there is no real paradox in this
double evolution, for the disappearance of the metasocial orders
infinitely extends the field of class conflicts and negates the second of the three components of the image of classes in the industrial societies. Moreover, the generalization of the industrial
societies diversified the nature of the ruling elites, multiplying in
particular the societies where these elites are state elites and
therefore nonbourgeoisie, a diversification that no longer permits us to identify the ruling class and the ruling elite.

One of the most urgent tasks of the sociology of action is to
discover the class relations where the landscape is no longer
dominated by classes acting as personages. The bourgeoisie and
the proletariat are no longer the heroes of industrialization.
Social classes are no longer recognizable; they can only be defined by class relations. Everywhere, apparatuses dominate territories or "masses," but neither the central apparatus nor the territorial collectivities can be seen as personages. The epoch of
mythology is passed; that of sociology is beginning.

VIII. BY CONFOUNDING STRUCTURE AND CHANGE IN A PHILOSOPHY OF EVOLUTION

1. There is no difference between explaining social facts by their place in .providential design, by principles of political philosophy, or by the meaning of history. Assuredly, in the latter, the metasocial order to which the social facts are related is in movement rather than frozen. But in all, social facts, that is, social relations, do not carry their own meaning; they belong to a higher order. When this order is conceived as movement from the simple to the complex, from the transmitted to the acquired, etc. social facts must be understood, according to presociological thought, by their place in the process of differentiation and of growing secularization. There is thus no difference between the concepts that analyze the social structure and those that explain change. The most simple example is that of the concept of modernization: a modern society is one in which the roles are strongly differentiated, in which there is a triumph of rationality, and so forth. The analysis of a "modern" society always leads back to notions that evoke the opposite image of a "traditional" society. The work of Talcott Parsons, whose influence has been considerable, is a good example of this narrow evolutionism associated with a functionalist analysis of social organization.

Society, as perceived by this type of social philosophy, is not defined by its actions, its social relations, its forms of social control. It is, fundamentally, defined by its modernity or traditionalism, by its place in the hierarchical ladder that leads from *Gemeinschaft* to *Gesellschaft*, from mechanical solidarity to organic solidarity, and so forth.

In a more concrete fashion, the actions of great actors of history were defined in historical terms. They created societies of "tomorrow," not different societies, but more advanced societies. The bourgeoisie sees itself succeeding the aristocracy, and the proletariat sees itself charged by history to succeed the bourgeoisie.

2. Once we realize that the social can only be explained by the social, by relations between actors defined by a mode of intervention of society on itself, the sociology of action can no longer be

identified with an evolutionist philosophy of history. First of all, there are forms of the self-production of society: historicity. Second, there are modes of passage from one type of society—I prefer to say one system of historical action—to another. Although we must not lose interest in social evolution, we must distinguish the analysis of the systems of social relations and those of the modes of passage between states of society. Structure and genesis must be completely separated.

This separation became possible only when an industrial society created itself in a way that was fundamentally removed from the British model. In spite of important differences, the French and German experiences belonged to the same category as the English. The Soviet revolution, however, invented a profoundly different path toward industrialization. Since then, the "paths" have so multiplied that a theory of convergence cannot be upheld. That would be like saying that only the roads were different but that they all led to Rome, that is, to a certain general type of social organization.

We therefore realize that it is not contradictory to speak of industrial society, on the one hand, and capitalist, socialist, or other paths toward industrialization, on the other.

An industrial society does not define itself by techniques but by class relations, by the capacity of a social category to transform the organization of work and to appropriate the resulting profits. This happens as much in the Soviet Union as it does in the United States. On the other hand, societies industrialized by a national bourgeoisie, by a nation-state, by a revolutionary party, or by an external bourgeoisie are profoundly different from one another. It therefore follows that capitalism and socialism are not stages of historical evolution, but different modes of industrialization.

This is a shocking formulation because it is contrary to the most widespread belief. I want to repeat it, therefore: capitalism and socialism are not modes of production; they are modes of industrialization.

The condition of workers in an industrial society has, consequently, two quite different aspects. The first is defined by the organization of work; the second by the degree to which this directly manifests the nature of the ruling elite. In a parallel fashion, in a capitalist society one cannot completely confound the industrializers, who exercise a domination of class, and the capitalists, who function in the market economy more than in the industrial economy.

Some are tempted to go further, to think that a sociology of action, unencumbered by a metasocial order, also should eliminate all references to social systems and to synchronic analysis. This entails recognizing but one single object of sociology: the analysis of the politics of change, the study of institutional decision making. This is in fact one of the fundamental orientations of the sociology of action, one that confronts the ideology of the rulers, the technocrats, which eliminates all references to social relations, particularly to relations of power. To reduce the sociology of action to an analysis of decisions amounts to identifying with the decision-makers and to forgetting the most fundamental principle of sociology: all conduct must be seen in light of the social relations that give it meaning. That is why the analysis of society as a system must remain dominant; the study of changes, diachronic analysis, although having its own autonomy, must remain subordinated to synchronic analysis.

IX. CONCLUSION

Sociological analysis of the industrial epoch elaborated three fundamental themes: the social system, the social conflicts, and the cultural orientations of action. Emile Durkheim, Karl Marx, and Max Weber, although not reducible to each respective theme, have become symbolic of each. These three themes were incompatible because the society in which they appeared did not conceive of itself as analyzable by itself. Two ideas contradictory to sociology still dominated.

The first idea was that the meaning of a social situation was external to the situation, that is, in a metasocial mode that some call "values" and others call "nature." Wondering about the economic and political success of the Western world, and thus about capitalism, rationalization, and secularization, Weber claimed an intervention of values—in his case religious values—and saw a tension between the ethic of conviction and that of responsibility in all collective action. Marx, beginning in his younger period, did not merely analyze the capitalist system. He referred to fundamental needs, to use-value, and to an image of society liberated from capitalist exploitation, which introduced a contradiction between nature and society that was only the proletarian interpretation of a general dualism (Weber provided the bourgeois interpretation). Finally, Durkheim, although introducing the idea of society as a system, saw it as an essence, a force that imposes itself on actors, not as a game of relations between actors.

The second idea that opposed the birth of sociological analysis was evolutionism and the philosophy of history that it implied. A society was defined by its place in evolution, the meaning of which was always associated with particular forms of progress—considered as a central principle of interpretation. The nineteenth century dreamed of modernity, progress, the future. Only slowly and with difficulty did social thought become sociological analysis. This is impossible to imagine without the works of Marx, Weber, and Durkheim and without a profound rupture with the principles which defined the historical setting of these thinkers in the culture of industrialization.

This transformation occurred through major crises, and we are still witnessing the challenges to sociological thought by various methodologies which are anti-sociological. In fact each of the three major themes "desociologizes" itself. Those who speak in terms of social conflicts and of the Marxist transition most often reject the elitism of the social order and return to utopias and to the weaknesses of utopian socialism. Those who speak of the problems of action are often "experts" who are close to the very power centers that they seek to understand. Finally, those who speak of the social system see it as an apparatus of reproduction and integration rather than as an arena of conflict and change.

The time has come to remember sociology. Society is a system, a system of action. Action is not only decision making; it is also aimed at cultural orientations in respect to conflicting social relations. Conflict is neither contradiction nor revolt; it is the social form of the historicity of the self-production of society. Little by little, moving on from dualism and evolutionism, societies' self-analyses take form over a long period of growth and crisis, atomic menace, totalitarianism, and revolutions; societies realize that they are the products of their own actions, not the manifestations of human nature, the meaning of history, or an original contradiction. From there, the specific approaches and the schools of thought lead to the birth of sociology.

PART II

THE CRITIQUE OF SOCIAL PROCESS: APPLYING THE CRITICAL PARADIGM

8.

CLASS STRUCTURE, CLASS MOBILITY, AND THE DISTRIBUTION OF HUMAN BEINGS

DANIEL BERTAUX

When I started working on "occupational choice," in about 1969, nobody told me about the one approach that would prove fruitful. European scholars were referring to "Marx, Durkheim, and Weber" as three key thinkers of equal importance and significance (an attitude that, given the forceful opposition of the last two to the first, is bewildering). American sociologists, considered masters of empirical research, paid only lip service to Weber and Durkheim and totally ignored Marx. (I should have realized that this conspicuous silence was a sure sign of something of interest.)

So I started reading the enormous literature on social mobility (95 percent was from the United States), and although I had trouble understanding what the authors were talking about and how it related to real societies, I blamed myself entirely—at least for a while. These years also saw the revival of the students' and workers' movements in France and Europe and other movements worldwide. It was as an intellectual, not especially as a sociologist, that I followed these movements and contacted some of them; they brought home to me the first basic principle of sociological thought, that is, that every social phenomenon is ultimately a product of some class relationship *(rapport de classe)*, and that to explain or understand a given social phenomenon means to reach its class core, its relation to the continuous class struggles on all levels; a task that, admittedly, is not always so straightforward as it seems.

I finally stopped reading Leo Goodman's clever irrelevancies and moved straight into the question of class. My idea was to get a clear understanding of this question, to draw from it an analysis of such phenomena as stratification and the family—two key questions for social mobility that I knew had been largely ignored by modern Marxism—and to augment my theoretical studies with empirical investigations. Then I would be in a position to deal with the "occupational choice" question seriously.

The first part of this paper concerns the notion of class structure. I shall present some concepts that are relevant to the study of "classes," although they run counter to some widely accepted ideas.

The second part of this paper develops an earlier concept,[1] that of the "process of production, distribution and consumption of human beings." This concept reorients toward a materialist approach sociological analysis of "the family" and the distribution of human beings.

Although very little will be said about social mobility or immobility per se, I believe that what is said will help lay solid foundations for the later study of these phenomena—foundations that have been lacking for too long now.

I. CLASS STRUCTURE, *APPAREILS D'ENCADREMENT,* AND THE APPROPRIATION OF SOCIAL RELATIONS

"It is always the direct relation between the masters of the conditions of production and the direct producers which reveals the innermost secret, the inner foundation of the entire social edifice—and therefore also of the political form of the relation between sovereignty and dependence, in short, of the particular form of the state," wrote Marx toward the end of his life.[2] Given what I know of the contemporary world, this is a correct assumption and it should be taken seriously.

In the so-called developed countries of the West, the fundamental relation is the capital-labor relation. This relation gives rise to the two "main" classes of the capitalist mode of production, that is, the bourgeoisie and the proletariat.[3]

Given nineteenth-century connotations of "bourgeoisie" and "proletariat," many writers today prefer to use "the ruling class" and "the working class," which, of course, are quite correct by themselves. However, I believe that these latter terms convey a thoroughly false assumption, one that is extremely damaging to the construction of class theory: the assumption that "the ruling class" and "the working class" are entities of the same nature, different only in their relative positions; something like two marbles of different colors, one standing above the other.

One thing does exist: class relationships. If sociology is the "study of social relationships," then it should place the study of class relationships at its core. This is, at least, how sociologists in France see sociology: both Marxists—like Poulantzas and Castells—*and* non-Marxists—like Alain Touraine and Pierre Bourdieu—use *les rapports de classe* as a central concept of their theories.

A class relationship (of exploitation and domination) constitutes a contradictory relation with a dominant pole and a dominated pole. Because of this fundamental characteristic, a class relationship determines totally different entities ("classes") at each pole.

Let us examine the capital-labor class relationship. Because they are on the dominant side of the class relationship, the members of the bourgeoisie can evolve a developed interclass organization, multiplying and diversifying the contacts among themselves in order to engage in a common practice against the dominated people ("It's a small world" is a typically bourgeois saying . . . and a statement of fact); on the other hand, because they are dominated, the people projected on the other side of the class relationship are "normally" unable to communicate, to create and develop relations among themselves, a common ideology, a common organization, a common practice that could not be anything less than an attempt to regain control of that historical movement that put them "under," that is, an attempt to abolish class relationships. In other words, where class relationships (exploitation-and-domination) do exist, the ruling class exists *for itself*, while the ruled class does not; it is only latent, potential. To define both entities by the same concept of "class" risks a chain of confusions.

Production relationships of course determine places (of owner of capital, on the one hand, of direct producer on the other) that are the foundation of the class phenomenon. But fifty thousand places of bourgeois do not make a bourgeoisie, no more than seven million places of workers make a working class. What makes a bourgeoisie is the network of relations that exists among the bourgeoisie, or, to put it in a better framework, it is the common practice of classs struggle that is allowed by class organization and, further, that reinforces it. Seven million workers could also be made into a class by a network of relations among themselves, arising out of a common practice, that is, an organization based on reinforcing common struggle. When sociologists look at the "degree of consciousness" of individual workers, make an arithmetic average of them to get the degree of "collective class consciousness," and thus conclude that the working class is "not revolutionary anymore," they miss the key point of the class phenomenon as a social, not a psychological phenomenon. If it were true (but it never has been) that in a given country there were no proletarian party or union and that the workers had largely adopted bourgeois ("middle-class") ideology ("values"), then instead do saying that the working class is not revolutionary" it would be more correct to say that "the workers are not revolutionary," and that the working class, as such, does not exist: millions of isolated "individuals" do not constitute a class.

Now what exactly is the class organization of the ruling class? Is it, as it would be for the dominated "class," the party? There are always a number of political (bourgeois) parties, but they are little more than extras on the theatrical scene of "politics." It is the *state,* actually, that constitutes the class organization of the ruling class; the state as the instrument of class struggle was forged during past struggles that presage future ones. Through the state, the bourgeoisie act collectively and exercise power.

The state is therefore not a subject, and no sociologist should ever use this word as a subject and write such sentences as the "The *state* does this, decides that, protects these, represses those. . . ." On the other hand, to conceive of the state as a mere instrument of repression in the all-powerful hands of the unified bourgeoisie may be misleading. Neither totally subject nor totally object—what, then, is the state?

It would, of course, be preposterous to pretend to propose a theory of the state. My interest is in the ways and means to construct such a theory; my interest is methodological. I want to suggest here that it is useful to start from "the direct relation between the masters of the conditions of production and the direct producers," that is, the capital-labor relation in the factory and the social organization that arises historically from this relation in the workplace—instead of starting from the highly different network of social relations that is called the state.

We are fortunate to have at our disposal a class-historical analysis of the various forms of social organization that the capital-labor relation had produced until the 1860s: it can be found in Marx's *Capital* in the famous section four of Book I. I cannot go through it here. Suffice to say that the historical process described by Marx is a process, not of building an "enterprise bureaucracy" in order to repress and/or manipulate the workers (a repressive-ideological apparatus), but of progressive expropriation from the workers, through the very dynamics of capital, of the control workers initially had over their tools. This process is also a process of progressive appropriation by capital of the control of the working process; it starts with the control of the collective process, goes on to the control of the workshop process, and finally reaches down to the control of the individual processes.

Initially composed of a set of craftsmen, the "collective worker" is split up into two contradictory entities: on the one hand, a set of unskilled workers do "manual" work, which in fact means that they do most of what has to be done (transformation and transportation) but have lost control over what they are doing; on the other hand, the "management" becomes the embodiment of the so-called intellectual part of the labor, that is, activities of conception, direction, controlling, and sanctioning of the whole process. Once the bosses had this apparatus, they could use it for repression and manipulation; for instance, once they controlled hiring, through departments of personnel, they could fire as well. If the departments of personnel and the *bureau des methodes* (which determine the organization of work and the work cadences) are indeed the backbone of "repression" in the factory, it would be reductive to think of them merely as repressive apparatuses "fulfilling repressive functions": by the very classist nature of the capital-labor relation, any task of organization that is undertaken from the standpoint of capital, inasmuch as it escapes being controlled by the workers, is repressive.[4]

Another way of looking at the same thing is by seeing that the boss (whether the owner or manager because he enacts the same logic of profit-maximization) is not only exploiting the workers but also is directing the whole process of production (a direction that could be exercised collectively by the workers, were it not for the capital-labor institutionalized relation). Thus, we need a concept that expresses the double nature of that social relation between boss and worker, a relation of both exploitation and direction ("leadership"): I propose to use the term *encadrement*.

The word *cadre* was first used to designate roles in an apparatus in France, in the Army of the First Republic: it is in 1796, seven years after the French bourgeoisie seized state power, that, according to the Robert dictionary, one finds the term *"cadre"* used to designate "the set of officers and non-commissioned officers who lead a body of soldiers." This is very interesting, considering that the relation between officers and soldiers is a double one; it is not only one of leadership but also one of control backed by the ultimate sanction: death.

Today, *cadres* is used by the bourgeoisie and everybody else to designate the "managerial staff," from the top executives down to, sometimes, the foremen. According to the Robert dictionary, this use of the term appeared in 1931 *(le personnel d'encadrement des entreprises")*. If the bourgeoisie was late conceptually in referring to its own practice, it was still ahead of sociologists, who still refer to those roles as *"les classes moyennes,"* the middle class(es), as if they were a class and as if they stood in some middle ground.[5]

I find it enlightening to apply this conception to the whole of society. The key hypothesis here is that the state stands in the same relation toward the workers (and, generally speaking, the people), on the one hand, and the ruling class, on the other, as the *appareil d'encadrement* of the capitalist enterprise stands toward the workers of this enterprise, on the one hand, and its boss, on the other. This relation is one of progressive expropriation/appropriation.

Once stated, the parallels become striking. At the level of society, the bourgeoisies are not only ruling class(es) but also are leading class(es), as for instance, Antonio Gramsci and Alain Touraine have stated. The scission of the collective worker into two contradictory parts, the "decisional" one playing the game according to bourgeois orders, is an outstanding characteristic of twentieth-century capitalist societies (the so-called rise of the middle classes). The atomization of unskilled, or rather, *deskilled* workers in the factory corresponds to the atomization of the people in the so-called mass society. And so on.

My argument would, of course, be more convincing if I could cite historical studies with a classist perspective; but, alas, the state of contemporary history is almost as sad as that of sociology. It is mostly in the work of Michel Foucault that historical analyses take a classist look at the formation of contemporary institutions (psychiatric, judicial, penal in France and Great Britain).[6] E.P. Thompson also hints of such processes as hypothesized here.[7] Moreover, the disappearance of a genuine working-class culture and its "replacement" by a so-called mass culture distributed from above[8] may be understood through the concepts of expropriation, appropriation, and *encadrement:* the mass media are not "ideological apparatuses" forcefully manipulating the so-called masses; they fulfill a "need," or rather, they give the illusion of fulfilling the need of sociability that working-class social life fulfilled previously. Bourgeois institutions are strong not only because they are repressive, but also because given the atomization of the people that prevents it from acting, they are needed.[9]

Incidentally, this view enables us to better understand both social processes that liberate the working class, as well as the people generally, and institutionalized relations that these processes establish between the producers: "reappropriation" is the key concept, and it means the expropriation of the expropriators—of not only the ownership of the means of production but also of every social process whose direction they have appropriated. Although this conception needs further development, part of its sociological/historical is already better defined than, say, the phrase "radically transforming ('to smash') the bourgeois state apparatuses and replacing them by proletarian state apparatuses," which is never defined.

II. THE GENERAL CONCEPT OF "ANTHROPONOMICAL PROCESS" AND ITS PARTICULAR FORM IN A CAPITALIST CLASS STRUCTURE

The classist conception of social structure, that is, its conception as a class structure, prepares the way for a sociologically meaningful approach to "social mobility"; but it is not sufficient. At least one more concept is needed: that of the process of distribution of people into social positions defined by the institutionalized social relationships (*rapports sociaux institués*).

The idea of a process of allocating people into social (or economic) positions has appeared and disappeared in the sociological literature and it is the most conservative sociologists and economists who have proposed it, for it does not fit into the liberal, achievement-oriented, individualistic ideology of most American sociologists or marginalist economists.

The concept I propose here, however, goes beyond merely formulating "process of allocation." Instead of considering "people" and "positions" as givens (only focusing on their allocation), I shall embrace not only the distribution but the production of people, as well as the consumption of people in the postions (consumption of people here means consumption of their vital energy, for example, in capitalism, their energy under the form of labor-power). In this view, their distribution appears as a mediating process between production and consumption; the concept of production-distribution-consumption of people as an entire process therefore arises. I propose to call the anthroponomical process (by analogy with the economical process, the process of production-distribution-consumption of goods and services), Anthroponomy.

It is surprising that such a concept is not already a part of the intellectual core of the "social sciences." Long ago, Engels hinted at it:

> According to the materialistic conception, the determining factor in history is, in the final instance, the production and reproduction of immediate life. This, again, is of a twofold character: on the one side, the production of the means of existence, of food, clothing, and shelter and the tools necessary for that production; on the other side, the production of human beings themselves, the propagation of the species.[10]

Thus, the idea has been expressed, but it remained undeveloped. Two reasons "explain" this theoretical lacuna. First, until very recently, little control over pregnancy (through contraceptive devices) was possible. Biological reproduction was thus a perfectly natural phenomenon. Second, the particular category of people who are the direct producers of this whole process, that is, the women, had no means to express themselves publicly and thus to develop a self-elaborated image, group consciousness, and organization. Their work was defined as something in itself natural, something inherent in women. When a women's movement reappeared in the late 1960s, the link with Lewis Morgan and Engels' old idea was quickly made.[11] See the introduction by Elizabeth B. Leacock to the reedition of Engels' work (1972). There is, I believe, a close link between the two reasons proposed here; that is, it was not by chance that the women's movement appeared when and where effective contraception was available.

Continuing my theoretical work, I arrived at the concept of
"production of human beings." Having redefined "social
mobility" as the "distribution of human beings into the social
structure," I was developing the idea when I happened to
reread Marx's famous methodological *Introduction to the Critique of Political Economy* and applied his treatment of the relations of production, consumption, and distribution of *goods* to
those of the production, consumption, and distribution of
human beings. [12]

Is anthroponomy just another barbaric neologism of the
social sciences? Could sociology be spared this concept? On
the contrary, it allows us to concentrate a large number of
previously unrelated concepts. At present, the various
moments of the anthroponomical process are designated by
such terms as natality, fertility, reproduction, socialization,
education, training, labor market, mobility, work, consumption,
and so forth; all of which tend to scatter attention. Because
these concepts have been relegated to different theoretical
fields, it is impossible to think of the process as a whole.

For instance, demography studies the initial production of
people (natality, fertility, and reproduction). Sociology is interested in these social agents as such, overlooking the fact
that these social agents were often caused by *social reasons,*
not natural or biological.

The production of a new human being makes use of
biological processes; yes, but to reduce it to this is as absurd
as reducing consumption to digestion or reducing work to
physiology (effort, fatigue, etc.): in all three cases, social relations trigger the process that give it its specific
characteristics and meaning. While the bases of these practices are indeed material—"material" means here, among
other things, physiological—their characteristics and their
meanings are always social. The idea, by the way, is not new; it
can be found in Marx and Engels' *The German Ideology:* "The
production of life, both of one's own by labour and of fresh life
by procreation, apears at once as a double relationship on the
one hand as a natural, on the other as a social relationship."

Child psychology, psychoanalysis, sociology of the family:
they all start off where demography leaves off, and they are
themselves followed by sociology of education, pedagogy,
adolescent psychology, and so forth. Further down, we find
economy of the work force (so-called human economy),
studies on the labor market, "social mobility" sociology,

social psychology (adaptation, identity, etc.); and so forth.

Each of these "social sciences" strongly emphasizes the practical side of "how to enable people to adapt themselves (or to be 'adapted') to the institutions"; one might even say that this emphasis is what these very different disciplines have in common.

What is called for, then, is one perspective that unifies these processes that transform human beings into social beings. The unity is not necessary because all the processes act on the same object—the living being—it is necessary because they all stem from the same source—through various mediations—that is, the historically determined class structure. This is why a unified perspective is needed and also why it has to be "positive," "scientific," and thoroughly *critical* as well: the fact that things could be different is a fact and as such constitutes an integral part of reality.[13]

Production of Human Beings

The whole process of production of human beings can be thought of as having two aspects: the material and the nonmaterial. The nonmaterial aspect is what is commonly referred to by the concepts of "psychology," "culture," or "ideology."[14]

The literature on the nonmaterial aspect is much more extensive than that on the material. The generally poor quality of this literature results, I believe, from this one-sided perspective. Here, however, I shall restrict myself to the other, one-sided perspective, that of the material aspect of the production of human beings, leaving the synthesis for later.

It seems that two phases may be distinguished in the material aspect of the process of production of human beings, or "anthropo-production." One is the initial phase, that is, the process by which a *new* human being is produced (conception and pregnancy). This phase interests demographers insofar as the numbers of viable embryos are concerned.

The second phase, from birth to death, has been fragmented into the separate disciplines of the social sciences. Curiously enough, while the demographic approach is very materialistic, that of the social sciences is extremely idealistic. Very little attention is paid to the actual processes through which the life of the child is produced and reproduced (e.g., eating, drinking, sleeping, playing, fighting, living, doing things); here psychology and psychoanalysis hold total hegemony.

When the human being goes to work, however, some concepts that permit formulating the "production of life" in materialistic terms do reappear in the literature: the concept of consumption, for instance. A better concept would be Marx's "reproduction of labor power," which is, however, an economic concept and should be taken with a grain of salt.

Given this state of affairs, I will limit myself here to an analysis of the process of "reproduction of labour power" of the individual workers and of the working class. This point of view is somewhat restricted, but I shall argue that it is a crucial one in that, in an attempt to completely control it, the ruling class established an institution, the so-called family, which in its turn determines the process of production of life in all social strata.[15]

Families as Units of Anthropo-Production

So far, we have conceptualized the various phenomena usually referred to as natality, education, consumption, as moments of a whole process of anthropo-production. To repeat, this term refers to both the initial production of human beings and the continuous process of their material and cultural reproduction and transformation through "time," that is, through social-historical practice.

Much of this process takes place within the framework of one particular institution, the so-called *family*. This means that the mediations between the process of anthropo-production as a socially determined phenomenon, on the one hand, and its ultimate results (class relationships), on the other, are found for the most part in the "family," the institution through which society determines children's lives.

Two points, which are somewhat foreign to the usual "sociology of the family," must be stressed here. First, contrary to appearances, "the family" as a structurally constant social unit (crossing class boundaries) does not exist.[16] What we observe are the effects, on various classist milieux, of one single institution, the familial institution as historically created by the ruling class. But this institution produces different effects (i.e., different types of families) in different classist milieux (different "social classes"). One should therefore not speak of the family as a transclass unit, but of *the familial institution* or of the various *classist types of families*.

Second, to understand the genesis and structure of the for-
malized relationships that constitute the familial institution, it is
fruitful to conceive of them as relations of production, that is, the
(institutionalized) social relationships that organize a particular
type of production, the production of human beings.

These observations open the door to a reanalysis of the familial
institution from a classist point of view. Baudelot and Establet
stress that "families" in various social classes, despite a common
appearance (Dad and Mom and the kids), constitute very different, contrasting systems of social relationships.[17]

To begin with, although each bourgeois family draws its
resources from a common fund, for example, a checking account, each worker's family relies on the daily employment of
the father. This basic fact determines the whole network of
"family relations."

For instance, the relation between father and son in the
capital-owning bourgeoisie is fundamentally based on capital-
inheritance: the son is socially and personally defined as the
future inheritor and constitutes for the father the (ideological)
meaning of his—in itself meaningless—accumulation of
capital. Workers' children, on the other hand, certainly do not
stand in the same relation to *their* fathers.

The relation of the wife to her husband is also bound to be
very different: in the working class, it is determined as a relation of direct production—the daily housework of the woman
is crucial to the reproduction of the labor power, that is, the
life of the man. This is not so among the bourgeoisie.

Fully developed, these hypotheses revolutionize the
"sociology of the family." For instance, they cast doubts on
the validity of sociological statements that are now applied to
all families—a drastic change in itself. One would have to
develop at least four different types of families, corresponding
to four different classist milieux and *thus* to four different life-
styles. The bourgeois-family type would be based on capital
accumulation and transmission. The working-class-family
type would be based on capital's demand of labor power
reproduction (from day to day, and from generation to generation), on the one hand, and on the workers' drive toward recon-
quest of at least *some* power over their own lives, on the other.
The small-production–family type (peasants, artisans, and
shopkeepers) would be based on precapitalistic relations of
production that do not separate capital and labor, capital's accumulation and labor-power reproduction (the label "family

production" says much more than it seems to at first glance).
The middle-strata–family type would be based on a career project, that is, the projection of self and children along slowly rising "career paths" institutionalized by the *appareil général d'encadrement.*[18]

This approach is much more promising than the conceptualization of the family (initial mistake) as an *appareil idéologi-
que d'état.*[19] No doubt the familial institution contributes
tremendously to securing and maintaining the ideological
order, not only through the familial ideology but also through
the practices it enforces on everybody, practices that cannot
but generate conservative ideas.[20] The familial institution,
however, widely differs from the other *appareils idéologiques:* all
of those, for example, the school, the churches, the media, are
composed like the state apparatus proper, of an army of full-
time members, officers on behalf of the bourgeoisie (*per-
manents de la bourgeoisie*), hierarchically organized and directed
by the ruling class. Not so for the family, though, because we
are all officers. This institution has no specialized personnel,
no bureaucracy, no single head; it is, so to speak, embedded
into the foundation of societies, while the *appareils idéologiques*
are part of the superstructure. This striking difference between
the family and the other *appareils* is dissipated when a
materialist approach is taken: the familial institution is created
by the ruling class to institutionalize particular social relations
through which it can control the process of anthropo-production,
which takes place at the level of the people themselves, without
the mediation of tools of production, and thus cannot be totally
expropriated from the people.

The idea of four classist types of families remains to be
developed concomitantly, determining if the enormous amount
of available data can be reinterpreted according to it. But such
an idea also raises new questions. For instance, how can the
ruling class (i.e., the bourgeoisie), which pretends to create
universal institutions, promulgate a universally valid legislation that promotes in various classes, and thus through
various consequences, its own particular interests? In analyzing the set of laws and norms that historically define the
familial institution, we find subsets that define rules for inheritance that are relevant to the bourgeoisie and secondly to
the small property-owning petty bourgeoisie and subsets that
define the responsibilities of wives toward husbands, of
parents toward children, the latter implicitly referring to the

working class. But then, provided these rules are actually enforced, a host of "problems" are created when they are applied to
those classes for which they were not written.[21]

We thus arrive at our second point: the conceptualization of
the familial institution as defining—for all classes—the relation of production to the process of production of human beings. I shall not attempt to study the laws of anthropo-
production in general or in capitalistic societies. Here I will
limit myself to investigating what should be the first step in
the analysis of the process.

Again starting with the capital-labor relation, we see that
labor is the crucial element in the enlarged reproduction of
capital; the production of labor is in turn a crucial element in
the capitalistic process. Therefore, from the point of view of
capital, it is necessity to control the production of labor-
power. When capital is in charge of a given social formation,
this point of view manifests itself in institutions. The familial
institution becomes the crucial tool for the control of labor-
power production. The relations of production of the people it
institutionalizes are meant to apply in the working class: they
are the main tools of capital's manpower policy. It is therefore
with the working class that we should start our study of the
production of human beings.

The Process of Anthropo-production in the Working-class Families and the Universal Oppression of Women

When we realize that social relationships, which the familial
institution creates and enforces in the working class, are relations of production (production of human beings), we see the
roles that these relations define in terms of a production process; not as roles in a theatrical game, but as roles that force
people to behave and to think of themselves as agents of a
productive process. An important point emerges from this approach: whether for the initial production of human beings, for
the reproduction of children's vital energy and production as
social beings, or for the reproduction of labor-power of adult
persons, the familial institution always designates the same
type of human being to carry the burden of production tasks:
women.

Until the women's movements exploded, their "activities" at
home were not recognized as work; on the contrary, it was

assumed that they were just fulfilling their "feminine nature."
This nature was, of course, thought of not in social terms but
in biological terms. Actually, nothing "natural" forces women,
either as a group or individually, to be solely responsible for
taking care of babies, bringing up children, and the cooking
and cleaning and mending for them until they are grown, as a full-
time job, not eight hours, but twenty-four hours a day.[22] Nor is it
natural that women should have to do *all* the housework (cooking, shopping, cleaning, washing, repairing, etc.) necessary to
produce their husbands' labor-power. If women now find themselves responsible for these types of work, it is not because of
their biological nature but because of the social relationships
(rapports sociaux) that define their position. It is only during the
nine months of pregnancy and in some cases the first year of
their children's lives, that the nature of women makes them chief
producers; but if it is their biological constitution that gives them
the monopoly of that production, it is society that decides—or attempts to decide—whether or not they are going to produce. The
ruling class, which is so fond of talking about the sacredness of
nature, in practice molds it to its very "unnatural" class interests.
One has only to look at the ongoing battle between various factions of the ruling class for control over women's bellies
(working-class women, that is) to understand that the bourgeoisie
is not at all afraid to interfere with nature.[23]

Hence, if women are constrained to do most of the work of
human production, it is not because of nature or because of
the oppression of men over women (this oppression, like that
of foremen over workers, itself results from some more fundamental social relation of which it is a *mediation*); the
historically determined, resistible, institutionalized, and thus
desinstitutionalizable system of social relations called the
family—as capital's instrument for constraining the working-
class women to produce human beings—is responsible for the
situation of *all* women.

Because this has not been clearly understood in the West, it
has been possible to argue that the "underdog" position of the
workers' wives was due to the so-called reactionary ideology
of their husbands concerning the sexual question. While there
are a number of immediate observations that support this
point of view (those that could contradict it are not emphasized in these types of studies), they are interpreted in the limited
framework of the home, that is, without considering what is
happening to the husbands-workers in the factories.

When *this* is taken into account, interpretations change. Let us suppose that capital wants as much energy as possible from the workers (a not altogether irrelevant hypothesis). In this case, workers return home from the factory completely exhausted, and some social organization has to exist that allows them rest in order to reproduce their labor-power: however, it takes more labor to do the shopping, cooking, and so forth. If workers work forty-five hours weekly in the factory and if it takes fifteen hours more to prepare the food, and so forth, it may be said that each worker uses sixty hours of labor-power to do all his work.

Now, does the worker's salary correspond to the goods and services that are necessary for him to reproduce his own labor-power? That would mean that he would have to earn enough money to eat in restaurants, pay somebody to clean his house, and so on: in Paris of the mid-1970's, for instance, that would take an absolute minimum of a hundred dollars per week, while the average salary is only about sixty dollars.

How can capital get away with paying labor at half of its value? It is precisely by not compensating workers for the extra work done at home, that is, paying them for the goods and services that are necessary for the workers to reproduce their labor-power. Capital's solution is "the family": a social organization through which workers' *wives* furnish all the above mentioned "services" (housework) for their husbands and for themselves—about twenty-five hours per week for one couple without children—while the reproduction of their *own* labor power is reduced to the very minimum: shelter is already paid for, there are no transportation costs, only food and clothes have to be purchased for the wife, whose cost will be counterbalanced by the shift in the husband's way of life: no more drinks at the local bar, no more movies or bowling alleys—in fact, no more social life. Sixty dollars is all that it takes, and besides, the worker has a "reproduction unit" ready to start producing future laborers.[24]

The supposition here is that it is absolutely necessary that both husband and wife act accordingly to the blueprint: the woman *must* accomplish the housework daily, the man *must* bring home all the pay. The trick is that it does not take any foreman to enforce these norms: the husband and wife enforce them on each other, each acts as foreman toward the other because it is necessary for his/her own survival. It is difficult to imagine a more alienating situation.

The situation is not symmetrical, however: it is the labor-power of the men that is capital's ultimate goal, the familial institution and ideology give power to the man in order to enable him to "get the work done." Hence, we arrive at the so-called authoritarian character of workers toward their wives, which looks so awful when looked at with middle-class eyes. The result of the above social-historical process is usually referred to as "the nuclear family."

To carry our example forward: children come along. Because sixty dollars are not enough to support them, the man works overtime at the factory, which further exhausts him; thus, the burden of taking care of the children rests entirely on the woman's energy. Hence, more and more, working-class children are alienated from their fathers; they do not share with them their working-class experience.

In earlier times, sons were usually brought up by their fathers, learning from them hunting, fishing, farming, or work as artisans, while mothers passed on to daughters the skills and culture of homemaking. This ensured the reproduction over the generations of the family culture of the social group. But with the division introduced in the nuclear, capital-determined family, no working-class culture could be transmitted spontaneously by a common practice, from father to son: mother to daughter; it had to be reexperienced and reinvented for each generation.

There is another important point: the nuclear form of the family concentrates all types of interpersonal relations into one very small group of people: the members of the nuclear family. Not only does it make conjugal life much more difficult (because of the overlapping of several types of relations); more important, it atomizes the working class into millions of isolated units. Solidarity fades away; privatization takes over. Thus, it is not only "the ruling ideology" that makes contemporary workers less revolutionary; nor is it due only to the standard of living that imperialism can afford to give to the skilled layer of the working group. In addition to bourgeoisie propaganda and monetary gains, the specific organization of social relationships that stems from the nuclear family in the working class encourages the atomization of the class, the disappearance (nonreproduction) of those social relations that, binding workers and workers' wives and workers' children together, transform them into members of a living social group.[25]

To end this section, it is interesting to see what secondary contradictions appear if the nuclear-type family is enforced on every class and every stratum.

In every social stratum, therefore, when men are not at work, they are at home; women do all the housework and single-handedly take care of the children; children are produced quasi-exclusively by their mothers and men have the power to enforce this type of family organization on their wives. But only in the working class does this appear as a "normal," if deplorable, way of life: outside of a genuine proletarian "solution," that is, inter-family solidarity and the reappropriation of the local "institutions," there is no other way to organize the husband-wife children relations.

But in other social strata, this type of family organization would generate a sense of absurdity, of unnecessary constraint. The bourgeoisie of course will be the first to make itself comfortable at home: servants will spare the wife the labor and leave her only its supervision; and the multiple tasks of class organization and class (bourgeois) struggle will provide the husband with a superabundance of excuses to stay away from home. For the children, however, the contradictory situation creates very interesting processes, which I cannot describe here. The first generations of middle strata, looking up toward the bourgeoisie as their reference group, will interiorize the bourgeois-professed morality and try very hard to live by it ("middle state" is the familiar word for what is actually the agents of the *appareils d'encadrement*).

It is for the new generations of the growing middle strata that something different happens: because men's domination over women is not necessary to the production of life in this stratum, conditions are created spawning women's liberation movements. Now, women's movements contain a revolutionary potential, but one can trust the instincts of the ruling class to repress this potential and strongly stress the "reformist" components (in the media, in the new legislation that it concedes). It seems very likely that one of the sources of women's movements is the frustration of middle-strata women seeing themselves trapped in an institution, the nuclear family, that constrains them unnecessarily, for it is obvious that in these strata men are not that tired that they could not do half of the housework and children's caretaking, thus freeing women of the dreariness of home life and allowing them to take up some of these middle-strata professional roles that provide at least an illusion of self-realization.

Reforms are worthwhile when they are initiated from below; and this one is important, for it suppresses a secondary contradiction between women and men of the middle strata. To change the social norms about the man-woman relation inside the middle-strata family also will induce a change in norms for nonmarried men and women, for example, girls and boys. Besides, if the movement is strong enough, it may force legislative changes that, because they are supposed to apply to all citizens, may help working-class women (e.g., the new laws on abortion; it is typical of bourgeois policy that in several countries the legalization of abortion has been accompanied by the creation of "committees" that decide if the women may have an abortion: the mere existence of such committees is a deterrent for working-class women). But one should not be surprised that working-class women do not always share with middle-strata women their enthusiasm for the "struggle against men" or even against male chauvinism: their real situation is different.[26]

A lot of work on these questions remains to be done. What is important, however, is that we start in the right direction. It seems to me that the conceptions of the production of human beings, of the families as units of this production, of family relationships as relations of production, make a good beginning.

Production of men and women is organized by society (i.e., the ruling class), with their *consumption* in view. Therefore, the next step would be to study the various patterns of consumption. This should be done even before we try to understand the process of distribution, not to mention social mobility, social immobility, and their social consequences. Inheritance of capital, not schooling, is the key process: the inheritance of capital, which is the main relation of distribution of human beings, is a relation of production, as it is the relation that distributes means of production to some people, projecting all the other people into the class position of proletariat, whether in necktie or in blue overalls.

NOTES

1. Daniel Bertaux, "Nouvelles perspectives sur la mobilité sociale en France," Proceedings of the Seventh World Congress of Sociology, 1970.
2. Karl Marx, *Das Capital*, Book 3.
3. There are not three main classes as Marx wrote about in his unfinished manuscript, "The Classes." For more on this point, see Pierre-Philippe Rey, *Les Alliances de Classes* (Paris: Maspéro, 1973), Part 1.
4. It has been argued that the true aim of the division of labor, the Taylorization of the process of production, is the division of the laborers. See the excellent papers by Stephen Marglin, "What Do Bosses Do?" "Origins and Functions of Hierarchy in Capitalist Production," Department of Economics, Harvard Uni-

versity, multigraph, 1970, and André Gorz et al., *Critique de la Division du Travail* (Paris: Editions du Seuil, 1973). The key idea in these papers is that the actual goal of the reorganization of the collective process of production is the disorganization of the collective of producers.

5. They are not standing, however, they are enacting, sometimes reluctantly and sometimes zealously, a class practice that is not their own. They could be thought of as means, the means that the ruling class constructs for its own practice; they are "in the middle" like the whip is in the middle of the coachman and the horses; they should be called not *classes moyennes* but *couches-moyens*.

6. Michel Foucault, *Surveiller et Punir* (Paris: Gallimard, 1975).

7. E. P. Thompson, *The Making of the English Working Class* (London: Victor Gollancz, 1963), and "Le Charivari Anglais," *Annales ESC* (March-April, 1972).

8. See Richard Hoggart, *The Uses of Literacy* (London: Chatto and Windus, 1959), for a vivid description of this process in Britain.

9. About progressive expropriation: I was able to witness throughout the years a process through which a particular village of the Pyrenees was expropriated from the power of making its own roads. Thirty years ago, they were maintaining them or opening new ones; now they pay taxes (which they did not pay before) to have specialists decide, in Paris—five hundred miles away—*which* roads should be done and to have a special apparatus of technicians and workers come up and make them. Of course, the roads are better; but they do not go where the peasants would like them to go. Instead of going to the fields, they go to tourist attractions.

10. Frederich Engels, *Origins of The Family, the Property and the State* (1884), Preface.

11. Ibid. See the introduction by Elizabeth B. Leacock in reprint issued by International Publishers, New York, 1972.

12. The raw result was included in a paper delivered at the Seventh World Congress of Sociology. Recently, I came across a number of very recent feminist studies, particularly, Maria Rosa Della Costa and Selma James, *The Power of Women and the Subversion of the Community* (Nottingham: Falling Wall Press, 1972), and was glad to discover that they were developing pretty much the same idea, but added to it a political dimension arising from their personal experiences and social praxis.

13. I know of one attempt to reconstruct the whole process of production of a human being, including the work done by himself: the monumental study of Jean-Paul Sartre on Flaubert, *L'Idiot de la Famille* (Paris: Gallimard, 1973). The methodological interest of this study widely exceeds the case of Flaubert.

14. Any social process has to be thought of as a whole, not as composed of two parts: the material and the nonmaterial. We are observing different aspects when we look at the same real process from different points of view. Because we cannot get more than one particular view of any real object at a time, idealism concludes that there must be as many real objects as there are points of view. On the other hand, mechanical materialism stresses a particular point of view as being "the truth." I am trying here to avoid both pitfalls.

15. Western demography has consistently ignored Marxist thought, while Western Marxists consistently ignored demographic questions. As a result, the conceptual field is in poor shape. Consider, for instance, the confusion introduced by the concept of reproduction as it is used today. Demographers use it to designate what is in fact the production of new human beings. This particular process of production is, as we have seen, at the same time a social and a biological process; socially, it is a process of production, but biologically, it is a process of reproduction (of the species). Thus, to use the term "reproduction" stresses the biological component and induces one implicitly to think about the whole process in biological terms.

Speaking about the process of (daily) reproduction of labor-power, the economists use the term "consumption." But while in a "critical political economy" approach the two terms are synonymous, the use of the term "consumption" in lieu of "reproduction" is not casual: it orients one towards the question of differential consumption (by social class), as if everybody who had to reproduce one's labor-power in similar ways had spent it in the same way. The next step then is to focus on differential symbolic consumption, with the result that the material aspect of consumption is soon completely forgotten, and the symbolic aspect is one-sidedly, if sometimes brilliantly, stressed. People whose lives are structured by the fact that they work in factories, mines, construction sites are no longer viewed in their working contexts but at home, where nothing distinguishes them from other citizens except that little tag, "worker."

16. This point comes from a few remarks made by Christian Baudelot and Roger Establet in their benchmark study on the French school "system," *L'École capitaliste en France* (Paris: Maspéro, 1971), pp. 231–236.

17. Ibid.

18. These ideas have been developed in Daniel Bertaux, *Destins personnels et rapports de classe* (Paris: Presses Universitaires de France, 1977).

19. Louis Althusser, "Idéologie et appéreils ideologiques d'état," *La Pensée*, No. 157 (June 1971); Nicos Poulantzas, *Fascisme et Dictature* (Paris: Maspero, 1972) and *Les Classes sociales dans le capitalisme d'aujourd'hui* (Paris: Editions du Seuil, 1974).

20. Daniel Bertaux, "Two and a Half Models of Social Structure," in *Social Stratification and Career Mobility,* ed. K. U. Mayer and Walter Muller (Paris: Mouton, 1972).

21. Maybe an explanation of the "double standard" in moral norms can be found here: norms edicted by the bourgeoisie are intended to apply to other social groups, not to itself. Another phenomenon, that is, the contemporary rebellion of women in the middle strata against an institution that they consider oppressive, also may be understood in this light as we shall see below.

22. See the ethnographic studies on so-called primitive societies and historical studies such as Philippe Ariès, *L'Enfant e la vie familiale sous l'ancien régime* (Paris: Plon, 1960), on the European Middle Age. Engels *The Origins of the Family,* remains an excellent introduction to the question; his study is based on the work of American anthropologist Lewis Morgan. Elizabeth B. Leacock has reviewed recent evidence for or against Engels' hypotheses as drawn from contemporary ethnography. Della Costa and James, *The Power of Women,* describes attempts by the Italian women's movement to resocialize the caretaking of children in making it a community activity.

23. It would be interesting to show which factions of the ruling class are natalist and which are Malthusian; history indicates that it depends on time and place. The key hypothesis is that of manpower policies that are hiding behind very strict but contradictory dogmas. Also the same class factions at once may be natalist for some categories—including usually themselves—and Malthusian for others; this is the case for the small group that is presently running the affairs of U.S. imperialism.

24. Let me emphasize again, it is sixty dollars for seventy hours of work, not forty-five hours. This is the initial mistake of many Marxist analyses of the salary and the blind spot that is responsible for the conceptualization of "housewives" as nonworking persons: this mistake is equivalent to adopting capital's point of view—or rather, capital's explicit ideology, not capital's practical and unspoken point of view, which considers workers' wives as highly productive, as indicated by laws that both constrain them and protect them against breakdown.

25. No empirical, that is, historical, evidence is offered here to sustain the supposition. However, various studies on the nineteenth-century European work-

ing class, either published or in progress, might be used to flesh out this
theoretical skeleton.

26. This point has been overlooked by some feminist writers, usually in the U.S.
movement; but it has been seen very clearly by other women, among them
Marlene Dixon, Della Costa and James, *The Power of Women*. The fact that
this point of view has not been prevalent in the women's movements is not
imputable primarily to these movements, but to the class-structured context
in which they develop and from which they tend to borrow their deep ideological structures.

9.
EPISTEMOLOGICAL PRACTICE AND THE SOCIAL SCIENCES*

MANUEL CASTELLS AND EMILIO DE IPOLA

INTRODUCTION

The 'social sciences,' faced with the upsurge of class-struggles all over the world, are at a crisis point.

Under the backlash of the general crisis of the dominant ideology in capitalist industrial societies, sociological 'theories' are being demystified by the implacable criticism of social practice; their techniques can only claim a very narrow field of application; their methodology has lost its high status as a general and universal scientific overlord and stands revealed as a catalogue of common-sense recipes. At a time when a confrontation of the researcher with his work, with the world which produces him and which he observes-and-practices, has been made inevitable by all the recent developments in social science research, a new principle of legitimacy (some might say, a new constraint), external to the research itself, has suddenly appeared: epistemology. The status of this new arrival from the celestial spheres of philosophy

*Originally published in *Economy and Society*. Vol. 5, No. 2, 1976. Reprinted by permission. Copyright © 1976

is all the more ambiguous because of its close participation in the destruction of the pillars on which the social sciences rested. This participation manifested itself as criticism addressed to certain principles of idealist philosophy that were implicit in the technical code of sociological scientificity. But when epistemology replaces the positivist methodology as the principle of legitimacy, the same metaphysical and anti-scientific process is taking place on a higher level. In fact epistemology continues to set itself up as a criterion of scientificity outside the bounds of actual research. The latter thus becomes merely a system of measurement connected with a set of predetermined standards instead of an activity to be judged by the fruitfulness of its results in relation to a theoretical and historical argument relevant to its own field of experience.

Thus the intervention of epistemology in the social sciences becomes at one and the same time a powerful instrument for the criticism of empiricist methodological normativity (which acts as a considerable obstacle to the development of research), and as the last bastion of sociological idealism.

These are so many claims demanding an explanation and a systematic theoretical development. Such a development would seek to examine the status of epistemological practice, the effects on the basic postulates implicit in the main tendencies of research of such a critique, and the proper limits of such a critique. We shall attempt to show by the use of analysis, on the one hand, the effects of division, rupture and exacerbation which are characteristic of the contradictions inherent in any epistemological intervention; and on the other hand, the subordinate, auxiliary role such an intervention is bound to take in comparison to actual scientific practice. All of which is in direct opposition to the widely held idea of epistemology as the *unifying* and *metatheoretical* foundation of the legitimacy of the social sciences.[1]

First of all, we must work out what the tools are, the conditions and the objectives of this type of epistemological intervention. The care taken over clarity and the avoidance of ambiguity (which contrasts with the vague rhetoric sometimes deliberately employed in epistemology) explains the somewhat schematic appearance of the text, which begins with a group of definitions and theses. The latter, which are intended to give a general outline of epistemological practice in the social sciences, should be considered *provisional* on two counts: first, because as with every theoretical product they are subject to correction and development; secondly, and more important, because the essence of epistemological intervention is to produce its effects on a *conjuncture* of scientific practices. It follows that epistemology, both in the categories it employs and in the theses it propounds, should take into account the shifts and variations in the areas in which it intervenes.

Once the working-tools of epistemology have been revealed, we shall analyse critically the principal *epistemological models* which implicitly orientate research in the social sciences.

Finally, we shall examine the relation between epistemological intervention and social and political practice, which will lead us to establish the *limits* inherent in this type of intervention.

I. POINTS OF DEPARTURE FOR A MATERIALIST EPISTEMOLOGY. DEFINITIONS AND THESES

Any attempt at epistemological intervention in the social sciences must provide itself with the necessary means, that is to say, with definitions capable of establishing the basic epistemological *categories* and the *theses* which express the fundamental propositions concerning the production of knowledge, scientific practices, and the epistemological obstacles hindering social research. The exposition of our argument in the form of a set of *theses* should not be seen as an indication of dogmatism, but rather as an attempt to answer the twofold demands of *clarity* and *economy*.

Definitions of Epistemological Categories

1. EPISTEMOLOGY: The exercising of vigilance in the (conceptual and methodological) operations of scientific activity. The aim of this vigilance being to render ineffective the epistemological obstacles which hinder the production of knowledge.[2]
2. THE PROCESS OF PRODUCTION OF KNOWLEDGE: The transformation of a given raw material (scientific knowledge and/or pre-scientific representation) into a given product (new scientific knowledge); this transformation would take place by the application of definite scientific agents of production using definite means of labor (concepts, theories, methods) in definite production conditions (both material and social).[3]

a) The category 'process of the production of knowledge' is an abstract one: such a process does not exist in a pure form, but is always linked with other processes of production within a *scientific practice* and in conjunction with a definite ideological practice.

b) Production conditions correspond essentially to what one means, in economic production when one talks about relations of production, i.e, the matrix that distributes the agents of production throughout the whole process.

c) The very fact that we are considering sciences in terms of the category 'process of production,' implies a challenging of the whole atomistic conception of knowledge. In fact all knowledge is by definition, inseparable from the *productive system* (articulation of the process of production) of which it is a product.

3. SCIENTIFIC PRACTICE: A complex of definite processes of production of knowledge the unifying principle of which is a common conceptual field (which forms part of a larger theoretico-ideological formation); these processes being organized and regulated by a system of norms and belonging to a set of institutional apparatuses.
Note: by 'institutional apparatuses,' we mean the unit of production and circulation of scientific knowledge (centres of research and education).[4]
4. KNOWLEDGE: A complex ensemble constituted, within a particular social structure, by the action of certain particular scientific practices in an ideological 'setting' (the latter being defined by inter-class relationships) in which knowledge (information) is produced, transmitted, appropriated, sanctioned and applied.
Note: The category 'knowledge' does not overlap with the category of scientific practice. Indeed, apart from the fact that all scientific practice contains ideological elements, it *also* belongs to a *certain socially defined organization of knowledge,* which in turn belongs to a system of institutional apparatuses which regulate scientific production in a given social formation. It is to this institutional system that we are referring when we speak of an ideological 'setting.'[5]
5. CONCEPT: Unit of meaning in a scientific discourse.
6. NOTION: Unit of meaning in an ideological discourse.
7. CATEGORY: Unit of meaning in an epistemological discourse.
8. THEORETICO-IDEOLOGICAL FORMATION: An articulated ensemble of concepts and notions which intervene as *means of*

labor, in the field of a particular scientific practice.

Note: In all scientific practice, as in all ideological practice, there exist certain processes by which discourse may be produced. But at the same time there are also some ideological elements present. The category 'theoretico-ideological formation' indicates this articulation of the conceptual and the ideological on the level of the means of production of scientific discourses.

9. EPISTEMOLOGICAL BREAK: Specific effect of the *irruption* into the ideologial formation of a process of production of scientific knowledge.

Notes on the history and influence of the category 'Epistemological Break'. The category 'epistemological break' is the culminating point of an important tradition of which the most brilliant developments can be traced back to Gaston Bachelard.[6] In the epistemological work of Bachelard the irruption of a process of production of knowledge is understood through a second category: that of 'rupture' which indicates a twofold discontinuity both produced by the emergence of a new scientific discipline in the history of knowledge, or possibly by the reformulation of the basic axioms of an already existing science.[7] Epistemological Discontinuity: is the specific effect produced by scientific work as such in relation to the 'evidence' of perception and common-sense.[8]

In both of these meanings, the category *rupture* cannot be dissociated from the complementary category of *epistemological obstacle.* The latter indicates what Bachelard's analyses refer to as the 'intellectual resistances' which hinder or pervert the production of scientific knowledge.[9] 'Anti-thoughts', 'web of persistence errors', 'resistance of thought to thought', these phrases (which list all the epistemological obstacles) stress the *subjective* origin of these obstacles. Indeed, according to Bachelard, these obstacles are nothing more than the product of the *imaginary relation* of the scientist to his own practice.[10] When it is not placed under strict surveillance, it is this 'relation' which leads ineluctably to systematic errors (theoretical hallucinations, logical fallacies, conceptual blanks) which harden into working habits, prejudices and beliefs, which constantly recur and which are deeply rooted in the practice of the scientist.

Having said this, Bachelard's analyses are essentially concerned with *describing* the functioning of certain types of epistemological obstacles, and the resultant effects in the sciences. On the other hand, with certain exceptions which we shall examine, he fails to explain satisfactorily the way in which these obstacles are formed and conditions in which their production periodically recurs.

Much the same can be said with regard to the category of *rupture*; Bachelard demonstrates very pertinently the efficacy and range of influence of certain localized 'ruptures' (in particular his analyses of the theory of relativity, of non-Euclidean geometry and of micro-physics), but he does not offer a full explanation of the real conditions (theoretical and historical) in which these 'ruptures' may be seen to be produced. This failure is the logical result of a basic lacuna in Bachelard's epistemological work: the lack of any developed and explicit reflection as to the forms in which scientific practice is articulated with other types of social practices (ideological, political or economic). In fact, Bachelard is not ignorant of this problem. But the generally unsystematic solutions he proposes often verge on psychologism and subjective idealism: such is the general implication of his reference to the libido of the scientist in order to explain the formation and recurrence of epistemological obstacles. It is also the case in his continual references to the 'scientific spirit' (where the word which dominates is 'spirit'), and to the 'scientific community', which should be understood as 'inter-subjectivity'. By these means he vaguely seeks to explain the conditions in which an epistemological rupture could emerge.[11]

The work of *Louis Althusser*, and of other philosophers adhering to the same trends of thought, is historically and theoretically closer to our own point of view; it has given a new value to Bachelard's epistemology, chiefly by attempting to understand certain of his theses in the light of dialectical materialism. Such work has the indisputable merit of attempting to answer those problems which were left in suspense by the work of Bachelard. Thus, on the one hand, epistemological obstacles were analyzed in the context of a general theory of ideology (defined according to its twofold effect); and on the other hand, the 'rupture' category (which is the name Althusser would give to the distinction between science and ideology) was considered in terms of the historico-social conditions in which it is realized.[12] In this way the processes whereby epistemological obstacles are formed, together with the mechanisms on which the science/ideology split is based to be *explained* rather than described.

However, these corrections and the use of hitherto unconsidered elements did not fail to pose new theoretical problems. We shall here refer only to the problem of the *concept* (or category . . .) *of ideology,* the status of which in Althusser's analyses is not only ambiguous but contradictory. Indeed, if ideology is defined according to its relation to science, it represents the opposite of scientific knowledge (generally, 'error'). As a result it is the irreconcilable enemy of the production of knowledge. Alternatively, if it is defined according to its social function, ideology is connected with 'a system of representations, notions, gestures and attitudes etc.'[13] of which the specific effect is to ensure social cohesion by means of the regulation of the link which unites individuals to their own endeavors through the position they occupy in the social structure. In this latter sense, it is an *indispensable* component of all social practice (and therefore, of all scientific practice).[14] Thus, this double system of reference leads necessarily to the contradictory conclusion by which ideology is at one and the same time the condition which allows for the production of scientific knowledge and the condition which prevents it, both an aid and a hindrance to science.[15]

This untenable conclusion is the result of a double mistake. According to Althusser:

a) In general, ideology *always* acts as an epistemological obstacle.

b) In general, ideology *always* acts as a cohesive factor in any social grouping.

Hence, from the *epistemological* point of view there is an a priori elimination of any possibility of a differential analysis of ideological effects on scientific practices, while from the point of view of *historical materialism* there is the exclusion of class-struggles from the domain of ideology.[16]

We personally think that any mechanical equating of ideologies to epistemological obstacles inhibits the possibility of a subsequent materialist intervention. In the interests of the latter, we propose a double affirmation:

a) Any ideology whatsoever does not always intervene in the domain of scientific practices as an epistemological obstacle.

b) Obstacles to the production of knowledge are not all ideological in nature.

Having said this, the discussion does not intend to effect a reversal of the positive contributions which have been made by Althusser and his disciples (we are thinking in particular of the valuable criticism of humanist subjectivism, even in its 'Marxist' disguise), nor does it intend to reject the category 'epistemological break'. We are not questioning the specificity of

the processes of irruption of knowledge which are opposed to
certain theoretical ideologies. But we do refuse the abstract,
general thesis of an absolute and universal opposition between
science and ideology, and the consequences such a distinction
entails. In a word, what is required is an analysis of the history of
sciences in their contradictory diversity.[17]

10. RECONSTRUCTION: The process of intra-scientific transformation in terms of which an established scientific practice totally
or partially revises its fundamental axioms. This reformulation,
even if it is 'total', does not invalidate the axioms which have
been revised, but simply gives them a new position in the overall
economy of the theory concerned.

11. EPISTEMOLOGICAL OBSTACLE: Any extra-scientific element or process which, *by intervention in a scientific practice,* slows
down, prevents, or perverts the production of knowledge.

Note: We define epistemological obstacles not by their 'origin' or
their 'nature', but by their *function* and their *effects.* These two
aspects are all-important, since, if it is true that any
epistemological obstacle is a factor which by its intervention
adversely affects the production of knowledge, it is not true that
any extra-scientific factor is an epistemological obstacle. The
specific nature of these latter extra-scientific factors is that they
operate in the guise of properly 'theoretical' modalities. This is
the reason why, even if every ideology is not an epistemological
obstacle, the principal obstacles of this type result from an intervention on the part, not of ideology in general, but of certain
typical ('theoretical') forms of existence of *certain* ideologies (at
least in the field of the 'social sciences').[18]

12. THEORETICAL IDEOLOGIES: Ideological systems which
'function' (that is to say, are socially recognized) as scientific
practices. They function by means of particular institutional apparatuses.[19]

Very   important   note: The   introduction   of   this   category
necessitates a more precise definition of the *concept of ideology*
which is logically antecedent to it. The definition that we put forward takes into account in particular, our polemical remarks on
the theory of ideology proposed by Althusser. Thus, by *ideologies,*
we mean: *the forms under which the class-struggle is seen to exist in
the realm of signifying practices* (discourses, gestures, habits, attitudes, modes of action, norms).

Theoretical ideologies are a particular type of the ideologies
defined above: ideologies which are recognized *institutionally* as
scientific activities. The recognition of this fact has particular

consequences as far as the function of theoretical ideologies is concerned, but does not alter their social role, which is to serve certain class-interests. Thus, the dominant 'theories' in the social sciences (which are, in fact, theoretical ideologies) have a capacity for reproducing themselves and for becoming entrenched, which is much less a result of their pertinence as theories than a result of their social function at the centre of the *knowledge* of the dominant classes. This function may be summed up as a form of repression, a silencing (if need be, by deforming it) of the historical materialist science of social structures, and consequently as a means of stifling the revolutionary ideology of the workers. It should be our concern to get beyond this state of affairs and to leave behind these two basic aspects of the knowledge of the exploited classes.

13. SCIENTISTS' SPONTANEOUS PHILOSOPHY: An assemblage of the representations, beliefs, attitudes and habits of scientists with regard to their own practice.[20] It can be considered as the epistemological equivalent of theoretical ideologies. However, its 'spontaneous' nature and the fluidity of its institutional recognition deprive it of the reflexive and deliberate nature proper to theoretical ideologies. All of which adds up to the efficacy of this philosophy as an epistemological obstacle.

Theses Concerning an Epistemological Intervention in the Social Sciences[21]

1. Science in general does not exist, because it belongs to the myth of a universal and historical rationality. There exist only scientific practices which are separate and unequally developed.[22]

2. Every discourse of science in general, which does not take into consideration the specific plurality and disparity of scientific practices, must be considered as an idealist epistemological discourse.[23]

3. Epistemology is not a science: epistemological categories and theses differ from scientific propositions and concepts. It is not a 'science of science', even though its methods are brought to bear on scientific practice. These methods are those which are expressed in the definitions of epistemological practice.[24]

4. In all scientific practice, there are always epistemological elements which act upon the unfolding of that practice, either as a hindrance or as an aid.

5. Epistemological practice can only intervene, or act upon, the epistemological elements which are present in any scientific practice.

6. There are typical forms of epistemological obstacles. These forms are the formal invariants, of which the actual epistemo logical obstacles, in each specific practice, constitute the particular variants.

7. In all scientific practice (and, generally, in the history of the production of knowledge) there are always certain dominant epistemological obstacles.

8. Any development of a scientific practice (epistemological break; partial or complete reconstruction) presupposes the criticism and the annulment of the dominant epistemological obstacle, by provoking in the same movement a displacement of the hierarchy of obstacles. This annulment is only temporary and partial. In the final instance, it depends on social practice.

9. In any scientific practice there are ideological elements, which act as aids or obstacles to the furthering of that practice.

10. The epistemological *discourse* (moment of epistemological *practice*) represents, as does the epistemolgoical practice itself, a specific (discursive) intervention upon the theoretical conjuncture which corresponds to a scientific practice. In consequence, conjunctural transformations imply a correlative transformation in the epistemological discourse.

The corollary of this thesis and of thesis no. 3 is that the epistemological question is basically different from that of scientific practices. A scientific problematic operates as a 'machine' for producing theories from concepts and rules of systematic construction. But on the other hand, an epistemological problematic is bereft of a 'model' from which one could produce the constitutive theses of its discourse. Epistemology works through interventions, the pertinence of which depends exclusively on its ability to structure them according to a progressive adjustment of the transformation of the theoretical conjuncture.

The theses we have just put forward are a condensation of those aspects which are common to every epistemological intervention. They should be complemented, as far as the social sciences are concerned, at least by the following theses.

11. In the social sciences, epistemological problems take the form of certain *theoretical ideologies* of which the chief ones are historicist humanism and positivism. These, in turn, interact among themselves to produce *ideological formations* of an equally particular nature: namely those sociological theories, economic theories, ethnological theories, etc., which are dominant from an institutional point of view: hence, functionalism, structuralism and their variants.

12. The chief epistemological obstacle in the social sciences to-day is *empiricism*.

13. This domination of the social sciences by empiricism should be understood in two ways:

    A). As a domination with regard to the opposite and con-temporary current: namely, formalism.

    B). As a domination of the theoretical ideologies and the ideological formations which have an empirical tendency with regard to the predominantly scientific trends.

14. As a general rule, the dominant theoretical ideologies in the social sciences are *positivism* and *historicist humanism*.

15. As a general rule, *functionalism* and *structuralism* (correla-tively with the strategic *neo-liberal* type of analysis) are the domi-nant ideological formations in the social sciences.

These theses, which are specifically aimed at the social sci-ences, represent the minimum point of departure for an interven-tion in this field. They need to be explained and developed. *That is the object of this text,* which hopes to demonstrate the specific-ity of an epistemological intervention by putting it into practice.

II. EPISTEMOLOGICAL MODELS IMPLICIT IN THE SOCIAL SCIENCES

The more a science (or an ideological formation institutional-ised as a science) is hesitant or inarticulated, the more it tends to legitimize itself by having recourse to general methodological bases which have been arrived at independently of the concrete conditions of existence which constitute it as a scientific prac-tice. The 'methodology of the social sciences' fulfills this exact function. It guarantees the 'objectivity' of a 'discovery' by its greater or lesser coincidence with a model of procedure deemed to be scientific. Hence, the norms of this type of methodology assume the status of magic formulae which are approved institu-tionally. At this point of the procedure, the underlying epistemo-logical models can be recognized as deep-rooted epistemological obstacles which must be overcome *in the practice* of science itself if we are to be able to create the theoretical conditions for a pro-duction of knowledge.

What exactly are these epistemological models? Any concrete research is subject to the influence of a complex combination of different epistemological obstacles. However, the definition of the basic elements of any combination of this type makes it easier to analyze. On the other hand, despite the diversity of the concrete forms of existence of these obstacles, it is possible to reduce them to two general epistemological 'models' which are in fact variants of the paradigm which we will call the *idealist philosophy of knowledge*. This philosophy can be summed up in three main theses.[25]

I. There is such a thing as an a-historical truth which has a prior existence in the order of 'reality'. All we have to do is extract it. It is not necessary to produce it.

II. The subject (discourse which possesses knowledge) and the object (of knowledge) are the first elements of scientific knowledge.

III. Scientific research is said to occur when there is an *equivalence* between the subject and the object of knowledge. This equivalence defines *truth,* which can be expressed in the following equation:

$$(\text{subject}) = (\text{object}) = \text{truth}.$$

Having said this, within the limit of this general equation there are typical forms which are tendentious variants of the invariant (subject) = (object) = Truth. These variants rely on the predominance of one of the two terms of the equation. Such a predominance can go so far as to completely do away with the second term. Therefore, starting from the original equation we arrive at two possible variants.

First variant:	= (object)	= truth
Second variant: (subject)	=	= truth

The first variant is known as *empiricism*. The second is called *formalism*.

These idealist epistemological tendencies take shape in the social sciences at the heart of particular 'theoretical ideologies' of which the two main ones are *historicist humanism* and *positivism*. These theoretical ideologies appear, in turn, in ideological formations that are called 'sociological theories'.

The analysis of the formalist and empiricist models, and of the forms under which they manifest themselves (especially within humanist and positivist ideologies), allow a proportional adjustment of the minimal elements (those which are necessary and sufficient) by a radical critique of epistemological obstacles in the practice of 'social sciences'.

Empiricism, the Dominant Obstacle in the Social Sciences

Empiricism is that representation of scientific practice which, by pre-supposing the existence of knowledge in the facts, deduces from the facts the objects of scientific research: to verify these facts, to group them together and to synthesize them by a process of abstraction which renders them susceptible to effective handling: that is to say, allows for their accumulation and communication. The empiricist model would therefore treat scientific work not as a process of transformation but as a process of *purification* of the stated fact, since it seeks to eliminate the contingent properties of the fact and thereby arrive at its 'essential determinations'.[26]

The basis of this model is the 'evidence theory', according to which scientific activity consists of first gathering and then analysing supposedly 'objective' information which pre-dates the actual activity (and the prejudices) of the researcher.

A very good illustration of this viewpoint is the synthesis arrived at by Johan Galtung in his work, which is a masterpiece of sociological empiricism. The text is based on the following proposition: 'Sociological evidence is obtained when a sociologist records facts about a section of social reality.'[27]

Once recorded, these facts are organized in a 'matrix of evidence' which combines the dimensions and the values which correspond to each 'analytical unit' or real object of research. The act of recording, therefore, transforms the fact into *evidence,* from which, by *inference* (that is to say, by a series of logical operations) the *concept* is obtained. The relations between the various pieces of evidence are expressed by means of conceptual relations which have been inferred from them and constitute *laws,* under the proviso that the fundamental principles of *fidelity* (precise nature of the observation) and *validity* (legitimate inference from the evidence) have been respected. Thus the overall process of the acquisition of knowledge is as follows:

Facts–Observations–Evidence–Relations between pieces of evidence–Indicators–Concepts–Relations between concepts–Theory.

What is essential in this model is the dominance of the *observed* over the theory (which in the last analysis is only a combination of facts) and not the sequential order of the operations involved. Hence Lazarsfeld's famous paper, which traces the passage from concepts to indicators[28] by the specifying of dimensions and the construction of indexes, remains essentially an expression of the same point of view. It is necessarily so, since what is termed a concept is 'an entity conceived in vague terms, which gives a meaning to the observed relations between phenomena'. In the same vein, the only possible criterion for establishing the equivalence of concepts and indicators is, in the last analysis, the fact that 'two different and equally *reasonable* indexes lead to similar or different relations between the variables being analyzed'.[29] All of which means, if we clarify, that the proposed equivalence (established by means of what Lazarsfeld calls an 'act of validation') can only be based on the interpretation of the researcher.

By virtue of this fact, even within its own point of view, sociological empiricism leads to irresolvable contradictions. If there are no objective criteria to prove the validity of the relation between concepts and indicators, how can one legitimize the inferential method, and consequently, the interpretation of the process under observation?[30]

The very logic of demonstration in experimental process clearly shows the absurdity of proposing relations which are not theoretically determined. Any system of relations neccessitates the presence of that condition which is known as the 'closed field', that is to say, of the chance distribution of the effects of those variables which have not been measured on the relations between the variables under study. Now, such a hypothesis demands a prior selection of these variables, but a selection which is theoretically determined, as well as an equally theoretical justification of the chance distribution of the effects of these variables. There is therefore no possibility of obtaining any information without a prior theorization which defines the nature of the information required, interprets it and articulates it to the proposed system of causality.[31] Indeed, in opposition to the thesis proposed by empiricism, theory is not an auxiliary or subordinate phenomenon with regard to the recording of evidence. Nor is it a mere additional elaborative process which glorifies the results of research at the end of the sequence. On the contrary, it is a means of production of scientific facts. There is no possibility of separating it from the evidence, nor of subordinating it to the evidence without destroying the various stages and the elementary principles of scientific research. Finally, and most important, there is no possibility of recording or observing without a prior categorization of what is to be observed. Such a categorization can only be based on a theory or on the language of the dominant ideologies which *in practice* come to grips with the phenomena under observation.[32] Without a transformation of the observation-process by theoretical work, one cannot establish a rigorous scientific language, failing which it is impossible to attribute any precise meaning to the co-variations which may be discernible between two facts.

The point is that in reality, there is no evidence which is not *constructed* in a process of production in which theory plays a fundamental role. Hence, by turning the 'gathering of evidence' into a pseudo-religion, the empiricist model fails to take into consideration the essential mechanisms for the production of knowledge. This state of affairs is all the more serious since at the present moment, empiricism is the dominant obstacle in the daily practice of the vast majority of researchers in the social sciences. Quite evidently, the reason for this situation follows from the social and institutional role which has fallen to these sciences. For a large part, the social sciences involve statistical operations which are intended to describe processes and situations on the basis of those notions which are current in the practice of administration. Empiricism serves them as a means of legitimization, elevating the tasks of bureaucracy to the status of scientific work, which prevents the questioning of their ideological content. Empiricism is not only an epistemological obstacle, but also an ideological weapon in the hands of the dominant classes. Its theoretical function (to defend and legitimize the social sciences as they exist at present) is in strict agreement with its social function: to serve *in this way*, the practical and thoretical interests of big capital.

Formalism

Empiricism has no 'enemies' in the social sciences. But it has a 'competitor' which is represented by the many variations of the formalist model. Formalism is a result of a systematic inversion of the standpoint of empiricism at the very heart of the paradigm which we have called the idealist theory of knowledge. Instead of failing to take stock of the specific moment of theoretical construction (as empiricism does), formalism tends to isolate it, and to subordinate to it the process of the effective production of knowledge (construction and *demonstration*). This subordination to the discourse is of a twofold nature: on the one hand it is concerned with the operations by which theoretical concepts are realized, and, on the other hand, it concerns the connection between material thus *constructed* and the social practices under observation.

In all the variants of the formalist obstacle, there is the exclusion of one of the two 'moments' which are necessary to all scientific research. This is either because scientific practice is conceived of as being limited to the elaboration of speculative constructions (first variant), or because theoretical reflection is considered *sufficient* in itself, by virtue of its internal coherence and logical rigour, as a means of engendering empirical propositions which are so evident that they can dispense with the process of experiment (second variant).

Having said this, it should be added that the claim of 'theory' to a status of self-sufficiency (a claim which is characteristic of formalism), is a *tendency* in the practice of the social sciences which is generally linked with a verbal recognition of the rights of empirical research while nevertheless defending a type of practice which is essentially determined by the autonomous development of discourse.

This, for example, is the case with George Gurvitch's 'dialectical hyper-empiricism'. It entails a radical, theoretical formalist stance which is in a direct line of descent from social philosophy. Its 'theory' is in fact a a monumental complex of classificatory stock-piling, the taxonomical coherence of which is highly dubious.[33] Moreover it is supported by vague hints at Bergson's philosophy and suggests that Gurvitch himself was 'imbued with such pious reverence that he has never dared to undertake a description or analysis of any concrete society'.[34]

It is understandable that such a theory has rarely oriented any empirical sociological research. But it would be a mistake to conclude that it is merely a case of pure inconsequential speculation. It would be a mistake not only because Gurvitch's work retains some influence in the teaching of sociology, but also and in particular, because his work legitimizes and sustains a deep-rooted tendency which sanctifies the widening of the distinction between reflection and empirical research while strengthening the idea that abstract speculation in itself and for its own sake represents a production of sociological knowledge.

Another equally exemplary and more prestigious illustration of the formalist obstacle is to be found in Talcott Parsons' so-called 'general theory of action'.[35] From the first moment of its formulation, this 'theory' (in which the classificatory categories play a fundamental role) has sought to contribute a unitary foundation for the 'sciences of action'. This project is already in itself an indication of formalism, since the foundation or basis of a science should not be sought in a theoretical construction but in the specificity of the material processes that one is attempting to understand. However, rather than remain on the level of a facile critique which has been established on several previous occasions (C.W. Mills) of the out-and-out idealism of this procedure, we would prefer to show the effects of its application to the analysis of a social practice, after the example provided by Parsons's study on 'modern medical practice'.[36] The latter is an example of one of the rare empirical applications of 'Parsonian Theory'. The aim of the research is to draw up a plan of those role-orientations which form the basis of action for social partners (patients as well as doctors) in the 'medical practice' of contemporary societies. But if these are the objectives, a cursory reading dispels any hope of finding an explanation or even an accurate description of the phenomena under study. This highlights a twofold inability resulting from this 'theory':

    a. An inability to provoke (or integrate into its conceptual framework) any empirical propositions which are not guilty of banality.

    b. An inability to question the characteristic commonplaces of dominant ideologies. On the contrary, these commonplaces are used by the theory and are thereby justified and strengthened.

Let us consider some of the passages from this text, which we consider to be abundantly eloquent in this respect (we leave the reader at complete liberty to place these quotations in whichsoever of the two categories he chooses, or to see in them possible examples of a conjunction of the two categories):

> Certainly by almost any definition health is included in the functional needs of the individual member of the society so that from the point of view of the functioning of the social system, too low a general level of health, too high an incidence of illness, is dysfunctional.
>
> One does not expect the physician as such to have better judgement about foreign policy or tax legislation than any other comparably intelligent and well-educated citizen.
>
> To see a person naked in a context where this is not usual, and to touch and manipulate their body, is a 'privilege' which calls for explanation in view of these considerations. Incentive or profit-motives are supposed to be completely absent from the medical world. This attitude is naturally

> shared with other professions, but it is stronger among doc-
> tors than in any other case, with the possible exception of
> the priesthood.
> Unlike the role of the business-man, the role of the doctor is
> collectivity oriented and not-self oriented.
> Illness is, in one of its major aspects, to be defined as a form
> of deviant behaviour.

These quotations are a sample of a very prevalent ideological
standpoint. They illustrate the double inability to which we were
previously alluding, namely: they are presented in the form of
evidence but they always remain on the level of an amalgam of
falsehood and banality while seeking to adopt the guise of an
esoteric terminology.

But more important for the point we are making is the way
these examples illustrate the 'auto-verification' mechanisms on
which a formalist-dominated corpus of theories relies. Indeed,
these statements (which are at one and the same time commonplace and mysterious) are nevertheless empirical propositions which should be examined as particular 'realizations' of the
general theory. Once this has been established, any 'realization'
of a theoretical system can be considered from two points of
view: because it produces a double effect: a) direct effect:
knowledge of the concrete object under analysis; b) indirect effect: that of demonstrating the very possibility of this realization
(that is to say, a demonstration of the *productivity* of the
theoretical system being tested). In Parsons's empirical research,
the first effect is obvious—it is a deformation of the process and a
fresh appeal to the evidence of social practice; but in relation to
the second effect a new and very important aspect crops up. It is
important because it typifies the whole formalist 'theory', and it is
the fact that the space of realization of the *theoretical* ideology occurs in the domain which coincides exactly with the domain of
the *practical* ideology (for example that the doctor has no profit-
motive, that his work is collectively orientated, that sickness is
aberrant behaviour). Hence Parsons's ideology itself creates the
conditions of its own viability, while the pseudo-evidence of the
proposed statements seems to provide an empirical demonstration of the theory.

It now becomes clear that Parsons' theoretical ideology is, in
the last analysis, nothing more than a sublimation of the dominant practical ideology. We can thus understand the nature of
this chimerical 'realization-demonstration' mechanism. It is

merely a *mirrored repetition* which has, as its effect, the reciprocal confirmation of both the theoretical and the practical ideology. The theoretical ideology verifies itself in the practical ideology of which it is a repetition; the practical ideology legitimizes itself in the theoretical ideology which perpetuates it.

It is logical that this rapid analysis of the formalist obstacle should lead to similar conclusions to those arrived at in our critique of empiricism. Formalism, also, functions at one and the same time as an epistemological obstacle and as an ideological weapon of the dominant classes. In its role as an epistemological obstacle it fails to consider scientific work as a *process of production*. On the contrary, it eliminates the importance of the experimental moment in scientific practice and sets up abstract speculation as both point of departure and point of arrival of the production of knowledge.[37]

In its role as ideological weapon, it attributes 'scientific' status to the most commonplace observations and the most outdated theories, like empiricism, the formalist obstacle is rooted in the close relation between its theoretical and social functions.

An Example of the Peaceful Coexistence Between Empiricism and Formalism: Structuralist Ideology

Our analysis of the formalist and empiricist obstacles allows us to contend that the opposition between these two epistemological models is more apparent than real. This is so simply because the divergences between them never overstep the limits of idealist epistemology which are common to both. This is extremely important because we can deduce from it that the inversion of the dominance, that is to say, the movement from empiricism to formalism which has taken place in certain sections of sociology and anthropology in no way alters their epistemological field.[38] On the contrary, it should be interpreted as a consolidating factor as far as idealist epistemology is concerned, in that it manages to overcome crises by effecting displacements *within its own field*.

In order to illustrate the complementary nature of the relation between empiricism and formalism, we have chosen a particularly edifying example: that of *structuralism*. We shall limit ourselves to one of its most significant aspects: Levi-Strauss's theory of 'models', in which the empiricist and formalist obstacles are called upon to play autonomous and complementary roles. The logic of structuralism calls for the peaceful coexistence of these two variants of idealist epistemology, in order to ensure that each one may take a predominant position at two separate stages of the development of this theory.

Hence *empiricism* is clearly present in the very definition of the model, and more especially in the setting out of the rules, which should be respected, according to Levi-Strauss, if we are to have any construction of pertinent scientific models. For example: '. . . . the model should be constituted so as to make immediately intelligible all the observed facts.'[39] This idea is connected, by a footnote at the bottom of the page, to the following text from Neumann and Morgenstern: 'Similarity to reality is needed to make the operation significant. And this similarity must usually be restricted to a few traits deemed *'essential pro tempore'*.[40]

To clarify, this means that a model is conceived of as the product of an abstracting process which, beginning with the actual object, reduces it to its 'essential' variables. The ability to recognize these aspects makes possible a sort of 'analogical reproduction' (a 'biased image', to use Barthe's term)[41] of the phenomenon under analysis. All considerations as to the nomenclature to be adopted when discussing this point are based on the two classic constants of empiricism:

a) The dichotomy between the essential and contingent is considered as having a physical reality.

b) The act of 'extraction' (called abstraction) of the essence of reality by the elimination of the contingent aspects. (Empiricism views this as the ultimate scientific operation.)

Formalism is also very much present in the structuralist theory of the model. Indeed, once the model has been established by an observation of facts and the application of given rules, a new series of operations comes into play but on a completely different level. It is what Levi-Strauss calls 'experimentation by means of models themselves'. At this point, it is a matter of determining the reactions of a model when it is affected by certain modifications, and at the same time, comparing among themselves modes of different types. Despite Levi-Strauss' vagueness in his formulation, we can establish certain bases for this 'experimentation by means of models' by applying it to other texts, in particular those which are concerned with the relations between the different 'levels' (or 'structures') of a society.[42] For Levi-Strauss the posing of this problem (which in an aberrant form is linked to the relations between infrastructure and superstructure) must be rooted in a basic premise: the fact that he is considering a whole complex of social structures as a 'group of transformations' characterized by formal correspondences and non-correspondences that have to be established. Such an aim demands that each 'level' (economic structure, system of kinship, language, myths, etc.) be the object of a *homogeneous* formalization, and that this formalization be as rigorous as possible. The proposed comparative study would be centered on the 'logical' characteristics of each structure, and would be rooted in the thesis which Levi-Strauss explicitly formulates, according to which the correspondences as well as any 'contradictions' which might crop up, 'all belong to the same group of transformations.'[43]

A program of formal research of this type would end up with the recomposition of what Levi-Strauss calls 'the order of orders', that is to say, the most abstract expression of relations between 'levels' which are susceptible to structural analysis.

Now, the key to the theory of the model is the fact that experimentation using models plays an essential role in the search for this 'order of orders'. In what perspective, therefore, would we place the type of research we have just outlined? One of Levi-Strauss' texts is particularly significant in this respect:

> If we grant, following Marxian thought, that infrastructures and superstructures are made up of multiple levels and that there are various types of transformations from one level to another, it becomes possible—in the final analysis, and on the condition that we *disregard content*—to characterize different types of societies in terms of the types of transformations which occur within them. These types of transformations amount to formulas showing the number, magnitude, direction and order of the convolutions that must be unravelled, so to speak, in order to uncover (logically, not normatively) an ideal homologous relationship between the different structural levels.[44]

We have to emphasize this abstraction of 'contents', which is essential to the proposed analysis, in order to demonstrate the presence of the formalist obstacle. It occupies a *dominant* position at this second level of structuralist research. This dominance follows directly from the hypothesis that the formal properties of the different structured levels are part of the same group of transformations. This claim is no accident. It is a direct reference to one of the basic postulates of Levi-Strauss' structuralism.

which is the universal nature of logical thought. This postulate determines the meaning of the key concepts of structuralist 'theory' (structure, unconsciousness, and their relationship), and at the same time plays a fundamental role as far as the actual research is concerned: it provides an a priori guarantee of the relevance of the operations involved in a structural analysis.

In fact, the claim in favour of the universality of logical thought authorizes:

a). In the first place, the rejection of 'content'; that is to say, in the long run, the historical specificity of the processes which take place within a social structure as well as the articulation of these processes within a particular conjuncture.

b). Secondly, the epistemological 'welding' of structuralist ideology which cuts short any fundamental objection to its concepts, its methods or its techniques. On this point, we can quote a very significant text:

I shall no doubt be accused of overinterpretation and oversimplification in my use of this method . . . I therefore say in advance to possible critics: what does this matter? For if the final aim of anthropology is to contribute to a better knowledge of objectified thought and its mechanism, it is in the last resort immaterial whether in this book the thought process of the South American Indians take shape through the medium of my thought, or whether mine take place through the medium of theirs. What matters is that the human mind, regardless of the identity of those who happen to be giving it expression, should display an increasingly intelligible structure as a result of the doubly reflexive forward movement of two thought processes acting one upon the other, either of which can in turn provide the spark or tinder whose conjunction will shed light on both.[45]

Beyond its 'literary' form, the meaning of this passage is clear: the 'structure of the human mind', universal logic, guarantees against all critiques, the profound relevance of structuralist aims. This is a masterpiece of formalist thought which is at least, highly convenient.

Two essential conclusions follow from this analysis:

a) Empiricism and formalism, as two variants of idealist epistemology, are not mutually exclusive nor do they necessarily contradict each other. On the contrary, the coexistence of these two obstacles is virtually a rule for all theoretical ideologies. At the very most, the latter are distinctive by virtue of their differential capacity for making such a coexistence harmonious. In this respect, structuralism provides a good example.

b) We may now add a new thesis to this subject: that the overthrow of these two obstacles is not to be achieved by balancing the amount of empiricism and formalism in any given recipe. Such a conciliation (which could be expressed in the formula: subject = object = truth) leads only to a simple addition of the two obstacles. 'Subject', 'object' and 'truth', being the basic categories of idealist epistemology, are not qualitatively transformed by mere combination. In order that they may really be overthrown, there must be a change in the very nature of the epistemological intervention.

III. EPISTEMOLOGICAL OBSTACLES AND THEORETICAL IDEOLOGIES: HUMANISM AND HISTORICISM IN THE SOCIAL SCIENCES

Epistemological obstacles arise in certain theoretical ideologies which increase their rationalizing capacity by coming into contact with the sources of their social determination by means of a close articulation with the dominant ideologies.

In the social sciences, the dominant theoretical ideologies are *positivism* and *historicist humanism*. Positivism is essentially characterized first by the abstract claim that science in general exists, and can be conceived of as an ahistorical entity. It comes across in its different classical and modern forms as a variable combination of the two epistemological obstacles we have been dealing with: empiricism and formalism. The stronger influence is usually provided by the empiricist branch (although this influence is more marked in traditional positivism than in 'logical neo-positivism'). On the other hand, historicist humanism, in so far as it constitutes an intervention in the domain of scientific practice, has very specific effects. That is not to say that it constitutes a new type of epistemological obstacle (in the final analysis, it is merely a variety of *empiricism*) but rather that its realization as an obstacle is brought to bear on individual and quite complex mechanisms. A particular type of approach to the problem is required if we are to be able to recognize and criticize these mechanisms.

Hence, even if theoretical ideologies realize and rationalize epistemological obstacles, it is the obstacles themselves and their practical expression which must constitute the object of an epistemological intervention; the obstacles and not the various idealist philosophies, the analysis of which is equivalent to establishing a theory of ideologies. Nevertheless, insofar as one of these philosophies, *historicist humanism,* plays a key part in the social sciences and takes on the shape of an epistemological obstacle by a unique process, there follows the necessity of establishing just what its specificity consists of and how great is its influence.

This theoretical ideology is characterized by a double claim, of which the two terms are mutually supporting:

1) There are no scientific laws, only explanations which are always contingent.
2) The only criterion of truth is a reference to practice, conceived of as a free and deliberate action performed by human beings.

Such a formulation is locsely akin to the attractive overtones of a spontaneous philosophy of social pragmatism,[46] the attractiveness of which is equally alluring to businessmen and to *certain* political activists. Let us consider the central arguments of epistemological historicism of which the most complete examination is to be found in the work of Max Weber.[47] By analyzing his theses we can both place in perspective the present-day arguments between 'scientists' and 'historicists', and also consider the theoretical conditions which transcend their differences.

As everyone knows, Weber begins with a fundamental distinction between the 'rationality of ends' and the 'rationality of means'. This leads to the distinction between the scientist and the politician, and to the affirmation of the ethical neutrality of a type of social sciences which is incapable of progressing beyond a limited role which consists of establishing the equivalence of ends and means. Thus, while the production of ends cannot be explained by itself since at its origins we have the free choice of individuals, science can still gain knowledge of the conditions in which these ends are brought about, exist and vary, by effecting a study of the significant configurations of concrete systems.

These 'ensembles' or societies, or epics are defined by a determined social content. They are not, therefore, concepts, but historical realities. They are at one and the same time units of analysis and the object of science.

It is possible to establish laws within these situations. But these laws are always relative to the society under consideration. The reason for this is apparent: since the observer is part of that which he is observing, he is incapable of distancing himself in such a way as to be able to analyze the explicative foundations of the ensemble to which he belongs. Since the only possibility of a relative objectivity (and therefore of scientific neutrality) is through a description of the internal mechanisms of a given situation, it is impossible to establish general laws and at the same time to explain the origins of those processes of social transformation which are in contradiction to the established order. (It is because of this thesis that, on a theoretical level, Weber's work has been able to act as a legitimizing basis for social functionalism: the 'theory' of the social system starts with institutionalized ends and uses them to study their realization at the level of means.)

The research methods which such a point of view calls for, are epistemologically equivalent to the point of view itself. Indeed, above all, it is a question of isolating a concrete historical phenomenon and of giving it significance by *imputing* certain causes to certain effects within a system of historically given social relations. The basic tool of this method is the *ideal type*. It is conceived of as firstly, 'concrete reality' in so far as it starts from the observation of something that exists, and secondly as 'abstraction' since what are particularly stressed are the dynamic lines of the observations. This stress is made in order to constitute an 'extreme case' which can act as reference point for comparison either with other types or between reality and the ideal established type. In so far as there is a particular meaning attached to each ideal type in terms of content, the analysis consists of the *imputation* of certain historical content to an observed reality by way of its greater or lesser correspondence with the ideal type which acts as a reference. Obviously research becomes more complicated when there is also the imputation of the relations between the types themselves and the social mechanisms involved in the production of the different types (*Economy and Society* provides many examples of this kind of procedure). But even the greatest complexity does not in any way change the status of the epistemological approach in question.

So, in order to be consistent with his overall view-point, Weber has to consider the question of the basis of science as an end. That is to say, according to which criteria is it possible to suggest that the established relation between ends and means in a given society has been scientifically arrived at, and does not arise from the subjectivity of the agent? Or at least, if ends are inexplicable and result from an unpredictable historical action, how can one uphold the claim for the existence of objective bases for scientific criteria? With great internal consistency, Weber denies, once again, the possibility of such objectivity and goes on to base scientific criteria in the subjective beliefs of the scientific community of each age, as to what is or is not science. In this way, the circle closes in on itself: beginning with a denial of the possibility of establishing non-contingent scientific laws, one arrives at a further denial—a refusal to accept the objectivity of the specific analysis of a determined reality which is thereby made to depend on the judgements of a particular social group called 'scientists'. This is the reason for Weber's emphasis on the indispensable ethical neutrality of the scientific community. If such a community exhibited particular social interest (for example, those of the ruling classes) there would be no limits to their subjectivism, and the imputation of effects to causes would conform to the pattern of those ideologies produced from a position held in the power-structure. We must acknowledge the generally recognized drawbacks to the theory that an area of human activity, that of intellectual work, be devoid of any influence as far as class-determination is concerned. Indeed, what would be the source of the social neutrality of scientists? In what way can they be detached from class interests? By way of conclusion we should note Weber's tremendous perspicacity, which enables him to go so far in his approach to scientism. On the other hand, political and ideological stances made it impossible for him to accept the ultimate consequences of his findings. Ultimately he was led to a shrewd compromise between social subjectivism and the (relative) objectivity of knowledge.

It was left to C. Wright Mills, Weber's most influential disciple in the whole of contemporary sociology, to make the decisive step and, in opposing empirical-formalist academicism, raise the banner of ideological conflict at the very heart of the social sciences. His theses, which are of considerable political importance, attack scientism from an idealist humanist position. Let us consider, by way of example, the famous definition of his intellectual aims that he proposed in *The Sociological Imagination*:

> Our work is closely and continuously concerned with historical reality and the meaning of that reality for individual men and women. Our aim is to define that reality and those meanings: it is in relation to these definitions that we must formulate the problems of the social sciences. Such a program demands that we should seek to attain an *entirely relative* understanding of the social structures which exist and have existed in the history of the world.

There is therefore no transformation of the real object (the raw material of knowledge) into a scientific object (the object of knowledge). There is a denial of the general applicability of any discovery, and in the final analysis, the accepted criterion is an ability to persuade. Scientific practice should hinge upon individual biographies, the history of political facts and the important problems of the modern world.

It is very tempting to adopt such a position in a world like that of American sociology which is dominated by banality, technologism, and the bureaucratization of research. Likewise, the notion that the power question constitutes the axis of social dynamics helps to put the problematic of the social sciences on a new and more relevant footing. But we have arrived at essentially correct theoretical and political positions by following an epistemological track which is based on a humanist and historicist presupposition, according to which it is impossible to conduct any objective study of social phenomena. In so far as a presupposition has a bearing on concrete gestures in the way research is conducted (always beginning with what has happened, placing too much emphasis on what has been said, interpreting and imputing what has been observed to ideological and moral criteria etc.) this kind of standpoint becomes an epistemological obstacle. It is akin to that type of empiricism which hinders the development of any practice that attempts to apply historical materialism.

Hence the same methodological principles are at the basis of two of the most influential trends in social sciences: social phenomenology[48] and social history. This fact alone indicates the ease with which they are assimilated by the academic establishment. In social phenomenology the absolute rule is case-study, punctuated here and there with more or less subtle observations. It is justified by a sort of primary vitality and by a preoccupation with leaving spontaneous forms of life' unmarked by abstract analysis. For its own part, social history institutionalizes high-quality journalism (with varying degrees of skillfulness). This reporting consists of a combination of a series of events and an all-embracing interpretative discourse which uses social facts as illustrations of a general social philosophy.

In criticizing these two trends there are two things to consider. On the one hand, there is the political and theoretical effect which they produce on a given conjuncture in the social sciences. On the other hand, there is the content they propose as a theoretical alternative within the scientific practice of the analysis of social relations. From a social point of view, the humanist 'critical sociology' has been an element of political liberation and theoretical regeneration in the stifling, constipated atmosphere of technocracy and establishment academics. But from the Marxist point of view, the *political alliances* with the humanist trend (which are essential in the present conjuncture) cannot be based on ideological ambiguity; they have to issue from a demarcation of humanist metaphysics and the consequences of such metaphysics on political and theoretical practice. Indeed, from the standpoint of social and theoretical spontaneity, certain essential operations are impossible. These include: the necessary break with the terms imposed by dominant institutional practice if we are to complete any scientific analysis of society; the reconstruction of the object; the process of experiment and control which is necessary to the production of knowledge; and especially the ability to establish *structural* and *conjunctural* laws. Not only are these operations impossible, but *in the context of this whole problematic,* it is false to propose in vague and general terms that the 'criterion of truth' depends on 'practice' (or the 'ability to persuade' as Mills puts it). What social practice or activity are we talking about? If we are referring to the condensed expression of social practice, i.e. political practice, what do we mean by saying that political practice establishes truth? It seems evident that such a criterion cannot be applied to the results achieved by this practice in the short term. But what time-limit should we set then? And who is to judge? The momentary victory (sometimes several decades) of fascism in some countries does not mean that we should consider its criminal theories as proven correct. And alternatively, the mistakes of the workers' movement do not entitle us to speak of a denial 'in practice' of the analyses of 'Capital', (as bourgeois ideologists are so ready to do).

But the apparent dead-end to which we seem to have been led is in fact no dead-end at all. This point has been amply clarified by Mao Tse Tung in his famous essay of 1937, *On Practice*.[49] In this work, he explains how the theoretical 'obscurities' derive rather from the social conditions surrounding the diffusion and the application of discoveries, than from the difficulties surrounding the theoretic work itself. In *On Practice* the production of knowledge is closely linked to social practice and in particular to political practice; but for Mao (in keeping with his Marxist-Leninist view-point) the 'criterion of practice' has a much deeper and more complete meaning than that which historicist humanism allows it. Indeed, even if practice is the decisive reference-point in all the various stages of the 'process of the development of knowledge', we only need to analyze these stages and it becomes evident that such a criterion is absolutely incompatible with any form of theoretical pragmatism, however well disguised. Unlike the historicist point of view, the analysis put forward by Mao does not rely on the criterion of 'practice' in order to break down distinctions or to drown the determination specific to each process in the sea of political spontaneity. For Mao, practice is the means of relating (rather than doing away with) the specificity of the different processes; more than that, practice (especially class-struggle) is the means by which the differentiation of the different processes is brought about. Hence, it is practical needs that lead us to make the leap from the 'perceptual knowledge', which can only grasp the 'apparent' side and the 'isolated' aspects of facts, to the *concept* which uncovers their fundamental determinations. In much the same way, there must be a passage from the concept to the *'logically defined' conclusions (laws)* which are capable of accounting for the internal link which joins together the different phenomena. But it should be remembered that all these distinctions which allow us to understand the different specificity involved in each process (and in each type of knowledge) by looking at the specific forms of its production, are justified only by practice.

> From the Marxist view point, theory is important; and its importance is fully expressed in Lenin's statement 'Without revolutionary theory there can be no revolutionary movement'. But Marxism emphasizes the importance of theory precisely and only because it can guide action.[50]

> Discover the truth through practice, and again through practice verify and develop the truth. Start from perceptual knowledge and actively develop it into rational knowledge;

then start from rational knowledge and actively guide revolutionary practice to change both the subjective and the objective world. Practice, knowledge, again practice, and again knowledge. This form repeats itself in endless cycles, and with each cycle the content of practice rises to a higher level. Such is the whole of the dialectical-materialist theory of knowledge, and such is the dialectical-materialist theory of the unity of knowing and doing.[51]

Hence in dialectical materialism the 'criterion of practice' refers to a materialist problematic of the production of knowledge. It is a problematic which takes into account the material conditions of such a production and the links it has with politics. There is no concern here for moral justification, as is the case with the historicist humanist conception. In this latter case, history (and the science of history) is merely the meaningful linking of human actions which always involve 'free choice' and are therefore 'unpredictable'.

The concrete consequences of historicist humanist views of scientific practice restrict the latter to mere descriptive chronicle and historical relativism. This has two effects:

1) On the theoretical level, it causes a constant oscillation between subjectivism and scientism.
2) On the political level, given the analyses are worked out on the basis of the trends that have already been outlined (since we have no knowledge of the production of conjunctural and structural laws), one ends up having no theoretical tools which are capable of orientating a transformation in historically determined social relations.

Having said this, the polemics of critical sociology and historicist humanism allow us to formulate the basic questions with which the process of production of knowledge is concerned, namely: Which science are we talking about? What are its aims? What are the material conditions of such a process of production? Indeed, if there are no methodologically justified *general norms,* which guarantee scientificity, but there is the possibility of a production of knowledge beyond the subjective grasp of a historical situation, what then defines a process of production of *knowledge?* Since we have dismissed as irrelevant those criteria which are exterior to scientific practice and which seek to describe its content, our answer can only be based on a materialist analysis of its conditions of production. The whole problem has therefore to be put on a new footing.

IV. ON MATERIALIST EPISTEMOLOGICAL PRACTICE

Since we have criticized the empiricist and formalist models and demystified their apparent extension in historicist ideology, should we not now offer a new model, which would this time be 'correct' and would correspond to materialist epistemology?

In fact, the preceding analyses have shown the absurdity of such an attempt. Materialist epistemological practice does not derive from a 'model' and cannot be thought out in terms of this idealist category.

This claim is connected with our previous remarks on the non-systematic nature of this conception of epistemology. A materialist epistemological intervention cannot be reduced to the application of pre-established rules according to a theoretical system: its relevance must be assessed after its effects and not after its ability to conform to any 'principle' whatsoever.

This does not mean that there are no criteria according to which such an intervention can be orientated. The tools and theses which we have briefly outlined are an attempt to provide the bases of such an intervention. But in keeping with our whole analysis, these criteria cannot be treated as independent of the theoretical conjuncture in which the epistemological intervention occurs. They are very much dependent on it.

A very important conclusion follows from all this: if it is true that there is no 'model' for a materialist epistemological practice, there are nevertheless moments which act as reference-points and sources of energy. In the present conjuncture these 'moments' are essentially:—*historical materialism* in so far as it is a science of the means of production and of social formations;—and the practice of *revolutionary struggle*. Let us consider the way in which these two closely related moments work themselves out.

We have said that the object of a materialist epistemological intervention is the theoretical conjuncture, that is to say, the 'present moment' which characterizes an ensemble of scientific practices.[52] If it is true that the 'present moment' can be analyzed on the basis of structural and conjunctural laws, we should be able to distinguish within it the articulation and the relation of forces which are present in any historical conjuncture. These are the shifts, the condensations, the contradictions, the dominant and subordinate poles etc. In particular, every theoretical conjuncture should be defined according to the factors determining the form of scientificity which plays the *dominant* role. These determining factors are crucial to epistemological practice. Logically, the form of dominant scientificity will be that particular theoretical referent in terms of which the practice will organize its interventions. We have only to examine the theoretical conjuncture if we wish to identify the *scientific* discipline which plays the chief part in all this. The answer to this question is clearly that the dominant scientific discipline is the science of history: historical materialism. However, the answer is not obvious but it can be theoretically justified: and any justification would have to be articulated in terms of a *political* standpoint. More precisely, the principal condition for the production of a theoretical justification of this type is the adoption of a political position.[53] It is at this point that we have to discuss the second source of materialist epistemology: the practice of class-struggle.

Indeed, only if one starts from a proletarian position can historical materialism come forward as the science which plays the chief role in our conjuncture, in so far as it constitutes the theoretical weapon of the fundamental process of contemporary history: socialist revolution.

It now becomes obvious that the two instances to which we referred are, in fact, a single one. The frame of reference of a materialist epistemological intervention is the fusion of Marxist theory and the working class movement, from the common view-point of class-struggle. This framework not only ensures the efficacy of the epistemological intervention but allows us to arrive at a consciousness of its *ranges* and its *limits*.

Indeed, materialist epistemological intervention in the 'social sciences' has an essentially critical role to play in the present conjuncture. Above all, it aims at preventing the theoretico-ideological struggle (for example, between historical materialism and functionalism) from slipping into the realms of the idealist philosophy of 'science'. The basic problem is to prevent the founding of 'science' on general methodological principles in order to begin a properly theoretical discussion within the social sciences by working towards a consolidation of the dominant pole of historical materialism. Such a discussion is not only a debate of ideas but also includes the process of experimentation as an integral part of the theoretical work.

Hence, the problem of the 'criteria of truth' which belongs to the 'theories of knowledge' is replaced by a concrete discussion of the historical conditions of production of any knowledge; that is to say, the establishing of structural laws and the analysis of the conjuncture in which these laws are verified and realized through practice.

If epistemology must appeal to one of the dimensions of 'sociological theory' (to historical materialism), we should also add that there is a need to integrate into this discussion not only the study of concepts and of means of experimentation but also the conditions through which a knowledge of the 'social' can be achieved. In the first place, this implies the study of the apparatuses which produce such a knowledge; secondly, it implies a connection between this process and the production of ideological discourse, in keeping with the thesis by which theory exists within theoretico-ideological formations; and finally in the way these two aspects are determined by class-struggle.

For example, to posit the possibility of 'producing' a historical materialism (in the form of concrete analyses of concrete situations) in conditions of production which are essentially determined by their involvement with the ideological apparatuses of the bourgeoisie (e.g., the University), is to fall back into scientism. In other words, it is to regress to the abstract relation of the intellectual to a scientific object defined in rigorous formal terms and with a faithfulness to certain texts. We should remember, in particular, that *historical materialism has been able to make no important discoveries without a direct link with the political conjuncture of the class-struggle.*[54] Nevertheless the opposite contention, according to which ideological apparatuses would entirely determine the content of the knowledge thus produced, is leftist and mechanist, in that it leads one to ignore certain of the effects produced by the class-struggle on the apparatuses of the dominant class. These effects, although they do not destroy the hegemony of this class, are very real.

More concretely (and here we are dealing with an actual case of epistemological intervention), one cannot deny the possibility of producing 'Marxism' in certain historical conditions, within the confines of the bourgeois university. (Obviously, we are not referring here to the 'academic Marxism' which was attacked by Lenin. Its appearance in solemn amphitheatres is rendered all the more easy in that it is completely cut off from popular struggles). But this type of theoretical practice thus realized is double conditioned.

1.   First, it is determined by the differing forces of the classes which are in struggle. The breaches which have opened up in the ideological apparatuses of the dominant class are a result of the political offensive of the exploited classes, and the ideological crisis of the dominant bloc itself (of particular significance as far as social sciences are concerned). Thus, most of the breaches which have appeared in the French university system of ideological domination result from the deep-rooted movement of revolt which broke out in May, 1968.

2. Secondly, it depends on the class-nature and the class-function of the ideological apparatuses under discussion. One should consider that the realization of some work within a given ideological framework has effects on the theoretical content of what is produced. This means that the positions occupied within these apparatuses cannot, of themselves, ensure that a theoretical practice be based on historical materialism. This practice can only exist if it derives, above all, from the class-struggle and *utilizes* bourgeois ideological apparatuses to strengthen its own position within the overall group of the dominated classes.

Indeed, the most important consequence that follows from our analysis as a whole is that only by aligning with the working class (which is linked to historical materialism by virtue of the fact that it is the last ascendant class) can one create the conditions in which the theory of society or the theory of class-struggle can be elaborated and put into effect. In addition, only the link with the working class allows an understanding of that which gives meaning to this historic task: the working out of a 'guide for action,' that is to say for the revolutionary transformation of society.

NOTES

1. Cf. E. de Ipola, "Lectura y Politica. A proposito de Althusser," in S. Sarsz *et al., Lectura de Althusser* (Buenos Aires: Ed. Galerna, 1970), pp. 320–324.
2. Cf. the definition of "philosophy" by Althusser in his *Cours de Philosophie pour Scientifiques,* —seminar notes, (Paris: Ecole Normale Superieure, 1967–1968).
3. Cf. L. Althusser, *For Marx* (London: Allen Lane, 1969), on the definition of "practice."
4. Cf. L. Althusser, "Ideologies et Appareils Ideologiques d'Etat," *La Pensee,* June 1970.

5. J. Ranciere, "Sobre la Teoria de la Ideologia," in Karsz, *Lectura de Althusser*, pp. 336–338.

6. Cf. Gaston Bachelard, *La Formation de l'Esprit Scientifique* (Paris: Urin, 1964); *Le Nouvel Esprit Scientifique* (Paris: P.U.F., 1949); *Le Rationalisme Applique* (Paris: P.U.F., 1966); and No. 42 of the journal, *L'Arc*, dedicated to Bachelard.

7. It should be noted that for Bachelard the category "rupture" includes both the categories, "epistemological break" and "reconstruction."

8. For our evaluation of Bachelard's contribution, we have relied upon Dominique Lecourt's book: *Pour une Critique de l'Epistemologie* (Paris: Maspero, 1972), especially the section "De Bachelard au Materialisme Historique" (which was originally published in *l'Arc*.

9. *Cf. Lecourt, Pour une Critique de l'Epistemologie*, p. 72.

10. Ibid., p. 27.

11. Ibid., p. 35.

12. On this point, see the chapter "On the Young Marx," in L. Althusser, *For Marx*, and especially, "The Conditions of Marx's Scientific Discovery," in *Theoretical Practice*, January 1973.

13. Cf. the definition of "ideologies pratiques" by Althusser in his *Cours de Philosophie pour Scientifiques*.

14. Cf. Althusser, *Pratique theoretique et lutte ideologique*.

15. Disciples of Althusser could possibly contend that such a conclusion is not "contradictory" but "dialectical" since ideology in general would be a "condition of possibility" of science insofar as it provides the "raw material" on which the scientific work bears. In turn, scientific work can transform the ideological raw material ("rupture"). However, this answer is only possible through a basic misconception. When Althusser claims that ideology is an essential part of any social pratice (including scientific practices), it is clear that the term "ideology" has the meaning of a "system of representations that ensures the realization by means of agents, of the tasks which are assigned to them by their position in the social structure." Now, scientific practice does not intervene upon this "system of representations" to produce the rupture. It works rather on ideological or determined theoretico-ideological formations, which imply the object of the science in question. The occurrence of rupture is not opposed to the "system of representations," but on the contrary presupposes it. Since Althusser simultaneously proposes the thesis by which ideology in general is opposed to science in general, his viewpoint suggests a logical rather than a dialectical contradiction.

16. Cf. Ranciere, "Sobre la Teoria de la Ideologia." In this discussion, we are exclusively concerned with the earlier work of Althusser and his team since this is all that has been fully elaborated. We have ignored certain declarations of intention that were subsequently published here and there and that seem to question the overall viewpoint adopted in the early work. This is the case with Althusser's post-scriptum to the article, "Ideologie et Appareils Ideologiques d'Etat" (1970), with his "Maoist" preface, published in Spanish, to the sixth edition of Marta Harnecker's book, *Los Conceptos Elementales del Materialismo Historico*, Siglo, XXI, Mexico, 1971, and with his last book *Reponse a John Lewis* (Paris: Maspero, 1973).

17. It does not seem to be true that the development of materialism can be promoted by prescriptive and generalizing phrases of this type: "For we are all agreed the problem is the defense of a science which really exists from the onslaught of ideology; it is to distinguish what is really science from what is really ideology. . . ." *For Marx*, p. 173.

18. *Certain* ideologies, that is to say; in the social sciences the ideologies and the *bourgeois* ideological social structures as they find expression on the dominant sociological, anthropological, economic, etc., theories.

19. This does not mean that certain techniques in the social sciences, although they imply these theoretical ideologies, cannot have a social utility above and beyond their use as ideological weapons.
20. Cf. Althusser, *Cours de Philosophie pour Scientifiques.*
21. We would like to point out that any of the theses we put forward owe much to Althusser,even though we have made some important modifications, which should be understood from our remarks on the value of the contradictions in his work.
22. This unequal development applies equally to the relation between different scientific practices.
23. This thesis does not invalidate all propositions of a general nature concerning scientific practice, but only those that presuppose the leveling of the specific differences between the different practices.
24. CF. L. Althusser, *Lenin and Philosophy* (London: New Left Books, 1971) p. 50; Alain Badion, *Le Concept du Modele* (Paris: Maspero, 1969), p. 11. The third thesis raises the problem of the connection between dialectical materialism and epistemology, which cannot be treated here. Let us simply say that the relation of epistemology to historical materialism and to class struggle is chiefly concerned with their takeover on a theoretical level. For a dialectical materialism, the aim is different: to help in ensuring the union of theory and practice under the dominance of practice. Dialectical materialism defines the strategic efficacy of epistemological intervention as well as its limits. If it is true that one should distinguish epistemological categories from scientific concepts, it is also true that there is a closer relationship between the language of epistemology and the language of the sciences in each conjuncture. In addition, as we illustrate further on, a materialist epistemological practice is defined specifically by the fact that it constantly takes into consideration the material and social conditions of the production of knowledge: a fact which closely links it with the science of means of production and with historical materialism.
25. Cf. Althusser, *Cours de Philosophie.*
26. The distinction between "appearance" and "essence" is one of the constants of empiricism. Cf. on this very point, Lenin, *Materialism and Empiriocriticism.*
27. Cf. Johan Galtung, *Theory and Methods of Social Research* (New York: Columbia University Press, 1967).
28. Cf. Paul Lazarsfeld, "Des Concepts aux Indices Empiriques," in P. Lazarsfeld, and R. Boudon, *Le Vocabulaire des Sciences Sociales* (Paris: Mouton, 1965), pp. 27–36. Indicator: means in empirical sociology of expressing a concept by reference to quantifiable information. For example, income level is an indicator to the position held in the class setup.
29. Cf. on the absence of criteria with which to validate the use of indicators, H. H. Blalock, "The Measurement Problem: A Gap Between the Language of Theory and Research," in H. H. Blalock and A. Blalock (eds.), *Methodology in Social Research* (New York: McGraw-Hill, 1969), pp. 155–198.
30. Cf. R. Boudon, *L'Analyse mathematique des faits sociaux* (Paris: Plon, 1967).
31. Cf. P. Bourdieu, J-C. Chamberedon, and J-C. Passeron, *Le Metier de Sociologue* (Paris: Mouton, 1968).
32. Cf. Althusser, *Sur le Travail Theorique.*
33. Thus, in Chapter 2, section VII, of the *Traite de Sociologie*, published under the direction of Georges Gurvitch (Paris: P.U.F., 1963), we find the following list of types of knowledge: (1) The perceptive knowledge of the external world. (2) The knowledge of the other, of Us, of groups and societies. (3) The knowledge of common sense. (4) Technical knowledge. (5) Political knowledge. (6) Scientific knowledge. (7) Philosophical knowledge. (p. 122).
    We believe that it would be very difficult to include the list itself as instance of the type of knowledge mentioned under the 6th heading or even the 3rd!

34. Levi-Strauss, *Structural Anthropology* (London: Allen Lane, 1968), p. 326.
35. In *The Structure of Social Action* (Glencoe: The Free Press, 1949).
36. See Chapter 10 of *The Social System* (Glencoe: The Free Press, 1959).
37. For a *logical* (and not epistemological) demonstration of the formalism inherent in functionalism, cf. G. Hempel, "The Logic of Functional Analysis," in Llewellyn Gross (ed.), *Symposium on Sociological Theory* (New York: Row, Peterson, 1959), pp. 271–288.
38. Cf. E. de Ipola, "Ethnologie et Historie dans l'Epistemologie Structuraliste," *Cabiers Internationaux de Sociologie,* Vol. 48 (Paris: P.U.F., 1970), pp. 37 ff.
39. Cf. Levi-Strauss, *Structural Anthropology,* p. 280.
40. Ibid., p. 316.
41. Cf. Roland Barthes, *Essais Critiques* (Paris: Editions du Seuil, 1963), p. 215.
42. Cf. *Structural Anthropology,* pp. 316 et seq.
43. Levi-Strauss uses historical materialism to justify his thesis. Ibid., p. 332.
44. Ibid., pp. 333–334.
45. Claude Levi-Strauss. *The Raw and the Cooked* (New York: Harper & Row, 1969).
46. Cf. Abraham Kaplan, *The Conduct of Inquiry* (San Francisco: Chandler, 1964).
47. Cf. Marx Weber, *Essais sur la Théorie de la Science* (Paris: Plon, 1965).
48. For this usage, see the work of the very powerful phenomenological current in contemporary American sociology: Garfinkel, Becker, Goffman, Glaser, Strauss, etc.; also, the current of "radical sociology" in the United States or the "Sociologie de l'evenement" proposed by Edgar Morin in France.
49. Mao Tse Tung, "On Practice," *Selected Readings* (Peking: Foreign Languages Press, 1971).
50. Ibid., p. 76.
51. Ibid., pp. 81–82.
52. Cf. on this point, E. Balibar and P. Macherey, "Materialisme Dialectique," in *Encyclopedia Universalis,* Vol. 16, Paris, 1971, p. 612.
53. As Marx himself points out in a discussion of his critique of Ricardo, scientific analysis presupposes the taking up of a class position (see Marx's *Postface* to the second edition of *Capital*).
54. See on this point: Mao, *"On Practice;"* A. Gramsci, "The Intellectuals," in *Selections from the Prison Notebooks* (London: Lawrence and Wishart, 1971): and Lenin's preface to the first edition of *Materialism and Empiriocriticism.*

10.
SOME REFLECTIONS ON THE MISERY OF THE WORK ETHIC

HANS PETER DREITZEL
*Translated by E. Bubser**

Leistung is one of those German words that Mark Twain would have liked, especially in luxuriant and hissing combinations like *Leistungsgesellschaft* and *Leistungsprinzip*. The Germans, anyway, do like it. It is pleasantly ambiguous.

A *Leistung* may be, among other things, the (better than average) performance of man or machine, a (more or less permanent) achievement, a cash contribution to a good cause. But whatever it means in a specific case, it always contains a solid slug of uplift: even the mere commitment to *Leistung* is almost proof that you are not going to be a failure. All this makes *Leistung* a good word for public speeches and a bad concept in sociology. If we employ it as a sociological concept, it is impossible to build a decent theory around it. On the other hand, it is so overwhelmingly popular in the German-speaking versions of the ideology of industrial society that it makes a good starting point for reflections that may shed some light on the work ethic from a new angle.

*Paul Breines also helped with the translation.

Leistung—let us for the moment say "performance"— is a very modern notion and indicates a change of attitude toward the necessity of human work that dates back only to the first phase of industrial development in Europe. With the Greeks and the Teutonic tribes, work was the proper occupation for bondsmen and slaves; in the Judeo-Christian tradition, work was the curse of Adam, the consequence of man's fall, which was always experienced with an envious glance at the work-free existence of animals (as long as they were "the animals of the field" and not in the service of man). This negative attitude toward work begins to change with the development of the acquisitive bourgeoisie, a change that has found its first and classic expression in the Protestant work ethic. This positive attitude toward work, which at present is culminating in the *Leistungsdenken,* the cult of performance, is inextricably bound up with the development of the bourgeoisie and the system of economy in which the bourgeoisie is at once the producer and the product: profit-oriented and market-dependent commodity production.

In accordance with this modern way of thinking, the most important analyses of capitalism have not only been organized around the concept of work, but also have maintained that it is *work* that marks the specific difference between man and animal, that the essential characteristic of man is work understood as a process through which, as Marx puts it, through his own activity man mediates, regulates and controls his interaction with nature.[1] The notion that man is forced by his own nature, by his bodily existence, to acquire the means for his subsistence by planned and controlled action on the surrounding nature, to appropriate *"den Naturstoff in einer für sein eigenes Leben brauchbaren Form,"*[2] to transform nature, in short; to work, has by now become one of the fundamental tenets of the European school of philosophical anthropology. Plessner, Portmann, Buitendkijk, Gehlen, and others[3] have pointed out the biological components of the "human condition" that have made man capable of reifying (and thus putting at his disposal) the surrounding world: our comparatively premature birth, which is followed by an "extrauterine" development; our upright walk, which has set hands and eyes free and so make possible the instrumental use of the body itself (an essential precondition for the use of tools); the unity of the senses, a precondition for the symbolic mediation of our relations to the surrounding world; our prolonged childhood, which makes us dependent on identifying with groups of others; and the necessity to make up for our lack of instinctual security and the complexities resulting from our "openness toward the world" by means of social institutions. But beyond this, there is still another highly significant point in the anthropological thinking of Marx: *human nature itself* is being changed by human work: When he (man) affects and alters nature through the movement (of the natural powers belonging to his physical make up), he transforms his own nature at the same time.[4] Man's exchange with nature, his social modes of work, shape and influence his "natural state." For our analysis of the *Leistungsgesellschaft*, the "performer society," this is a very important remark: the range of inner experience for the *Leistungsmensch*, the "performer," is already reduced by the very structure of his bodily existence.

The positive attitude toward work has been induced by drastic changes in the modes of production. Under agricultural conditions, the peasant's work did not consist of a conscious manipulation of nature because the product of this type of work was still dependent on quite uncontrolled natural events: the seasons, the weather, the growth rhythms of plants, the feeding and breeding habits of animals, to mention just a few. Things look different in the manufacturer's workshop, however, and still more different under the conditions of machine production: here the change from raw material into finished product gives visible proof of man's power to transform and appropriate nature. And so, with the growth of industrial production, the concept of work acquired a unique rank in human thinking. The ground for this had already been prepared by the bourgeois insistence on the benefits of individual performance; this eventually grew into a universal feeling that man could rid himself of all the darker and more doubtful sides of his existence by resolute application to work. The idea of *Machbarkeit*, the "can do" attitude, not only toward things but also toward human relations, came to determine modern man's relations to nature and society.[5] The concept of *Leistung* bears witness to this modern consciousness: each piece of successful performance demonstrates a new degree (or so it seems) of man's control over his own and external nature.

In the first place, *Leistung* signifies a certain characteristic of man, that is, the process *and* the results of his work. But the immense popularity of this signifies more; it implies a certain model of social organization. It is at this point that it becomes sociologically relevant. Notions that a society employs for self-interpretation are always sociologically significant because whatever we believe about ourselves (or *make* ourselves and others believe) is already part of the social reality we shall have to analyze. This notion of *Leistung* gains its relevance for sociological analysis when it solidifies into a principle of social order that, because of its ideological character, has real social consequences.

Quite obviously, *Leistungsprinzip,* merit as a function of individual achievement, has not only legitimized bourgeois prosperity but also has contributed to the demolition of privileges of birth and guild restrictions; more than anything else, it marks the emancipatory potential of the developing bourgeoisie. In a world dominated by aristocratic and guild privileges, "To each according to his needs" had the force of a liberating, even a revolutionary slogan. And today, long after the beginning of the acquisitive bourgeoisie and long after acquisitiveness became a generally accepted norm, its productivity-raising force is acknowledged even by those who always had to fight for what the propertied class gained automatically from their invested capital: a real bonus for good performance. In the course of time, the *Leistungsprinzip* developed into *the* universally dominating norm of bourgeois society. The most important institutions that have been shaped by its influence are "free" enterprise and its entrepreneurs, the linking of workers' productivity to their wages, and education. In each of these institutions, we can see the gradual expansion of the performance principle and traces of its original ambivalence: profits express the achievement of the entrepreneur, namely, to get maximum surplus value out of the original producers (labor) and to reinvest this surplus value successfully. The absolute (not relative) rise of the wage level expressed the ability of labor to raise productivity sufficiently to reach a livable balance between effort and compensation *and* to sell their socially necessary work by political and economic means at a better price than under conditions of pure competitive capitalism. Educational institutions carry a political obligation to reproduce a certain quantity of qualified labor and to grant a chance (however small) of social mobility founded on individual achievements. The rise of the *Leistungsprinzip* as the ultimate criterion for status allocation in our social system originally had, as we have seen, emancipatory effects; it opposed egalitarianism against the privileges of birth and guild regulations.[6] But on the other hand, its expansion under the bourgeoisie has been possible only because a free labor market is a necessary precondition for capitalist industrial development. The fact that everybody can sell his labor on the free market is (even today) the only guarantee for a sufficient and flexible labor supply. And although this principle has always been limited—even before state interventions in late capitalism (for instance, by the pauperization of agricultural workers and by limitations imposed on certain industries in certain regions)—its importance is not diminished by the development of a mobile class society.

Leistungsgesellschaft, performance society, is a society where labor is a commodity that is exchanged on the market for the means to gratify the wants and needs of the laborer. Hegel has already said this in his Philosophy of Law –

> The mediation to prepare and to acquire particularized means appropriate for particularized needs is the work which the material directly supplied by nature specifies for these manifold purposes by the most various processes.[7]

His formulation shows the close connection between performance and consumption of our present century. Hegel himself, of course, still thought of a society of small manufacturers, where everybody has free and equal access to the market. He considers the mutual interdependence of manufacturers caused by the progressive division of labor and the growing market orientation of production to be a guarantee of the public good. In this dependence and reciprocality of labor and the satisfaction of needs, subjective selfishness is transformed into a contribution to the satisfaction of the needs of all others, the mediation of the particular through the general as dialectical movements, such that as each individual seeks to acquire, produce and enjoy for himself, he precisely thereby produces and acquires for the benefit of others.[8] The misery of the workers who have nothing to sell except their labor, and the ever-increasing concentration of economic power due to capital accumulation and the growing need for even more massive investments are not registered in this picture. But of course, we could not expect that much foresight from Hegel. Things became different later on, however, when the idyllic picture of many small manufacturers in equal competition in a free market turned into a bourgeois illusion, which, for instance, still persists in the capital savings policy for workers advocated by the German Christian Democrats. Considering the fact that about 85 percent of the present West German population are wage earners in industrial or state jobs, this (and similar schemes for "worker capitalism") is simply ideological makebelieve.

The performance principle, without industrialization, can only be enforced at first by an egalitarian and motivating force; in the later stages of industrialization, however, it metamorphizes into its opposite: from an emancipatory principle that increases man's rule over nature, it changes into an ideological principle that stabilizes the rule of man over man. The surplus value resulting from individual performance is appropriated by the owners of the means of production, which results in a continuous proliferation of class antagonisms, and these in turn deprive the performance principle of its motivating force (if we except the dying species of individual entrepreneurs), turning it into a wage earner's strait-jacket: in the place of the principle, we now have performance norms—and the fight against these is part of the worker's daily routine.

At this point, however, we must turn to the impact of the performance principle on the educational institutions: a continuously increasing demand for better qualified labor is part of industrial development. And because no modern society can exist without a certain average level of education, compulsory education is one of the fundamental institutions of industrial society. Beyond this, the manufacturing and service industries require considerable quantities of highly qualified specialized manpower, which can be supplied only by institutions of higher education—if, and this is another important precondition, access to these institutions is not unduly restricted. Performance knowledge and performance ability therefore become more important than real achievements[9] because the requirements of a system governed by ever-changing and newly created needs and by ruthless competition can be met only by the training of both specialist and non-specialist abilities. (The contradictions inherent in this goal explain much of the permanent crisis in our educational institutions.) The important point is that the performance principle embodied in performance knowledge and performance abilities creates new and solidifies old inequalities. Even if there were no class-determined education barriers (the most important of which are raised by early childhood socialization within a certain milieu), and even if specialist training did not produce its own inequalities, a perfect application of the performance principle would result in the social implementation of a *natural* inequality, and this inequality would be especially inhuman because there is no appeal against nature. British sociologist Michael Young has developed a kind of negative utopia, in which individual income and prestige are strictly coupled to individual I.Q.[10] What this proves is not so much how cruel uncontrolled nature can be but rather how inhuman are the seemingly natural but in fact socially determined performance abilities and capacity for success of the individual.[11] The initial inequality of chances among individuals is not only determined by regional, religious, or family differences but also by the highly unequal chances to dispose individually of the surplus value produced by one's labor. If a society removes *this* inequality of chances, as has been attempted by the socialist countries, then the demand for control over nature must be carried so far (and be so successful) that the differences in abilities because of age, sex, intelligence, or health are not adjusted in a merely mechanical fashion.

Because the performance principle contains an ineradicable ambivalence, the political postulate that performance society and its full development must be secured obviously has ideological functions. First, it masks the fact that even in capitalist industrial society "ascribed status" plays an essential role in the acquisition and securing of social power and consumption privileges. Sociology distinguishes between "ascribed status" and "acquired status"[12]: "ascribed status" results from certain natural or quasi-natural properties, for example, membership in the superior sex, in a venerable age group, or in one of the great families; whereas "acquired status" results from personal abilities and accomplishments. In modern society, acquired status is more important for the individual's social position than ascribed status, although the language level in the home, the parents' material position, and certain *traditional* privileges of the father's profession rather accurately predict the future intellectual and material positions of the children.[13] Individual accomplishments play a role only if his family background provides material security during the process of education *and* a motivational structure that enables him to experience the postponement of gratification as meaningful. The open society in this sense is a fiction aimed at the legitimization of established inequalities. At the same time, however, the rapid and unpredictable changes in demand for specialist talent have called, albeit hesitantly, for a permanent reform of our educational system, one that will bring all reserves of potentially qualified labor into the labor market.[14]

Second, all the current invocations of *Leistungsgesellschaft,* of the performance society, keep silent on the main uncertainty connected with this concept: the evaluation of a given individual performance. All objective attempts to measure performance (i.e., in industrial work, in pupils learning achievements, or even in scientific work) have been remarkably unsuccessful. In industry, attempts to develop objective norms have been restricted to ever more intensive exploitation of labor. During the 1920's, Taylor's attempts to categorize work into motion sequences that avoid friction, delays, and wasted energy, and the resulting measures of performance, were, as Elton Mayo recognized in his Hawthorne study on work problems, of doubtful value.[15] This study (which inaugurated the so-called human-relations movement in industrial psychology) demonstrated that job satisfaction, "company climate," tensions within working teams, and material job conditions, among other factors decisively influence worker productivity. Obviously the human organism revolts against Taylor-type rationality and demands satisfactory status, prestige relations, and a recognizably meaningful content for his work. Considering the principle of capitalist production, which aims at the most intensive exploitation of labor, that is, maximum productivity per worker, the rational consequence introduced social job benefits, pseudohierarchies, and make-believe worker participation. With this, however, nothing has changed the material dependence of workers, and so direct material inducements will play a large role, especially in shift work and piecework (and this, by the way, holds for the productivity-conscious socialist societies, too). The whole wage system has become so complex that it is hardly comprehensible for the individual worker and bears no relation to individual productivity—if we except pure piecework and its special hardships.[16] Ergonomics failed to find an objective measure for human performance because all definable concepts of performance are dependent on value judgments. The dominance of the performance principle in industry means in practical terms that workers are subjected to a system of work norms that is coupled with a wage system that contains a host of value judgments on bodily strength, intelligence, education, ability, personality, age, sex, milieu, and so on, and above all on the unconditional commitment to material success. A recent German textbook on ergonomics states: "Ergonomics has tried with the greatest possible care to find objective and testable criteria for determining that performance which was to be used as standard value, as standard performance."

At each step our discipline increases the number of the components of human performance, the number of characteristics which mark differences in performance. Unfortunately, however, the ecotechnic system of ergonomics never succeeds in its efforts to escape the region of value judgments.[17] The authors add that this is due mainly to the supremacy accorded to material success in our system. However problematical the measurement of objective performance and performance knowledge may be, for the sociologist it is important that even in an unadulterated performance society status allotment contains an element that is irreducible to factual accomplishments, namely, the individual or collective ability to succeed.[18] Performance does not gain (material or ideal) rewards just because it results in a piece of shaped matter or an intellectual construct. In order to induce social approval and positive sanctions, performance must be made highly visible; the buyer in the market and the public that allots prestige must be convinced that the product is useful and profitable, and this conviction tends to be more or less independent of the factual existence of these characteristics. This was seen in 1930 by psychologist Gustav Ichheiser,[19] who introduced the distinction between *Leistungstüchtigkeit* and *Erfolgstüchtigkeit,* the ability to perform and the ability to succeed, respectively. The ability to perform comprises all those properties and modes of behavior that tend to have positive effects on the factual requirements and the social expectations connected with a certain type of job; the ability to succeed comprises properties and behavior directed at public acknowledgment, first of a certain achievement and second of the performer's personality.[20] To achieve what is usually called success, both abilities must be combined. Only in certain limited cases is one of them completely absent: the charlatan tries to get by without any factual performance, and if he succeeds, this is due to the always present subjective element in our social system of performance evaluation; the "neglected genius," on the other hand, can claim accomplishments that do not become socially pertinent because, from pride or from sheer inability, he holds the market of vanities in contempt and keeps his light hidden. This duality of expectations directed at professional roles that combine performance norms and success norms reveals the hidden dialectics of success. Usually, norm fulfillment for just one set of norms will not be sufficient for success; it takes an adaptation—sometimes equilibristic—to often conflicting expectations concerning role behavior to achieve this aim, the combination of performance and sucess, the transformation of performance into success. In our social structure, success is dependent on certain job-specific achievement norms, and if these are fulfilled, further advance inside professional hierarchies is dependent on hierarchy-specific success norms that demand a quite specific presentation of the expected performance qualifications. Some time ago, the wrong type of dress or the wrong type of wife could put an academic career in jeopardy; today it would only show a certain degree of worldly innocence and even a touch of totalitarian rigidity to condemn the evils of the ability to succeed without taking notice of its brighter sides, for a certain degree of moral and sensual corruptibility and corruption is an unfailing symptom for the humanness of human associations.

It might, for instance, show that recent plans to shorten courses at German universities drastically and to subject students to more frequent achievement controls will very probably only produce an unusual number of psychological disturbances in students, a result that can hardly be in the interest of a society that is so dependent on its academic elite. Perhaps we should recall Adorno's definition that talent is just "luckily sublimated rage"—rage, that is, against repressive performance norms, which is certainly worlds apart from a willing identification with these norms. On the other hand, one also must admit that the norms of the ability to succeed serve to cement social inequalities.

This cementing happens in two ways. First, there is the phenomenon that Ichheiser has called the "self-veiling of success," namely, the ex post facto ideological legitimization of one's ability to succeed by equating success with the ability to perform. Thus, the most successful are often the most ardent advocates of performance society. Tycoons who owe their successes to good financial connections, unscrupulous exploitation, and ruthless infighting with the competition spread the myth of their own hard work and its fruits through the media, and so are among the best propagandists for the open performance society. Second, the skills that comprise the ability to succeed are highly class specific, that is, dependent on family background, and this means that people who start out privileged have the best chances to achieve certain positions. How difficult such achievements are for those who did not learn the right attitudes and habits at home is documented in stories about the uncivilized behavior of the newly rich; for the sociologist, it explains much of the typical overadaptations to the norms of the class just entered, comparatively authoritarian attitudes, rigidity, and inflexibility that so often can be observed in social overachievers.

So the performance principle no longer favors the individual's life chances; rather, it serves as a subtly veiled legitimization of continuing social inequalities. This ideological function, however, does not exhaust the present misery of the performance principle. Its dominant role as a norm that determines all chances of need gratification results from the fact that, under the conditions of capitalist division of labor, abstract performance has become independent from the concrete contents of performance, and that this "alienated" performance determines the standard of self-assertion in the competitive labor market. This development (together with its internal contradictions) is a natural consequence of the essence of capitalist production: because of increasing capital concentration, the interests of capital grow more and more independent from the interests of labor; that is, the economic meaning of work consists in the accumulation of capital, in the transformation of surplus value into capital, and in the growing distanciation of abstract work from its concrete contents. From the economic point of view, what counts is the exchange value of commodities; their use value is important only insofar as it is necessary to maintain or create a certain level of demand. Thus, the value of work is reduced to effort per time unit, plus the costs of the investment necessary for the required qualification of the worker, and these costs are often paid with the workers' tax money. The abstractness of performance and its valuation, the indifference toward the product created by work, becomes visible in the extreme forms of the division of labor and in the general alienation of the worker from his product. It is important to realize that this development is not restricted to industrial work (primary production). The abstract performance principle dominates nearly all professions and spheres of life: it regiments governmental and industrial bureaucracies, the independent petit-bourgeois harassed by competition, and (if we look at the intended education reforms) work in the academic sphere, which so far has been cushioned by traditional professional privileges. To the degree that processes of production and its distribution are *verwissenschaftlich,* "scientized" or submitted to calculated functional rationality, abstract criteria of performance govern the corresponding spheres of social activity, including "the reproduction of labor" (here we mean higher education). This is true partly because this reproduction is just one aspect of the selling of the commodity, labor, and partly because the service professions in this highly differentiated sector must secure their material existence against competition from other sectors.

The abstractness of the required performance brought about by the separation of productive activity from product is symptomatic of a process called the "desensualization" of work. This is due to a division of labor into a sequence of steps, each of which has lost any visible connection with the final product and its use. Desensualization does not hold only for industrial work but also for bureaucratic work, where it is aggravated by progressive mechanization and automation. Furthermore, this division of labor inhibits the worker's identification with his product, which, to a certain degree, is a psychological need whose gratification increaes productivity. In some places, this has been recognized; for example, Volvo, a Swedish manufacturer of cars, has abandoned the assembly line in some workshops and has replaced it with work teams that develop their own nonmechanical forms of cooperation. This raises a point that is quite often overlooked in discussions about the performance principle and alienation; namely, the most important aspect is not the individual abstractness of performance and the separation between the individual worker and his work, but rather the work chances and work situation of cooperating groups and collectives. The splitting of the production process into individual bits of performance implied by the performance principle is an expression of the abstractness of work, on the one hand, and of the interest in inhibiting the solidarity of workers, on the other hand. This division and reduction of work to the level of the lonely individual, which in industry always has met limits imposed by mechanical and organizational requirements, has proliferated in office work (i.e., the production and distribution of information). The modern secretarial pool, which has been propagated and introduced with much ideological furor, is an example. Its main function is to rationalize and to improve performance control. With academics, "lonely work" is one of the most stable items in the inventory of their false consciousness. How far the ideology of the bourgeois personality, combined with solid material interest, can reduce performance is shown by the overwhelming opposition of doctors against group practices.

The instrumental attitude toward work,[21] the conscious notion that work is performed only because it increases chances of consumption, is a widespread *modus deficiens* of functional rationality. It is caused by the preeminence of exchange values over use values within the capitalist system of production and distribution. But it also appears in socialist countries that have not developed economically viable criteria for the use value of commodities, or putting it differently, that have not found economic and political solutions for the problem of adapting production and distribution to the real needs of man. Actually, even functional rationality has to consider mechanical and organizational rigidities that, together with the predominance of the exchange value of products, determine our daily lives in a threefold way: by the norm of *affective neutrality,* by the *temporalization* of action sequences, and by the *spatial segmentation* of action spheres. These categories are protected from spontaneous irruptions by our internalization of external constraints. The desensualization of work expressed by the performance principle dominates our social life in all its aspects.

Let us look at a few examples of this. Affective neutrality, the suppression of libidinous impulses, is taken for granted, not only in work situations, but also in innumerable social interactions. Only artists can afford to surrender emotionally to their process of production because their products express an emotional relation toward the world. A dreamy assembly line worker, a stoned crane operator, a lovesick pilot, a driver under stress, a lonely and depressed telephone operator, a sexually frustrated secretary are real and sometimes deadly dangers to the functional integrity of those action systems we are forced to depend on daily. Under these aspects, the romantic idea of an *allseitige* state of society giving free reign to the "complete sensual man" is not much help. Quite obviously, a high degree of affective control (beginning with elementary bodily functions and extending beyond deferred gratifications) is a functional necessity for a society at our present stage of technological and organizational complexity. The question, however, is whether or not the bourgeoisie has developed (for historical reasons) rigidities that go far beyond the functional necessities, and whether or not these rigidities cause a host of physical disturbances that are highly dysfunctional to productivity. The answer, I think, is obvious.

One of the most important mechanisms of affective control is the temporalization of action sequences. We not only live by the clock; it controls our lives more than any tyranny. During the first phase of industrialization in the Catholic Rhineland, the first strikes occurred when Protestant factory owners tried to cut down on the quite great number of Catholic holidays.[22] Since then, the time clock has become an everyday reality for all industrial workers, and this general temporalization not only schedules our workdays but also our weeks, months, years (with holidays and Christmas shopping season). Only death, which is timeless although not unlike a temporal principle of finality that governs all organic life, is exempt from the schedule (some see a connection between temporalization and the rule of the market faithfully enough to think that the early purchase of a cemetery plot is eminently rational). For our society, death is fundamentally a regrettable accident after which everybody returns to his regular agenda, except, of course, those who have died. This embarrassed suppression of death corresponds to an attitude that values the appointment calendar as a status symbol and that divides the contemplative and libidinous aspects of human life because they cannot be planned. The German proverb *Dienst ist Dienst und Schnaps ist Schnaps* (work is work and fun is fun) marks a state of mind that has solidified the temporalization of our lives into a norm whose reifying character consciously separates work and sensuality.

The spatial separation of action spheres, combined with time separations, guarantees that work and sensuality will not mix. The job (or the school) has rules that further the production process: nobody goes to the washroom without excusing himself; eating and drinking are performed in the company cafeteria at the proper time; personal likes or dislikes do not enter into team cooperation; in other words, one does not behave as if one were at home. At home—no longer in nature—is where Goethe's "*Here am I human; here should I be so*," still holds, provided, of course, one does not have a nagging wife (or husband), too-noisy kids, or next-door neighbors who are making an awful racket. The separation between private and public sphere, which has matured during several centuries of the developing bourgeois world, has now reached the point where human sensuality has been reduced to sexual behavior inside the bedroom. Fathers and mothers disappear daily behind factory entrances and office walls that mark the boundaries of industrial feudalism, into a world that is closed to all outsiders—and among these outsiders are family members, children, and friends. The sphere of public life has been almost totally reduced to regimented streams of traffic if we except the artificial stimulations and pseudogratifications dispensed in consumption factories and holiday zoos; the private sphere shrinks toward an "at-home" intimacy of already mutilated impulses neurotically fixated at an overburdened partner. Modern town planning and architecture manifest this spatial separation between work and sensuality in indestructible concrete. The (let us hope) discredited dogma of town planners that "disentangled" the functions of city life has transformed our cities into a maze leading to and from work, where any sign of sensuality is exotic at best and a breach of public order at worst.

All this, however, is not so poignant as one expects; the external compulsions have been internalized during a long process of civilization.[23] If people had not been "broken in," unrest and revolt would have erupted long ago. We are hardly aware of how far we have internalized the external compulsions that suppress our sensuality. In most cases, this manifests itself as "neurotic return of the suppressed," by which nature takes its revenge: psychosomatic diseases, functional disturbances, and generalized psychic discomfort.[24]

What we have seen so far shows (among other things) the modern attitude toward nature: for the capitalist market mechanism and its correlate, bourgeois consciousness, internal and external nature is an inexhaustible source of energy, and the ruthless exploitation of this source of energy is justified by man's "supposed" mastery over nature. In fact, however, this exploitation has served the purpose of capital accumulation and the rule of man over man. At first, the wealth of exploitable external resources dominated, and even men were seen as a somehow "external," physically exploitable resource. The first phase of industrialization could afford this physical exploitation. The requirements of production were largely dependent on the workers' muscle power, and although the workers' average life expectancy (and consequently working life) was short, the supply of unskilled workers seemed inexhaustible. Today, the situation has changed, and even the huge worker migrations inside Europe count for little. First, the workers themselves enforced certain protective measures, and second, qualification requirements have risen and are still rising, so work has become a comparatively expensive commodity. Nevertheless, changes in attitude toward the internal, that is, our own nature, proceed slower and with greater difficulty than the realization that our external resources of raw materials and energy are limited and endangered by our present modes of consumption and production, as for example, is the case with water. Psychic disturbances are diseases like other diseases and should be treated as such, although this is an idea that has been painfully slow in emerging (as evidenced by the enormous trouble it has taken to get psychotherapy covered by medical insurance). Now the ecology movement and the slow realization of how far physical devastation has spread, seem to prepare the way for a changed attitude toward nature, an attitude adumbrated in the—again and again suppressed—category of sensuality, which historically has been espoused by romantics and philosophical materialists, especially Feuerbach.

Materialism, especially post-romantic materialism, was one of the first philosophies directed against the Cartesian dualism that had dominated the modern age, and in this, it has been the precursor of philosophical anthropology, which explicates the body-mind unity of man in scientific terms. In place of Descartes' "I think, therefore I am," the materialist substitutes "I work, therefore I am," and this means a metabolic exchange between man and nature, sensuality as a fundamental trait of man's relation toward nature. Man is "open" toward the world, but this does not mean that a disorderly stream of sense-data impinges on his organs, in the image of the old empiricists that still dominates the rigid picture-theory of official Soviet epistemology. It also does not mean that the relation between man and the world is mediated by the categories inherent in the transcendental ego, as the idealists thought. It means, instead, that the relation between man and the world is "mediated by immediate sensuality," by the fact that we *are* a body and *have* a body. As Feuerbach puts it, "In no way is man's ego 'by itself' as such 'open to the world,' but through itself as physical being. Against the absolved I, the body is objective world. Through the body the I is not I but object. One's physical being means to be in the world. So many senses, so many pores, so much nakedness. The body is the porous I.[25] In the original mode of givenness of the world, subject and object, I and world are simultaneously present in the body."[26] The central role of man's bodily existence in the mediation of man's relation to nature has been covered, on the one hand, by the persistent influence of idealistic philosophy (which, one must not forget, has played a useful role in the development of capitalism) and, on the other hand, by the foreshortened concept of praxis that arises from Leninism, which tends to mean little more than the balance sheet of technological progress as approved by the party.

The ruthless subjugation of nature was unknown to non-European cultures. In Europe, however, this attitude was presaged by the Christian demythologization of nature; it was fully developed by the logic of the capitalist market economy. Today, the first signs of a postmodern relation toward nature are surfacing in the consciousness and the behavior patterns of youth subcultures whose members sense that mastery of man over nature implies mastery of man over man. This principled refusal of course has its potentially regressive aspect. The mere rejection of techniques and civilization and all active interference with external and internal nature neglects the massive problems connected with maintaining our natural resources; only rational behavior can deal with them. More important, however, this refusal does not take into account the fact that man's own nature in his exchange with external nature has become artificial, that, for man, nature in the specific shapes of his needs and their gratification already appears "humanized." In man's natural artificiality, nature has produced its own opposite; and the relation between man and nature can only consist in a mutual mediation. And that means that complete submission to nature blocks the sources of human existence just as complete mastery over nature does.

The elements of a postmodern consciousness in our counterculture are inseparably bound up with premodern and antimodern attitudes that accompanied industrial society from its beginnings. The main tenet of counterculture is the rejection of functional or instrumental rationality, of techniques and bureaucracy. This is a reaction against the "disenchanted" world that Max Weber analyzed (and called "a den of servility"). The counterculture rejects the work ethic (i.e., the morality of the performance principle), stresses creativity, shrinks the metric time perspective into the "here and now," and gives a negative value to making things and a positive value to letting things grow and develop by themselves. Its aim is to reunify the separated behavior spheres of private and public life, of work and sensuality; it favors spontaneous consensus over systematic discussion, voluntary action over ritualized self-control, and *Gemeinschaft* (quasi-natural community) over *Gesellschaft* (rational association). Even beyond the inner circles of counterculture, one can observe a spreading desocialization of needs: identity is being constructed more on physiological properties like sex or ethnic origin which therefore achieve political significance. The individual's bodily existence appears as the final legitimizing ground of social action, and consequently, ascriptive status and acquired status exchange their former conservative and progressive meanings. In contrast to the class society of the nineteenth century, the silent majority today is conservative, and the political opposition is split up into a multitude of vociferous minorities. And finally, the self-realization of a literally naked self inside a present and participating group has become the sociopolitical aim of Progressivism that claims allegiance to Rousseau's suppressed tradition by radically invoking nature against societal rule.

In certain spheres of action, because functional rationality of behavior remains imperative for industrial and bureaucratic societies, the societal dissociation of pleasure and performance

marks a fundamental contradiction in our capitalist mode of production. This is true for socialist societies as well, at least as long
as they change property relations by radical political and administrative democratization. In capitalist societies, where the
class struggle has been institutionally anaesthetized, this fundamental contradiction takes the shape of a series of antinomies
that mark the friction points and the germs of future conflicts.
We have already noted the antinomy between strict affective control in the public sphere and that in the private sphere, where
stunted sensual needs have to be gratified in the intimacy of the
bedroom. We hardly ever realize how massive is the amount of
drive suppression required by our performance society because
the mere voyeurism of stunted libidinous impulses is supported
by generally tolerated compensatory performance aids, such as
pseudoliberating pornography and pseudoscientific phar-
macological concoctions. A corresponding antinomy appears in
the market sphere, where there is a strict separation between increasingly empty work and consumption, where commodity
aesthetics produces a semblance of use value that is less and less
sufficient to mark the mere exchange value, and so again
frustrates even our compensatory drive fixations.[27] Certainly, one
of the strongest effects of the performance ideology is that the
victims do not realize the internal connection between the lack of
gratification in work and the pseudogratifications in consumption. And finally, the fundamental contradiction between
pleasure and performance manifests itself on a massive scale in
the frictions of our political order: here the interest of the commodity economy in rapidly decaying use values and the production of useless and/or destructive commodities (in order to maximize capital turnover) imposes itself on a welfare state that has
to bear not only the costs for the reproduction and socialization
of labor but also the costs of a (more or less) functioning industrial infrastructure. Together with these obligations, the state
has accepted the responsibility for the ideological procurement
of mass loyalty toward a system riddled by a permanent legitimacy crisis.[28] These contradictions (which nowadays emerge as
political crises whenever the material standard of living is in
danger) manifest themselves in, among other things, the equivo-
cations of the concept "performance," which has come to mean
at once work performance, that is, increased productivity, and
social performance, that is, guaranteed reproduction of labor.

    In the future, this contradiction of our industrial societies most
likely will grow in intensity. We are moving in the direction of

what Alain Touraine called a programmed society containing temporarily, spatially, and socially defined "hedonist ghettos"; the question is whether these will do the job and control the conflict that results from the separation of work and sensuality. This will partly depend on whether it will be possible to develop organizational forms for the articulation and support of sensual needs. One of the main obstacles to this will be the fact that exploitation, stress, and underprivileged conditions are no longer characteristic of a definite social group; they are conditions every one of us is subject to. Formerly, the limits of political action and the articulation of needs were marked by class barriers, and political-economy was the key to the structure of the capitalist system. Today, however, social classes capable of political action no longer exist; we have class relations that everybody enters into individually and that are managed bureaucratically by the very institutionalization of class conflict.[29] And so sociological analysis is faced with the task of elucidating (in contrast to the current predominance of political-economical categories) the political meaning of the subjective constitution of our social relations—seen in its relation to the technical and organizational determinants of the production process. This analysis will show that the dissociation of pleasure and performance can be overcome only by strategies aimed at two central structural elements of our social condition: first, a dissolution of the rigid drive suppression and/or neurotic fixation with substitute objects and, second, a replacement of the commodity-conditioned loneliness and instrumentalization of work with collective modes of production and consumption.

NOTES

1. Karl Marx, *Das Kapital* (Berlin: 1962, Book 1).
2. Ibid.
3. See Helmuth Plessner, *Die Stufen des Organischen und der Mensch* (Berlin/Leipzig: 1928); Adolph Portmann, *Biologische Fragmente zu einer Lehre vom Menschen* (Basel: 1944); F.J.J. Buytendijk, *Allgemeine Theorie der menschlichen Haltung und Bewegung* (Heidelberg: 1956); Arnold Gehlen, *Der Mensch* (Bonn: 1950).
4. Marx, *Das Kapital.*
5. See Hans Freyer, *Theorie des gegenwärtigen Zeitalters* (Stuttgart: 1955), pp. 15 ff.
6. See Claus Offe, *Leistungsprinzip und industrielle Arbeit* (Frankfurt: 1970).
7. G.W.F. Hegel, *Grundlinien der Philosophie des Rechts,* p. 196.
8. Ibid., p. 199
9. See Hans Peter Dreitzel, *Elitebegriff und Sozialstruktur* (Stuttgart: 1961), esp. Chapter 7.

10. Michael Young, *The Rise of the Meritocracy, 1870–2033: An Essay on Education and Equality* (London: 1958).

11. On the question of the social determination of intelligence, see Hugh Mehan, *Assessing Children's School Performance,* in Hans Peter Dreitzel, *Childhood and Socialization* (New York: Macmillan, 1973).

12. The difference between "ascribed status" and "achieved status" was first elaborated by Ralph Linton, *The Study of Man* (New York: 1936).

13. See P. M. Roeder, A. Pasdzierny, and W. Wolf, *Sozialstatus und Schulerfolg* (Heidelberg: 1965).

14. See for this development Gunnar Heinsohn, *Vorschulerziehung Heute?* (Frankfurt: 1971).

15. See Elton Mayo, *The School Problems of an Industrial Civilization* (New York: 1945); F. J. Roethlisberger and W. J. Dickinson, *Management and the Worker* (New York: 1942).

16. Marx, *Das Kapital,* Book 1, pp. 574 ff.

17. H. Pornschlegel, R. Birkwald, and H. Wiesner, *Menschliche Leistung und Arbeitsergebnis* (Köln: 1967), p. 82.

18. See the chapter "Die Dialektik des Erfolgs" in Dreitzel, *Elitebegriff und Sozialstruktur.*

19. Gustav Ichheiser, *Kritik des Erfolgs: Eine soziologische Untersuchung* (Leipzig: 1930).

20. Dreitzel, p. 100.

21. See John Goldthorpe and David Lockwood, *Der wohlabende Arbeiter* (Munich: Goldmann, 1970).

22. David Riesman, *Work and Leisure: Fusion or Polarity? in Abundance for What?* (New York: 1969).

23. See Norbert Elias, *Uber den Prozess der Zivilisation* (Stuttgart: 1970). English translation: *The Civilizing Process* (New York: Urizen Press, 1977).

24. See, for instance, as a first overview, Hans Strokzka, *Einfuhrung in die Sozialpsychiatrie* (Hamburg: 1965).

25. Ludwig Feuerbach, *Der Anfang der Philosophie.* Quoted in Alfred Schmidt, *Emanzipatorische Sinnlichkeit—Ludwig Feuerbach's anthropologischer Materialismus* (Munich: 1973), p. 122.

26. Ibid.

27. For this argument, see W. F. Haug, *Kritik der Warenästhetik* (Frankfurt: 1970).

28. For this problem, see Jürgen Habermas, *Legitimationsprobleme im Spätekapitalismus* Frankfurt: 1973). English translation: *Legitimation Crisis* (Boston: 1975).

29. See Claus Offe, "Political Authority and Class Structure—An Analysis of Late Capitalist Societies," *International Journal of Sociology* (Spring 1972): 81.

11.
SOCIOLOGY AND THE PRESSING DEMAND
FOR SOCIAL PARTICIPATION

FRANCO FERRAROTTI

I. In their famous *Soziologische Excurse,* Max Horkheimer and
Theodor W. Adorno insist on a notion of "sociology as a science
of resignation to the *status quo,*" which does not seem quite
tenable today. Taking a retrospective view, they remark that,
sociology, or to put it more precisely, the "doctrine of society,"
was at the beginning far from being totally free of philosophical
elements. They quote from a fundamental text of classical
philosophy, the *Republic,* to show that Plato's intent was to
outline the good life in a perfect society as it was conceived of by
a patrician citizen of Athens with a conservative bent. Horkheimer and Adorno early capitalize on the platonic use of value
judgments about the constitution of the polity and refer directly
to the autobiographical *Seventh Letter* to prove how, in the
platonic doctrine of society, direct observations and personal experiences were incorporated from Plato's own missions as a
technical expert to Egypt and Sicily and Socrates' death

sentence. According to them, sociology cannot confine itself to the simple gathering and arrangement of facts. Factual information and experience, although necessary at first, must be transcended; it must be evaluated in order to arrive at a guideline to political decision and social action. This could be acceptable if Horkheimer and Adorno were not so philosophically inclined to obliterate empirical research and fieldwork to the benefit of abstract speculation.

The notion of sociology as a science subservient to facts seems to derive, at least as far as Horkheimer and Adorno are concerned, from a reductive view of positivism in the light of an abstract dialectical approach that is biased in favor of a purely, or primarily, cultural consideration of social phenomena. This cultural consideration is linked with the idea of a global approach, that is, the study of social phenomena within the framework of their characteristic totality instead of exploring them as separate items, which although heuristically advisable or even indispensable, misses their final, and total, meaning. As suggestive as they are, Horkheimer and Adorno's conceptions do not do justice to the fundamental and liberating function of historical positivism vis-a-vis traditional religious beliefs and metaphysical speculation. Their eloquent strictures about positivistic sociology as being essentially captive to purely factual statements and therefore .devoid of any operational value overlook an important problem that Auguste Comte repeatedly dealt with: "Knowledge, for What?" Comte's cherished motto was: "To know in order to predict; to predict in order to act and to intervene."

Far from being the "science of resignation," sociology today is the science of social crisis. It offers a tool through which a social crisis can become an important positive contribution in establishing a controllable link between the decisions of those in power and the aspirations of the so-called underlying population. There is an epiphanic function of social crisis that sociology can retain and maximize. The institutional crisis of technically developed societies delineates shortcomings of the existing institutional fabric. The Watergate affair in the United States and the "continuous conflictuality" in Western Europe point to a relatively new phenomenon. We used to complain about general political apathy; now we see that political participation through established formal political behavior and organization is no longer adequate. It has to be complemented, and somehow guaranteed, by *social* participation. On the other hand, a growing body of evidence shows that the existing institutional set-up cannot accommodate the new and pressing demand for social participation. Old bureaucratic practices and structures are about to collapse. A feeling of helplessness spreads among the oligarchic functionaries and policymakers. Formal task definition is no longer sufficient. A new legitimation is needed. Where can we get it and how?

II. Soviet sociologist S. A. Efirov has severely criticized my notion of "sociology as participation." I would like to counter by saying that the idea of "sociology as participation" is to be confused neither with the generic empathy of the philanthropist nor with the participant observation approach, no matter how valuable these can be. With the term "sociology as participation," I indicate an approach that goes well beyond the early positivistic, or perhaps I should say mechanistic, approach to social research, whereby the researcher stands, by definition, in a superior position to the "object" investigated, with the sad result that he often investigates his own shadow, that is, his own principles of preference. As such, sociology as participation simply means that, in order to ensure reliable research findings, a two-way relationship has to be established between researcher and researched; therefore, any comfortable, but in the end mystifying, reification of society as a rigid social system must be abandoned. I do not think that Efirov has understood the methodological and substantive implications of sociology as participation. He has exclusively, almost obsessively, concentrated on its disruptive consequences to the formal institutional social fabric. He fears a surge of antistate feeling, with the radical political opposition it implies, and in what he calls my "eclectic theorizing," he detects camouflaged expression of the anarchosyndicalism that was so widespread in Italy and France at the turn of the century and some sort of anarchistic nostalgia that is a mortal threat to the established order. However, I answer my conservative Soviet critic by saying that a social consensus incapable of tolerating a sphere of mild informality and indetermination is insecure, if not fragile. If I suffer from nostalgia for the anarchic dream of a direct democracy, maybe Efirov suffers from a medieval nostalgia for the supremely simplified and orderly world represented by the forced identification of state and society.

It is a fact, however, that even old societies that labor under a heavy medieval and feudal past, such as in Europe, "state" and "public" do not coincide. Actually, a new sense of what is public is slowly emerging, while social and formally political elements are growing farther apart. In short, more politics is going on out-

side of politics than inside the traditional organizations, such as
political parties and trade unions. Formal political representation
is lagging behind the orientation and the requests of the broader
civil society. Even in countries with well-established democratic
governments, where nobody openly criticizes representation, one
notices a certain amount of uneasiness. In Europe, a certain
malaise is undeniable. Representation is under attack. Anti-and
extraparliamentary groups are very vocal; so vocal, in fact, that
they have succeeded in electing their representatives to the national parliament. As ridiculous, contradictory, or paradoxical as
this might seem, we cannot let it go unnoticed. Representative
democracy is more and more out of pace with society. There is a
crisis of representivity. Institutions have lost their links with
ideal tensions and with everyday experiences of individuals. I
would not agree with some student and feminist movements that
have simplistically proclaimed that the "personal is political,"
but it is true that a dialectical connection between the personal
and the political has to be found again if a renovation or a
refounding of democratic institutions is to be possible. The ideal
that a democratic regime is best and only ensured through
regular electoral process is far from sufficient. Every institutional
complex today is striving for a new kind of social participation
and individual, personal recognition. Democracy as a pure and
simple decision-making mechanism, that is, as a machine based
on a special kind of engineering and legal procedure irrespective
of social substance and economic content, is no longer enough.
The traditional double standard whereby democratic citizens,
like Christians, are equal in heaven but unequal on earth, that is,
equal in the heaven of abstract formal democratic rights but unequal on the practical ground of economic interests and relative
affluence, is no longer tenable.

In all the major spheres of social life—inside the family and at
work, in the schools and in the professions—participation,
equality, and recognition emerge as the central values, and the
rising demands coming from the underlying population must be
satisfied. It is not the absurd anarchic dream that my Soviet critic
fears; it is the simple request that democracy be something more
than empty formula or ritualistic behavior.

III.   However widespread and universal it is, the concept of
participation remains elusive. In essence, it implies a sense of
"togetherness," of "being part" of a transcending whole, a
member of a community; at the same time, it means taking sides,
making a choice, choosing a party. There are also operational dif-

ficulties of a practical nature. Although, without social participation, economic development would probably result only in economic expansion and private profit maximization, it is doubtful that representative government would automatically transform itself into a tool of the producers. Moreover, it seems that the logic of development for industrial societies is not necessarily compatible with the basic rules of democracy, of indirect representative and parliamentary democracy, not to mention direct and self-governing democracy. The high degree of interdependence and the rational calculation that go with an industrial system based on middle- and high-level technical operations constitute a serious difficulty for any kind of democratically governed society.

These difficulties are real. Yet the demand for social participation stands out as the great novelty of the second half of the twentieth century. History is no longer only the history of great men and their deeds: *historia rerum gestarum*. It is "social" history. Colonial countries become emerging countries; excluded social classes gain access to cultural and political life. The crucial, decisive characteristics of our time arise from neither technical progress, as unprecedented as it is, nor scientific exploit. The most important fact is that for the first time people and entire continents that had been isolated from the mainstream of human life have finally made their entrance into history. They are no longer so much lifeless matter, the objects rather than the subjects of historical action.

Traditional societies, whether pre- or paleotechnical, characteristically consider history as a given fact, as a "natural situation" that is, by definition, outside human initiative. These people, in other words, rather than playing an active part in history, are passively subjected to its results. Certain currents of Western culture have long regarded this passive state as the logical and inevitable outcome of a natural, mental, and civil inferiority of such races, which they regard as human only in the biological sense. By projecting onto other human civilizations and groups its own particular values, especially its technical achievements, Western culture has set itself up as the touchstone and ideal for all other human groups, which are indiscriminately reduced, even while they are exploited, to the rank of "subjects to be educated." But it is here where we run into a fatal contradiction: just when Western culture puts forward its way of life as the exclusive ideal, it prevents, because of this ethnocentricity, any real communication with other cultures. The flow of information is blocked or, at best, it functions only in one direction, from above downward. Western culture is moving toward its own historical destruction insofar as it finds it impossible to understand others because they are different.

IV. This extraordinary and novel entry into the history of people and nations that were hitherto excluded gives a peculiar connotation to our time. Something profoundly significant has developed in the international relationships between different nations and cultures; the epoch of vertical imperialism has given way to the age of interior colonization. Within individual countries, new forms of exploitation of man by man are found. Our mental schemes, the images that support the conceptual structure of our reasoning, have fallen hopelessly behind the evolution of the objective world. A new "political demand," and the corresponding request for participation, lies at the heart of the contemporary institutional crisis. This crisis marks a moment of anguish and indicates a breaking point, but it also is a moment of epiphany. It tears apart, true, but it also opens and lays bare.

We are living in an age when men are linked by a constant flux of explicit, politically relevant communications, on a worldwide scale: a synchronic world in which anything happening in Southeast Asia has a direct influence and effect on North America; in which a word whispered in Peking reechoes in Rome and New York, in Tokyo and Paris. The things we used to learn by rubbing shoulders with our neighbors are learned today through satellite messages. But we have still to realize this; we know it with our minds, but we must *realize* it existentially. We are still thinking of the exploitation of man by man, of one social class by another, in nineteenth-century terms. At this rate, we shall move into the twentieth century when in fact it is drawing to a close.

Nineteenth-century exploitation is based on certain assumptions. It invents the autonomy of civil society in respect to both the economic system and the political institutions. On this basis, it constructs the notion of the individual as a free agent, capable of making his own contracts. All are equal in the market, whether capitalist or proletariat: the one as the buyer of labor, the other as the seller. Nineteenth-century exploitation is based on this purely juridical and formal equality. The difference between the modern worker-slave as compared with the classic slave of Greco-Roman times is purely juridical. The slave belonged physically and emotionally to the family of his master; he was the *famulus*. The worker in modern times is formally free; he belongs only to himself and can work and bargain; he is part of a free and imper-

sonal market. But in fact, he is heavily tied down in all his attitudes; he cannot survive except by selling his labor, and the
fruit of the labor he has sold corresponds exactly to the disadvantage in which he finds himself in relation to his employer in terms
of bargaining pressures, urgency, and direct and indirect influence that can be brought to bear. This is the origin of the
nineteenth-century picture of the proletariat as a poor class,
modestly dressed, receiving a humble and precarious wage,
forced to be sober and simple along the lines of the populist image that was so ably described in Henry George's book *Progress
and Poverty* and in the novels of Charles Dickens. As compared
with present-day exploitation, nineteenth-century exploitation
was direct and genuine. It was immediately observable. It dealt
with measurable quantities in terms of physical force, muscular
energy, rhythms and times of operation, working hours, and so
on. In effect, it was exploitation based on purchase by the
capitalist and sale by the worker of *Arbeitskraft,* physical labor.
*Exploitation today is less direct, but it goes deeper. Physical labor is
no longer sold, rather the entire man and particularly his mental
outlook are sold.* It is not a question of muscular force; it involves
nervous energy, and although rarely tiring, it can be stultifying
and soul destroying. Exploitation today cannot be measured in
terms of quantity, but it requires a qualitative reorientation of
labor activity. Physical obedience is no longer sufficient; what is
wanted is psychological identification.

This is a paradox. The abundance and wealth of one part of·
mankind are paid for by all the rest. But this abundance is
widespread and continues to expand. It gives rise to phenomena
that overzealous and overoptimistic sociologists have hastened
to designate important phenomena of "anticipatory participation" by means of consumption, as a way of tranquilizing the con-
sciences and suffocating the guilts of satiate humanity. Is it not
important that today the lady and her maid buy and wear the
same make of nylons? Is this not the beginning of the end of
social inequality? The obvious answer is that it is not. But the
analysis must cut deeper. Within the structure of that part of
humanity that has progressed, new forms of exploitation must be
examined, together with the manipulation that is effected
through an inculcation of unreal needs and the artificial creation
of the "customer." The typology of this new exploitation hinges
not on the back-breaking sixteen hours of hard labor per day,
which we find so effectively described in the last chapters of Book
I of *Das Kapital,* but on the new, really crucial variables of modern

life: isolation, segregation, solitude, neglect, exclusion.

To be exploited in the modern world means to be on the fringes, to be cut off. Our everyday experience and common sense might seem to contradict this conclusion, for mass media continues to spread. Decisions at all levels of organized association are more numerous, more clamorous, more widely known. But access to a center where these decisions are taken is more difficult. The center is remote: its arbitrary nature is consecrated by mystery. It is even hard to determine exactly where it is located and who takes part in the decision-making process. The message of power risks becoming the "message of the emperor." Kafka's solitary prophetic intuition has today become a sensation that is widely shared. Let us set aside, without pausing even to glance at them, the philosophical and sociological theories by which the various power elites defend themselves. Then a curious and, in many ways, an unexpected fact must be pointed out. *Power today exploits and oppresses not by the use of direct action, which can be objectively and logically assessed on the basis of the goals (and results effectively obtained), but simply by ignoring, by failing to intervene, by refusing to take action, by taking refuge behind complex and perfectionist procedures through which formalism and paralysis come to each other's aid. The most serious sins of power today are sins of omission.* Today, the genuine reactionary is not the man who has a gallows erected or who applauds the censor, but the man who prevents action, who preaches resignation, and who urges others to put their trust in a spontaneous, automatic evolution.

This is why social participation is so important. But what kind of participation?

In an article of 1959, French sociologist Yves Delamotte carefully elaborated a typology in which three types of participation can be logically accommodated: the "idyllic," the "institutional," and the "conflictual." Such a typology, as inclusive as it is, that is, capable of enclosing paternalistic participation and joint consultation as well as *Mitbestimmung* and the various patterns of collective bargaining, is not sensitive enough to the qualitative, structural differences among the specific social and economic contexts. Moreover, it lacks, or is silent about, the political dimension, although other typologies are even more restrictive. For example, Paul Blumberg, in his *Sociology of Participation,* is especially concerned with workers' participation and job satisfaction, but he does not pay too much attention to the political and economic system within which the work activity develops itself; in the end, he believes that the impulse to participate is in itself good and that what is styled "self-government" is always and necessarily a true, authentic democratic process.

There are, however, a few caveats on which social research can throw a bit of light and save us from mystifying traps. In the first place, how much does the impulse to participate represent a genuine ground swell and how much does it represent a new dimension of elite, counterelite, or intraelite struggle? It is a fact that the impulse to participate is concentrated wherever there is an educated middle class. The proportion of bourgeois elements who share in participatory activities is extremely high. They have time on their hands; they have the necessary knowledge and know-how. Working-class peers are working or, if unemployed, are busy looking for work. In many countries, participatory experiments seem to have been designed to fit the bourgeoisie. Those who favor them will perhaps constitute a new, relatively closed elite.

Second, it is an open question whether or not a society, as it becomes more "democratic" and perhaps incorporates Jacobean habits, can avoid the tyranny of plebiscitary democracy and assemblages.

And so we come back to the basic question: What kind of participation? Genuine or spurious? To be genuine, participation must be a process involving decisions that are not only technical or methodological but that concern the ultimate goals of social and political life. Thus, social participation complements the traditional democratic process and leads from purely formal to participatory democracy. This necessarily implies a new concept of the state, one that is based on equal access of all social classes and ethnic groups to major political and economic decisions. Moreover, it enters into the planning process, which is imperative if the vested interests are to be offset and the shortcomings of technocracy are to be avoided. In short, it listens to and exposes citizens' specific needs and aspirations.

Naturally, this seems too good to be true. But, especially for Europe, it seems to be the only answer. The Napoleonic centralized state is neither effective in terms achieving general goals nor respectful of local habits. European policymakers are clearly caught up in a dilemma. On the one hand, there is the exigency of a metanational state, that is, a united European organization. On the other, there is a need to rediscover what are today called the "cut-off languages," the dialects, the local manners—not in terms of picturesque local color but an actual way of life, a fundamental source of legitimation for political and economic power.

12.
SPACE: SOCIAL PRODUCT AND USE VALUE

HENRI LEFEBVRE
Translated by J. W. Freiberg

"To change life-style," "to change society," these phrases mean nothing if there is no production of an appropriated space.

"To produce space," these are surprising words: the production of space, in concept and in reality, has only recently appeared, mainly, in the explosion of the historical city, the general urbanization of society, the problems of spacial organization, and so forth. Today, the analysis of production shows that we have passed from the *production of things in space* to the *production of space itself*.

This passage from production in space to production of space occurred because of the growth of the productive forces themselves and because of the direct intervention of knowledge in material production. This knowledge eventually becomes knowledge about space, information on the totality of space. Production *in* space is not disappearing, but it is oriented differently. One can speak of an economy of flow: the flow of energy, the flow of raw materials, the flow of manpower, the flow of information, and so forth. The units of industrial and agricultural production are no longer independent and isolated.

From this follows an important consequence: the planning of the modern economy tends to become spatial planning. Urbanism and territorial management are only elements of this spatial planning, the effects of it are felt everywhere, although this has been particularly the case in France.

Space is social; it involves assigning more or less appropriated places to the social relations of reproduction, namely, the bio-physiological relations between the sexes, the ages, the specified organization of the family, and to the relations of production, namely, the division of labor and its organization.

The past has left its marks, its inscriptions, but space is always a present space, a current totality, with its links and connections to action. In fact, the production and the product are inseparable sides of one process.

Social space is explained by neither nature (the climate and the topology), history, nor "culture." Furthermore, productive forces do not constitute a space or a time. Mediations and mediators interpose themselves; with their reasons derived from knowledge, from ideology, from meaning systems.

Is space a social relation? Yes, certainly, but it is inherent in the relation of property (the ownership of land, in particular), it is also linked to the productive forces that fashion this land. Space is permeated with social relations; it is not only supported by social relations, but it also is producing and produced by social relations.

Space has its own reality in the current mode of production and society, with the same claims and in the same global process as merchandise, money, and capital.

Natural space is irreversibly gone. And although it of course remains as the origin of the social process, nature is now reduced to materials on which society's productive forces operate.

Each society is born within the framework of a given mode of production, with the inherent peculiarities to this framework molding its space. Spatial practice defines its space, it poses it and presupposes it in a dialectical interaction.

Social space has thus always been a social product, but this was not recognized. Societies thought that they received and transmitted natural space.

All social space has a history that begins from this natural base: indeed, nature is always and everywhere characterized by particularities (climates, topologies, etc.).

But if there is a history of space, if there is a specificity to space according to periods, societies, modes and relations of production, then there is a space of capitalism, that is, of the society managed and dominated by the bourgeoisie.

I. CAPITALIST SPACE

Capitalism and neocapitalism have produced an *abstract space* that is a reflection of the world of business on both a national and international level, as well as the power of money and the "politique" of the state. This abstract space depends on vast networks of banks, businesses, and great centers of production. There also is the spatial intervention of highways, airports, and information networks. In this space, the cradle of accumulation, the place of richness, the subject of history, the center of historical space, in other words, the city, has exploded.

Space as a whole enters into the modernized mode of capitalist production: it is utilized to produce surplus value. The ground, the underground, the air, and even the light enter into both the productive forces and the products. The urban fabric, with its multiple networks of communication and exchange, is part of the means of production. The city and its various installations (ports, train stations, etc.) are part of capital.

Abstract space reveals its oppressive and repressive capacities in relation to time. It rejects time as an abstraction—except when it concerns work, the producer of things and of surplus value. Time is reduced to constraints of space: schedules, runs, crossings, loads.

1. The Different Functions of Capitalist Space

—means of production

Space is a means of production: the network of exchanges and the flow of raw materials and energy that make up space also are determined by space. The means of production, themselves a product, cannot be separated from the forces of production, techniques, and knowledge; from the international division of social labor; from nature; or from the state and other superstructures.

The city, the urban space, and the urban reality cannot be conceived simply as the sum of the places of the consumption of goods (merchandise) and the places of production (enterprises).

The spatial arrangement of a city, a region, a nation, or a continent increases productive forces, just as do the equipment and machines in a factory or in a business, but at another level. One uses space just as one uses a machine.

—an object of consumption

Space as a whole is consumed for production just as are industrial buildings and sites, machines, raw materials, and labor power.

When we go to the mountains or to the beach, we consume a space. When the inhabitants of industrialized Europe descend to the Mediterranean, which has beome their space for leisure, they pass from the space of production to the consumption of space.

—a political instrument

Space has become for the state a political instrument of primary importance. The state uses space in such a way that it ensures its control of places, its strict hierarchy, the homogeneity of the whole, and the segregation of the parts. It is thus an administratively controlled and even a policed space. The hierarchy of spaces corresponds to that of social classes, and if there exist ghettos for all classes, those of the working class are merely more isolated than those of the others.

—the intervention of class struggle

Class struggle intervenes in the production of space, today more than ever. Only class conflict can prevent abstract space from spreading itself across the planet and therefore erasing all spatial differences. Only class action can produce differences that oppose what is internal to economic growth, namely, strategy, logic, and system.

Thus, in the current mode of production, social space is considered among the *productive forces and the means of production, among the social relations of production and, especially, their reproduction.*

History emerges on a world level and it therefore produces a space at this level: the formation of a world market, an international generalization of the state and its problems, new relations between society and space. World space is the *field* in which our epoch is created.

With this world space, and with new contradictions effacing old contradictions, new aggravations will appear; for example, the international relations between states and their confrontational strategies.

2. The Contradictions of Capitalist Space

This space, produced by capitalism and by its state, has its own contradictions.

—a major contradiction

The major contradiction of space arises from *the pulverization of space* by private property, the demand for interchangeable fragments, and *the scientific and technical (informational) capacity to treat space on ever more vast levels.* The contradiction "center/periphery" results from the contradiction of "global/partial" since all global constructs lead to the establishment of a concentrated centrality.

—a space oriented toward the reproducible . . .

Oriented toward the reproduction of the social relations of production, the production of space enacts a logic of homogeneity and a strategy of the repetitive. But this bureaucratic space con-. flicts with its own conditions and with its own results. When space is of this nature, occupied, controlled, and oriented toward the reproducible, it soon sees itself surrounded by the nonreproducible: nature, the site, the locality, the regional, the national, even the world level.

The activity of the base, discontinuous, multiple, soon proposes a return to precapitalist space. Sometimes proposing a counterspace, it pushes toward the explosion of all spaces organized by the state-bureaucratic rationality.

. . . and negating the differences

This formal and quantified abstract space negates all differences, those that come from nature and history as well as those that come from the body, ages, sexes, and ethnicities. The significance of such factors dissimulates and explodes the very

functioning of capitalism. The dominant space, that of the centers of richness and power, is forced to fashion the dominated
spaces, that of the periphery.

In the space of neocapitalism, the economic and the political
tend to converge, without, however, the political mastering the
economic. Conflicts are therefore manifested between the hegemonical state—which is still not the master of things—and the
owners of these things.

3. The Generalized Explosion of Spaces

Because of these contradictions, we find ourselves faced with
an extraordinary, little-noticed phenomenon: *the explosion of
spaces.* Neither capitalism nor the state can maintain the chaotic,
contradictory space they have produced. We can witness, at all
levels, this explosion of space.

> —At the level of the immediate and the lived, space is ex-
> ploding on all sides, whether this be living space, per-
> sonal space, scholastic space, prison space, army space,
> or hospital space. Everywhere, people are realizing that
> spatial relations also are social relations.

> —At the level of cities, we see not only the explosion of
> the historical city but also that of all the administrative
> frameworks in which they had wanted to enclose the ur-
> ban phenomenon.

> —At the level of regions, the peripheries are fighting for
> their autonomy or for a certain degree of independence.
> They undertake actions that challenge their subordina-
> tion to the state, economic and political centralization.

> —Finally, at the international level, not only the actions
> of the so-called supranational companies, but also those
> of the great world strategies, prepare for and render in-
> evitable new explosions of space. The Mediterranean is
> an excellent example because if it has become a strategic
> space it is only after the accumulation of many factors.
> This network, which contained the oldest commercial
> relations of the world, which gave us our great cities and
> ports, recently, has been completely transformed into a
> space of leisure for industrial Europe. Still more recently,

this space has been crossed by the flow of energy and raw materials. Finally, it has become a nearly overindustrialized space with enormous complexes installed on its periphery, not only at Fos, but also at Sagunte and at Tarente. These phenomena represent extraordinary alterations of the space and enable us to study the problems already posed by the transformations of contemporary space.

4. Social Movements that Question the Use of Space

In all the industrialized countries, a very old movement exists that comes from demands concerning work, businesses, and work places; however, it seems that current movements are arising on a world level, which, while still divided, incomplete, and largely unconscious of themselves, call for a reorganization of space other than the places of work.

These are *consumer movements.* In the United States, they are very frequent, numerous, and more or less question the use of space.

They reveal that:

—Space is not merely economic, in which all the parts are interchangeable and have exchange value.

—Space is not merely a political instrument for homogenizing all parts of society.

On the contrary, they show that:

—Space remains a model, a perpetual prototype of use value resisting the generalizations of exchange and exchange value in a capitalist economy under the authority of a homogenizing state.

—Space is a use value, but even more so is *time* to which it is intimately linked because time is our life, our fundamental use value. Time has disappeared in the social space of modernity. Lived time loses form and social interest except for the time of work. Economic space subordinates time, whereas political space eradicates it because it is threatening to existing power relations. The primacy of the economic, and still more, of the political, leads to the supremacy of space over time.

One of the most important points for the power of the left is to support consumer movements that have not yet found their voice and that are very often enclosed in such narrow frameworks that the political significance of their actions escapes them.

One of the political roles for the left, then, is to *use the class struggle in space.*

II. TOWARD A SOCIALIST SPACE

Like the societies that preceded it, socialist society must produce its space, but in full consciousness of its concepts and potential problems.

It is currently popular to say that Marxism is old-fashioned, that it is less relevant for history. However, it is precisely today, more than ever, that we cannot analyze world phenomena except in the light of the fundamental categories of Marxism, being ready to modify them to specific situations.

Although space is not analyzed in *Capital,* certain concepts, such as exchange value and use value, today apply to space. At present, we must use the distinction, which Marx did not introduce, between the domination and the appropriation of nature. This conflict unfolds in space: in dominated spaces and appropriated spaces. Even more than in Marx's time, nature is the source of all use value.

Should we socialize space? Certainly not; it is already socialized in the framework of the existing society and mode of production. A society that is transforming itself into socialism cannot accept (even during the transitional period) space as it is produced by capitalism. To do so means accepting the existing political and social structures; it leads only to a dead end. It accepts the reproduction of the relations of production; thus, in the end, it is the same, and however it would be hierarchialized and controlled, it would still reflect the former social hierarchy.

A "different" society invents, creates, produces new forms of space, but the relations of property and production now block these possibilities. Some want socialism in the industrialized countries to continue with growth and accumulation, that is, with the production of things in space. Others want to break this mode of production. But the productive forces have changed enormously, passing from the production of things in space to the production of space. It is necessary then to proceed to the ultimate consequences of this qualitative leap. This involves the process of quantitative growth, not to break it, but to unleash its full potential.

The production of socialist space means the end of the private property and the state's political domination of space, *which implies the passage from domination to appropriation and the primacy of use over exchange.*

Furthermore, capitalist and neocapitalist space is a space of quantification and growing homogeneity, a merchandised space where all the elements are exchangeable and thus interchangeable; a police space in which the state tolerates no resistance and no obstacles. Economic space and political space thus converge toward the elimination of all differences.

Insofar as we can conceive it, given certain current tendencies, socialist space will be a *space of differences.*

1. The Determining Role of Social Movements

There is reason to believe that only the convergence and the conjunction of the worker and peasant movements, linked to the production of things and material work and those who use space, will enable the world to change. Relative to the possession and management of space, urban social movements do not have the continuous character and institutional promise of those that come from the factories, units, and branches of production. Yet if the pressure from the base (the consumers) occurs with enough force, it will influence production in general toward space and toward the social needs of this base. The action of those interested parties would determine the social needs, which would then no longer be determined by the "experts." The notions of equipment and environment would thus break free from their technocratic and capitalistic context. However, the spontaneous explosion of the social "base," although revolutionary and profound, would not be sufficient to produce an adequate, operational definition of space in socialist society. It would, however, be an integral part of these determinations. But the management of social space, like that of nature, can only be collective and practical, controlled by the base, that is, democratic. The "interested" parties, the ones "concerned," would intervene, manage, and control it. But first, they would lead to the end—the explosion—of all imposed space.

2. A General Self-Management

The reconstruction of the "low to high" of social space, previously produced from "high to low," implies general self-management, that is, at the various levels, complementing that of the units and instances of production. Only in this way can the socialization of the means of production include the issue of space. To do otherwise, to define "socialist space" as natural space or as communes living on a privileged space or by "conviviality," is to confuse the end with the means, the goal with the stages; it is, in other words, abstract utopianism.

Production in a socialist society is defined by Marx as production for social needs. These social needs, in great part, concern space: housing, equipment, transportation, reorganization of urban space, and so forth. These extend the capitalist tendency to produce space while radically modifying the product. This is what contributes to the transformation of daily life, to the definition of development more in social than in individual terms, without the exclusion of the latter. The individual in a socialist society *has the right to a space*, as well as the right to urban life as the center of social life and of so-called cultural activities, and so forth.

The beginning of this transformation has to wait for the thought, the imagination, the creativity, which in turn depend on surmounting the separation between "public" and "private," by dissipating the illusions about the social and the collective confounded with "public charity," and so forth.

Socialist politics of space can resolve the contradictions of space only by adding them to the other economic and social contradictions. Of course, the pressure from the base and the self-management of space cannot restrict themselves to a reformism.

Turning the world "back on its feet," according to Marx, implies overturning dominant spaces, placing appropriation over domination, demand over command, and use over exchange. Self-management reveals itself to be both the means and the end, a phase of the fight and its objective. In the transformed space, there can and must be a redefinition of the relations between productive activities and the return to the internal market, oriented deliberately toward issues of space. It is space as a whole that would be redefined, that would bring about a conversion and subversion.

3. A Redefinition of Space as a Function of Use Value
—how are these revolutionary processes foreseen?

If the current situation does not reduce itself to an economic crisis, but instead calls for a profound modification of the society and the civilization, it still offers a point of reference from which the transformation can begin. The modification can be thus defined: space produced from the perspective of the priority of the means of exchange and transportation will be produced from the perspective of the priority of use value. The revolution of space implies and amplifies the concept of revolution, defined as a change in the ownership of the means of production. It gives a new dimension to it, starting from the suppression of a particularly dangerous form of private property, that of space: underground space, ground space, aerial space, planetary space, and even interplanetary space.

The so-called transitional formulas—state control of land, nationalizations, municipalizations—have not succeeded. But how can we limit and suppress the ownership of space? Perhaps by remembering the writings of Marx and Engels: one day, which will indeed come, the private ownership of land, of nature and its resources, will seem as absurd, as odious, as ridiculous as the possession of one human by another.

The problems relating to the "pollution of the environment," which are seen by ecologists as primary, are indeed important, but they are secondary. In this perspective, the real problems of society and its transformation are diverted toward a naturalism: take, for example, the biologism involved in treating human space as animal space.

In conclusion, a transformation of society presupposes the possession and collective management of space by a permanent intervention of "interested parties," even with their multiple and sometimes contradictory interests. This orientation tends to overcome the separations and disassociations in space between a work (unique) and a commodity (repeated).

This is an orientation. Nothing more and nothing less. But it does point out a meaning. Namely, something is perceived, a direction is conceived, a living movement makes its way toward the horizon. But it is nothing that yet resembles a system.

13.
SOCIAL CLASS, POLITICAL POWER, AND THE STATE: THEIR IMPLICATIONS IN MEDICINE

VICENTE NAVARRO

A CRITIQUE OF CONTEMPORARY THEORIES OF THE WESTERN SYSTEM OF POWER

Part I

THE ASSUMED HOMOGENIZATION OF CONTEMPORARY WESTERN SOCIETIES

Economic, political, and sociological analyses of contemporary Western societies find that, as result of welfare state policies, social mobility, and an enlargement of opportunities, these societies are being recast in a mold of middle-class conditions and life-styles that obviate their characterization as class and capitalist societies. Indeed, it is assumed that, because of welfare state and Keynesian economic policies, a substantial redistribution of wealth and income has taken place, with inequalities of consumption narrowing and opportunities for individual advancement broadening. To that effect, an extensive literature has demonstrated the narrowing and even disappearance of class differentials in the consumption of goods and services, including health services. For example, in a popular and influential volume on the British National Health Service (NHS), Cochrane[1] indicates that, because of the NHS, differences in the consumption of medical care by social class have virtually disappeared in Great Britain. He takes Titmuss[2] and Tudor Hart[3] to task for their undue concern about class inequalities and inequities because, according to him, there are far more important inequities to worry about.[4] Similarly, Bice and Associates have postulated that Medicaid and other antipoverty programs in the United States have rendered class differentials in medical care consumption a thing of the past. And if any differences do exist, they are more likely to be skewed in favor of the lower than the upper echelon of our social spectrum.[5] Actually, in a thorough and well-known analysis of equity in the health sectors in the United Kingdom, United States, and Sweden, social class as a cause of cleavage and of differential consumption is not even mentioned.[6]

Such analyses assume that there is a process of social fluidity and mobility so open and all-encompassing that distinctions between classes are being blurred as never before, making the whole category of class irrelevant. In the process, social heredity and birth are dramatically weakened as variables of success, while merit and learning—and perhaps just a little bit of luck—are passwords for access to the ever-increasing number of new opportunities. According to one of the main theorists of this paradigm, Western developed societies are

> relatively open so that an individual or group is able to find its niche in society in some reasonable relationship to its efforts, ability, and aspirations within the accepted rules of the game.[7]

Because of this homogenization and the opportunities it engendered, the working class and what used to be its chronic underconsumption of goods and services have, for all practical purposes, vanished. For some, like Anderson, that process started decades ago, when the middle class was (and still is) the source of entrepreneurial, technical, and managerial skills, which exploited natural resources, developed the economy, and thus began to create a social surplus that spilled over into other endeavors such as the arts, education, health services, and warring for national honor and expansion.[8]

The transformation of society into a middle-class society does not imply, of course, that there has been a complete homogenization of consumption. But while it is recognized that some sectors of society, namely, the poor, remain marginal, it is assumed that their marginality is both provisional and correctable.[9]

It is further assumed that the process of homogenization has been accompanied, and even facilitated, by a change in values. Individual achievement, hard drive, competitiveness, and family security, values usually identified with the middle class, are now thought to have become widely accepted by manual workers. Thus, class consciousness increasingly is being replaced by a concern for status and for a middle-class pattern of consumption. And as Westergaard has indicated, "In this psychological analysis of class perceptions, loyalties of the world of work are replaced by loyalties of the hearth."[10] Furthermore, this vanishing of class consciousness is supposed to be accompanied by a dilution and disappearance of the working-class culture. They—the working class—have thus practically disappeared; they have been absorbed by our middle-class or mass society.

It is worth noting that the above interpretation is prevalent not only among conservative and liberal circles[11] but also among large sectors of the left. Among many others, most of the analysts of the Frankfurt School in Europe,[12] and Marcuse[13] and Aronowitz in the United States,[14] have expressed the belief that the working class in developed capitalist societies, which they once saw as the only potential leverage for change, has lost that potential and instead has been absorbed into society, becoming merely a part of the larger consuming masses. Those masses, they say, are concerned mainly with a narrow personal interest in consumption, have become politically apathetic, and are being manipulated by the ruling or corporate elite. According to these writers, the distribution, nature, and composition of our resources—including medical resources—are not so much a result of class struggle—a passé category of concern only to "vulgar" Marxists—but that of the manipulation of societal consumption by the corporate elite and its different components, including the medical and other professions and bureaucracies.

In summary, then, according to the majority of conservative and liberal social analysts, including many left wing writers, social class has lost its importance as a category of social analysis that explains not only the nature of Western societies but also their different patterns of production and consumption. As a result of that belief, these analyses have concluded that class inequalities in the distribution and consumption of resources have been superseded by persisting or newly created inequalities, such as those of age, sex, and regional imbalance.[15]

Middle-Class—Mass Society, Political Power, and the State: An Analysis of Theories

A most important consequence of the prevalent belief that we are a middle-class society—or, in its newer version, that we are a mass society—is the idea that class struggle has been superseded. Instead, it is assumed that conflict and struggle exist, not among classes, but among groups and elites. And it is believed that the nature and outcome of those conflicts—and not of class struggle—explain the nature and content of Western developed societies, including the composition and distribution of societal resources, such as medical resources. This set of beliefs is reflected in doctrines that try to explain the distribution of political power in Western societies. One doctrine includes different variations of paradigms that are usually referred to as the theories of countervailing pluralist power; the other encompasses those theories that are known as the power elite paradigms. Because of the frequency with which both groups of theories appear in analyses of our society, including medical care, let me summarize them here.

Countervailing Pluralist Theories of Power

According to these, our societies have neither dominant classes nor dominant groups or elites. Instead, competing blocks of interests exist, with none having a dominant control over the state,[16] which is assumed to be an independent entity. In the words of one proponent of this theory:

government becomes more or less another group or interest in cooperation, competition, and negotiation with the private individual or groups.[17]

In that explanation, different competing blocks balance each other, and no particular group or interest weighs too heavily on the state; in other words, power is diffuse. Furthermore, it is this competition among interests, supervised and arbitrated by the state, that guarantees against the concentration of power. The resulting system thus offers all active and legitimate groups the opportunity to make themselves heard at any crucial stage in the decision-making process.[18] And this "being heard" takes place primarily through a parliamentarian system in which a plurality of ideas are openly exchanged, complementary to the free allocation of resources in the marketplace, following, for the most part, the rules of laissez-faire. It is, of course, recognized that the system is far from perfect. But in any case, those societies are thought to have already achieved a model of democracy in light of which the notion of "ruling class" or even "power elite" is ludicrous, completely irrelevant, and of concern only to ideologues.

The main weakness of such paradigms, however, is not so much their postulate that competition exists; more importantly, they are unmindful of the fact that such competition is continuously skewed in favor of some groups and against others. Indeed, as Schattschneider indicated:

> the flaw in the pluralistic heaven is that the heavenly chorus sings with a very special accent . . . the system is askew, loaded, and unbalanced in favor of a fraction of a minority.[19]

As the power elite theorists have empirically shown, the different organs of the state are heavily influenced and in some instances dominated by specific power groups. In that respect, the pluralist's failure to recognize the consistent dominance of our state organs by specific groups is certainly not shared by the majority of the U.S. population, who believe, for example, that both political parties are in favor of big business and that America's major corporations dominate and determine the behavior of our public officials and of the different branches of the state.[20]

Power Elite Theories

The weaknesses of pluralist theories have led to the development of such analytical. paradigms as the power elite theories.
According to these, pluralism applies only to a very limited segment of our societies, that is, a small number of elite groups that
essentially dominate the different branches of the state.

Although there is considerable variation among power elite
theorists, all of them use similar conceptualization and methodology: first, they identify the groups or elites that play a dominant
role in the different sectors of the state; second they analyze how
that power is exercised and through what mechanisms of state
intervention; and third, they describe the benefits those groups
derive because of their intervention. This method of analysis has
been especially prevalent in the study of the medical care
sector,[21] where the actors, that is, hospitals, universities,
insurance companies, physicians, and so forth, are seen as
competing power groups in their quest for dominance and/or
influence over the different agencies of the state. According to
this analysis, the battlefield is the control of knowledge,
licensure, instruments of care, fund, and so forth. The proponents of the power elite theory have indeed provided extremely
valuable empirical information for the analysis of the health sector in Western societies. However, their focus on the health sector
has combined with their seeming unawareness of social class to
seriously limit the value of their theories. Indeed, as I have indicated elsewhere, in order to understand the behavior and dynamics of the actors in the health sector, we have to understand
their positions within the overall economic and political scheme
of our societies, that is, their class positions.[22] In this respect, the
power elite theories are limited because they fail to recognize
that those elites are segments of a dominant class and that, when
considered systematically, they possess a high degree of cohesion and solidarity, with common interests and common purposes that far transcend their specific differences and
disagreements. Consequently, these theorists do not consider
the nonactors and the nondecisions, which may be far more important than the visible actors and the actual decisions. In other
words, among power groups or elites, competitive conflict (as the
pluralist theorists believe) or not-so-competitive conflict (as the
power elite theorists postulate) takes place within a set of class
relations and within a well-defined capitalist structure, the

maintenance and reproduction of which is the primary role of the state: the object of that competition. This state role established a set of constraints in that competition (which I will detail later) that is of paramount importance in understanding the nature of both the conflict and the system. And again, as I will show later, in the competition among groups and elites, the nonactors and nondecisions are as important as the actors and the decisions, if not more so. In fact, both non-decisions and decisions respond to the dynamics of Western societies—societies that I will redefine as capitalist.[23]

Another weakness of the power elite theories—a weakness that the structuralists (described later on) attempt to remedy—is that the nature of the system may be defined as one of conflict resolution among different groups of actors and individuals whose *behavior* and *motivation* determine the very nature of the conflict. In that respect, such analyses may interpret personalities and their motivations as the predominant forces in those conflicts.[24]

Bureaucratic and Professional Control Theories

A new variation of these power elite theories defined the nature of our societies and the sectors within them as resulting from the ideological manipulation of our populations by the bureaucracies (including the professional bureaucracies), which have taken the place of the capitalist class as the main agencies of oppression. According to these theories, industrialization has so reshaped the nature of our societies that power, assumed to be divorced from ownership of capital, has passed from the owners of capital—the capitalists—to the managers of that capital and from there to the technocrats, those who have the skills and knowledge to operate the major social edifices of industrialism, the bureaucracies. The new elite, then, is composed of the bureaucrats. In medicine, for example, Illich,[25] one of the main proponents of this theory, assumes that the nature of medicine and medical care results from the manipulation of medical resources (including the ideology of medicine) by the medical bureaucracy, which, in order to perpetuate its power, has created an addiction to medicine that legitimizes the medical profession's control over the population. More recently, powerful voices in international agencies have supported this interpretation.[26] Since I have discussed this theory and its political ramifications elsewhere,[27] I do not intend to reiterate its main conceptual, methodological, and political weakness, except to say that, while the medical profession is very much a part of the problem, it is not *the* problem. Indeed, a historical, empirical and political analysis of the health sector indicates that (1) the most predominant force in determining the nature of medicine and the resulting iatrogenices and dependencies has not been the medical profession but the capitalist system and the capitalist class; (2) for the most part, the medical professionals are the administrators and not the creators of these dependencies; and (3) this interpretation of bureaucratic and professional power and control leads to a strategy that ultimately strengthens the ideological construct of capitalism.[28] Regarding the first two points, Susser has convincingly shown that medical problems are defined and strategies for solving them are implemented by responding to the needs of society as perceived and defined by the powerful. And this process of continuous redefinition takes place in spite of the medical profession's resitance to those changes.[29] In the hierarchy of determinants, the medical profession is secondary to a higher level of dominance. However, bureaucratic control theorists are unaware of this and focus instead on the medical profession. Indeed, reliance, self-care, and the autonomy of the individual are solutions that suggest that the individual is ultimately responsible for his or her own health. But this individual solution to what is basically a collective problem (the way power is distributed in society) strengthens the tenet of bourgeois individualism, the ethical construct of capitalism wherein one has to be free to do whatever one wants—to buy and sell, to accumulate wealth or to live in poverty, to work or to idle, to be healthy or to be sick. Because this interpretation does not conflict with the tenets of the capitalist system, we frequently find rebellious authors, such as Illich, with strange bedfellows, such as President Ford. Recall, for example, President Ford's great stress on self-care, health education, and change in life-styles as the primary health strategies.[30] In summary, these authors, conservatives and rebels alike, see changes in the individual, not changes in the system of class relations and its system of production, as the primary solution. Their main weakness, of course, is their unawareness of the rationale and requirements of the capitalist system—itself the primary creator of dependencies—which determines the nature and perpetuation of sickness in our societies.[31]

A Critique of Some Marxist Theories of Political Power and of the State

Because pluralist and power elite theories cannot fully explain our continuously and increasingly "in-crisis" societies, and because socialist movements are expanding all over the world, new analyses, which recognize the nature and structure of capitalism as their "variables," are appearing. All of them use Marx (not Weber, as the previous theories did) as their point of departure. Because of the great importance of these theories, let me outline them according to three subgroups: (1) economic determinism; (2) structural determinism; and (3) corporate statism.

Economic Determinism

Miliband[32] and Poulantzas,[33] among others, are included in this group of theorists, who assume that whatever happens or does not happen in political life depends *exclusively* on what is going on at the economic level of society. In other words, the laws of economic development determine, linearly and mechanistically, the laws of political and social development; that is, the economic needs of capitalism determine the nature of our political systems. Capitalism, once reduced to its economic dimensions, unavoidably and fatalistically evolves according to its own internal economic laws. In this scheme, state intervention is seen primarily as smoothing down the possible contradictions and bottlenecks that handicap the evolution of the economic mode of production. Economic determinism thus interprets the medical sector in Western developed societies in two ways. The first, prevalent in the literature of political economy, perceives the changes in the nature, form, and distribution of medical resources as being exclusively determined by the economic needs of the capitalist system. The second maintains that changes in the mode of production in medicine reflect changes in the mode of production of capitalism, that is, from petty commodity production (cottage industry) to large-scale commodity production (monopoly capital). According to these theories, the organizational evolution of medicine (from cottage medicine to corporate medicine) is exclusively determined by the changes in the mode of production of medicine, which follow and replicate the different stages of the economic development of capitalism.

These contributions have exposed the economic nature and function of the health sector, breaking with the prevalent Hegelian and idealistic interpretations that saw medicine evolving because of personalities and values, without realizing the purpose of those values within the rationality of the economic system. On the other hand, these contributions have viewed history as a fatalistic and deterministic process, not, as Marx saw it, as a dialectical one.[34] Indeed, to allow for the importance and even primacy of the economic base does not reduce history to its economic laws of motion. There are other factors and other levels, such as politics, religion, medicine, and so forth, that continuously interact with the economic base and with themselves and thus contribute to the formation of history. As Engels wrote:

> Political, religious, juridical, philosophical, literary, artistic, etc. [and I would add medical] development is based on economic development. But all these react upon one another and also upon the economic bases. It is not that the economic situation is *cause, solely active,* while everything else is only passive effect. There is, rather, interaction on the basis of economic necessity, which *ultimately* always asserts itself.[35]

Let me underline here that by criticizing the economic determinists I do not detract from the extremely important and primary role that their analyses have had in understanding the realm of the possible in our societies. According to Marx:

> Men make their own history, but they do not make it just as they please; they do not make it under circumstances chosen by themselves but under circumstances directly encountered, given and transmitted from the past.[36]

And among those, economic circumstances are of primary importance. Consequently, as I have stressed elsewhere,[37] there is a great need to study the material bases of history in order to understand the evolution of medicine. In that respect, I am an historical materialist and proud of it. My criticism of the economic determinists should be read primarily as a criticism of their seeming unmindfulness to the importance of other factors besides economics in determining why and in what form changes in capitalism and its medicine take place.

Structural Determinism

Structural determinists, while aware of the limitations of economic determinism, still believe that there are objective laws of motion in capitalism that *wholly* determine how classes and their substrata operate. Heavily influenced by Althusser,[38] Godelier,[39] Poulantzas,[40] and other French structuralists, those theorists[41] who assume that who is in government, for example, or "what groups dominate what state boards," is not important since the laws of the system (its objective relations) are so constraining that intergroup conflicts and relations are of little consequence and that the structure of the capitalist system explains and/or constrains everything. Here, we find ourselves at the other extreme of the power elite theoreticians. Indeed, while the power elite analysts do not realize the importance of the structure of capitalism in their analysis of the competition between elites, the structural determinists believe that everything is explained by structure and its inherent objective relations. At the highest level of abstraction, structural determinism leads to the statement that the structure of the capitalist system is the source of all our problems. But this understanding yields little unless those categories, structures, and relations are disaggregated and their political nature and implications are verified empirically. In other words, capitalism does not exist without a capitalist class, and that class is composed of different segments that interact dialectically. The specific form that capitalism takes depends on the nature of the class struggle and on the internecine struggles among segments within the capitalist class. Actually, not only does the structure of capitalism condition the class struggle but more importantly, and conversely, the class struggle[42] and the conflict between factions within the capitalist class condition and determine the structure of capitalism.[43] Not to be aware of the latter aspect might lead, as Miliband rightly indicates, to the conclusion that there are no differences between a state ruled by fascists and one ruled by social democrats since both are capitalist systems.

Corporate Statism

Another body of theory, corporate statism, views the state as the direct instrument of the capitalist class or one of its components, the corporate class.[44] Here, Marx and Engels' statement that "the modern state is but a committee for managing the common affairs of the whole bourgeoisie"[45] means that the state not only acts on behalf of but at the behest of the capitalist class. In that interpretation, the state and the capitalist class, or a segment within it, the corporate class, are in a symbiotic relationship. It is interesting to note that this theory of the corporate state, as Gough has said, is especially prevalent today in the United States because, among other political items, a Rockefeller became vice-president of the country and because the personal penetration of corporate groups into the organs of the state is very deep indeed.[46] Thus, it is tempting to believe that the state acts not only on behalf of but also at the behest of the capitalist class and the evolution of all sectors, including the medical, results from the manipulation of the agencies of the state by different segments of the capitalist class and its dependent upper-middle class, including the professions. Similar analyses and interpretations appear in the United Kingdom, France, and Germany, particularly (although not exclusively) when conservative governments are in power.

These theories are limited because they are seemingly unaware that there is a clear distinction between "on behalf of" and "at the behest of." In fact, the state, to better serve the capitalist class, needs to be autonomous (but not, as I will explain later, independent). And the degree of that autonomy depends primarily on the level and form of class struggle, including, for example, the existence of a political party based on and supported by the working class. Indeed, the absence of a political arm of American labor has made capital subject to far fewer restrictions in the United States than it has been, say, in Britain or in Europe. And this had led to the predominance of members of the capitalist class in the different organs of the state, including its executive and legislative branches. But that predominance, empirically shown in all sectors of the state, is not tantamount to direct control, as I will show later. The failure to recognize this fact leads to dismissing the state as a proper battlefield, that is, to a rejection of participation in the parliamentary system to advance working-class programs.

Part II

THE STATE

State Intervention

Having critiqued the prevalent interpretations of political power and the state, let me now outline my own interpretation of the state, both within and outside the health sector.

My first postulate is that the state is the configuration of and relationships among public institutions, whose primary role is the reproduction of an economic system based on private ownership of the means of production, that is, the capitalist economy. Let me say here that I am well-aware that the prevalent mythology that, due to the dramatic expansion of the public sector since World War II (presumably because of the Keynesian revolution), maintains that our economies are no longer capitalist but mixed. Empirical evidence shows, however, that in none of the so-called mixed economies does the state own more than a subsidiary and complementary part of the means of production. Therefore, as Miliband correctly points out, to speak of "mixed economies" in this context is to "attribute a special and quite misleading meaning to the notion of mixture."[47] We do indeed have a capitalist system with a capitalist class whose power derives from its ownership of and control over the means of production. And the state's primary function is to maintain the conditions for the survival and growth of that economic system. For example, both Labor and Conservative governments in the United Kingdom and Democratic and Republican administrations in the United States have indicated that their primary role and concern is the "health" of the economy, with everything else conditional on its survival and growth. To have social services or to expand their benefits depends on having a "healthy" economy. The assumption that is made, of course, is that the welfare of the people depends, first and foremost, on the welfare of the econony. But economy is synonymous with capitalist economy, and there the capitalist class reigns.

How does the state maintain the conditions for the economy to operate? In many different ways, the most important of which are:

    1. *The development of what is usually referred to as the infrastructure of production,* that is, the development of

those goods and services that are essential preconditions for the working of the capitalist system such as:
a. *technical* preconditions for the actual process of
   production (e.g., roads, railways, environmental
   and sanitation services, postal service, etc.);
b. *social* preconditions of this same process (e.g., law
   and order, a stable currency system, etc.); and
c. conditions for the *reproduction of labor* (e.g.,
   education and some preventive health services).[48]

These goods and services have one important characteristic in
common: they are too costly or too risky for one individual or
corporation to buy (in the sense that making a profit would be too
uncertain and that the possibilities of monopolizing their use
would be very limited).[49]

2. *The defense of the capitalist system* through:
   a. the actual delivery of goods and services in
      response to different pressures mediated in the
      political process, of which the most important
      pressures are those generated by the class
      struggle. The provision of services is aimed (not
      always successfully) at increasing the level of
      cohesion among classes and groups in a society
      and avoiding its disruption. Thus, for example,
      social legislation has been implemented
      historically at moments of labor unrest. As Henry
      Sigerist wrote:

Social-security legislation came in waves and followed a
certain pattern; strong political parties representing the
interests of the workers seemed a potential threat to the
existing order, or at least to the traditional system of
production, and an acute scare such as that created by the
French Commune stirred Conservatives into action and
social security legislation was enacted. In England at the
beginning of our century the second industrial revolution
was very strongly felt. The Labor party entered Parliament
and from a two-party country England developed into a
three-party country. The Russian revolution of 1905 was
suppressed to be sure, but seemed a dress rehearsal for
other revolutions to follow. Social legislation was enacted
not by the Socialists but by Lloyd George and Churchill.[50]

And as Balfour said in 1895, "Social legislation is not merely to be distinguished from Socialist legislation, but it is most direct opposite and its most effective antidote."[51]

        b. the development and/or maintenance of the value-generating institutions, such as the media, academia, and others, which sustain a system of values that, while appearing natural, universal, or commonsensical, are actually most convenient to the survival of that economic system, (e.g., individualism and competitiveness). Part of this value system is the primacy of the private sector and profit making as the societal and ethical pillars of its ideological construct. Consequently, all profitable activities should be left to the private sector, and conversely, all activities should be geared, to the highest degree possible, to the generation of profit. The public should intervene only when the private activity is too costly or too risky, or, in the penultimate hour, when it has failed.

   3.   *The control over physical force* to be used against internal and external threats against the system.

It is important to note that for the state to be able to establish the first two conditions it must be perceived, at least by the majority of the population, as being neutral, above classes, and serving common interests. In that respect, its claims to put the health of the economy first are legitimized as benefiting everyone. Calls for austerity and sacrifice are, in theory, calls for all because we are all in the same boat, that is, the capitalist economy. As Offe said, "the existence of a capitalist state presupposes the systematic denial of its nature as a capitalist state."[52] When that legitimation disintegrates and when the supposedly classless nature of the state is challenged, the state resorts to the third condition.

What Defines a State as Capitalist?

The capitalist character of the state is attributable not to its being the state of the capitalist class (or its corporate component as some corporate statists postulate) but because its primary role is to define, support, and encourage the capitalist economy, upon whose health (or lack of it) everything else is assumed to depend. Therefore, what establishes governments as capitalist is not so much that members of the capitalist class predominate in them (e.g., from 1889 to 1961, over 60 percent of the members of the U.S. Cabinet and over 35 percent of the British Cabinet were businessmen of one sort or another[53]) but, most importantly:

1. That they give primacy not to the interests of specific capitalist groups but to the interests of the capitalist economy as a whole, whose sanctity is deemed above the interests of specific groups of classes; and
2. That when the needs of the economy and other needs, such as human satisfaction, conflict, the former takes priority over the latter. The dramatic cuts in allocations for social services in both Wilson's and Ford's 1977 fiscal budgets are examples. In both cases, cuts were justified because they were perceived as essential to saving the troubled economies of the United Kingdom and the United States.[54]

In summary, to see these policies as resulting from individual malevolence or capitalist manipulation of government is limited and erroneous. Such policies result because these governments perceive that the economy, to whose health we are all supposedly tied, has to be straightened out before "we can think of other matters." This behavior, not the specific motivation of individuals or the manipulation of groups, establishes those policies as capitalist. The fact that the policies required to save the capitalist system are made even aginst the interests of specific capitalist groups—as during the New Deal—does not make them any less capitalistic. Actually, the state is better able to represent the interests of the capitalist class *as a whole* when it can be politically autonomous from specific short- or even long-term economic interests of particular factions of that class.

The Characteristics of the Capitalist State

Having explained (1) that states in Western developed societies are capitalist states and (2) why the state must have relative autonomy from the capitalist class, let me now establish how the dominance of that class over the state takes place, that is, the mechanisms that establish the dominance of that class, the bourgeoisie, over the state. These mechanisms are (1) the dependence of the state on the successful development of the capitalist economies; (2) the class origins of the top members of the organs of the state; (3) the ideology of the state; and (4) the structure of the state and separation of powers.

The Dependence of the State on the Successful Development of the Capitalist Economies

The size and scope of state activities depend on the successful development of the economy. State activities are funded through revenues collected via *taxes* on wages and profits and through *credit,* especially from increasing the national debt. And the mass of wages, profits, and credit depends very much on the "health" of the economy.[55] Thus, when the latter suffers, the former shrinks. Consequently, since state resources depend on capital accumulation, it is of paramount importance for the state that the process of capital accumulation—the axle that keeps the economy moving—expands as unobstructed and as smoothly as politically possible. As Offe has written, "accumulation acts as the most powerful constraint criterion, but not necessarily as the determinant of content, of the policy-making process.[56] This dependency of state activities and resources on the overall health of the economy is clearly shown in the present fiscal crises of the state. Let us consider, for instance, how social security and large numbers of health programs are affected by the health of the economy.

The funding of both types of programs is very seriously handicapped in the present economic crunch since less revenue flows into the Treasury's coffers, from whence comes the money to pay for them. And this scarcity of revenue is felt most intensely precisely when these programs are needed the most because of increased unemployment, earlier retirement, more sickness, and so forth. It is precisely when the state needs to provide those services to show that "it works and takes care of people" that it can least afford to do so: capital is needed to save the economy and cannot be diverted into social expenditures. Thus, when, for purposes of legitimization, the state needs to appear most classless is the very time when its class nature appears most clearly.

This dependence of the state and its state apparatus on the "health" of the economy is of paramount importance to understanding not only national but also international governmental policies. Indeed, the integration and increasing interdependence of their economies make nation-states even more vulnerable and dependent on the "health" of the world capitalist system. The dependence of state policies on international economic demands is exemplified in the reported pressure that administrators of the Marshall Plan brought to bear on successive British governments to reduce the size of their public sector, including NHS expenditures. Indeed, Marshall Plan aid was made conditional on increasing military expenditures, liberalizing trade, and cutting social programs, including housing, health, and education.[57] The development of the social programs was subordinated and made conditional to the liberalization of trade and the expansion of military expenditures.

The Class Origins of the Top Members of The Organs of the State

The class origins of the top members of the state organs have been well documented by, among others Domhoff[58] in the United States and Miliband[59] in the United Kingdom. Similarly, Tudor Hart[60] in Britain and I myself[61] in the United States have shown the pattern of class dominance in the main organs of the medical care sectors. Here again, what determines the class composition of the state is the class nature of our societies, not vice versa, that is, what imparts a capitalist character to the state is its function, not its composition.[62] In a class society, it is "natural" that those in positions of power belong to the capitalist class either by origin, association, or common conviction. As Mandel indicated, "The Capitalist state machine . . . possesses a hierarchical organization corresponding to the order of the capitalist society itself."[63]

Here, let me add a note that is of great importance and that concerns the key significance of the composition and ideology of the state. A debate between Poulantzas and Miliband centered on the importance of that composition in defining, explaining, and understanding the nature of the state.[64] Poulantzas maintains the state is characterized as capitalist by its function, as mentioned before, not its composition. I fully agree with that (and so, for that matter, does Miliband). But Poulantzas goes still further, postulating that even if all the members of the state, including its apparatus, were *not* members of the capitalist class by origin, that is, if they were working class, that state would still be capitalist. I find this position most un-Marxian, linear and non-dialectical, and deterministic. Besides, it is wrong. Indeed, the high degree of abstraction and generalization that French structuralists indulge in, and their disregard for empirical verification, lead them to miss the point: in not one of the capitalist societies (including assumedly socialist Sweden) do members of the working class have more than a minimal role in the top corridors of the state and its apparatus.[65] And as long as those societies are capitalist, those "on the top" will be members of the capitalist class. Moreover, and as Miliband rightly points out, because of this failure to analyze the actual composition of the state and its meaning in policy formulation, the French structuralists blur the distinction between a state run by fascists and one run by social democrats since both are capitalist. Let me add a personal note here: as one who has lived under both fascist and social democratic regimes, I can testify that there are differences. This difference, for example, led the major underground Marxist parties in Spain to support   the reestablishment of bourgeois democracy.[66] Actually, *bourgeois democracy is not irrelevant; rather, it is dramatically insufficient.*

The Ideology of the State

The class nature and class position of the state and its apparatus are reflected in the top echelons of the civil service, which espouse an ideology that gives that apparatus its internal cohesiveness and logic. That ideology is the one of the capitalist class. Indeed, "success" in the civil service is not related to competence so much as it is to the degree to which performance conforms to the tenets of those in power. It is utterly inconceivable, for example, that someone rejecting or resisting the existing social order and its norms of thought and action could reach the top of the state apparatus. Indeed:

> Convinced and active pacifists do not usually become generals, and it is absolutely certain that they do not become Chiefs of General Staff. To imagine that the bourgeois state apparatus could be used for a socialist

transformation of capitalist society is as illusory as to suppose that an army could be dissolved with the aid of
"pacifist generals."[67]

Similarly, it is unimaginable that the Secretary of Health, Education and Welfare in the United States or the senior medical officer
in Britain would believe in a classless society, with worker and
community control of the health institutions.

In summary, members of the state apparatus must hold a certain set of beliefs. One example is the belief required of
them—and, for the most part, gladly held—regarding the
primacy of the private sector. In fact, some of the strongest opponents of public ownership are individuals serving the state apparatus. For example, the New York City Health Commissioner
supported the absorption of the New York municipal hospitals by
the voluntary private ones.[68] Needless to say, the frequent   turnover and exchange of job opportunities between the public and
private sectors, with public officials waiting for beneficial retirement to the private sector, further contributes to what is already a
natural condition and consequence of the internal logic of the
system.[69]

I am aware, of course, that some argue that civil servants just
reflect the overall values of the society and that, for the most
part, they are above specific economic or class interests. Indeed,
as I indicated earlier, this appearance of being above class interests is of paramount importance to legitimizing both their
conduct and the state apparatus. Empirical evidence shows,
however, that their ideas are the ideas of the powerful in society,
among which are the primacy of the private sector and the need
to strengthen the capitalist system, usually expressed in terms of
"strengthening the economy." The same applies, incidentally,
to the bodies set up by the state apparatus. Many studies have
shown that most advisory, policy-making bodies in the branches
of the state are dominated by members who uphold bourgeois
positions. In the health sector, for example, the National Health
Planning Council, appointed by the Secretary of Health, Education and Welfare, is composed of members who are well-known
advocates in the sanctity of the private sector. In fact, one of the
leading forces on that council (which is the main federal health
planning agency) is a defense and support of the reintegration of
the *private* market forces in the medical care sector.[70] "Free
marketeers" in command of the top health planning advisory
body! Similarly, out of nearly one hundred members of the

special advisory board on national health insurance set up by the U.S. Congress, very few are known supporters of any form of national health service or of worker control in the health sector.[71] And this is so despite the fact that 22 percent of Americans have declared their support for a completely federally financed and owned health system,[72] and 62 percent expressed the need for worker control.[73] Needless to say, in order to serve the legitimization function, those advisory bodies must seem balanced, professional, and, for the most part, absent of "ideologies," most certainly that of class interest.

The Structure of the State and the Separation of Powers

The most important determinant of class power in capitalist societies is inherent in the structure of the state itself and in its principle of separation of powers, wherein the bodies responsible for implementing policies are separate from those responsible for deciding and formulating those policies. This decision making and formulation, however, takes place indirectly—by so-called representatives of the people seated in the executive and legislative branches of government—not directly by the people themselves. Thus, Western democracies are indirect democracies and, we may add, incomplete democracies. Indeed, due to the skewed nature of political debate, political parties that challenge the basic assumption of the capitalist sytem are systematically hindered from participating in the electoral system and are seriously handicapped from presenting their views, to the advantage of those parties that do accept the system.

Moreover, the indirect character of Western democracies is being strengthened by the remarkable shift of decision making from the legislative to the executive branch of government and to the central administrative machinery, a shift that has left an indelible imprint on most Western parliamentarian and congressional systems. Moreover, this shift of power is directly related to the shift from competitive to monopolistic modes of production. Indeed, the increasing concentration of state policy within the executive branch and the central administration corresponds, not so much to the requirements of the increasingly complex postindustrial societies, but to the increased centralization of economic power and its dominance over both the executive and the administrative branches of government. Actually, the increased centralization of economic and management policies in

the NHS (with the 1974 reorganization)[74] and of health planning
in the United States (reflected in the National Health Planning
Act of 1975)[75] are state responses to pressures by the monopolistic segments in both societies to do something about the "mess"
in the health and social sectors.[76] Not infrequently, this process
of centralization and increased bureaucratization further
strengthens the tendency, inherent in the internal rationale of the
capitalist system, to separate the governors from the governed
and the administrators from those administered, or, as Lenin indicated, to separate the state from society.[77]

Politics in bourgeois democracies, therefore, takes place in the
realm of the politicians—the experts—not in people's everyday
lives. As a recent international commission on Western
democracies found, Western democracies work best when the
citizenry is passive and somewhat apathetic and when its input into the political process takes place only through a limited electoral system.[78] Thus, the electoral system legitimizes the political
process, despite the lack of the people's input in their own gover-
nance. In consequence, as Wolfe indicated, the electoral aim is
the replication of a political institution "which claims primary
responsibility for reproducing alienated politics, that is, for maintaining a political system based upon the extraction and imposi-
tion of power from people."[79] Not surprisingly then, and as part of
the increased consciousness of the population and the intensification of class struggle, that process of legitimization is
quickly losing its validity. In fact, a primary problem in Western
societies is the political alienation of increased masses of the
population from the political system, which in the case of the
United States, is the majority. Indeed, a recent public opinion
poll prepared for the U.S. Congress indicated that:

> the most striking verdict rendered by the American
> people—and disputed by their leaders—is a negative
> one. A majority of Americans display a degree of aliena-
> tion and discontent with government. . . . Those citizens
> who thought something was "deeply wrong" with their
> country had become a national majority.
>   . . . And for the first time in the ten years of opinion
> sampling by the Harris Survey, the growing trend of pub-
> lic opinion toward disenchantment with government
> swept more than half of all Americans with it.[80]

And that disenchantment has been increasing, not decreasing According to the University of Michigan's Survey Research Data, there was a growing decline of public trust in government between 1964 and 1970 and an equally sharp rise in the feeling that government is run only by and for the rich.[81]

The Characteristics and Consequences of State Intervention in the Health Sector

Having explained the characteristics of state intervention in capitalist societies, let me now focus on the specific characteristics of state intervention in the health sector.[82]

The Reproduction of Class Structure

Within the health sector, the state replicates the class hierarchy that characterizes capitalist societies. Accordingly, the distribution of functions and responsibilites follows class, sex, and racial lines, with, for example, physicians being primarily upper-middle-class white males; nurses, lower-middle- or working-class females; and auxiliary health workers, working-class females. And as I have shown elsewhere, both the distribution of skills and knowledge and the control of technology are aimed at strengthening the class relations within the health sector.[83] To assume, as Illich and others do, that control over technology is what gives the medical profession its power is to be unhistorical and unempirical. A study of underlying causes shows that the hierarchy was already there and that technology strengthened it, not vice versa. Needless to say, both the hierarchy and the technology strengthen each other in a dialectical fashion, that is, each has influence on the other. But in that dialectical relationship, hierarchy based on class takes precedence over the other.[84]

The Reproduction of Bourgeois Ideology

State intervention replicates the ideology of medicine, which is subsumed in the ideology of capitalism, that is, liberalism and individualism. And this ideology of medicine takes two forms, one of which is the mechanistic conception of medicine; that is, disease is an imbalance of the components of the machine-like body. As McKeown has eloquently presented it, the most prevalent approach to medicine, Flexnerianism, has been (and still is) that "a living organism could be regarded as a machine which might be taken apart and reassembled if its structure and functions were fully understood."[85] The second form, which derives from the first, is that disease is primarily individual, and thus, the therapeutic response to it is individually oriented. Increasing historical evidence suggests that the victory of Flexnerianism in U.S. medicine paralleled the increasing influence of corporate America on the state. Similarly, the vision of scientific medicine in Europe in the late nineteenth century was a victory of the individualistic-mechanistic view over that of the environmentalist-structuralist (advocated by the revolutionary Virchow), replicating in the health sector the conflict between Weberian and Marxist interpretations of reality.

While most diseases arose from conditions of nascent capitalism,[86] an ideology that "faulted" the individual and that emphasized individual therapy clearly absolved the economic and political environment from responsibility and channeled potential rebellion against that environment to an individual and thus less threatening level. The ideology of medicine individualized a collective causality that by its very nature required a collective answer.

Flexnerian medicine today serves a similar apologist function. Let us analyze, for example, three major health problems in today's capitalist societies.

1. Alienation of individuals in society, which is responsible for a large majority of the psychosomatic conditions seen in medical practices, arises from their lack of control over their own work and over societal institutions.[87] Work, for example, is not a source of creativity or self-expression; rather, it is a means for obtaining satisfaction elsewhere—in the world of consumption, where self-expression is supposed to take place. But such self-expression can never be realized since the world of consumption is based on the stimulation of wants; as Marcuse has indicated, we all have to aspire to more when, in fact, more always has to be inaccessible.[88] The capitalist system creates a continuous process of alienation and frustration that is reflected in despair, disease, and unease.

2. Occupational diseases have been defined as the "new plague in modern societies."[89] The etiology of those diseases resides in the control of the labor process by capital, not by labor, with profit making taking priority over job safety and workers' satisfaction. Moreover, occupational diseases are, for the most part, environmentally determined.

3. Cancer, in the overwhelming majority of cases, is determined by environmental conditions,[90] with individuals living in industrial working-class neighborhoods facing a much greater risk of dying of cancer than those who live in residential areas. (In Baltimore, for example, the incidence of lung cancer is four times higher among residents of industrial areas.[91])

These are just three examples of the economic and political etiology of disease, and this etiology is as apparent today as when our diseases were predominantly infections. But, and as one would expect, the powerful in society either deny or obscure this reality. Instead, the problem is perceived as individual, and the nature of intervention is individually oriented (health education in prevention and clinical medicine in cure).[92] Consequently, one of today's most active state policies is to encourage and stimulate those health programs, such as health education, that are aimed at bringing about changes in the individual, not in the economic or political environment.[93] It is assumed that

> . . . it is increasingly evident that many health problems are related to behavior . . . and that . . . the greatest potential for improving health is through changes in what people do and do not do for themselves.[94]

Interestingly, while much of the disease affecting the working class in Engels' time was supposedly due to the poor moral fiber of the workers and their families, the poor health of that class and of the majority of the population today is assumed to be due to their lack of concern and their poor health education. In both cases, the solution is *individual* prevention and *individual* therapy.

The Reproduction of Alienation

Developed capitalist societies are increasingly characterized by division of labor, both in the production and in the legitimation spheres, with the consequent separation of powers between governors and governed, administrators and administrated, experts and laymen, and skilled and unskilled. Similarly, bourgeois medicine assumes a division of labor in which the citizenry receives the care and the experts provide and administer the therapy. The expropriation of political power from the citizenry, as well as the absence of control over the product and nature of their work, is accompanied by the expropriation of control over the nature and definition of health from the patient and potential patient. It is the bureaucracy—the medical profession—that is supposed to administer and conquer disease. In this respect, the medical profession is assigned an impossible task, that is, to solve something that, because of its economic and political nature, is beyond its control to solve. From the health maintenance point of view, then, the medical care system is failing. And there is no way around that. But this failure does not mean that medicine does not serve a useful purpose. On the contrary, medicine is indeed socially useful because the majority of people believe that politically caused conditions can be individually solved by medical intervention. And from the point of view of the capitalist system, that is the actual utility of medicine: it contributes to the legitimization of capitalism and therefore serves the interests of the capitalist system and of the capitalist class.

The expropriation of political power, work, and health takes place not only individually but collectively; that is, expropriation is imposed on the collectivity of citizens. And it is the collective nature of that expropriation that requires not an individual but a collective response. But the aim of capitalist medicine is to reduce a collective phenomenon to an individual one. In this respect, the present self-care strategies are strengthening the long term legitimization of capitalism.

Part III

The Mode of State Intervention
in the Health Sector

Mechanisms of State Intervention

Having discussed the nature, role and characteristics of the capitalist state, let us now analyze the specific mechanisms of state intervention. And let us begin by arbitrarily dividing those interventions into two levels: negative and positive selection mechanisms.

Negative Selection Mechanisms

By negative selection, I mean that mode of intervention that systematically and continually excludes strategies that conflict with the class nature of the capitalist society. This negative intervention takes place through (1) structural selective mechanisms; (2) ideological mechanisms; (3) decision-making mechanisms; and (4) repressive coercion mechanisms.[95]

Structural Selective Mechanisms

Structural selective mechanisms exclude alternatives that threaten the capitalist system and are inherent in the nature of the capitalist state. Offe mentions, for example, the constitutionally guaranteed right to private property, which excludes state conflict with that right and with the class nature determined by that right. In fact, the overall priority given to property and capital accumulation explains why, when health and property conflict, the latter usually takes priority over the former. For example, the appalling lack of legislation protecting workers in most capitalist societies (including Social Democratic Sweden) contrasts dramatically with the large array of laws protecting private property and its owners. This is put very clearly by A. Miller, head of the United Mine Workers of America:

> If a factory worker drives his car recklessly and cripples a factory owner, the worker looses his license to drive, receives a heavy fine, and may spend some time in jail. But if a factory owner runs his business recklessly and cripples 500 workers with mercury poisoning, he rarely loses his license to do business and never goes to jail. He may not even have to pay a fine.[96]

Actually, the dramatic cuts in the already meager funds for federal occupational programs in the United States indicate that when capital accumulation and property conflict with health the latter is, by definition, the loser.[97] The outrage voiced by the French establishment when a French factory owner was jailed for negligence shows that this "benign neglect" for workers but strong concern for owners and property is not unique to the United States.

Negative selective mechanisms also appear in the assumption that all health programs and reforms have to take place within the set of class relations prevalent in capitalist societies. For example, in Britain, Bevan's Labor party strategy for implementing the NHS (a victory for the British working class) assumed that class relations in Britain were unalterable. Indeed, the creating of NHS took place within the structure of capitalist Britain, respecting the class distribution of power both outside and within the health sector. In fact, Bevan relied very heavily on the consultants (who clearly were of upper-class extraction and position) to break the General Practitioner's resistance against the implementation of the NHS. As he proudly indicated, "I bought them with gold."[98] The strategy of nationalizing the health sector in order to break with the class structure both outside and within the health sector, as Lenin did in the Soviet Union, was not even considered.[99] Moreover, to reassure the medical profession in general, and the consultants in particular, they were given dominant influence over planning, regulation, and administration of the health sector.[100] Actually, these mechanisms of class reassurances also operated in other nationalized sectors. As Coates has shown, the men chosen by the Labor government in the 1940's to lead the nationalized industries were all members of the managerial and ownership class of the former private industries.[101] Shearer demonstrated that the same occurred in the United States.[102] In summary, in all Western capitalist societies, nationalization has taken place within the set of class relations prevalent in those societies.

Ideological Mechanisms

Ideological mechanisms exclude from the realm of debate those ideologies that conflict with the system. In other words, not only programs and policies are being excluded but, more importantly, also conflicting ideologies. This is clearly shown in the lack of attention to and research into areas that conflict with the requirements and needs of capitalist systems. Reflecting the bourgeois bias of the medical research establishment, for example, priority is given to the assumedly individual causes of disease. One instance, among others, is that most research on heart disease—one of the main killers in society—has focused on diet, exercise, and genetic inheritance. On the study of these etiologies, millions of pounds, dollars, marks, and francs have been spent. However, in a fifteen-year study of aging, it was found that the most important predictor of longevity was work satisfaction. Let me quote from that report:

> In an impressive 15-year study of aging, the strongest predictor of longevity was work satisfaction. The second best predictor was overall "happiness." Other factors are undoubtedly important—diet, exercise, medical care, and genetic inheritance. But research findings suggest that these factors may account for only about 25% of the risk factors in heart disease, the major cause of death. That is, if cholesterol, blood pressure, smoking, glucose level, serum uric acid, and so forth, were perfectly controlled, only about one-fourth of coronary heart disease could be controlled. Although research on this problem has not led to conclusive answers, it appears that work role, work conditions, and other social factors may contribute heavily to this "unexplained" 75% of risk factors.[103]

But very few studies have investigated these sociopolitical factors. Indeed, studies on such subjects as work satisfaction are threatening to those who control the work process since, as Braverman has clearly shown, it is the capitalist process of production that actually produces alienations.[104] To change the former means to question the latter.

In summary, the most prevalent mechanism of state intervention is the exclusion of ideologies that question or threaten the basic assumptions of the capitalist system, that is, unthinkable alternatives.

Decision-Making Mechanisms

Decision-making processes are weighted heavily in favor of certain groups and classes, and thus against others. For example,, the mechanism of selecting and appointing members to the new regional and area health planning and administrative agencies in Britain[105] and to the health system agencies in the United States[106] favor individuals of the corporate and upper-middle classes—to the detriment of members of the lower-middle and working classes.

Repressive Coercion Mechanisms

Repressive coercion mechanisms take place either by using direct force or, more importantly, by cutting (and thus nullifying) those programs that may conflict with sources of power within the state organism (e.g., the cutting of the Office of Economic Opportunity because it developed into an alternative source of power to local government in the United States).

Positive Selection Mechanisms

By positive selection, I mean the type of state intervention that generates, stimulates, and determines a positive response to overall capital accumulation, rather than a negative one that excluded anticapitalist possibilities. Offe distinguished between two such types of intervention—allocative and productive.[107] In the former, the state regulates and coordinates the allocation of resources that have already been produced; in the latter, the state becomes directly involved in the production of goods and services.

Allocative Intervention Policies

Allocative intervention policies are based on the ability of the state to influence, guide, and even direct the main activities of society, including the most important one, capital accumulation. These policies are effected primarily (although not exclusively) through laws, which make certain behavior mandatory, and through regulations, which legalize certain claims. Examples of the former in the health sector are laws requiring doctors to register contagious disease with their state health department and employers to install protective devices to prevent industrial accidents; examples of the latter are regulations determining that certain categories of people receive health insurance.[108] Both laws and regulations are determined and dictated in the world of politics. As Offe indicates, in allocative functions "policy and politics are not differentiated."[109] And as such, those state policies are determined by pressure groups and factions within the dominant class.

Here, we have to ask ourselves an important question. How exactly do we study those allocative policies and their class character? The most frequently used method is to analyze, either in specific government policies or in historical events, how the different classes and their components use *interpersonal relationships* to influence with the organs of the state and its intermediary institutions, such as political parties, professional associations, and so forth.[110]

Productive Intervention Policies

Productive intervention policies enable the state directly to participate in the production of resources, for example, medical education, production of drugs in nationalized industries, management of public hospitals, medical research. In these activities; the state produces the resources. Before analyzing these activities, let me clarify a number of points that bear on the presentation of these productive activities.

1. The distinction between allocative and productive policies is not always clear-cut. Frequently, health policies include elements of both.

2. Most allocative functions are administered by the state apparatus, that is, the civil service or the administrative branch of the executive, while most productive functions usually take place outside the administrative bodies of the state apparatus. For example, in the production of medical knowledge—research and teaching—the allocative functions are carried out by an administrative branch of the state apparatus, while their actual production is carried out by medical schools and research institutions that, although public institutions, are not directly run by the branch of the state apparatus in charge of the allocative function.

3. Since World War II, both allocative and productive policies have increased dramatically in all capitalist countries, with the productive becoming more prevalent than the allocative. An example in the medical sector occurred when state intervention in education shifted from an allocative function (e.g., subsidies, tax benefits) to actual production (e.g., nationalization of medical schools and research institutions). Similarly, the health sector is moving from national insurance schemes (allocative) to national health services (productive). Britain in 1948; Quebec, Canada, in 1968; and Italy in the 1970s are all examples of that trend. In all capitalist countries, there has been an impressive growth of state intervention, primarily productive intervention, as measured by either public expenditures or public employment. Moreover, this growth has taken place primarily in the social (including health) services sector. In a survey of expenditures carried out by the Organization of Economic Cooperation and Development among its member countries, for example, it was concluded that public expenditures had grown and will continue to grow very dramatically, both proportionally and absolutely and that the major characteristics of those changes are very substantial growth in (a) social services expenditures (including education, health, and social security); (b) capital investments in the infrastructure (e.g., roads); and (c) state aid to private industries.[111] And in this growth of expenditures, the health sector occupies a prominent place. Again, where information for the 1950s and 1960s is available health expenditures have grown faster than gross national product.[112] (See Table 1 for a sample of countries.)

Table 1
Health Expenditures as Percentage of Gross
National Product, 1950–73

	1950	1960	1970	1973
England and Wales	4.1	3.9	4.9	5.3
United States	4.6	5.2	7.1	7.7
France	2.9	4.0	5.5	5.8
West Germany	—	4.5	—	—
Sweden	—	3.5	6.6	—

Source: Maxwell, Health Care, p. 68.

Similarly, in terms of employment, the social services sectors (including health) have been the fastest growing. Having described that growth, let me now analyze its nature and consequences.

THE REASONS FOR THE GROWTH OF STATE INTERVENTION

The health sector in developed capitalist countries has grown because social needs, as determined by capital accumulation and by the level of class struggle, have grown.

The Growth of Social Needs as Demanded by the Process of Capital Accumulation

The primary role of state intervention is to facilitate the process of capital accumulation, that is, to stimulate and strengthen the economy. Let us now discuss the main characteristics of that process and analyze how they determine what is required from the different agencies of the state. A primary characteristic of that process of accumulation is its concentration. Indeed, insurance, banking, manufacturing, and other sectors of economic life are in the hands of an increasingly smaller number of corporations.[113] That concentration has many consequences, the most important of which is that technology and industrial development are directed to best serve the needs of that concentration in such areas as:

1. *Division of labor, with its continuous demand for specialization,* fragments the process of production and,

ultimately, as Braverman has indicated, the producer himself. This specialization demands a great involvement and investment from the state in order to guarantee the reproduction of labor needed for the system. Similarly, in the health sector, the state allocates and produces the human resources needed for the delivery of health care, thereby stimulating an increased specialization of labor, which is necessary to sustain and legitimize the growing concentration, industrialization, and hierarchicalization of that sector. In summary, and as expressed in Figure 1, increased economic concentration requires an increased concentration of political power because increased state intervention is needed to facilitate the type of industrialization demanded by that economic concentration—an industrialization that influences and determines the type of specialized medicine that is prevalent today.

I believe that the relationships among these categories to be dialectical, not linear, with a pattern of dominance that is expressed by the main direction of the arrow.

FIGURE 1: The Dialectical Relationship Between Concentration of Economic Power and Industrialization of Society (Including Medicine)

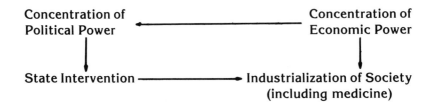

2. *All sectors of economic life are invaded by corporate capital.* Indeed the process of capital accumulation, in its search for profits, invades all sectors of economic life, including social services such as health,[114] education,[115] transportation.[116] As Mandel indicated:

The logic of late capitalism is . . . to convert idle capital into service capital and simultaneously to replace service capital with commodities; transport services with private cars; theatre and film services with private television sets; tomorrow, television programmes and educational instruction with videocassettes.[117]

> In summary, contemporary capitalism tends to convert public services into commodities that are bought and sold on the private market. Reflecting that tendency is the push, both by conservatives in the United Kingdom and by conservatives and liberals in the United States, to shift the delivery of health services permanently back to the private sector (supposedly to make them more efficient and more profitable). And in this scheme, the payment for services is public, while the appropriation of profit is private. In brief, the state sector is footing the bill for the profit of capital.

3. *The spheres of social life are invaded by corporate capital and its process of industrialization,* causing dislocation, diswelfare, and insecurity that state intervention, through social services (including medicine), is supposed to mitigate. The most important example, of course, is the alienation that industrialization causes in the working population—an alienation that reflects itself in psychosomatic conditions, which medicine is supposed to care for and cure. Similarly, occupational diseases, the new plague of developed societies, and environmental damage are, for the most part, also caused by industrialization but, according to bourgeois ideology, individually cured through medical intervention. In summary, the concentration of economic activities and its consequent process of industrialization create a process of diswelfare that, in turn, determines and requires the growth of state services.

4. *The spheres of private life are invaded by corporate capital,* with the commodification of all processes of interpersonal relationships, from sex to the pursuit of happiness. Indeed, according to corporate ideology, happiness depends on the amount and type of consumption, that is, on what the citizen has, not on what he or she does.

5. *The population is increasingly proletarianized,* including
    the medical profession. The health professionals,
    once independent entrepreneurs, become employees
    of private medical corporations (as in the United
    States) or employees of the state (as in the majority of
    European capitalist countries). In both cases, that
    process of proletarianization is stimulated by the
    state, with the assistance and stimulus of the cor-
    porate segments of the capitalist class.[118]

6. *Resources are increasingly concentrated in urban areas*
    because it is needed for the realization of capital. This
    process of urbanization necessitates a growth in the
    allocative functions of the state (e.g., land use legisla-
    tion and city planning) and of productive functions
    (e.g., roads and sanitation) in order to support, guide,
    and direct that process in a way that is responsive to
    the needs of capital accumulation. It is worth
    underlining here that the majority of infrastructure
    services are consumed by components of capital, not
    by private households. For example, three-quarters
    of the U.S. water supply is consumed by industry and
    agriculture (mainly corporate), while private
    households consume less than one quarter. Water
    supply, however, is paid for largely from funds com-
    ing from the latter, not from the former.[119]

In summary, then, the economic concentration typical of the
present stage of capitalism—usually referred to as monopoly
capitalism—determines (1) an invasion by corporate capital of all
spheres of economic, social, and private life and (2) a specific
type of technological development and industrialization (both of
which are summarized in Figure 2) that requires increased state
intervention to (a) stimulate and facilitate that concentration and
(b) rectify the dislocation of general well-being created by that
concentration.

Moreover, this process of economic concentration and its concomitant industrialization determine a model of production and
distribution in medicine that replicates the characteristics of the
process of economic production and distribution, that is,
specialization, concentration, urbanization, and a technical
orientation. The nature of medicine, then, and its relation to the
overall process of production determine its *characteristics.* And its

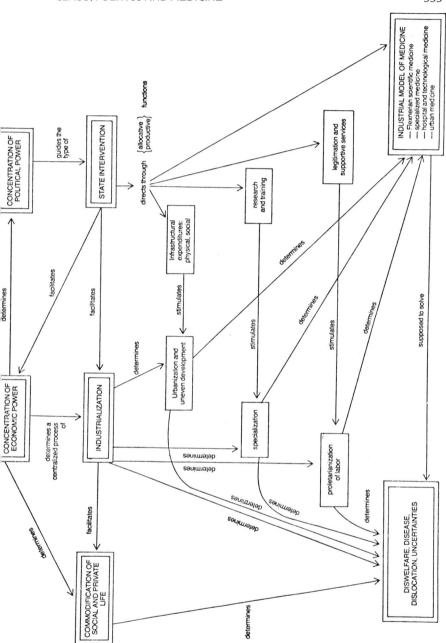

FIGURE 2: The Dialectical Relationship
Between Society and Medicine

position within that process of production explains its *function,* namely, to take care of and solve the unsolvable—the diswelfare and dysfunctions created by that very process of production.

The Level of Class Struggle

The tendencies explained above result from the growth of capital accumulation that occurs within the context of a continuous conflict between capital and labor, that is, between the capitalist class and the working class. Indeed, the working class continuously tries to extract significant concessions from the state, over and above what the state considers sufficient for the needs of capital accumulation. For example, it is impossible to explain the creation of the NHS in Britain without understanding the relationship of class forces in Britain and the wartime radicalization of the working class that had challenged "the survival of capitalism." According to Forsyth:

> rightly or wrongly the British Government at the outbreak of war could not be sure that large sections of the working class were entirely satisfied about the reasons for fighting the war. . . . For the sake of public morale the Government tried to make it clear that after the war things were going to be very different from the heartbreak conditions of the "thirties."[120]

The much-heralded consensus among Labour and Conservative politicians for national health service resulted from the radicalization of the working class, on the one hand, and the instinct of self-preservation by the capitalist class and the state, on the other.[121] Indeed, labor movements have historically viewed social services (including health) as part of the *social wage,* to be defended and increased in the same way that *money wages* are. In fact, Wilensky has shown how the size of social wages depends on the level of militancy of the labor movements.[122] Thus, contrary to popular belief, the size and nature of social services is higher in France and Italy than in Scandinavia or even in Britain.[123] And I attribute this to the higher militancy of the unions in those countries and to the existence of Socialist and Communist parties (whose platforms are, at least in theory, anticapitalist). Moreover, the almost total absence of comprehensive social benefits in the United States is undoubtedly due to the lack of an organized left-wing party.

Therefore, in the labor-capital conflict, the labor movement demands: (1) increased social wages, the comprehensiveness and level of which depend on the strength of working-class pressure; (2) jobs to counteract the unemployment characteristic of contemporary capitalism (in that respect, the large increase in public employment—particularly at the provincial, state, or local level —is a response to that demand for the state to absorb surplus population); (3) additional services, such as welfare, social security, and unemployment insurance, to smooth down and cushion the dislocation, uncertainty, and diswelfare created by the process of capital accumulation; (4) worker control of the process of production;[124] and (5) public ownership of the means of production, which has meant that even governing social democratic parties are forced to pay lip service to that objective.[125]

In summary, then, the nature and growth of the state in contemporary capitalist societies can be attributed to the increased *social needs of capital* and the increased *social demands of labor*. In order to understand the nature of any state policy, including health policy, our analysis must be placed within those parameters. Having said that, let me clarify two points:

First, no single factor explains social policy. Rather, it is explained by the combination of factors already mentioned. And the nature and number of those combinations depend on the *historical* origins of each factor, the *political* form determining each factor's relation to others and its *function* in that specific social formation.

Second, there is no clear-cut dichotomy between the social needs of capital and the social demands of labor. Any given policy can serve both. Indeed, social policies that serve the interests of the working class can be adapted to benefit the interests of the dominant class. As Miliband and others have shown so well, the "bias of the system" has always ensured that social policies can be deflected to suit the capitalist class. Indeed, history shows that concessions won by labor in the class struggle become, *in the absence of further struggle,* modified to serve the interests of the capitalist class.

The Present Fiscal Crisis of the State: A Last Note on the Health Sector of Contemporary Capitalism

I end this article, then, again underlining the two main characteristics of contemporary capitalism, that is, the concentration of capital and the consequent growth of the state. In this scenario, the growth of the state (and the growth of medicine within it) is both a cause and an effect of the expansion of monopoly capital. In Marxist terms, the growing socialization of production necessitates greater state intervention to ensure private capital accumulation and profitability. But this growth of state intervention and expenditures requires ever-increasing revenues that are forever insufficient. Thus, the continuous fiscal crisis of the state.[126]

The nature of this crisis determines the type of state response, the main characteristics of which are (1) a cutting of social wages; (2) an increasing demand for planning the economy, which requires still further centralization of power; and (3) an increasing demand for rationalization of the system, with growing demand for higher productivity and efficiency.

These three characteristics of state response to it fiscal crises also are reflected in the medical sector. First, cuts are made in health expenditures because the capitalist class must "save the economy" at whatever cost, putting first and foremost the need for private capital accumulation. Therefore, a political struggle occurs over the state's goal to cut social wages, in particular those portions of medical care, care of the elderly, and welfare services that are considered by capital as contributing least to the productivity of the system. Such cuts are justified by the need to shift capital from unproductive to productive sectors, thereby increasing private capital accumulation. Consequently, these cuts in health and social services are accompanied by increased assistance to private industry. Needless to say, the working class (although not always its leaders) has resisted these cuts because social wages are considered as a necessary complement to money wages. One instance, among others, of this resistance is the strike of coal miners in Yorkshire to protest cuts in the NHS and to support a pay raise for nurses.

Second, increasing centralization by the state (primarily by the executive branch and its administrative apparatus) directs social and health policy. Examples of the centralization are the reorganization of NHS in Great Britain and the health planning apparatus in the United States. This centralization manifests itself as (1) the creation of regional and local bodies (e.g., health system agencies in the United States and area health authorities in Great

Britain) that bypass local governments and are accountable to the central government and (2) a shift of power from the legislative to the executive branch of government, with an increasing allocation of decision-making power to agencies of the state apparatus (e.g., major decisions in the health sector are increasingly made by the Office of Management and Budget of the White House).

Finally, the increased demand to rationalize the system forces the central government to develop mechanisms of cost control and alternative ways of organizing the delivery system (e.g., emphasis on primary care) and different types of personnel (e.g., nurse practitioners) who can do the job "cheaper." In all these reforms, a primary motive is the reduction of costs. Underlying these changes, there also are ideological changes, with both an increasing focus on individual behavior as responsible for improving health and a growing skepticism concerning the effectiveness of medical intervention.

These, then, are the main characteristics of the medical sector in Western capitalist societies today, as determined by the historical, political, and functional factors discussed in this article.

I have tried to show that if we are to understand the nature, composition, distribution, and function of the medical care sector in Western developed capitalist societies, we must first understand the distribution of power in those societies and the nature, role, and instrumentality of the state. This understanding makes us realize that (1) the so-called diluted category of social class is still needed to understand the distribution of power in our societies and (2) class struggle, far from being an outmoded concept of interest only to "vulgar" Marxists, is most relevant indeed and is as needed today to understand the nature of our societies and our health sector as it was when Marx and Engels wrote that "class struggle is the motor of history."

Needless to say, this interpretation is a minority voice in our Western academic setting. It is in conflict with the prevalent explanations of the health sector, and this accounts for its exclusion from the realm of debate. Still, its veracity will be affirmed not by its "popularity" in the corridors of power but in its verification on the terrain of history. It is because of this that I dedicate this article to all those with whom I share a praxis aimed at building up a society of truly free and self-governing men and women—a society in which, as Marx indicated, the state (and I would add medicine) will be converted "from an organ superimposed upon society into one completely subordinated to it."[127]

NOTES

1. A. L. Cochrane, *Effectiveness and Efficiency: Random Reflection on Health Services* (London: The Nuffield Provincial Hospitals Trust, 1972), p. 70.
2. R. Titmuss, *Commitment to Welfare* (London: Unwin University Books, 1968).
3. J. Tudor Hart, "The Inverse Care Law," *The Lancet,* Vol. 1, No. 7696 (1971): 405-412.
4. For an answer and critique of Cochrane's dismissal of class inequities of consumption, see J. Tudor Hart, "An Assault on All Custom," *International Journal of Health Services,* Vol. 3, No. 1 (1973): 101-104.
5. For a representative reference, see T. W. Bice, R. L. Eichhorn, and P. D. Fox, "Socioeconomic Status and Use of Physician Services: A Reconsideration," *Medical Care,* Vol. 10, No. 3 (1972): 261-271. For an answer and a critique of equalization of consumption by social class in the United States, see S. E. Berki, "Comments on 'Socioeconomic Status and Use of Physician Services: A Reconsideration,'" *Medical Care,* Vol. 11, No. 3 (1973): 259.
6. O. Anderson, *Health Care: Can There Be Equity? The United States, Sweden, and England* (New York: John Wiley and Sons, 1972).
7. Ibid., p. 26.
8. Ibid., pp. 24-25.
9. It is worth underlining that the category *poor* is presented unconnected with any class linkage. The fact that all poor people are, by association, employment, or unemployment, members of the working class is dismissed since the category of *working class* has assumedly disappeared altogether.
10. H. H. Westergaard, "Sociology: The Myth of Classlessness," in *Ideology in Social Science,* ed. R. Blackburn (New York: Fontana, 1972), p. 121.
11. In this text, the American terms "conservative" and "liberal" will be used interchangeably with the European term "bourgeois." Conservative, liberal, or bourgeois positions are those that do not question but rather build on the basic assumptions of capitalism.
12. J. Habermas, *Toward a Rational Society: Student Protest, Science and Politics* (Boston: Beacon Press, 1971).
13. H. Marcuse, *One-Dimensional Man* (Boston: Beacon Press, 1964).
14. S. Aronowitz, *False Promises: The Shaping of American Working-Class Consciousness* (New York: McGraw-Hill Book Co., 1973).
15. "Equality in the Health Services," in Cochrane, *Effectiveness and Efficiency,* p. 70. The assumption that Cochrane makes in dismissing class inequalities and instead focusing on age and regional ones is that age and regional differences are independent from and unrelated to class differences. This assumption, however, is erroneous. For example, if we analyze the interregional differences in availability of human health resources in the NHS, we see that those regions with higher percentages of the working class (and primarily of the low-income strata within it) also are the ones with lower availability of resources. See A. Learmouth, "Regional Disparities in the Health Sector," *Health* (London: The Open University Press, 1972).
16. In the term "state," I include the executive and legislative branches of government as well as the state apparatus, that is, the administrative bureaucracy, the judiciary, the army, and the police. Also, it is important to clarify that I consider the state far more than the mere aggregate of those institutions. Rather, it includes the set of relationships between and among those institutions and with other ones that it guides and directs (such as the medical institutions). These relationships are aimed, as I will show later on, at perpetuating and reproducing the system of production and its concomitant class relations. To understand the nature of the state in Western societies, three excellent volumes are: R. Miliband, *The State in Capitalist Society* (London: Weidenfeld and Nicolson, 1970); N. Poulantzas, *Political Power and*

Social Classes (London: New Left Books, 1973); and N. Poulantzas, *Classes in Contemporary Capitalism* (London: New Left Books, 1975).

17. Anderson, *Health Care,* p. 28. It is worth indicating that Anderson, as many others in political sociology, seems to confuse the government with the state. Indeed, the functions listed by Anderson as functions of the government (p. 29) are actually the functions of the state. The executive and legislative branches of the state (the government) are only part of the overall structure of the state. For a further expansion of this point, see "The State System and the State Elite," in Miliband, *The State in Capitalist Society,* p. 49.

18. There are many authors who uphold variants of this theory. The most representative is R. A. Dahl, *A Preface to Democratic Theory* (Chicago: University of Chicago Press, 1956). In medical care literature, the most representative is Anderson, *Health Care,* whose inheritance from Dahl is acknowledged, and V. Fuchs, *Who Shall Live: Health, Economics and Social Choice* (New York: Basic Books, 1975).

19. E. E. Schattschneider, *The Semi-Sovereign People: A Realistic View of Democracy in America* (New York: Holt, Rinehart and Winston, 1960), p. 31.

20. Hart poll results reported in M. Bender, "Will the Bicentennial See the Death of Free Enterprise?" *The New York Times,* January 4, 1976, p. 27.

21. Representative of this analysis in the United States are the most informative volumes by R. Alford, *Health Care Politics* (Chicago: University of Chicago Press, 1975); and T. Marmor, *The Politics of Medicare* (Chicago: Aldine Publishing Co., 1973). In the United Kingdom, representatives are J. Willcocks, *The Creation of the National Health Service: A Study of Pressure Groups and a Major Social Policy Decision* (London: Routledge and Kegan Paul, 1967); and H. Eckstein, *The English Health Service: Its Origins, Structure and Achievement* (Cambridge: Harvard University Press, 1958).

22. V. Navarro, "The Political Economy of Medical Care," *International Journal of Health Services,* Vol. 5, No. 1 (1975): 65–94.

23. For a further explanation of the rationality of capitalism, see M. Godelier, *Rationality and Irrationality in Economics* (New York: Monthly Review Press, 1973).

24. For an expanded critique of power elite theories, see N. Poulantzas, "The Problems of the Capitalist State," *New Left Review,* No. 58 (November, December, 1969). Also, "Economic Elites and Dominant Class" in R. Miliband, *The State in Capitalist Society,* p. 23.

25. I. Illich, *Medical Nemesis: The Expropriation of Health* (London: Calder and Boyars, 1975). A similar paradigm is presented in E. Freidson, *Doctoring Together: A Study of Professional Social Control* (New York: Elsevier, 1975).

26. H. Mahler, "Health—A Demystification of Medical Technology," *The Lancet,* Vol. 2, No. 7940 (1975): 829–833.

27. V. Navarro, "The Industrialization of Fetishism or the Fetishism of Industrialization: A Critique of Ivan Illich," *Social Science and Medicine,* Vol. 9, No. 7 (1975): 351–363.

28. Ibid.

29. M. Susser, "Ethical Components in the Definition of Health," *International Journal of Health Services,* Vol. 4, No. 3 (1974): 539–548.

30. President Gerald Ford, *State of the Union Message* (Washington, D.C.: U.S. Government Printing Office, January 1976).

31. For an expansion on this point, see Navarro, "The Industrialization of Fetishism or the Fetishism of Industrialization."

32. Miliband, *The State in Capitalist Society.*

33. Poulantzas, "The Problems of the Capitalist State."

34. See R. Miliband, "Marx and the State," in *The Socialist Register, 1965,* Ed. R. Miliband and J. Saville (London: The Merlin Press, 1966), p. 278.

35. Letter from F. Engels to J. Bloch, September 21, 1890, in K. Marx and F. Engels, *Selected Correspondence* (Moscow: 1963), p. 498.

36. K. Marx, *The Eighteenth Brumaire of Louis Bonaparte* (New York: International Publishers, 1969), p. 15.

37. "Introduction," in V. Navarro, *The Political Economy of Social Security and Medical Care in the USSR,* forthcoming.

38. L. Althusser and E. Balibar, *Reading Capital* (New York: Pantheon Books, 1970).

39. M. Godelier, *Rationality and Irrationality in Economics.*

40. Poulantzas, *Political Power and Social Classes.*

41. The best reference on structuralism in the health sector is the excellent article by M. Renaud, "On the Structural Constraints to State Intervention in Health," *International Journal of Health Services,* Vol. 5, No. 4 (1975): 559–571. Also, Jean-Claude Polack, *La médecine du Capital* (Paris: Maspéro, 1970).

42. By class struggle I mean the realization of the economic, political, and social conflict between social classes and primarily between the capitalist class and the working class. According to bourgeois theory, there is no intrinsic conflict between capital and labor. Rather, they are supposed to complement each other. According to Marxist theory, to which I subscribe, there is an intrinsic conflict between both. The advantage of one presupposes the disadvantage of the other. Actually, not only Marxists but leading representatives of capital have subscribed to this paradigm. None other than Gates, the closest advisor to J. D. Rockefeller, indicated that "The plank between Capital and Labor is stiff. If labor goes up, capital comes down; if capital goes up, labor goes down. There are no two ways about it, it is impossible, utterly impossible, unthinkable, unimaginable that labor as a whole can have increase of wages except capital as a whole shall have a decrease of interest and rent." (F. Gates, "Capital and Labor," undated memorandum. Gates Collection, Rockefeller Foundation Archives.) And this paradigm is verified by data representing the distribution of national income, that is, when income to labor increases, income to capital declines, and vice versa. See A. Glyn and B. Sutcliffe, *British Capitalism: Workers and the Profit Squeeze* (Middlesex: Penguin Books, 1972).

43. R. Miliband, "Reply to N. Poulantzas," *New Left Review,* No. 59 (1970); also, R. Miliband, "Poulantzas and the Capitalist State," *New Left Review,* No. 82 (1973); and E. Laclau, "Poulantzas-Miliband Debate," *Economy and Society,* Vol. 4, No. 1 (1975).

44. One of the most informative and instructive discussions of the nature of corporate state theories is by J. O'Connor, *The Corporations and the State* (New York: Harper Books, 1974). Also, by the same author, *The Fiscal Crisis of the State* (New York: St. Martin's Press, 1973). For a French version of corporate statism, see P. Herzog, *Politique Economique* (Paris: Maspéro, 1971).

45. Marx and F. Engels, *The Communist Manifesto* (New York: International Publishing Company, 1960).

46. J. Gough, "Review of 'The Fiscal Crisis of the State.'" *Bulletin of the Conference of Socialist Economists,* Vol. 4, No. 1 (1975): 823.

47. Miliband, *The State in Capitalist Society,* p. 11.

48. "State in Late Capitalism," in E. Mandel, *Late Capitalism,* (London: New Left Books, 1975), p. 476.

49. C. Offe, "The Theory of the Capitalist State and the Problem of Policy Formation," in *Stress and Contradiction in Modern Capitalism,* ed. L. Lindberg et al. (London: Lexington Books, 1975), p. 126.

50. H. E. Sigerist, *Landmarks in the History of Hygiene* (London: Oxford University Press, 1956). Quoted in M. Terris, "Crisis and Change in America's Health System," *American Journal of Public Health,* Vol. 63, No. 4 (1973): 313-318.

51. Quoted in V. George and P. Wilding, "Social Values, Social Class and Social Polity," *Social and Economic Administration,* Vol. 6, No. 3 (1972): 236-248.

52. Offe, *The Theory of the Capitalist State*, p. 127.
53. For the analyses of businessmen predominant in the governmental corridors of power, see H. D. Lasswell, et al., *The Comparative Study of Elites* (Stanford: Stanford University Press, 1952). p. 30; C. W. Mills, *The Power Elite* (New York: Oxford University Press, 1956); and W. L. Guttsman, *The British Political Elite* (London: MacGibbon and Kee, 1963).
54. P. K. Kilborn, "Britain Slashes Spending on Social-Welfare Items," *The New York Times*, February 21, 1976; "The Budget: A Special Analysis," Special issue of the *National Journal*, Vol. 8, No. 5 (1976).
55. For an analysis of the increased reliance of state expenditures on credit, see Chapter 13, "Permanent Inflation," in Mandel, *Late Capitalism*, pp. 409-437.
56. Offe, *The Theory of the Capitalist State*, p. 126.
57. D. Coates, *The Labour Party and the Struggle for Socialism* (London: Cambridge University Press, 1975), p. 68.
58. G. W. Domhoff, *The Higher Circles: The Governing Class in America* (New York: Vintage Books, 1971).
59. Miliband, *The State in Capitalist Society*.
60. J. Tudor Hart, "Industry and the Health Services," Letter to the Editor, *The Lancet*, No. 7829 (1973): 611.
61. V. Navarro, "The Political Economy of Medical Care: An Explanation of the Composition, Nature and Functions of the Present Health Sector of the United States," *International Journal of Health Services*, Vol. 5, No. 1 (1975): 65-94.
62. The function is what determines the class position; the origin is what determines the class situation. See "Social Classes and Their Extended Reproduction," in Poulantzas, *Classes in Contemporary Capitalism*, pp. 13-35.
63. Mandel, *Late Capitalism*, p. 492.
64. This debate is reproduced in Blackburn, *Ideology in Social Science*, pp. 239-262.
65. The number of workers' sons and daughters among the top Swedish politico-bureaucratic echelons was less than 9 percent in 1961. G. Therborn, "Power in the Kingdom of Sweden," *International Socialist Journal*, Vol. 2, No. 59 (1965): 490-494.
66. See Democratic Junta and Democratic Convergency programs for the support of Marxist parties to the democratization of Spain, *Cambio*, January 1976.
67. Mandel, *Late Capitalism*, p. 494.
68. A. A. Appelbaum, "New York City Hospitals: The Financial Crunch," *Hospitals*, Vol. 50, No. 2 (1976): 59.
69. Examples of top officials in the health agencies of the state retiring to work for commercial insurance and drug companies, private health institutions, and so forth, are many, and have been well documented, primarily by the "power elite" analysts.
70. For a critique of the market ideologies in the health sector, see V. Navarro, "National Health Insurance and the Strategy for Change," *Health and Society, The Milbank memorial Fund Quarterly*, Vol. 51, No. 2 (1973): 223-251.
71. "Revised List of NHI Advisory Panel Members Issued," *Washington Information: National Health Insurance*, Bulletin 2-5 (June 1975).
72. Cambridge Survey polls, *Health Security News*, January 1976.
73. Complete Hart polls, published in *Common Sense* (September 1, 1975): 16-17. Also quoted in Bender, "Will the Bicentennial See the Death of Free Enterprise?"
74. H.M.S.O., *National Health Service Reorganization:* England, 1972.
75. That centralization takes place with the central government bypassing state and local authorities by appointing ad hoc bodies appointed by and ultimately accountable to them.
76. For an expansion of the political consequence of economic concentration,

see I. Gough, "State Expenditure in Advanced Capitalism," *New Left Review,* No. 92 (1975): 53–92.

77. V. Lenin, *The State and Revolution* (New York: International Publishers Co., 1932).

78. *Governability of Democracies: Report of the Trilateral Task Force* (New York: Trilateral Commission, 1975). For an excellent critique of this report, See A. Wolfe, "Capitalism Shows Its Force," *The Nation,* Vol. 221, No. 18 (1975): 557–563.

79. A. Wolfe, "New Directions in the Marxist Theory of Politics," *Politics and Society,* Vol. 4, No. 2 (1974): 149.

80. Committee on Government Operations, U.S. Senate, *Confidence and Concern. Citizens View American Government: A Survey of Public Attitudes,* Part I, (Washington, D.C.: U.S. Government Printing Office, 1973), p. VI.

81. A. H. Miller, "Political Issues and Trust in Government: 1964–1970," *American Political Science Review,* Vol. 68 (September 1974).

82. Let me clarify that the health sector is increasingly part of the state because (1) the production and allocation of health resources is perceived in most Western capitalist societies as a public responsibility, where the chartering of resources and services has to be approved by the public sector; (2) training, research, and delivery of services are increasingly financed from public funds; and (3) the ideology and organization of medicine build on and strengthen the replication of class relations in our society and thus reinforce the capitalist system. In that respect, the ideology of the capitalist system, guaranteed by the nature of state intervention, is embodied in the medical institutions and in the ideology of medicine. Indeed, as Gramsci indicated, the state directs and involves itself in most spheres of political, economic, and social life, and the ideological influence of the state apparatus far transcends the sector that we usually refer to as the public sector. And medicine is very much a part of it, regardless of whether those medical institutions are, legally speaking, private or public. In the Gramscian sense, I am thus including in the public sector institutions influenced by the state apparatus, not only medicine, but academia, schools, and the media. (A. Gramsci, *Prison Notebooks* [New York: International Publishers, 1971].)

83. Navarro, "The Industrialization of Fetishism or the Fetishism of Industrialization."

84. For an excellent analysis of this point, see H. Braverman, *Labor and Monopoly Capital* (New York: Monthly Review Press, 1975).

85. T. McKeown, "A Historical Appraisal of the Medical Task," in *Medical History and Medical Care: A Symposium of Perspectives,* ed. T. McKeown (London: Oxford University Press, 1971), p. 29.

86. See the excellent description by Engels of the conditions among the English working class to see the effect of nascent capitalism on the health of the population. F. Engels, *The Condition of the Working Class in England,* trans. W. Henderson and W. Chaloner (Stanford: Stanford University Press, 1958).

87. For further discussion, see V. Navarro, "The Underdevelopment of Health of Working America: Causes, Consequences and Possible Solutions," *American Journal of Public Health,* Vol. 66 (5), 1976.

88. Marcuse, *One-Dimensional Man.*

89. A. Miller, "The Wages of Neglect: Death and Disease in the American Workplace," *American Journal of Public Health,* Vol. 65, No. 11 (1975): 1217–1220.

90. J. Cairns, "The Cancer Problem," *Scientific American,* Vol. 233, No. 5 (November 1975); and E. C. Hammond, "Epidemiologic Basis for Cancer Prevention," *Cancer,* Vol. 33, No. 6 (1974).

91. Dr. G. Matanoski, "Lung Cancer by Census Tracts in the City of Baltimore," *The Johns Hopkins Gazette* (March 4, 1976).

92. The most recent addition to this literature is Fuchs, *Who Shall Live?*

93. See, among other examples, M. Lalonde, *A New Perspective on the Health of*

Canadians: A Working Document (Government of Canada, Government Printing Office, 1975).

94. V. Fuchs, "Health Care and the United States Economic System," *Milbank Memorial Fund Quarterly, Health and Society,* No. 50 (1972): 299.

95. In this text, I am using a modified version of Offe's categories. For a presentation of Offe's theories of state intervention, see C. Offe, "Political Authority and Class Structures—An Analysis of State Capitalist Societies," *International Journal of Sociology,* Vol. 2, No. 1 (1972): 73-108. Also, C. Offe, "The Abolition of Market Control and the Problem of Legitimacy," *Kapitalistate,* Vol. 1 (1973): 109, and C. Offe and V. Ronge, "Theses on the Theory of the State," in this volume. For a critique of Offe's work, see S. S. Biermann, V. Christiansen, and K. Dohse, "Class Domination and the Political System: A Critical Interpretation of Recent Contributions by Claus Offe," *Kapitalistate,* Vol. 2 (1973): 60, and E. G. Rusconi, "Marxism in West Germany," and W. Muller and C. Neususs, "The Illusion of State Socialism"—both in *Telos,* No. 25 (1975).

96. A. Miller, "The Wages of Neglect," p. 1219.

97. See the present cuts in OSHA, where the rationale is that they are too expensive and that they interfere with the process of capital accumulation. D. Burnham, "Ford Termed Cool to 3 Key Agencies," *The New York Times,* January 16, 1976, p. 1.

98. See J. Tudor Hart, "Primary Care in the Industrial Areas of Britain: Evolution and Current Problems," *International Journal of Health Services,* Vol. 2, No. 3 (1972): 349-365, and J. Tudor Hart, "Bevan and the Doctors," Book Review of *Aneurin Bevan: A Biography* by M. Foot, *The Lancet,* No. 7839 (1973): 1196-1197.

99. For Lenin's strategy in health services, see "Leninism and Medicine," in Navarro, *The Political Economy of Social Security and Medical Care in the USSR.*

100. For an excellent analysis of the professional dominance in the NHS, see J. Robson, "The NHS Company Inc.? The Social Consequences of the Professional Dominance in the National Health Service," *International Journal of Health Services,* Vol. 3, No. 3 (1973): 413-426. Also, P. Draper and T. Smart, "Social Science and Health Policy in the United Kingdom: Some Contributions of the Social Sciences to the Bureaucratization of the National Health Service," *International Journal of Health Services,* Vol. 4, No. 3 (1974): 453-470.

101. D. Coates, *The Labour Party and the Struggle for Socialism* (London: Cambridge University Press, 1975), p. 48.

102. D. Shearer, "The Salt of Public Enterprise," *The Nation,* February 21, 1976.

103. *Work in America.* Report of a Special Task Force to the Secretary of Health, Education and Welfare (Cambridge: M.I.T. Press, 1973), pp. 77-79.

104. H. Braverman, *Labor and Monopoly Capital.*

105. J. Tudor Hart, "Industry and the Health Service," Letter to the Editor, *The Lancet,* No. 7829 (1973): 611.

106. V. Navarro, "The Political Economy of Medical Care," *International Journal of Health Services,* Vol. 5, No. 1 (1975): 65-93.

107. Offe, "The Theory of the Capitalist State," p. 128.

108. Ibid.

109. Ibid.

110. The best and most detailed study of the nature of the state and the distribution of power is Miliband, *The State in Capitalist Society.*

111. Organization of Economic Cooperation and Development, *Expenditure Trends in OECD Countries, 1960-1980,* mentioned in Ivan Gough, pp. 62-62.

112. R. Maxwell, *Health Care, The Growing Dilemma: Needs Versus Resources in Western Europe, The U.S. and the USSR* (New York: McKinsey and Company, 1975), p. 18.

113. See P. Sweezy and P. A. Baran, *Monopoly Capital* (New York: Monthly Review

Press, 1966).

114. For the increased dominance of financial capital in the funding of medical care in the United States, see V. Navarro, "The Political Economy of Medical Care," *International Journal of Health Services*, Vol. 5, No. 1 (1975): 65-94.

115. S. Bowles and H. Gintis, *Schooling in Capitalist America: Educational Reform and the Contradictions of Economic Life* (New York: Basic Books, 1976).

116. G. Yago, *State Policy, Corporate Planning and Transportation Needs* (Madison: University of Wisconsin, 1974), mimeo.

117. Mandel, *Late Capitalism*, p. 406.

118. Editorial, "Doctors and the State," *Wall Street Journal*, January 16, 1976.

119. O'Connor, *The Fiscal Crisis of the State*, p. 175.

120. G. Forsyth, *Doctors and State Medicine: A Study of the British Health Service* (London: Pitman and Sons, 1973), p. 16.

121. Needless to say, while radicalization triggered the creation of the NHS, the implementation of that legislation was skewed to favor and replicate the class structure and hierarchicalization of labor prevalent then, as today. Indeed, the concession by the capitalist class and victory by the working class could not conflict—or conflict as little as possible—with (1) the class structure of Britain and (2) with the process of capital accumulation that determined it.

122. H. L. Wilensky, *The Welfare State and Equality* (Berkeley: University of California Press, 1975).

123. One indicator, among others, is the percentage of gross national product spent on social security in 1965: Italy, 17.5; France 18.3; Sweden, 17.5; Britain, 14.4; Norway, 12.6; Denmark, 13.9; United States, 7.9. In *The Cost of Social Security, 1964-66* (Geneva: International Labor Organization, 1972), pp. 317-323.

124. For an interesting account of the evolution of workers' demands to control the process of work in Italy, see J. B. Proctor and R. Proctor, "Capitalist Development: Class Struggle and Crisis in Italy, 1945-1975," *Monthly Review*, Vol. 27 (1976): 21-36. It is worth underlining that the demand for worker control—different from worker participation—has arisen in most Western capitalist societies from the base, not the top, of the labor movement.

125. See, for example, Clause 4 of the *Governing Constitution of the British Labour Party*, which reads that the primary aim of the party is "to secure for the workers by hand or by brain the full fruits of their industry and the most equitable distribution thereof that may be possible, upon the basis of the common ownership of the means of production, distribution and exchange, and the best obtainable system of popular administration and control of each industry or service."

126. For an excellent elaboration of this point, see O'Connor, *The Fiscal Crisis of the State*.

127. K. Marx, *Critique of the Gotha Program* (New York: International Publishers, 1938).

14.
THESES ON THE THEORY OF THE STATE*

CLAUS OFFE AND VOLKER RONGE

The following notes give a brief outline of some of the theoretically relevant findings which the authors have made in two empirical studies of reformist state policies in West Germany. These studies were concerned with the reform of vocational training and with a new programmatic approach to research and development policies. We believe that such case studies of certain state policies in specific policy areas are necessary to gain both theoretical understanding and political perspectives which cannot be gained either through deductive reasoning or immediate experience. For the sake of convenience, the organization of the argument is divided into eight points. These remarks are intended to provoke discussion and debate and are, of course, tentative in nature.

    1. In Marxist theories of the state, there is a cleavage

*Originally published in *New German Critique,* No. 6, Fall 1975, 137–147. Reprinted by permission. Copyright © 1975.

between two approaches. One approach suggests that there is a particular *instrumental* relationship between the *ruling class* (capital as a whole) on the one side and the state apparatus on the other side. The state thus becomes an instrument for promoting the common interests of the ruling class. We believe that this view is gravely misleading—including the version that is offered in the doctrine of "state monopoly capitalism" with its stereotyped proposition of a "merger of the monopolies and the state apparatus." The alternative view is that the state does not patronize certain interests, and is not allied, with certain classes. Rather, what the state protects and sanctions is a set of *rules* and *social relationships* which are presupposed by the class rule of the capitalist class. The state does not defend the interests of one class, but the *common* interests of all members of a *capitalist class society.*

2. The concept of the capitalist state describes an institutional form of political power which contains the following four major elements:

(a) political power is prohibited from organizing production according to its own political criteria; property is *private* (be it property in labor power or property in means of production). Hence, it is not from political power, but from private freedom that decisions over the use of the means of production emerge.

(b) political power depends indirectly—through the mechanisms of taxation and dependence on the capital market—on the volume of private accumulation. The occupant of a power position in a capitalist state is in fact powerless *unless* the volume of the accumulation process allows that individual to derive the material resources (through taxation) necessary to promote any political ends.

(c) Since the state *depends* on a process of accumulation which is beyond its power to *organize,* every occupant of state power is basically interested in promoting those conditions must conducive to accumulation. This interest does not result from alliance of a particular government with particular classes also interested in accumulation, nor does it result from any political power of the capitalist class which "puts pressure" on the incumbents of state power to pursue its class interest. Rather, it results from an *institutional self-interest* of the state which is conditioned by the fact that the state is *denied* the power to control the flow of those resources which are indispensable for the *use* of state power. The agents of accumulation are not indispensable for the *use* of state power. The agents of accumulation are not interested in "using" the power of the state, but the state must be interested—for the sake of its own power—in guaranteeing and safeguarding a "healthy" accumulation process upon which it depends.

(d) In democratic political regimes, any political group or party can win control over institutional state power only to the extent that it wins sufficient electoral support in general elections. This mechanism plays a key role in disguising the fact that the material resources of state power, and the ways in which these are used, depends upon the revenues derived from the accumulation process and not upon the preferences of the general electorate. There is a dual determination of political power in the capitalist state: by its institutional *form,* access to political power is determined through the rules of democratic and representative government, by its material *content,* the use of political power is controlled by the course and the further requirements of the accumulation process.

3. Is there any method by which these divergent constitutional requirements of the capitalist state can be reconciled through the policies of a particular government? Yes, there is *one.* If the conditions can be created through which *every* citizen becomes a participant in *commodity relationships,* all of the four structural elements of the capitalist state are taken into account. As long as every owner of a unit of value can successfully exchange his/her solid value as a commodity, there is no need for the state to intervene

in economic decision making; there is no lack of
material resources needed by the state; there is no
problem in maintaining a steady process of accumulation (which is only the net result of equivalent
exchange between the owners of capital and the
owners of labor power); and there is no problem in
maintaining political support for a political party
which manages to create this universe of commodities. It is only to the extent that values fail to
operate in the commodity form that the structure of
the capitalist state becomes problematic. The commodity form is the general point of equilibrium of the
capitalist state. At the same time, accumulation
takes place as long as every value appears in the
form of a commodity. The link between the political
and the economic structure of capitalist society is the
commodity form. Both substructures depend upon
the universalization of this form for their viability.

4. The key problem, however, lies in the fact that the
    dynamics of capitalist development seem to exhibit a
    constant tendency to *paralyze* the commodity form of
    value. Values cease to exist in the commodity form as
    soon as they cease seeking exchange for money or
    other values. To be sure, in an economic world con-
    sisting of commodities one can never be certain that
    one particular item offered on the market for sale will
    actually find a buyer. But in this simple case the
    failure of a value offered for exchange is supposed to
    be *self-corrective*: the owner of the exchange-seeking
    value will either be forced to lower the price or to of-
    fer an alternative good the use value of which has
    higher changes of being bought. At least in the world
    of Jean Baptiste Say, an economy consisting of com-
    modities is self-perpetuating: the failure of a good as
    a commodity leads to other goods less likely to fail.
    Similarly, parts of labor and parts of capital which
    are, as it were, temporarily thrown out of the com-
    modity form in the course of an economic depres-
    sion, create through the very fact of their idleness,
    the preconditions for a new boom (at least if there is
    downward flexibility of prices). The functioning of
    this "healthy" self-corrective mechanism, however,

does not seem to be the regular case, particularly in advanced capitalist societies. Marxist economic theory has developed various, though controversial, theorems which could explain such failure of self-corrective mechanisms. For example, it is assumed that monopolization of the economy leads to downward inflexibility of prices on the one side, and, to a constant flow of what Baran and Sweezy have called "surplus profit" on the other, i.e., monopolistic profits unsuccessfully in search of investment outlets. Another explanation is based on the increasingly social character of production in capitalism. This means increasing division of labor within and among capitalist enterprises, hence increased specialization of every single unit of capital and labor, and hence diminished flexibility and adaptivity to alternative uses. Thirdly it has been argued that the periodic destruction of large parts of value through unfettered economic crises is by itself a healthy economic mechanism which will improve chances for the remaining values to "perform" as commodities, but that the conflict associated with such "cleansing off" of superfluous values tends to become explosive to the extent that it has to be prevented by state intervention and Keynesian policies. Whatever may be the correct and complete explanation, there is plenty of everyday evidence to the effect that both labor and capital are thrown out of the commodity form, and that there is little basis for any confidence that they will be reintegrated into exchange relationships automatically.

5. It is equally evident that the most abstract and inclusive common denominator of state activities and state intervention in advanced capitalist societies is to *guard the commodity form of individual economic actors*. This, again, does not directly mean guarding the general interests of a particular class, but guarding the general interest of all classes on the basis of capitalist exchange relationships ("*Tausch als universale Verkehrsform*"). For instance, it would be a mistake to argue that state policies of education and training are designed to provide the necessary man-

power for certain industries, since no one, least of all
the state bureaucracy, has any reliable information as
to what industry will need what type of skills at what
time, or in what numbers. Such policies are instead
designed to provide a *maximum of exchange opportunities* to both labor and capital, so that individuals
of both classes can enter into capitalist relationships
of production with each other. Likewise, research and
development policies designed and funded by the
state are by no means directed towards concrete
beneficiaries (e.g., industries which can use the
resulting technologies, or users of specific "civilian"
technologies). These policies are designed to open up
new markets, to shield the domestic economy
against the intrusion of foreign competitors—briefly,
to create and maintain the commodity form of value,
in whose absence values become non-existent in a
capitalist society.

6. The overwhelming concern of all state policies with
the problem of guarding the commodity form of
value is a *relatively new strategy* which in some
capitalist states, like the U.S., is still subject to substantial political and ideological controversies. What
are the alternative strategies open to the state in
order to deal with the structural problem of failure of
values to perform as commodities? The most "ancient" method seems to be *inaction,* i.e., hoping for
the self-corrective mechanism in the course of which
those units of value that have dropped out of the commodity form are supposed to return to the market.
The assumption is that the more unpleasant unemployment (of labor or capital) is, the sooner the
owners of those values will return to the marketplace.
The flaw in this logic lies, however, in trusting that
owners of values do *not* have another option than to
return to the commodity form. They do in fact have
such options, of which emigration, delinquency and
political revolt are only a few historical examples.

The second method is *subsidies and alimentation.* In
this case, those owners of labor power and owners of

capital who have lost their chance to participate in exchange relationships are allowed to survive under conditions artificially created by the state. Their economic existence is protected although they have dropped out of the commodity form, or they are prevented from dropping out because they are granted a claim for income derived from sources other than the sale of value. The problem with this "welfare state" type of dealing with "decommodified" values is that it becomes too costly in fiscal terms, thus sharpening the fiscal crisis of the state. Subsidizing the owners of values that have become obsolete as commodities is particularly costly for the state because it implies a category of expenditures which are by no means self-financing. They do not increase, but rather diminish the basis of future state revenues. On the basis of these considerations, we wish to argue that the more and more dominant, more and more exclusive strategy of the capitalist state is to solve the problem of the obsolescence of the commodity form by *creating* conditions under which values can function as commodities. More specifically, these attempts develop in three directions: first, the saleability of *labor power* is enhanced through measures and programs directed towards education, training, regional mobility and general adaptivity of labor power. Second, the saleability of *capital* and manufactured goods is enhanced through transnational integration of capital and product markets, research and development policies, regional development policies, etc. Third, those *sectors of the economy* (which can be specified by industry, by region, by labor market segments) which are unable to survive within the commodity form on their own strength are allowed by plan to fall victim to market pressures and at the same time they are urged to modernize, i.e., to transform themselves into "marketable" goods. We suggest that the term *"administrative recommodification"* might be an appropriate label for this most advanced strategy of the capitalist state; it is basically different from both the "laissez faire" and "welfare state-protective" types of strategy sketched out above.

7. Policies which pursue the goal of reorganizing, main-
    taining and generalizing exchange relationships
    make use of a specific sequence of *instruments*. These
    instruments can be categorized in the following way.
    First, we find *regulations and incentives* applied which
    are designed to control "destructive" competition
    and to make competitors subject to rules which allow
    for the economic survival of their respective market
    partners. Usually these regulations consist in
    measures and laws which try to protect the "weaker"
    party in an exchange relationship, or which support
    this party through various incentives. Second, we find
    the large category of *public infrastructure investment*
    which is designed to help broad categories of com-
    modity owners (again: both labor and capital) to
    engage in exchange relationships. Typical examples
    are schools of all kinds, transportation facilities,
    energy plants, and measures for urban and regional
    development. Third, we find attempts to introduce
    compulsory schemes of joint decision making and joint
    financing which are designed to force market part-
    ners to agree upon conditions of mutually acceptable
    exchange in an organized way, *outside* the exchange
    process itself, so that the outcome is reliable for both
    sides. Such compulsory schemes of mutual accom-
    modation are to be found not only in the area of wage
    bargaining, but equally in areas like housing, educa-
    tion, and environmental protection.

8. Such attempts to stabilize and universalize the com-
    modity form and exchange process by political and
    administrative means leads to a number of specific
    structural contradictions of state capitalist societies
    which in turn can become the focus of social conflict
    and political struggle. Such contradictions can be
    found on the economic, political and ideological
    levels of society: On the *economic level,* the very state
    policies which are designed to maintain and promote
    universal exchange relationships have the effect of
    threatening the continuity of those relationships. For
    all three of the above-mentioned instruments of
    economic policy making (regulations, infrastructure
    and compulsive accommodation) deprive the owners

of capital of value to varying degrees either in the form of *capital* that is just "taxed away," or in the form of *labor,* or in the form of their *freedom* to utilize both of these in the way they deem most profitable. To the extent such state policies of "administrative recom-modification" are "effective," they are bound to put a burden upon the owners of capital which has the paradoxical effect of making them *ineffective.* Since, in a capitalist society, all exchange relationships de-pend upon the willingness of owners of money capital to invest, i.e., to exchange money capital for constant capital and variable capital; since this willingness depends upon the expected profitability of invest-ment; and since all observable state policies of recommodification do have the side-effect of depriv-ing capital of either capital or labor power or the freedom to use both in profitable ways, the cure turns out to be worse than the illness. That is to say, refor-mist policies of the capitalist state by no means un-equivocally "serve" the interests of the capitalist class: very often they are met by the most vigorous resistance and opposition of this class. Social con-flicts and political struggles do not, of course, emerge automatically from this contradiction. They are waged by political forces which are willing and able to defend the reformist policies of the capitalist state against the obstructive resistance of the capitalist class itself.

A second structural contradiction is related to the organization *power structures* created by such state strategies. It has often been observed by both liberal and Marxist social scientists that those sectors of the economy which are not immediately controlled by market mechanisms tend to expand (both in terms of labor power employed and value absorbed) in ad-vanced capitalist social structures. The most obvious example is public administration and all the agencies that are created and controlled by it (like schools, transportation facilities, post offices, hospitals, public service institutions, welfare bureaucracies, the military, etc.). What is the explanation for the growth of the share of these organizations? In the most simplified form, the state's attempts to maintain and

universalize the commodity form do require organizations which cease to be subject to the commodity
form in their own mode of operation.

This can be demonstrated in the case of teachers. Although it
is true that their labor power is *hired* for wage, it is not true that
the *purpose* of their labor is to produce commodities for sale
(which is the case in commercial enterprises). The purpose of
their labor is, rather, to produce such use-values (skills, etc.)
which put commodity owners (e.g., workers) in a position to actually sell their commodities. Therefore, schools do not *sell* their
"products" (which hence do not assume the form of commodities), although they help to maintain and to *improve the
saleability* of the commodities of the *recipients* of their products.
But to the recipients the products of educational activities (i.e.,
the work of teachers) are distributed through channels different
from exchange. The same is true in such organizations as public
housing authorities, hospitals, transportation systems, prisons
and other parts of the administrative apparatus. Although we
often find nominal *fees* (as opposed to equivalent *prices*) as a
mechanism playing a role in the distribution of their products
and services, the prevailing mechanism is by no means *sale* but
such things as legal claims, legal compulsion, acknowledged
need or simply free use.

One of the most debated and most controversial issues in the
fields of liberal public economics and political science is just
what mechanism of production and distribution of "public
goods" could be substituted for the exchange mechanism that is
inapplicable in the area of public production—an increasing part
of production designed to maintain and to universalize the commodity form of property.

This strategy of *maintaining* the commodity form presupposes
the growth of state-organized production facilities *exempt* from
the commodity form. This, again, is a contradiction only in the
structural sense—a source of possible conflicts and destabilizing
developments which in turn remain contingent upon political action. This contradiction can give rise to social conflicts and political struggles which try to gain popular control over exactly those
"weakest links" in the world of commodities. Although it is a puz-
zle to many Marxists who consider themselves "orthodox," it still
is hardly deniable that the major social conflicts and political
struggles that have taken place during the decade of the sixties

did *not* take place within exchange relationships between labor and capital, but took place as conflicts over the control over the service organizations that *serve* the commodity form without themselves being *part* of the commodity nexus. Conflicts in schools, universities, prisons, military organizations, housing authorities and hospitals are cases in point. We suggest that an explanation of this fact can be based on the consideration that such organizations represent the most advanced forms of erosion of the commodity form within capitalist exchange relationships themselves.

A third contradiction can be located on the ideological level, or in the normative and moral infrastructure of capitalist society. The commodity form does presuppose two related norms with which individual actors must comply. First they must be willing to utilize the opportunities open to them, and they must constantly strive to improve their exchange position (*possessiveness*); and second, they must be willing to accept whatever material outcome emerges from their particular exchange relationship—particularly if this outcome is unfavorable to them. Such outcomes must, in other words, be attributed to either natural events or the virtues and failures of the individual (*individualism*).

For a capitalist commodity economy to function, the normative syndrome of possessive individualism must be the basis both of the behavior of the actor as well as of his interpretations of the actual and future behavior of others. Our point is now that the contradiction of state capitalism on the ideological level results in the *subversion* of this normative syndrome of possessive individualism. To the extent that exchange relationships are prepared and maintained through visible political and administrative acts of the state, the actual exchange value any unit of property (be it in labor or capital) achieves on the market can be seen at least as much determined through *political* measures as through the *individual* way of managing one's property and resources. These resources themselves thus come to be seen as something resulting from, and contingent upon, political measures. Whether or not one receives exchange value for one's labor power, and how much of it, becomes—on the level of normative orientation—less a matter of adequate state policies in such areas as education, training, and regional development. Similarly, for the owner of capital, his market success does not depend upon his preparedness to take risks, his inventiveness and his ability to anticipate changes in demand, but instead upon state policies in such areas as tariffs, research and development, infrastructure supply and regional development. The structural weakening of the moral fiber of a capitalist commodity society—which is caused by the very attempts to stabilize and universalize the commodity through policy measures—again does not imply any automatic tendency toward crises or the "breakdown" of capitalism. It can, however, become the focus of social conflict and political struggle which is oriented towards overcoming the obsolete commodity relationships as the organizing principle of social reproduction.

15.
THE POLITICAL CRISIS AND THE CRISIS OF THE STATE*

NICOS POULANTZAS
Translated by J. W. Freiberg

In this essay, I will clarify certain methodological points that are essential to understand before both the transformations and the crisis of the capitalist state in the current situation of monopoly capitalism can be analyzed. I will pose certain problems facing this analysis and sketch some directions for further research.

Thus announcing my plan I immediately face a problem in establishing a theoretical line for the research: the transformations that affect the state apparatuses in the developed capitalist countries and that permit us to speak of new forms of the capitalist state are not reducible to specific characteristics. Certain transformations suggest general characteristics that come from the current crisis of capitalism and that concern the reproduc-

*Originally published in *La Crise de l'Etat,* Presses Universitaire de France, Paris, 1976. Reprinted by permission. Copyright © 1976.

tion of capitalism; in other words, even if the crisis of capitalism and the crisis of the state were eventually reabsorbed, these profound modifications of the state apparatus would nonetheless persist. This also means, on the other hand, that this crisis is articulated to the more general transformation relevant to the form of the state in the current phase of monopoly capitalism and that the characteristics of the crisis of the state that effect these states are part of these more general transformations.

I. ON THE CONCEPT OF CRISIS

The distinction between the reproduction phase of capitalism and the crisis of capitalism, and thus the distinction between the transformations of the state relevant to this phase and those relevant to the crisis of the state, require a more precise definition of "crisis." This definition is necessary because of the current overuse of the term, which embraces economic crisis, political crisis, ideological crisis, and the relationships among these. Proceeding from this profusion, let us ask ourselves about the different types of crises of capitalism, particularly, about the precise characteristics and modes of the current political crisis and the crisis of the state.

1. One can delimit the concept of crisis already at the level which is called economic crisis by realizing that it is necessary to do so to avoid a double danger:

    a. The economic and bourgeois-sociological conception of crisis, now so popular, which views crisis as a dysfunctional moment that ruptures an otherwise harmonious functioning of the "system," a moment that will pass when equilibrium is reestablished.This narrow conception excludes the contradictions and class struggles that are inherent in the reproduction of capitalism. Now, because historically the average rate of profit tends to fall insofar as the relations of capitalist production conflict with the exploited class, we know for a fact that economic crises are not only inherent to the fundamental capital labor contradiction but also fulfill an organic role: these crises function as periodic and savage purges of capitalism to counter the tendency for the average rate of profit to fall. Massive devaluations and permanently increased productivity and rates of exploitation work to elevate the average rate of profit. This means, on the one hand, that economic crisis, far from being moments of disarticulation, (dysfunctions of the economic "system,") are necessary to the survival and the reproduction of capitalism. It follows that not just any economic crisis can automatically bring down capitalism, but only those that translate themselves into *political crises,* for then the issue *can be* the overthrowing of capitalism. On the other hand, it also means that crises are not accidental explosions of anomic or heterogeneous elements in the otherwise normally functioning, equilibrated, and harmonious system, but that the generic elements of crises (due to class struggle) are always at work in the reproduction of capitalism.

b. The mechanistic, evolutionistic and economistic conception of the crisis, dominant in the Communist International between the two world wars, still makes itself felt in its repercussions and made the way for an economistic catastrophe (its political implications also were very severe). This conception, starting from the point that the reproduction of capitalist relations, particularly in the imperialist-monopoly capitalist stage, because of the new contradictions, would accentuate the tendency of the rate of profit to fall, included in an organic and intensified fashion some elements of crisis and concluded that crisis was constantly present. The conception thus stretched the concept of crisis to the point where it covered a stage or phase of the reproduction of capitalism; the Third International viewed this state of monopoly capitalism as one of constantly present crisis, a conception that in fact led to the notion of "the general crisis of capitalism" and to the use to which this was put. In its contemporary form, this conception considers the current reproduction of monopoly capitalism as a phase of "general crisis" continuing to the end of capitalism, that is, as a permanent crisis of capitalism. Economism pictures capitalism insofar as it reproduces itself, to automatically accentuate its own "rotting" and to be presently in its last phase of reproduction (which is always, as if by chance, the one in which the analyst finds himself), and that this coincides with a permanent crisis. In one fashion or another, it always comes out the same: this time (a "this time" that is beginning to get a bit repetitive) the crisis is the real general crisis, the final and apocalyptic crisis. It should be evident that capitalism can always (although depending on class struggles this could be *cannot*) reabsorb these crises and prolong its reproduction. What is important to remember here is that this conception dissolves the specificity of the concept of crisis because in this sense capitalism was always in crisis.

We can, with these precautions, situate the first problem underlying the makeup of the concept of crisis: if it is indeed true that the generic elements of crisis are present and permanently at work in the reproduction of capitalist relations, more particularly in its current phase, it would nevertheless be necessary to limit this concept to a particular situation of a condensation of contradictions. This means that the elements of the crisis permanently existing in the reproduction of capitalism must be grasped in their function as real transformations in the state and phase that cut across capitalism but that also point to the situation of a condensation of contradictions that can be called "crises." These crises therefore carry the marks of the period that occur throughout capitalism without so much as watering it down; and this is also true for the current crisis. In brief, all teleological concepts of crisis must be mistrusted: the end of capitalism does not depend on any crisis whatsoever but on the issue of the class struggles that manifest themselves therein.

2. What has just been said for the economic crisis also is true, *mutatis mutandis,* for political crises, of which the crisis of the state is a constituent element.

In effect, here, we also find the two dangers I spoke of earlier:

a. The bourgeois-sociological and political science conceptions of political crisis and the crisis of the state. This crisis is considered as a "dysfunctional" moment rudely breaking the naturally equilibrated "political system" that otherwise functions in a harmonious and internally self-regulating fashion. From traditional functionalism to the currently popular "systems" approach, in the end it is always the same story: the underlying vision ignores class struggle when conceptualizing an integrated pluralist society of "powers" and "counterpowers," the "institutionalization of social conflicts," and so forth. This not only makes it impossible to realize the proper place of the political crises but also, precisely to the extent that they reduce sociopolitical "conflicts" to those of ideas and opinions, to speak of political crises in terms other than "crises of values" or crises of "legitimization." So in fact: first, the generic elements of political crisis, due to class struggle, are inherent in the reproduction of institutionalized political power; and second, the political crisis and crisis of the state although slackening in certain aspects, play an organic role in the reproduction of class domination because, unless the struggle leads to the transition to socialism, this crisis can establish the way (sometimes the only way) for the restoration of an unsteady class hegemony and the way (sometimes the only way) for a transformation-adaptation of the capitalist state to the new realities of class conflict.

b. The prevailing conception, at the end of a certain period of the Communist International (post-Leninist, to simplify), the effects of which are still felt, leads, when applied to the political crisis and the crisis of the state, to the same experiences as when it is applied to the economic crisis. Starting with the point that the political domain, particularly in the imperialist stage, carried permanent generic elements of political crisis because of the class struggle, the analysis concluded with the conception of this stage as that of a constantly present political crisis with a conception of the state as being in permanent open crisis. This also has dissolved the specificity of the concept of political crisis, which has had some serious effects: as far as the political crisis is concerned, because of the impossibility of a theoretical elaboration of the concept of crisis in this context, the identification of all political crisis with "revolutionary situations," which was almost constantly declared until the Seventh Congress (1935) of the International, opened the way to the Popular Fronts. As far as the state is concerned this conception had some effects, in particular from 1928 to 1935, when it culminated in the conception of the transformations of the capitalist states relevant to this stage and phase of the reproduction of capitalism as a crisis of these states—the fascistization of these states made during the supposed permanent "revolutionary crisis." Thus, the democratic-parliamentary forms under which certain of these transformations took place were identified with the fascist form of state and were dependent on a political crisis of specific characteristics.

We can, therefore, delimit the problems posed by the concept of political crisis: although the political domain, including that of the state apparatus, carries permanently within it, particularly under capitalism in its current phase, generic elements of crisis, we must reserve the concept of political crisis for the field of a particular situation of the condensation of contradictions even if the crises appear in general and permanent contexts, of instability that are thoroughly singular. In brief, political crisis consists of a series of particular traits, resulting in this condensation of contradictions in their political struggles with the state apparatus.

3. This elucidation of political crisis in its turn poses
a series of new problems: to begin with, that of the
relations between the economic crisis and the
political crisis. In effect, contradicting the "economist" conception, an economic crisis does not
automatically translate itself into a political crisis or a
crisis of the state because the political is not a simple
reflection of the economic; the capitalist state is
marked by a relative "separation" from the relations
of production, the accumulation of capital, and the
extraction of surplus value, a separation that constitutes in a specific field a proper organizational
structure. The political conflict of social classes over
power and the state apparatus is, moreover, not
reducible to the economic conflict; it also is inscribed
in a specific field. From this it follows that:

a. The political crisis, accompanying the political
conflict of classes and the state apparatus, has a
series of particular traits that can only be grasped
in specific frames of reference; this means that an
economic crisis does not necessarily translate
itself into a political crisis.

b. We can witness political crises that are in tune with
the fundamental coordinates of the reproduction
of the relations of production and the conflicts
over exploitation but that are not related to any
economic crisis whatsover; nothing is more false
than to believe that a political crisis, an intensification of class conflict at the political level, can only
"result" from an economic crisis.

c. An economic crisis *can* translate itself into a
political crisis, and this is precisely what is currently happening in certain capitalist countries. In
order to designate these crises that envelope the
ensemble of the social relations, we will reserve a
particular term: the crisis of hegemony, following
Gramsci, or structural crisis, following a current
term. In effect, the structural character of the current crisis does not reside only in its peculiarities
as an economic crisis but also in its repercussions
as a political crisis and a crisis of the state. It is still
necessary to discuss any ambiguity that the term

of "structural crisis" risks gliding over. We must not take "structural" in the usual sense that designates "structure" according to the degree of its permanence as opposed to "conjuncture," meaning that which is secondary and ephemeral, because we risk succumbing to the danger I already have mentioned, that is, understanding by structural crisis a permanent trait of capitalism in its current phase, seeing in this the final crisis of capitalism, and thus diluting the specificity of the concept of crisis. We can only continue to use this term if we reserve it to the field of a particular conjunction and by precisely designating how the crisis affects the ensemble of social relations (economic crisis and political crisis) and manifests itself in a conjuncture of a situation that reveals and condenses the inherent contradictions in the social structure. In other words, we must make the very notion of structural crisis relative: if the current economic crisis distinguishes itself from the simple cyclical economic crises of capitalism, it does not constitute a structural crisis or a crisis of hegemony except for certain capitalist countries where it translates itself into a political-ideological crisis in the proper sense of the term.

d. Economic crisis, then, can translate itself into political crisis. But this does not imply a chronological concordance, that is, a simultaneity of the two crises and their own processes. Because of the specificity of the political field, we often find displacements between the two crises, each with its own rhythm. The political crisis and the crisis of the state can come later than the economic crises, that is, wait until it culminates, occur when it is losing its intensity (this was the case for the political crisis in Germany, which led in 1933 to the accession of Nazism, and for the political crisis in France, which led to the accession of the Popular Front in 1936), or even after it has been reabsorbed. It is important to note that where the signs of economic "recovery" are doubted is indeed a situation of political crises. But political crisis also can precede economic crisis, articulating it (always according to its divergencies) as in the case of the prolonged and current effects in France of May 1968, a time when the economic crisis, even supposing that it had actually begun, was still far from producing any massive effects. Finally, political crisis can precede economic crisis and can even constitute a principal factor of it (as was the case in Chile under Allende).

4. Finally, it is necessary to mention some supplementary points concerning political crisis.

   a. We can determine the general characteristics of a political crisis and a crisis of the state, that is, grasp the general sense of the concept. But proceeding from this conceptualization of the political crisis, we can specify some particular species of this crisis: political crises, for example, can be identified neither with a revolutionary situation nor with a crisis of fascistization; these, while indeed containing general characteristics of political crisis, constitute particular types specified by their own traits. This is currently quite important insofar as we sometimes have the tendency to identify the political crisis–crisis of the state with a process of fascistization.

   b. A political crisis, while being a precise conjunctural situation, cannot be reduced to an instantaneous conflagration but instead constitutes a real process with its own rhythm, to its own strong times and weak times, highs and lows, and that often can spread itself over a long period: it is this very process that consists of a particular conjunctural situation of condensation of contradictions.

   c. The political crisis contains, as one of its own elements, the crisis of the state, but it is not reducible to this which is contrary to all current "institutionalist-functionalist" — "system" analyses of bourgeois sociology and political science, which see in the political crisis an aspect of the crisis of institutions or the "political system." The politi-

cal crisis consists principally in substantial
modifications of the relations of force of class conflict, modifications which themselves specifically
determine the exact elements of crisis at the heart
of the state apparatus. These elements are formed
by the contradictions between the classes in conflict, the configurations of class alliances of the
power bloc and of the exploited-dominated
classes, the emergence of new social forces, the
relations between the organizational forms and the
representation of classes, and the new contradictions between the power bloc and certain of the
dominated classes, that support the power bloc,
and so forth.

Now, these traits that constitute the political
crisis in class struggle determine the crisis at the
center of the state apparatus, but because of the
relative autonomy of the capitalist state in relation
to the power bloc and because of its own organizational framework that tends specifically to separate it from the economic space, this determination is neither direct nor one-directional. The political crisis in class relations always expresses itself
at the center of the state in a specific manner and
by a series of mediations.

d. I have until now spoken only of political crisis in its
relation with economic crisis. It is now necessary
to face the question of ideological crisis, and I advance the following proposition: the political crisis
always articulates an ideological crisis that is itself
a constituent element of the political crisis.

First of all, the relations of ideological domination-
subordination are themselves directly present not only in the
reproduction but also in the constitution of social classes, whose
position at the heart of the social division of labor does not reduce to the relations of production, although these play a determining role. This role of ideology is all the more important in the
constitution of the classes into social forces, that is, in the position of the classes in the heart of a given conjuncture of their conflict, a conjuncture that is the proper place of a political crisis:
ideological relations are directly part of the relations of force

among the classes, in the configuration of alliances, in the forms of organization-representation that these classes use, in the relations between the power bloc and the dominated classes, and so forth.

Furthermore, the ideological relations, notably the dominant ideology, are organically present in the very constitution of the state apparatus, which reproduces the dominant ideology in its relations to other ideologies, or subensembles of the dominated classes. In effect, ideology does not consist only of ideas; it is incarnated (Gramsci) in the material practices, the morals, the customs, the way of life of social formation. As such, and insofar as the ideological relations themselves constitute relations of power that are absolutely essential to class domination, the dominant ideology materializes and incarnates itself in the state apparatus.

On the one hand, the dominant classes cannot dominate the exploited classes by the monopolistic use of violence; dominance must always be represented as legitimate by state manipulation of the dominant ideology, which provokes a certain consensus on the part of certain classes and factions of dominated classes. On the other hand, from the perspective of the power bloc, the state has a role of organizing, unifying and installing its own political interests in light of the struggles of dominated classes: from the perspective of the dominated classes themselves, who make direct appeal to the dominant ideology, the state has a role of unification-representation. Finally, in the form of functioning-inculcation that it uses in the interior and even at the very heart of the state apparatus, the dominant ideology constitutes an indispensable "cement" unifying the personnel of the diverse state apparatuses, enabling it to function "in the service" of the dominant classes.

Therefore, political crisis, both in modifying the relations of force in class conflict and in the internal ruptures that it provokes at the center of the state apparatus, necessarily articulates crisis of legitimization: notably, the political crisis articulates a crisis of dominant ideology, as this materializes itself not only in the ideological state apparatuses (church, mass media, cultural apparatus, educational apparatus, etc.) but also in the state apparatus of economic intervention and its repressive apparatuses (army, police, justice, etc.).

POULANTZAS

II. THE STATE AND THE ECONOMY

Having examined the political crisis in its aspects of crisis of
the state, it is now necessary to clarify certain supplementary
points concerning the capitalist state, particularly in its current
phase of monopoly capitalism.

1. First of all, let us consider the relations between the
    state and the economy. We must stress here that the
    space of the relations of production, exploitation, and
    extraction of surplus work (that of reproduction and
    of the accumulation of capital and the extraction of
    surplus value in the capitalist mode of production)
    has never constituted, neither in other modes of pro-
    duction (precapitalist) nor in the capitalist mode pro-
    duction, a hermetic and partitioned level, that is, self-
    producible and in possession of its own laws of inter-
    nal functioning. It is necessary, in effect, to move
    away from an economist-formalist conception, which
    views the economy as composed of invariant ele-
    ments throughout the diverse modes of production, a
    self-producible, internally self-regulated space. In ad-
    dition to eliminating the role of class struggle, which
    is at the very heart of the relations of production, this
    conception considers the space or the field of the
    economy (and, conversely, that of the state) as im-
    mutable, possessing intrinsic limits traced by the pro-
    cess of its alleged self-reproduction across all modes
    of production.
       When the relations between the state and the
    economy are considered as essentially external, this
    can be presented under different forms: (a) under the
    form of traditional economism, attached to a descrip-
    tive and topological representation of relations be-
    tween the "base" and the superstructure, which con-
    siders the state as a simple appendage-reflection of
    the economy: the relation between the state and the
    economy would consist, at best, in the famous "ac-
    tion and reaction" of the state on an economic base
    essentially considered as self-sufficient; (b) under the
    more subtle form, the social ensemble is represented
    in "instances" or "levels" by nature or by essence
    "autonomous," intrinsic spaces that cut across the

diverse modes of production, the essence of these instances being a presupposition for putting them at
the center of a mode of production.

To move on from this conception, I want to advance certain propositions:

a. The political-state (although it is equally true for
   ideology) was always, even if under different forms
   for different modes of production, constitutively
   "present" in the relations of production and, thus,
   in their reproduction, including the premonopolist
   stage of capitalism. This is true in spite of a series
   of illusions that deemed that the "liberal state" did
   not intervene in the economy except to maintain
   the "exterior conditions" of production. Although
   the place of the state in relation to the economy is
   certainly modified according to the diverse modes
   of production, this place is always the modality of
   a presence and specific action of the state and is at
   the very heart of the relations of production and of
   their reproduction.

b. It follows that the space, the object, and thus the
   concepts of economy and state do not and cannot
   have either the same extension or the same field in
   the diverse modes of production. Even at an abstract level, the several modes of production do
   not constitute purely economic forms; instead,
   they constitute different combinations of "economic" elements, in themselves invariant but
   moving in a closed space with intrinsic limits;
   moreover, they do not constitute combinations
   between these elements and invariant elements of
   other instances (ideology, the state) which are
   themselves considered to be in immutable spaces.
   It is the mode of production, the unity of the
   ensemble of economic, political, and ideological
   determinations that delimits these spaces,
   designates their field, and defines their respective
   elements: they are defined by their internal relations.

c. However, in respect to the relations between the
   state and the economy, the capitalist mode of production presents a characteristic specificity that is

different from the perspective of the precapitalist modes of production; that is, a relative separation exists between the state and the economy, in the capitalist sense of these terms. This separation is linked to the relations of capitalist production, specifically to the depossession of the workers from the objects and means of their labor; it also is linked to the constitution of the classes and to their conflict under capitalism. This separation begins with the "narrow overlapping" (Marx) of the state and the economy in the precapitalist modes of production, which is at the base of the institutional framework of the capitalist state because it traces its new spaces and respective fields from the economy and the state.

In considering these remarks, however, we realize that this separation is capitalist not only because of its autonomous nature but also because there is no effective externality of the state and the economy, with the state only intervening in the economy from the outside. This separation pervades the history of capitalism; it does not impede it, however. Even at the premonopolist stage of capitalism, the constitutive role of the state in the relations of capitalist production was only the precise form that recovers, under capitalism, the specific and constitutive presence of the state in the relations of production and, therefore, in their reproduction.

d. Now it is necessary to propose a supplementary proposition: this separation of the state and the economy transforms itself, without being abolished, in accordance with the stages and phases of capitalism. In effect, the space, the object, and thus the content of the concepts of politics and of economy change not only under diverse modes of production but also in the stages and phases of capitalism itself.

It is in the "transformed form" of this separation and in the changes in these enlarge spaces (due to the changes in the relations of capitalist production) *that the decisive role of the State is inscribed in the very cycle of reproduction and accumulation of capital in the current phase of monopoly capitalism,* a role qualitatively different than what it fulfilled in earlier capitalism. Therefore, to the extent that a series of domains (qualification of the work force, urbanism, transportation, health, environment, etc.) becomes integrated in the growth of the very space of the accumulation of capital, and insofar as entire economic sectors of capital (public and nationalized) become integrated in the growth of the space of the state, the relations between the two and the functions of the state in relation to the economy become modified. But these changes do not obliterate the relative separation of the state and the economy. Notably, this separation marks the structural limits of the "intervention" of the state in the economy.

e. This is the only way to situate the meaning of the current interventions of the state in the economy and their limits (*who* intervenes; *where,* and *how?*) and also to perceive the current relations between the economic crisis and the political crisis–crisis of the state. I have already mentioned several important elements from this perspective.

First, insofar as the respective spaces of the state and the economy are currently changing, and insofar as state intervention in the economy is different than it was in the past, the repercussions of the economic crisis in the political crisis change in the sense that, on the one hand, the economic crisis translates itself into political crisis in a more direct and organic way than in the past and, on the other hand, the interventions of the state in the economy themselves become productive factors of economic crisis; second, however, insofar as the separation of the state and the economy is maintained, even though it is transformed, the interventions of the state in the economy, including efforts to overcome an economic crisis, always present limits that correspond to the reproduction-accumulation of capital, which in turn corresponds to the very structure of the state. This explains the impossibility of current "organized-planned" capitalism, which attempts to succeed in avoiding, mastering, or "managing" the crises by the skewing of the state interventions. Furthermore, the political crisis–crisis of the state is always situated in a specific field in relation to an economic crisis: the current economic crisis, although different from cyclical crises of capitalism, does not necessarily translate itself into a political crisis—crisis of the state.

2. a. The transformations of the relations between the state and the economy, the new economic role of the state, and thus the new relations between economic crisis and political crisis lead back to substantial modifications of the capitalist relations of production on both the world and the national levels; these modifications underlie such processes as the concentration of capital. Focusing research on the capitalist relations of production and their transformations leads us to break with the economist conception of these relations, particularly insofar as, in exactly situating the content of these two forms, we must grasp the preexistence of the relations of production over the "productive forces" preexisting because the process of producing is the effect. As far as the relations of production are concerned, we are led to consider them as the social division of labor, not as the simple crystallization of a process of the productive forces as such: this is precisely what allows us to grasp the capitalist separation of the state and the economy as a specific presence of politics (and of ideology) in the relations of production and the social division of labor in capitalism. In other words, the current modifications of the role of the state in the recovering economy amount to the biasing of changes in the relations of production, in substantial changes in the reproduction of labor power and of the division of labor (understanding as part of this the new forms of the division manual labor–intellectual labor). This appears elsewhere as the priority of the production of production and the relations of production over the relations of circulation of capital in the cycle of the ensemble of reproduction of social capital (production–consumption–distribution of the social product). The economic crisis and the relations between this and

the political crisis–crisis of the state are constantly spreading out over the whole of the cycle of reproduction of social capital, situating themselves in the first place in the new relations of the state, on the one hand, and in the relations of production and the division of labor, on the other, contrary to a current tendency to see the crisis only in the single space of circulation and to see the crisis of the state as simply a crisis of legitimacy.

b. Therefore, examining this new relation of the state and the economy, of the political crisis and the economic crisis, takes us directly to the tendency of the rate of profit to fall and therefore to directly consider the particular conditions of the functioning of this tendency in the current phase of capitalism. In the first place, the current crisis of the state must be situated in the efforts taken by the state to counter this tendency. In relation to the dominant countertendency, the role of the state raises the rate of exploitation and surplus value which returns us to the very heart of class conflict about exploitation (the dominant displacement towards the intensive exploitation of work and relative surplus value, technological innovations, and industrial restructurations, the process of qualification-dequalification of the labor force, the extension and modification of the very space of reproduction and the "management" of the labor force, etc.). The role of the state in this countertendency also consists of devaluing part of the overaccumulated capital (public and nationalized) in order to raise the average rate of profit and produces considerable transfers of surplus value from fractions of capital to others and leads back to intense class struggles within the dominant class. Furthermore, the current functioning of this tendency thus explains the fact that the elements of the crisis are accentuated in the current phase of capitalism, the crisis itself being situated in a context of particular instability characterizing the ensemble of this phase.

c. I will not go any further on this subject, for what I have said is enough to show one decisive point for the study of the political crisis–crisis of the state in its relations to the economy and the crisis of the economy: these relations cannot be taken as relations between the state and some unconscious "laws" of the economy; instead, they lead back directly to the class struggles lodged in the very heart of the relations of production and exploitation. To understand the crisis of the state in its relation to the economy and to the economic crisis means, in the final analysis, understanding the relations between the economic struggle (economic crisis) and the political struggles of classes (political crisis) *and to understand the manner in which class contradictions have repercussions in the very heart of the state apparatus.*

III. THE STATE AND CLASS RELATIONS

Now, in order to understand how class contradictions (economic crisis and political-ideological crisis) have repercussions in the heart of the state (state crisis), it is necessary to make some supplementary remarks on the very nature of the state and its relations to social classes, in particular, in the current phase of monopoly capitalism.

1. a. The capitalist state must represent the long-term political interests of the whole of bourgeoisie (the idea of the capitalist collective) under the hegemony of one of its factions, currently, monopoly capital. This implies that, first, the bourgeoisie is always presented as divided in class fractions: monopoly capital and nonmonopoly capital; (monopoly capital is not an integrated entity but designates a contradictory and unequal process of "fusion" between diverse fractions of capital). Second, taken as a whole, these fractions of the bourgeoisie, which are to a certain degree increasingly unequal, enjoy a political domination as part of the power bloc; third, the capitalist state must

always hold a relative autonomy in relation to any given fraction of the power bloc in order to assume its role as political organizer of the general interest of the bourgeoisie (from "the unstable equilibrium of compromise" between these fractions, said Gramsci) under the hegemony of one of its fractions: and fourth, the current forms of the process of monopolization and hegemony particular to monopoly capital over the whole of the bourgeoisie restrict the limits of the relative autonomy of the state in relation to monopoly capital and to the field of the compromises it makes with other fractions of the bourgeoisie.

Now, how can we prove that state politics act in favor of the power bloc? This is only another way of asking how class contradictions echo at the center of the state, a question that is at the heart of the problem of the crisis of the state. To understand this question, the state must not be considered as an intrinsic entity, but, as is also true for "capital" itself, it must be considered as a *relation,* more exactly, as a material condensation (apparatus) of a relation of force between classes and fractions of classes as they are expressed in a specific manner (the relative separation of the state and the economy giving way to the very institutions of the capitalist state) at the very heart of the state. Understanding the state as a relation avoids the impasses of the pseudo-dilemma between the state conceived as a thing and the state conceived as a subject. The state as a thing is the old instrumentalist conception that views the state as a passive, if not a neutral, tool totally manipulated by a single fraction, in which case the state has no autonomy. The state as a subject: the state has absolute autonomy and functions of its own will. This conception started with Hegel; was revitalized by Weber; is the dominant current of bourgeois political sociology (the "institutionalist-functionalist" current); and carries this autonomy to the power itself, which is supposed to restrain the state, those in power, and the state bureaucracy or political elites. In effect, this tendency endows the institutions-apparatuses with power, when in fact the state apparatuses possess no power, because state power cannot be understood only in terms of the power of certain classes and fractions of classes to whose interest the state corresponds.

What is more important here is to see that in both cases (state conceived as thing and as subject) the relation of state to social classes and, in particular, state to classes and dominant fractions is understood as a relation of externality: either the dominant classes submit the state (thing) to itself by a game of "influences" and "pressure groups" or the state (subject) submits the dominant classes to itself. In this relation of externality, state and dominant classes are considered as two intrinsic entities, one "confronting" the other, one having "power" while the other does not. Either the dominant class "absorbs" the state by emptying it of its own power (state as thing) or the state "resists" the dominant class and takes power for its own purposes (state as subject).

Let us now postulate that the state is a relation; so saying, we return to our original problem: the state's relative autonomy and its role in establishing the general interests of the bourgeoisie and the hegemony of one fraction (currently monopoly capital), in brief the *"politique"** of the state, cannot be explained by its own power or by its rationalizing will. *Politique* is established because of class contradictions that are inscribed in the very structure of the state—the state therefore is a relation. In effect, when we understand that the state is a material condensation of a relation of force between classes and fractions of class, it becomes obvious that class contradictions thoroughly constitute and permeate the state. In other words, the state, destined to reproduce class divisions, is not and cannot be state-thing or state-subject, a monolithic bloc without fissures; because of its very structure, it is divided. But in what specific forms are these class contradictions found, particularly, those between fractions of the power bloc that constitute the state? They manifest themselves in the form of internal contradictions between the diverse branches and apparatuses of the state, while having a privileged representative of a particular interest of the power

*Translator's note: The French word *"politique"* is at times synonymous with "politics," and with "policy." Rather than say "political line" or some such concoction, I retain the French.

bloc: executive and parliament, army, justice, regional-municipal and central apparatuses, various ideological apparatuses, and so forth.

In this framework, the state establishes the general and long-term interests of the power bloc (the unstable equilibrium of compromises) under the hegemony of a given fraction of monopoly capitalism. The concrete functioning of its autonomy, which is limited in the face of monopoly capitalism, seems to be a process whereby these intrastate contradictions interact, a process that, at least for the short term, seems prodigiously incoherent and chaotic. However, what is really at work is a process of structural selectivity: a contradictory process of decisions and of "nondecision," of priorities and counterpriorities, each branch and apparatus often short-circuiting the others. The politics of the state are therefore established by a process of interstate contradictions insofar as they constitute class contradictions.

All this is therefore translated into considerable divisions and internal contradictions that accrue in the state personnel and that question the state's own unity, but that, here also, take a specific form. They occur in the organizational framework of the state apparatus, but following the line of its relative autonomy, they do not correspond exactly to the divisions in class conflict. Notably, these divisions often take the form of "quarrels" among members of of various apparatuses and branches of the state. In this context, this poses the problem of the *unity* of the power of the state, that is, the problem of its global *politique* in favor of monopoly capital. This unity is not established by a simple physical seizure of the state by the magnates of monopoly capital and their coherent will. Instead, this contradictory process implicates the state in institutional transformations that cannot, by their nature, be favorable to other than monopoly interests. These transformations can take several shapes: a complex domination of an apparatus or branch of the state (a ministry that, for example, crystallizes monopoly interests over other branches and state apparatuses, centers of resistance of other fractions of the power bloc); a *transstate network* that covers and short circuits the various apparatuses and branches of the state, a web that crystallizes, by its very nature, the monopoly interests; finally, the circuits of formation and functioning of the body—special detachments of high state functionaries endowed with a high degree of mobility not only within the state but also between the state and monopoly concerns (Ecole Polytechnique, Ecole National d'Ad-

ministration,* etc.), which, by constant bias of important institutional transformations, are charged with (and led to) implementing policies in favor of monopoly capital.

> b. The nature of the capitalist state, particularly as it
> manifests itself in the current phase of monopoly
> capitalism, must be grasped before the translation
> of political crisis into a crisis of the state can be
> understood. In effect, on the side of the power
> bloc, the political crisis accentuates the internal
> contradictions among its constituent fractions,
> politicizes these contradictions, challenges the
> hegemony of one fraction by other fractions, and
> often modifies the relations of force between the
> various parts of this bloc. This concomitantly in-
> volves an ideological crisis leading to a rupture of
> the representatives-represented link between the
> classes and the class fractions of the power bloc
> among not only their political parties but also
> among certain other state apparatuses that repre-
> sent them. The role of the state as organizer of the
> power bloc is then challenged. These contradic-
> tions, specific to a political crisis of the power bloc,
> have certain repercussions at the heart of the state
> in the form of accrued internal contradictions be-
> tween branches and apparatuses of the state: com-
> plex displacements of dominance and functions
> from one branch and apparatus to others; breaks
> between centers of real power and those of formal
> power; increased ideological role of representative
> apparatuses accompanying the expanded use of
> state violence; deterioration of the organizational
> role of the state, from certain apparatuses par-
> ticularly destined to this role (notably political par-
> ties) to others (the administration, the army); the
> passing and short-circuiting of "official" state ap-
> paratuses by a series of parallel networks; substan-
> tial overturning of the laws, which, among other
> things, limits the field of action of the state appar-
> atuses and regulates their relations; and important

*Two of the "Grandes Ecoles" that educate France's elite, particularly its
"technocrats." Trans.

changes in the personnel of the state. These cannot be reduced to a simple crisis of the political scene; they are manifested by an incoherency that characterizes the politics of state that maintains its relative autonomy and restores a toppling class hegemony.

2. a. These characteristics of the crisis of the state can only be studied from the perspective of the dominated classes. In effect, in exercising repression and physical violence, the state apparatuses conserve and reproduce class domination; they also organize class hegemony by allowing for provisional compromises between the power bloc and certain dominated classes and by installing an ideological "consensus" of the dominant class. By permanently disorganizing-dividing the dominated classes, by polarizing them toward the power bloc, and by short-circuiting their own political organization, the state apparatuses organize-unify the power bloc. The relative autonomy of the capitalist state is essential in order for the hegemony of power to be organized over the dominated classes.

This also is inscribed in the organizational framework of the capitalist state as a relation: the state concentrates the relation of force not only between fractions of the power bloc *but also between the power bloc and the dominated classes.* Of course, this latter relation does not crystallize in the state apparatuses in the same way as the former relations; due to the unity of state power, as the power of class domination, the dominated classes do not exist in the state because of the bias of the apparatuses that concentrate the real power of these classes. However, this does not mean that the struggles of the dominated classes are "exterior" to the state and that the contradictions between the dominant classes and the dominated classes remain contradictions between the state, on the one hand, and the dominated classes "outside" the state, on the other. In fact, the struggle between the dominant and the dominated classes cuts across the state apparatuses insofar as these apparatuses materialize and concentrate the power from the dominant classes and class fractions in their contradictions with the dominated classes.

Thus, the precise configuration of the ensemble of the state apparatuses—the relation of dominance-subordination between the branches and apparatuses of the state, the ideological or repressive role of a given apparatus, the exact structure of each apparatus or branch of the state (army, justice, administration, school, church, etc.)—depends not only on the internal relations of force in the power bloc but also on the role they fulfill in respect to the dominated classes. If, for example, a given apparatus plays the dominant role at the heart of the state (political party, administration, army),it generally is not only because it concentrates the power of the hegemonical fraction of the power bloc but also because, simultaneously, it concentrates in itself the political-ideological role of the state with respect to the dominated classes. Moreover, the more important the role of the state in class hegemony, in the division and disorganization of the popular masses, the more that role consists of organizing compromises between the power bloc and the dominated classes (particularly the petty bourgeoisie and the rural popular classes) in order to set them up as *supporting classes* of the power bloc and to short circuit their alliance with the working class. This is expressed in the very organizational framework of a given state apparatus, which exactly fulfills this function; for example, in France, the educational apparatus does this for the petty bourgeoisie, while the army does it for the rural popular classes.

Finally, the contradictions between the power bloc and the dominated classes directly intervenes in the contradictions between the dominant classes and the fractions of which it is composed: for example, the tendency of the falling rate of profit, a primordial element of division at the center of the power bloc, ultimately is only an expression of the struggles of the dominated classes against exploitation. It follows not only that the various fractions of the power bloc (monopoly capital, nonmonopoly capital, industrial capital, commercial capital, etc.) have different contradictions with the popular masses but also that their strategies with respect to them are different. A given policy of the state results from a process of contradictions not only between fractions of the power bloc but also between it and the dominated classes.

b. We return to the political crisis. For the dominated classes, this manifests itself (here again, it is necessary to distinguish between various sorts of political crisis) in a considerable intensification of their struggles: these struggles are politicized and the relations of force between the power bloc and dominated classes are modified; the relations of the power bloc and supporting classes are broken and emerge as effective social forces; ideological crisis enables the dominated classes to challenge the "consensus" of the dominant classes and their representation-regimentation biased by the state apparatuses (which accentuates the objective possibilities of alliance and union of the popular masses); their autonomous political organization and the accrued weight of their own class organizations are accentuated, as well as the articulation of the political crisis and the economic crisis that restrains the objective possibilities of compromise between the power bloc and the dominated classes and accentuates the divisions at the heart of the power bloc with respect to strategies toward the dominated classes. This series of contradictions expresses itself at the very heart of the state (the state is a relation) and is a factor in determining the characteristics of the state crisis: accrued internal contradictions between branches and apparatuses of the state, complex displacement of dominance between apparatuses, permutations of function, accentuations of the ideological role of a given apparatus accompanying the reinforcement in the use of state violence, and so forth. These all bear witness to efforts of the state to restore a toppling class hegemony.

IV. THE STATE PERSONNEL

I have so far stressed the aspect of the state crisis that affects its institutions and apparatuses and that is fundamental to this crisis. This state crisis also is manifested in another aspect, a crisis of the state personnel (politicians, functionaries, judges, military men, police, teachers, etc.), in brief, a crisis of the state bureaucracy. In effect, the political crisis is translated to the very heart of the state personnel in several manners: (1) insofar as it is an institutional crisis of the state, that is, precisely insofar as the ensemble of the state apparatuses is reorganized; (2) insofar as there is an accentuation of the class struggles and contradictions as expressed at the heart of the state personnel; and (3) insofar as there are increased demands and struggles of the state personnel.

To understand this, we must first see clearly that the state personnel themselves hold a class position (they are not a separate social group) and they are divided because of this. The higher spheres of personnel of the state apparatuses have membership in the bourgeois class; the intermediates and subordinates, in the petty bourgeoisie. These positions must be distinguished from the class origins of this personnel, that is, the classes from which this personnel come. But this personnel nevertheless constitutes a specific social category, possessing, across its class divisions, its own unity, because of the organizational framework of the capitalist state apparatus (separation of the state and the economy) and because of its relative autonomy from the dominant classes, which goes back to the very role of this personnel in elaborating and implementing the policies of the state.

Thus, the characteristics of the political crisis, that is, of the class struggles that correspond to it, necessarily impregnate the state personnel because of their class membership, the intensification of the divisions and contradictions at the heart of the power bloc, the politicization of these contradictions, the ruptured links of representation between the classes and dominant fractions and their political representatives, the conflicting diversification of the strategies and tactics of the dominated classes, and the particularly contradictory characteristics of the policies of the state which have repercussions at the heart of the higher spheres of state personnel, just as the characteristics of the political crisis of the dominated classes, notably the petty bourgeoisie (recalling its role as a supporting class of the power bloc) have repercussions at the heart of the intermediate and subordinate ranks of this personnel.

All this is therefore translated into considerable divisions and internal contradictions that accrue in the state personnel and that question the state's own unity, but that, here also, take a specific form. They occur in the organizational framework of the state apparatus, but following the line of its relative autonomy, they do not correspond exactly to the divisions in class conflict. Notably, these divisions often take the form of "quarrels" among members of various apparatuses and branches of the states that result from fissures and reorganizations arising from the institutional crisis of the state. Or they take the form of quarrels between "leagues," "factions," "great bodies of the state" at the very center of each branch and apparatus. Even when class positions have repercussions at the heart of the state personnel, more precisely, when there is politicization of this personnel, one part leaning, let us say, "to the left," another "to the right," this follows specific paths: notably, those of ideological crisis. In effect, the dominant ideology, which the state reproduces and inculcates, also functions to constitute the internal cement of the state apparatuses and of the unity of their personnel, a personnel that (Gramsci saw this clearly), because of the general role of organization, representation, and hegemony of the state, make up, in its ensemble, part of the "intellectuals." This ideology, the internal cement of the state personnel, is precisely that of the neutral-state representing the interest of the general will, arbitrating among the conflicting classes: the administration or judiciary as above the classes, the army, pillar of the "nation," the police, the "order of the Republic," the "freedom" of the "citizens," the administration as the motor of "efficacity" and of the general "well-being" and so on. The ideological crisis, in its relations to the political crisis, places a veil over the real nature of the state and as such is experienced at the very heart of the state personnel. To this we must add, of course, the particular effects of the ideological crisis on the personnel of the ideological apparatuses (schools, church, mass media, cultural apparatus, etc.) that rupture the links between the power bloc and its "organic intellectuals."

The divisions and contradictions at the heart of the state personnel, repercussions of their positions in class conflict, do not therefore follow a simple line of cleavage between the intermediate and subordinate levels, on the one hand, and the higher personnel spheres, on the other; the cleavage is indeed more important, but these divisions cut vertically through the state hierarchy. These contradictions are further articulated in a complex fashion in the demands of "corporatist" struggles of the state personnel, struggles that intensify in the general context of the political crisis.

V. IMPERIALISM AND THE NATION-STATE

Finally, an important problem for the analysis of both the political crisis and the current crisis of the state involves the imperialist context, and, therefore, the current phase of imperialism (which is only the other face of the current phase of monopoly capitalism) and its repercussions on the very form of the nation-state.

The current phase of imperialism is characterized, more and more, by the internationalization of capital and work processes, therefore by the dominant imperialist relations of production (notably in the United States) as they reproduce themselves at the very heart of other social formations, by an induced reproduction of these relations. This tendency also manifests itself in the relations between the dominant imperialism, that of the United States, and the other imperialist countries, notably Europe, by producing a specific *dependency* of these countries on the dominant imperialism. This internalization also works for the imperialist relations of the foreign capital within the power blocs of these social formations and affects their state, a state that intervenes in the reproduction of the dominant imperialist relations at the heart of its own social formation.

Thus, the nation-state and its formations undergo important modifications in order to take charge of this internationalization of capital. On the other hand, the current phase of imperialism and this internationalization do not detract from the importance of the nation-state in this process. This does not mean that there is a process of internationalization that takes place "above" the states and that either replaces the role of nation-states by that of "economic powers" (multinational corporations) or implies the birth of an effective supranational state (United Europe of the American superstate). Indeed, the more there is class struggle between the dominant class and the dominated class, of which the state condenses the relations of force, the more this struggle is essentially situated in the frame of the national space and takes a national form.

I return to the current crisis in order to make one last far-reaching remark. It is, on the one hand, evident that the current crisis concerns the whole of capitalism-imperialism; this means that "external factors," in the sense of external contradictions, intervene at the very center of the various social formations, where the reproduction of capitalism and the existence of the imperialist chain actually occur. But in the economic crisis, and more particularly in the political crisis, where the economic crisis is translated into political crisis, *the internal contradictions take primacy over the external factors, and this is also true for the crisis of the nation-state in the social formations where one finds such crisis.* Thus, to pose the primacy of internal factors, a primacy that not only concerns a situation of crisis but goes much further, one must break with the mechanist and quasi-topological (if not "geographical") conception of the relation between internal and external factors. One cannot, in the current phase of imperialism, speak of external factors that act purely on the "outside" and "isolated," internal factors that support the former. To accept the primary of internal factors means that the coordinates of the "external" imperialist chain to each country, including the relations of world forces, the role of a given great power, and so forth, only act on these countries when they are internalized, that is, when they become inserted in and modify the relations of force between the classes of these countries and when they articulate the specific contradictions, contradictions that appear, in certain of their aspects, as the induced reproduction of contradictions in the imperialist chain at the centers of the various countries. In this sense, to speak of the primacy of internal factors is to discover the real role that imperialism plays—unequal development—in the evolution of the various social formations and also in their political crisis and the crises of their own nation-states. This also contributes a fact already mentioned: the current economic crisis is not necessarily transforming itself, for all countries involved, into a political crisis–crisis of the state, and, where this is the case, the various political crises have, according to the different countries, differences between them and manifest these under very different forms (in different spaces of political crises).

VI. THE CURRENT CRISIS OF THE STATE

I will conclude this essay by making, according to the theoretical directions established above, some remarks on the current political crisis; where it is taking place, it presents the traditional characteristics of the political crisis, about which I will here only mention certain new aspects. In effect, it is situated in the context of an economic crisis distinct from the simple cyclical crises of capitalism. This poses a series of problems concerning the economic crisis itself, problems I do not consider in this essay. But these problems concern: (1) the accentuation of the generic elements of political-ideological crisis, and accentuation belonging to the current phase of monopoly capitalism and also touching the ensemble of capitalist countries; (2) the political-ideological crisis and the crisis of the state in the very sense in which it is currently experienced in certain capitalist countries, in brief, the "structural" character of this crisis in these countries. This structural character resides, as I have already noted, in the repercussion of the economic crisis in political-ideological crisis (crisis of hegemony) at the very heart of certain countries, that is, in the current relations between the economic crisis and the crisis of the state.

1. In effect, one of the most important problems is the fact that, because of the new economic role of the state and the transformations of the spaces of *politique* and economy (transformations in the separation of the state and the economy), a whole series of these state functions consists of implementing the counter-tendencies to the tendency of the rate of profit to fall (to some extent to avoid the crisis), thus becoming themselves involved to a point where the state cannot avoid committing factors productive of a crisis that, *by this very fact, goes beyond the simple economic crisis.* I want to call attention to certain new aspects of the problem.

   a. The considerable accentuation of internal contradictions of the power bloc (contradictions at the very heart of monopoly capital, between this and nonmonopoly capital, between industrial capital and bank and commercial capital; etc.) is an important element in the political crisis insofar as it already has translated itself into an instability of hegemony. To understand this element in its full impact, we cannot lose sight of the current conditions of the internationalization of capital: the indirect reproduction and internalization of foreign capital at the heart of the various social formations produce important internal dislocations by making a place at the center of these formations for the emergence of a new division, that I have called internal bourgeois, which, although linked to external capital (it is not a true national bourgeoisie), presents important contradictions with itself, and a comprador bourgeoisie entirely dependent on (and integrated to) this foreign capital. This line of division does not always duplicate the "monopoly capital-nonmonopoly capital," cleavage but it often cuts across these capitals. This already constitutes a supplementary factor that destabilizes hegemony, especially if inter-imperialist contradictions, accentuated in a crisis period, are reproduced directly at the very heart of the power blocs of the various countries. Now the current "economic" functions of the state (devalorization of certain parts of capital, industrial restructurations to raise the rate of relative surplus value, an increasing role in favor of the centralization of capital, selective aid to certain capitals, the decisive place of the nation-state in the process of the internationalization of capital) are accentuated precisely in the context of the economic crisis, favoring more than ever the severe "corporate economics" of certain fractions of capital at the expense of others. This direct overlapping of the state in the economic contradictions, with its snowball effects, serves only to increase and deepen the political fissures of the power bloc and becomes, therefore, a direct factor of political crisis in permanently questioning the role of the state in establishing the general political interests of the power bloc.

b. The organic "intervention" of the state in a series of domains that, although previously marginal, are now in the process of being integrated into the very space of the reproduction and accumulation of capital (urbanism, transportation, health care, "environment," etc.) has considerably politicized the struggle of the popular masses in these fields, insofar as these masses are directly confronted by the state. Already an important element of political crisis, these struggles are accentuated by state interventions, which among other things, aim to raise the rate of (relative) surplus value by the capitalist reproduction-qualification of the labor force, while casting off their disguise of "social policy." These interventions therefore reduce the elements of crisis (a current example of this is aid to the unemployed). This is all the more true since the new petty bourgeoisie or middle-level-salaried workers are, by their nature, particularly sensitive to the objectives of a struggle in these domains; the base of their alliance with the working class is therefore considerably extended. In brief, we are now experiencing the demythification of the providential state or the state of well-being.

c. The role of the state favors foreign or transnational capital, a role accentuated in a context of crisis (look at the current relaxation of the European bourgeoisie under the American economic-political umbrella) and increases the unequal development of capitalism at the heart of each national social formation, where the reproduction of foreign capital occurs, notably by creating new "poles of development" of certain regions at the expense of others. Arising from this are the phenomena of ruptures of the "national unity," of the nation sustained by the state bourgeoisie, by the massive development of regionalist movements that have a political character and that, as ambiguous as they often are, nevertheless constitute important elements of the current political crisis.

d. In addition, the current role of the state confronts the economic crisis in the strictest sense of the term. It seems to me that the new problem in this regard is the following: Insofar as the state extensively intervenes in the very reproduction of capital and insofar as the economic crises are organic and necessary factors of this reproduction, the state has probably succeeded in limiting the "wild" aspect of economic crises (like that of the 1930s, for example), but only insofar as it takes charge of the functions formally fulfilled by these "wild crises." Without exaggerating this paradox, we can say that all this occurs as if it were henceforth the state that becomes the prime mover of these "rampant" economic crises (a current example is unemployment and inflation directly orchestrated by the state), even though this should not be seen only, or even principally, as a conscious strategy of the bourgeoisie, but as the objective result of the current role of the state, whereas in the past the state seemed content to limit the social damage of the extreme economic crises. The effect of this, here also, is a considerable politicization (against state policy) of the struggles of the popular masses in the context of the economic crisis.

These remarks, however, are only a beginning; to understand the current political crisis, we must study it in the ensemble of its characteristics while also insisting on certain new forms under which the characteristics currently present themselves; notably the new forms of rupture between the bourgeoisie and the petty bourgeoisie, a particularly important rupture that is taking a totally different form than in the past insofar as it henceforth concerns the new salaried petty bourgeoisie (the famous "tertiaries"), where the objective polarization on the side of the working class is, because of its class position, altogether more important than was that of the traditional petty bourgeoisie (small merchants and artisans); the emergence of new struggles on fronts often called "secondary," the struggles of women, immigrant workers, students, and so forth; the new elements of the ideological crisis, a crisis not experienced before under capitalism, especially in the dominant countries.

Thus, to understand the current political crisis thoroughly, we need a concrete examination of each capitalist country in which it is occurring; in effect, certain facts I just mentioned arise, more generally, from the current phase of capitalism itself: they are concerned with *the accentuation of the generic elements of the crisis,* an accentuation characterizing the ensemble of the current phase, which is marked by a particular instability. But these elements are only translated into a political crisis when they are articulated and condensed in the conjuncture of only certain capitalist countries, while the ensemble of these countries are touched by the accentuation of the generic elements of the crisis.

2. This last remark leads us to wonder about the repercussion of the political crisis, wherever it is taking place, on the crisis of the state, which in turn compels us to look at the transformations that, to different degrees, currently affect the state apparatuses of the dominant capitalist countries. These transformations also can be understood as state reactions to, among other things, the political crisis, including its own crisis, because it is currently experiencing, in this case, a blockage of its efforts to quietly install itself in the management of its own crisis, an explosion that the English call "crisis of the crisis management" or "crisis of the management of the crisis."

But as I have said, these transformations also are due, among other things, to the crisis of the state, which leads us back to a problem that I posed at the beginning of this text. In effect, certain transformations come from more general factors of the current phase of monopoly capitalism and of its own permanent coordinates (including the accentuation of the elements of crisis and its characteristic instability). These transformations therefore follow the same lines as the adaptation of the state as it is faced with the new realities of the class struggles of this phase and thus lead not simply to an occasional authoritarian turning of the bourgeois state but to the constitution of a new form of the capitalist state with characteristics appropriate to the "authoritarian state" or "strong state" that could signify simply that a certain form of "democratic policy" has at last arrived for capitalism. It is under these transformations that we find, in certain of these states, the specific characteristics of the crisis of the state articulated. This not only means that all states undergoing transformations toward this new form of "authoritarian" state will necessarily experience a crisis of the state but also that their transformation toward an "authoritarian" state will persist even after this crisis is eventually reabsorbed. Furthermore, in the case of an eventual end to the crisis of the state by its absorption, this crisis will appear to be the way for a transformation-adaptation by specific and necessary means of the capitalist state to the new realities of the class struggle (new form of the capitalist state). The next question, that often comes up—"Is what is happening a crisis or an adaptation (modernization) of the state?"— poses, in certain respects, a false dilemma: perhaps it is exactly where a crisis is in fact occurring that the capitalist state is led to an adaptation-"modernization."

Considering the general level of this discussion it is not possible for me to elucidate these transformations of the state that, in a concrete case, are brought up on a first order (new form of the state adapted to the new realities of the phase) or on a second order (reaction of the state faced with the political crisis and its own crisis). I will be content here to call attention to certain aspects of the process in order to reveal the breadth of the problem, without explicitly establishing, much less simplifying, the relations of the process with the coordinates that determine it: processes that accentuate elements of preceding phases and of a series of new elements that coexist in the state of monopoly capitalism.

    a. The prodigious concentration of power in the executive at the expense of not only "popular" parliamentary representation but also a series of networks founded on popular suffrage, on both central and local or regional levels.

    b. The organic confusion of three powers (executive, legislative, and judicial) and the constant encroachment on the fields of action and competence of the apparatuses or branches that correspond to them (police and justice, for example); the "separation" of these powers, always somewhat fictional anyway, is really nothing more than a fundamental ideology of bourgeois power.

    c. The accelerated pace of the state's arbitrary policies that restrict citizens' political liberties and that connote, on the one hand, a complete political-ideological overturning of the traditional limits between the "public" and the "private" and, on the other, substantial modifications of the very notion of the politics of

the "individual person" that structure a new field,
which M. Foucault in his *Surveiller et Punir* called
anatomic politics or the microphysiology of power.

d. The precipitous decline of the role of bourgeois
political parties and the displacement of their
political-organizational functions (both from the
perspective of the power bloc and from that of the
dominated classes) in favor of the administration and
bureaucracy of the state. This process involves the
direct politicization of the personnel of the state apparatuses, which is accompanied by the displacement of the dominant ideology toward
"technocratism" in all its variations, the privileged
form by which the state legitimizes itself via the bias
of the administrative apparatus.

e. The accentuation of the use of state violence (both in
the sense of physical violence and in that of "symbolic violence"), which accompanies not only the accentuation of the ideological role of the state
(cultural apparatus, mass media, etc., in brief, apparatuses of the "internalization of repression") but
also the displacement of the ideological apparatuses
(teaching, family, etc.) in relation to the repressive
apparatuses themselves (e.g., the army or the police
whose "civilizing" mission never ceases to be
glorified), all of which implies a major reorganization
of the repressive apparatuses.

f. In direct relation with the preceding characteristics,
the creation of a vast network of new circuits of
"social control" (extended police surveillance,
psychological-psychoanalytic divisions, social
welfare controls), which has been subtly and diffusely
established in the social texture.

This is how the extension of surveillance takes the form that R.
Castel, in *Le Psychoanalism,* calls, "deinstitutionalization"; the
setting up of ideology and repression and processes of "non-
enclosing" in respect to the special apparatuses (asylums,
prisons, and various places of detention) destined to isolate the
supposed "abnormals-deviants-dangerous," opening them by extending their concern to the whole of the social body. This im-

plies, of course, that the ensemble of the social body is considered "abnormal" and "dangerous," guilt passing from accomplished act to mere intent, repression extending from punishment to policies of prevention.

g. The overthrow of the legal system and of the juridical ideology corresponding to the traditional "state of law" in order to account for the institutional transformations.

h. The dislocation in each branch and apparatus of the state (army, police, administration, justice, ideological apparatuses) between formal and open networks, on the one hand, and impervious nuclei directly controlled by the summits of the executive, on the other, and the constant displacement of the centers of real power from the former to the latter. This implies transmutation from the principle of public knowledge to that of secrecy, of which the Watergate affair is only a sampling.

i. The massive development, directly orchestrated by the heights of the state itself, and the increased organizational role of the parallel state networks, paid for publicly, semipublicly, or para-publicly-privately, which must simultaneously function to unify and direct the nuclei of the state apparatuses and which thus also constitute reserves for sociopolitical confrontations.

j. The prodigious and characteristic incoherence of the current state policies, which are constantly reduced to contradictory, spasmodic micropolitics, what one calls "blind piloting" or, more notably, "absence of a global social project," on the part of the state and its various governmental majorities. This is characteristic of the state policies from the perspective of both the power bloc and the dominated classes; it is from here that we arrive at the current forms of "reform-repression" that mark the policies of the Western capitalist states.

BIBLIOGRAPHY

Alford, R. *Health Care Politics.* Chicago: University of Chicago Press, 1975.

Althusser, L. and Balibar, E. *Reading Capital.* New York: Pantheon Books, 1970.

Anderson, O. *Health Care: Can There Be Equity? The United States, Sweden and England.* New York: John Wiley and Sons, 1972.

Appelbaum, A. "New York City Hospitals: The Financial Crunch." *Hospitals,* 50 (2), 1976.

Aronowitz, S. *False Promises: The Shaping of American Working-Class Consciousness.* New York: McGraw Hill Book Co., 1973.

Bender, M. "Will the Bicentennial See the Death of Free Enterprise?" *The New York Times,* January 4, 1976, p. 27.

Berki, S. E. "Comments on 'Socioeconomic Status and Use of Physician Services: A Reconsideration,'" *Medical Care,* 11 (3), 1973.

Bice, T. W., et. al. "Socioeconomic Status and Use of Physician Services: A Reconsideration," *Medical Care,* 10 (3): 261-271, 1972.

Blackburn, R. (ed.) *Ideology in Social Science.* New York: Fontana, 1972.

Bowles, S. and Gintis, H. *Schooling in Capitalist America: Educational Reform and the Contradictions of Economic Life.* New York: Basic Books, 1976.

Braverman, H. *Labor and Monopoly Capital.* New York and London: Monthly Review Press, 1975.

Cairns, J. "The Cancer Problem," *Scientific American,* 233 (5), 1975.

Coates, D. *The Labor Party and the Struggle for Socialism.* London and New York: Cambridge University Press, 1975.

Cochrane, A. L. *Effectiveness and Efficiency: Random Reflections on Health Services.* London: The Nuffield Provincial Hospitals Trust, 1972.

Committee on Government Operations, U.S. Senate. *Confidence and Concern: Citizens View American Government. A Survey of Public Attitudes,* Part I. Washington, D.C.: Government Printing Office, 1973.

Dahl, R. A. *A Preface to Democratic Theory.* Chicago: University of Chicago Press, 1956.

Dohse, K. "Class Domination and the Political System: A Critical Interpretation of Recent Contributions by Claus Offe," *Kapitalistate,* 2: 60-70, 1973.

Domhoff, G. W. *Higher Circles: The Governing Class in America.* New York: Vintage Books, 1971.

Draper, P. and Smart, T. "Social Science and Health Policy in the United Kingdom: Some Contributions of the Social Sciences to the Bureaucratization of the National Health Service," *International Journal of Health Services,* 4 (3): 453-470, 1974.

Eckstein, H. *The English Health Service: Its Origins, Structure and Achievement.* Cambridge: Harvard University Press, 1958.

Editors. "The Budget: A Special Analysis," *National Journal,* 8(5), 1976.

Editors. "Doctors and the State," *Wall Street Journal,* January 16, 1976.

Engels, F. *The Condition of the Working Class in England.* Stanford, Ca.: Stanford University Press, 1958.

Ford, G. *State of the Union Message.* Washington: Government Printing Office, January, 1976.

Forsyth, G. *Doctors and State Medicine: A Study of the British Health Service.* London: Pitman & Sons, 1973.

Freidson, E. *Doctoring Together: A Study of Professional Social Control.* New York: Elsevier, 1975.

Fuchs, V. "Health Care and the United States Economic System," *Milbank Memorial Fund Quarterly, Health and Society,* 50, 1972.

———, *Who Shall Live: Health, Economics and Social Choice.* New York: Basic Books, 1975.

Glyn, A. and Sutcliffe, B. *British Capitalism, Workers and the Profit Squeeze.* Middlesex: Penguin Books, 1972.

George, V. and Wilding, P. "Social Values, Social Class and Social Policy," *Social and Economic Administration,* 6(3): 236-248, 1972.

Godelier, M. *Rationality and Irrationality in Economics.* New York and London: Monthly Review Press, 1973.

Gough, J. "Review of 'The Fiscal Crisis of the State,'" *Bulletin of the Conference of Socialist Economists,* 4 (1), 1975.

————, "State Expenditure in Advanced Capitalism," *New Left Review,* 92: 53-92, 1975.

Gramsci, A. *Prison Notebook,* New York: International Publishers, 1971.

Guttsman, W. L. *The British Political Elite.* London: MacGibbon and Kee, 1963.

Habermas, J. *Toward A Rational Society: Student Protest, Science and Politics.* Boston: Beacon Press, 1971.

Hammond, E. C. "Epidemiologic Basis for Cancer Prevention," *Cancer,* 33(6), 1974.

Hart, J. Tudor. "An Assault on All Custom," *International Journal of Health Services,* 3(1): 101-104, 1973.

————, "Bevan and the Doctors," *The Lancet,* 2, (7839): 1196-1197, 1973.

————, "Industry and the Health Service," *The Lancet,* 2 (7829): 611, 1973.

————, "The Inverse Care Law," *The Lancet,* 1 (7696): 405-412, 1971.

————, "Primary Care in the Industrial Areas of Britain: Evolution and Current Problems," *International Journal of Health Services,* 2(3): 349-365, 1972.

Herzog, P. *Politique Economique.* Paris: Maspero, 1971.

Illich, I. *Medical Nemesis: The Expropriation of Health.* London: Calder and Boyars, 1975.

International Labor Organization, *The Cost of Social Security, 1964-66.* Geneva: ILO, 1972.

Kilborn, P. K. "Britain Slashes Spending on Social Welfare Items," *The New York Times,* February 21, 1976.

Laclau, E. "Poulantzas-Miliband Debate," *Economy and Society,* 4(1): 87-110, 1975.

Lalonde, M. *A New Perspective on the Health of Canadians: A Working Document.* Canada: Government Printing Office, 1975.

Lasswell, H. D. et. al. *The Comparative Study of Elites.* Stanford, Ca.: Stanford University Press, 1952.

Learmonth, A. *Health.* London: The Open University Press, 1972.

Lenin, V. I. *The State and Revolution.* New York: International Publishers, 1932.

Mahler, H. "Health: A Demystification of Medical Technology," *The Lancet,* 2 (7940): 829-833, 1975.

Mandel, E. *Late Capitalism.* London: New Left Books, 1975.

Marcuse, H. *One Dimensional Man.* Boston: Beacon Press, 1964.

Marmor, T. *The Politics of Medicare.* Chicago: Aldine Publishing Co., 1973.

Marx, K. *Critique of the Gotha Program.* New York: International Publishers, 1938.

———, *The 18th Brumaire of Louis Bonaparte.* New York: International Publishers, 1963.

Marx, K. and Engels, F. *The Communist Manifesto.* New York: International Publishers, 1960.

———, *The Selected Correspondence, 1846-1895.* New York: International Publishers, 1942.

Matanoski, G. "Lung Cancer by Census Tracts in the City of Baltimore," *The Johns Hopkins Gazette,* March 4, 1976.

Maxwell, R. *Health Care, The Growing Dilemma: Needs Versus Resources in Western Europe, the U.S. and the USSR.* New York: McKinsey and Co., 1975.

McKeown, T. (ed.). *Medical History and Medical Care: A Symposium of Perspectives.* New York and London: Oxford University Press, 1971.

Miliband, R. "Poulantzas and the Capitalist State," *New Left Review,* 82: 83-92, 1973.

———, "Reply to N. Poulantzas," *New Left Review,* 59: 53-60, 1970.

———, *The State in Capitalist Society.* London: Weidenfeld and Nicolson, 1970.

Miliband, R. and Saville, J. (eds.). *The Socialist Register, 1965.* London: Merlin Press, 1966.

Miller, A. "The Wages of Neglect: Death and Disease in the American Workplace," *American Journal of Public Health,* 65 (11): 1217-1220, 1975.

Miller, A. H. "Political Issues and Trust in Government: 1964-1970," *American Political Science Review,* 68: 951-972, 1974.

Mills, C. W. *The Power Elite.* New York: Oxford University Press, 1956.

Muller, W. and Neususs, C. "The Illusion of State Socialism and the Contradiction Between Wage Labor and Capital," *Telos,* 25: 13-90, 1975.

Navarro, V. "The Industrialization of Fetishism or the Fetishism of Industrialization: A Critique of Ivan Illich," *Social Science and Medicine,* 9(7), 351-363, 1975.

———, "National Health Insurance and the Strategy for Change," *Health and Society, The Milbank Memorial Fund Quarterly,* 51(2): 223-251, 1973.

———, "The Political Economy of Medical Care: An Explanation of the Composition, Nature and Functions of the Present Health Sector of the United States," *International Journal of Health Services,* 5(1): 65-94, 1975.

———, *The Political Economy of Social Security and Medical Care in the USSR.* (In process)

———, "The Underdevelopment of Health of Working America: Causes, Consequences and Possible Solutions," *American Journal of Public Health,* (in press), 1976.

O'Connor, J. *The Corporations and the State.* New York: Harper Books, 1974.

———, *The Fiscal Crisis of the State.* New York: St. Martin's Press, 1973.

Offe, C. "The Abolition of Market Control and the Problem of Legitimacy," *Kapitalistate,* 1: 109-116, 1973.

———, "Political authority and Class Structures—An Analysis of State Capitalist Societies," *International Journal of Sociology,* 2(1): 73-108, 1972.

———, "The Theory of the Capitalist State and the Problem of Policy Formation," in Lindberg, L. et. al. (eds.). *Stress and Contradiction in Modern Capitalism,* London: Lexington Books, 1975.

Offe, C. and Ronge, V. "Theses on the Theory of the State," *New German Critique,* 6: 137-147, 1975.

Polack, J. C. *La Médecine du Capital.* Paris: Maspero, 1970.

Poulantzas, N. *Classes in Contemporary Capitalism.* London: New Left Books, 1975.

———, *Political Power and Social Classes.* London: New Left Books, 1973.

———, "The Problems of the Capitalist State," *New Left Review,* 58, 1969.

Proctor, J. B. and Proctor, R. "Capitalist Development: Class Struggle and Crisis in Italy, 1945-1975," *Monthly Review,* 27: 21-36, 1976.

Renaud, M. "On the Structural Constraints to State Intervention in Health," *International Journal of Health Services,* 5(4): 559-571, 1975.

Robson, J. "The NHS Company, Inc.? The Social Consequence of the Professional Dominance in the National Health Service," *International Journal of Health Services,* 3(3): 413-426, 1973.

Rusconi, G. E. "Marxism in West Germany," *Telos,* 25: 6-12, 1975.

Schattschneider, E. E. *The Semi-Sovereign People: A Realistic View of Democracy in America.* New York: Holt, Rinehart and Winston, 1960.

Shearer, D. "The Salt of Public Enterprise," *The Nation,* February 21, 1965.

Sigerist, H. E. *Landmarks in the History of Hygiene.* London: Oxford University Press, 1956.

Special Task Force to the Secretary of Health, Education and Welfare. *Work in America.* Cambridge: M.I.T. Press, 1973.

Susser, M. "Ethical Components in the Definition of Health," *International Journal of Health Services,* 4(3): 539-548, 1974.

Sweezy, P. and Baran, P. A. *Monopoly Capital.* New York and London: Monthly Review Press, 1966.

Terris, M. "Crisis and Change in America's Health System," *American Journal of Public Health,* 63(4): 313-318, 1973.

Therborn, G. "Power in the Kingdom of Sweden." *International Socialist Journal,* 2(10): 490-494, 1965.

Titmuss, R. *Commitment to Welfare.* London: Unwin University Books, 1968.

Trilateral Commission. *Governability of Democracies, Report of the Trilateral Task Force.* New York, 1975.

Westergaard, J. H. "Sociology: The Myth of Classlessness," in R. Blackburn (ed.), *Ideology in Social Science.* New York: Fontana, 1972.

Wilensky, H. L. *The Welfare State and Equality.* Berkeley and Los Angeles: University of California Press, 1975.

Willcocks, J. *The Creation of the National Health Service. A Study of Pressure Groups and a Major Social Policy Decision.* London: Routledge and Kegan Paul, 1967.

Wolfe, A. "Capitalism Shows Its Force," *The Nation,* 221(18): 557-563, 1975.

———, "New Directions in the Marxist Theory of Politics," *Politics and Society,* 4(2): 131-160, 1974.

Yago, G. *State Policy, Corporate Planning and Transportation Needs.* University of Wisconsin, Madison, 1974 (unpublished manuscript).